FOR REX AND FOR BELGIUM

FOR

REX

AND FOR

BELGIUM

LÉON DEGRELLE AND WALLOON POLITICAL & MILITARY COLLABORATION 1940–45

Eddy de Bruyne

&

Marc Rikmenspoel

HELION & COMPANY

Helion & Company Limited
26 Willow Road
Solihull
West Midlands
B91 1UE
England
Tel. 0121 705 3393
Fax 0121 711 4075
Email: publishing@helion.co.uk
Website: http://www.helion.co.uk

Published by Helion & Company Limited 2004

Designed and typeset by Carnegie Publishing Ltd, Lancaster, Lancashire
Printed by The Cromwell Press, Trowbridge, Wiltshire

ISBN 1 874622 32 9

British Library Cataloguing-in-Publication Data
A catalogue record for this book is available from the British Library

The publishers apologise for the poor quality of some of the images contained in this book. However, it was felt that their inclusion was very important on the grounds of historical research and interest. In addition, please note that many images have had to be reproduced at a small size due to the poor quality of the original.

Dedication

Marc Rikmenspoel thanks Eddy De Bruyne for the opportunity to participate in this project, and further thanks Duncan and Wilfrid Rogers for taking on its publication. Marc dedicates his part to his late grandparents, and offers a special salute to the memory of Earl Murray. Hoka hey, Mitakola! Mitakuye Oyasin.

To Liliane for her precious help and support – Eddy de Bruyne.

Contents

Preface

The name Léon Degrelle is well known, both in Belgium and abroad. Degrelle was active in pre-war Belgian politics, and became notorious during World War II for collaborating with the German occupiers of his country. He was frequently written about and photographed for the German and Belgian censored news and propaganda. As a result, photos of Degrelle are common, and appear in numerous post-war works.

In exile in Spain after the war, Degrelle wrote his memoir of the war years, based mainly on memory and a few personal notes.

This book, which eventually saw English translation as *Campaign in Russia: The Waffen-SS on the Eastern Front*, was widely translated and read, and then widely quoted, its contents being taken for granted. The consequence is that Degrelle is a well-known figure to students of the war, especially in the English-language world, which has seen an unabated flood of World War II book releases continue into the new millennium.

When Degrelle is discussed, it is usually in the context of his military service and that of his fellow Walloon volunteers in the German military. He and they are recognized as brave and determined soldiers, yet primary source material on which to base such judgments is lacking. One book seems merely to quote from another. I too have written about Degrelle, and had to rely on secondary sources, ones that I now realize are biased and inaccurate.

In this era we are not shocked to discover that a politician may have stretched the truth to some degree. Degrelle was a politician before he was a soldier, and as the book in your hands will show, he remained a politician during his wartime and post-war careers. He shaped his books and speeches to put himself in the best possible light. This is understandable, and even to be expected. The danger is that his errors and omissions have never been countered, at least in English, with documented, reliable information. Thus, they have entered the historical record, and rendered inaccurate portions of many works.

Walloon Collaboration specialist Eddy De Bruyne, a Belgian researcher and a correspondent to the Brussels based *CEGES* for more than 15 years, has devoted most of his time to studying Degrelle, Degrelle's Rexist political party, and the Walloon civil and military collaboration during the World War II era. By sorting through mounds of documentary material in the original French and German – including never before explored classified and restricted material not open to the public, via interviews and contact with survivors of that time, to start with Léon Degrelle himself, he has assembled unsurpassed knowledge on the topic. Eddy De Bruyne has shared that information in several books and innumerable articles written in French. In his capacity of Walloon Military Collaboration expert he has also participated in several TV programmes.

This material received no attention in the English-language world. However, Eddy De Bruyne, as he is quite aware that Degrelle and his fellow soldiers are well known overseas, decided to combine elements from several of his works in French into one introductory yet thorough English book, a release that would shed a new light on Degrelle's war-time years. At the same time, the purpose of this publication is twofold: to complete the information on the one hand, and on the other hand to correct the errors previously presented on Degrelle and the military unit and also introduce English readers to the civil and political aspects of Rex and its collaboration.

It has been my privilege to assist in the translation and editing of this book. In reality, it was the best opportunity to educate myself ahead of all of the lucky readers who will now follow a tragic story from Belgian history.

Thank you Eddy, for letting me be a small part of this!

Marc Rikmenspoel
Fort Collins, Colorado, 25 November 2001

Foreword

When speaking of collaboration during WWII in Belgium one faces two realities deriving from its political, cultural and ethnic components: Flanders, that is the Flemish-Dutch speaking part of Belgium and Wallonia, or the French-speaking provinces of the country.

This book deals with the Walloon military, cultural and political collaboration during WWII, explored to a much lesser extent than its Flemish counterpart. And there are good reasons for this!

Unlike the Flemish collaboration striving for separatism and independence thanks to the presence of the Germans in occupied Belgium, the French-speaking collaboration never was motivated by a similar (Walloon) nationalism. On the contrary, it focused on one single person: Léon Degrelle, anti-Communism being the apparent common denominator between the two communities. Apart from a very short period after the war, the Flemish collaborators and more particularly the former Eastern Front veterans could openly confess their past via writing and publishing. This is quite impossible in Wallonia where Rexists (by way of amalgam all former Walloon Eastern Front veterans are looked upon as Rexists!) are decried by most traditionally left-wing classes of French-speaking society. Until recently, the only literature dealing with the *Légion Wallonie* were the books written by Degrelle himself. In addition, if the books by Degrelle are reliable as far as the chronology of the facts reported is concerned, for the substance they do not stand up to a critical examination by the historian.

During and after the war, Degrelle made the utmost of his idealism when speaking of his anti-Communist crusade. The crude truth is that the vast majority of the Rexists who volunteered for the *Légion Wallonie* in the first two years of its existence were true idealists convinced as they were to fight for a good cause: the Fatherland (not Wallonia but Belgium) and the preservation of Christianity, whereas Degrelle, in reality, only collaborated with the Germans with the hope to play a (major) role in Belgian politics from which he had been banned already before the war.

After coming back from the Vernet camp (France) in July 1940, he again tried to step into politics. He even contacted Cardinal Van Roey – who a few years earlier had severely condemned him by means of a clerical letter, imploring the prelate for his help in republishing the *Pays Réel* (the *Real Country*). All his efforts were vain until an unexpected event showed up: the invasion of the Soviet Union ... It so to speak saved Degrelle from a political drowning.

If Degrelle and the *Légion Wallonie*, and later on the *5. Sturmbrigade Wallonien* and the *28.SS-Frw.Gren.Div.Wallonien*, proved to be an important faction of political and military collaboration in French-speaking Belgium ... it was far from being the whole collaboration. Not only the Rex Movement but also smaller collaborating groups fiercely competed with a view to getting the favour of the German occupying authorities.

PART I

Political, Intellectual and Cultural Collaboration in Wallonia, 1940–44

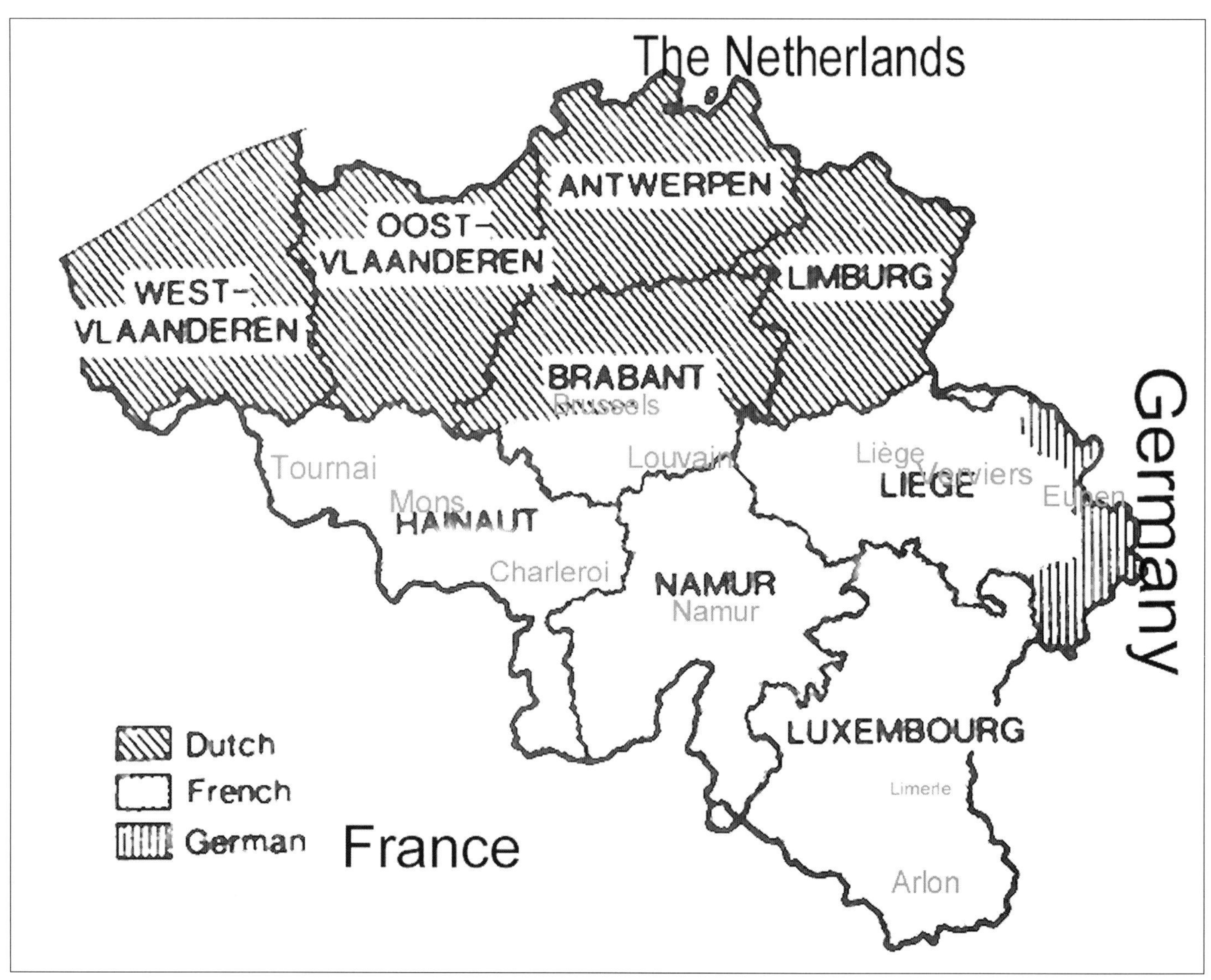

Map of Belgium

CHAPTER I

Pre-War Walloon Fascist Movements

Fig. 1.1. Paul Hoornaert wearing the *L.N.* militia uniform. (*Collection F. Balace*).

A. The National Legion

The First World War generated a number of nationalist, Germanophobe, anti-Marxist and Belgian unitarian royalist movements in French-speaking Belgium. Among the latter emerged the *Légion Nationale*, an extreme right movement launched on 1 May 1922, as a WWI veteran organization by a group of discontented former servicemen. A talented lawyer by the name of Paul Hoornaert (Liège 1888-Sonnenburg Concentration Camp 1945) took over this group in 1924. He organized and developed it in a substantial way.

Hoornaert served as a *lieutenant-patrouilleur* during WWI, clearing up the trenches of remaining enemy after offensive operations and was therefore distinguished and highly decorated. After the war, he intended to oppose parliamentarian democracy, liberalism and all forms of Communism in the same way he had fought the invader for four years.

It did not take long before the *Légion Nationale* (National Legion) absorbed other small nationalist groups, such as the *Faisceau belge* (Belgian Fasces) and the *Jeunesses Nationales* (National Youth). Hoornaert became the leader of the movement in 1927.

The *Légion Nationale* was the first League to stress the importance of having a paramilitary organization, a militia first known under the abbreviations *S.P.* (*Service de Protection*), later on *G.M.* (*Groupes Mobiles*) and finally, in 1934 – for legal reasons in order to avoid penal charges since uniformed groupings had been forbidden – *Blue Shirts* (*Chemises Bleues*), numbering 4 to 5,000 members under Fernand Dirix (1910–1983), Hoornaert's deputy chief. In 1940, Dirix was to become the general secretary of the *Légion Nationale* until he joined the underground Secret Army in 1941. Unlike his chief, Dirix survived the war.

Hoornaert's *New Order* was of corporatist and nationalist essence. It rejected anything pertaining to Nazi Germany and its philosophy. On the other hand, Hoornaert had become a fervent admirer of Mussolini since he had taken part in the International Fascist Meeting in Montreux, Switzerland, organized by the *C.A.U.R.* (*Comitati d'Azione par l'Universalita di Roma*) in December 1934. From that moment on he supported Italian intervention in Abyssinia. Through the *C.A.U.R.* he got in touch with the Young Spanish Phalange headed by José Antonio Primo de Rivera and sent volunteers to fight for the Nationalist cause in Spain.

In 1940, there was an unsuccessful attempt to create a unified party with Joris van Severen, leader of the Flemish Fascist corporatist and authoritarian *Verdinaso* (*Verbond van Dietse Nationaal-Solidaristen* – Union of the Netherlandish

Un grand mouvement
d'ordre nouveau est en marche...

Qu'est-ce que la
Légion Nationale ?

UNE DOCTRINE, UNE FOI,
UNE ORGANISATION, UNE ACTION

par Paul HOORNAERT
Chef du Mouvement

JUILLET 1935 Prix : 1,25 Franc

Editions Légion Nationale, Siège Central :
Boulevard de la Sauvenière, 38, Liége.

Fig. 1.2.

National Solidarists), a movement that was the most akin to the *Légion Nationale*.

In spite of the fact Hoornaert was promised a high-ranking position in the Rex Movement, the *Légion Nationale*, on behalf of its Germanophobia, refused to cooperate with Degrelle and the Rexist Movement.

The German invasion split up the movement. A majority, the elder veteran members, joined the Resistance, withdrew or just waited for the war to end. Only a very small minority of younger members thought the German occupation would offer a better chance for the recognition of an authoritarian corporatist New Order regime. Among them was Dr Gaston Haelbrecht, leader of the Youth Movement of the *Légion Nationale*.[1]

In 1941, the *Légion Nationale* had become part of the mobile reserve of the Resistance. Hoornaert was arrested on 24 April 1942, charged with organizing military exercises and stockpiling arms and ammunition. He was sent to the Sonnenburg Concentration Camp in Germany, where he died on 2 February 1945.

Apart from its vertical organization in zones and federations – there were about 15 homes or *Maisons Nationales* – the *L.N.*, like any corporatist institution, also had its horizontal structure.

The *Légion Nationale* had two daily newspapers, one in French and one in Dutch.

B. The Rex Movement

1. Léon Degrelle

Born in Bouillon on 15 June 1906 in the province Luxemburg, near the French border, Léon Degrelle was a bright and

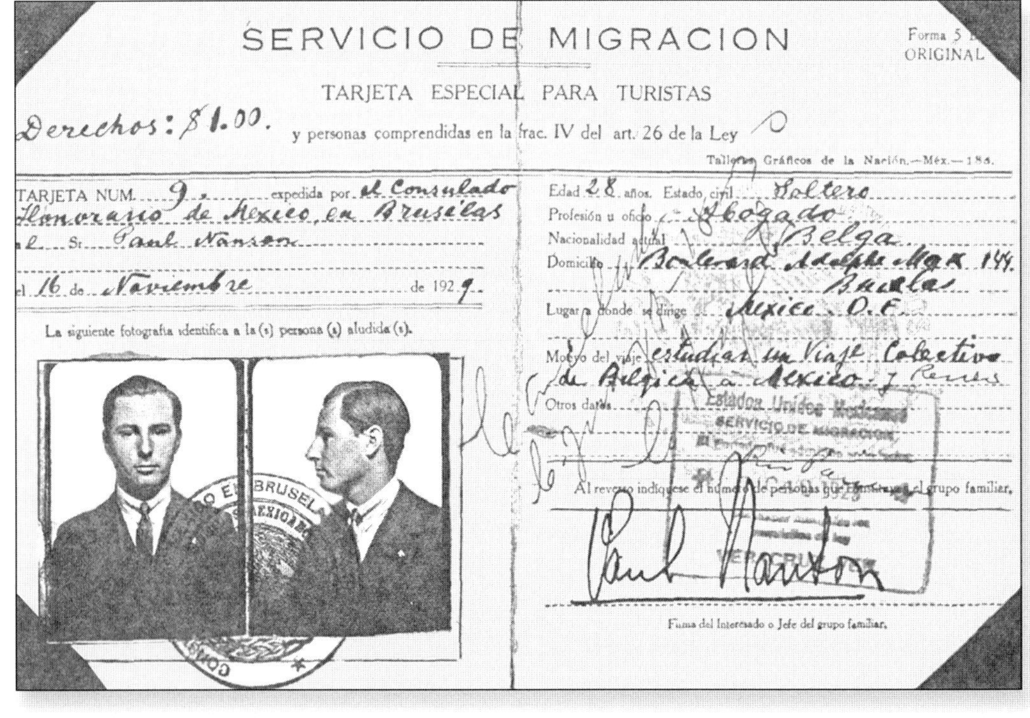

SERVICIO DE MIGRACION

Forma 5 B
ORIGINAL

TARJETA ESPECIAL PARA TURISTAS

Derechos: $1.00. y personas comprendidas en la frac. IV del art. 26 de la Ley

TARJETA NUM. 9 expedida por el Consulado Honorario de Mexico en Bruselas al Sr. Paul Nanson el 16 de Noviembre de 1929.

La siguiente fotografía identifica a la (s) persona (s) aludida (s).

Edad 28 años. Estado civil Soltero

Profesión u oficio Abogado

Nacionalidad actual Belga

Domicilio Boulevard Adolphe Max 144 Bruselas

Lugar a donde se dirige Mexico D.F.

Motivo del viaje estudiar un Viaje Colectivo de Belgica a Mexico

Otros datos

Al reverso indíquese el número de personas que forman el grupo familiar.

Paul Nanson

Firma del Interesado o Jefe del grupo familiar.

Fig. 1.3. Degrelle's visa to Mexico bears the name of Paul Nanson, a former fellow student of the University of Louvain. Note his profession listed as *Abogado* (lawyer) and the reason for his trip *Estudias en viaje colectivo de Belgica a Mexico* – Studies made to take notes on a journey from Belgium to Mexico (*Private collection*).

Fig. 1.4. The early Rexist cross and crown emblem.

yet inconstant person, whose decisions were often guided by the impulses of the moment. He died in Spain on 31 March 1994. First educated (1921–24) in a Jesuit school (*Notre Dame de la Paix*), in Namur, he later studied law at the Louvain University. However, as he was more interested in editing the students' magazine *L'Avant Garde*, he failed to get his degree.[2]

In his early twenties he emerged as one of the leaders of the Louvain University Catholic Students Association and soon got entirely involved in the Catholic Association of the Belgian Catholic Youth (*A.J.C.B. – Association Catholique de la Jeunesse Belge*) thanks to *Monseigneur* Louis Picard, director and chaplain of the *A.J.C.B.* In March 1929, he was given the editorship of the movement's organ *Cahiers de la Jeunesse Catholique* (Journal of the Catholic Youth). After writing a series of articles thwarting anti-clericalism in Mexico he visited that country *incognito*.

There has been a great deal of controversy over whether or not he actually visited Mexico. Well, he actually did. Travelling under the name of Paul Nanson,[3] a lawyer and collaborator of the *Avant-Garde*, a visa had been issued at the Mexican embassy at Brussels on 9 November 1929. Sailing aboard the steamer *Rio Panuco* he left Hamburg for Vera Cruz (via Havanna) on 19 November 1929, and arrived mid-December 1929. With the money he earned from selling his articles to an American editor, Degrelle rapidly visited the U.S.A. and Canada. By February 1930 he was back in Louvain.[4]

Late October 1930, Mgr Picard asked

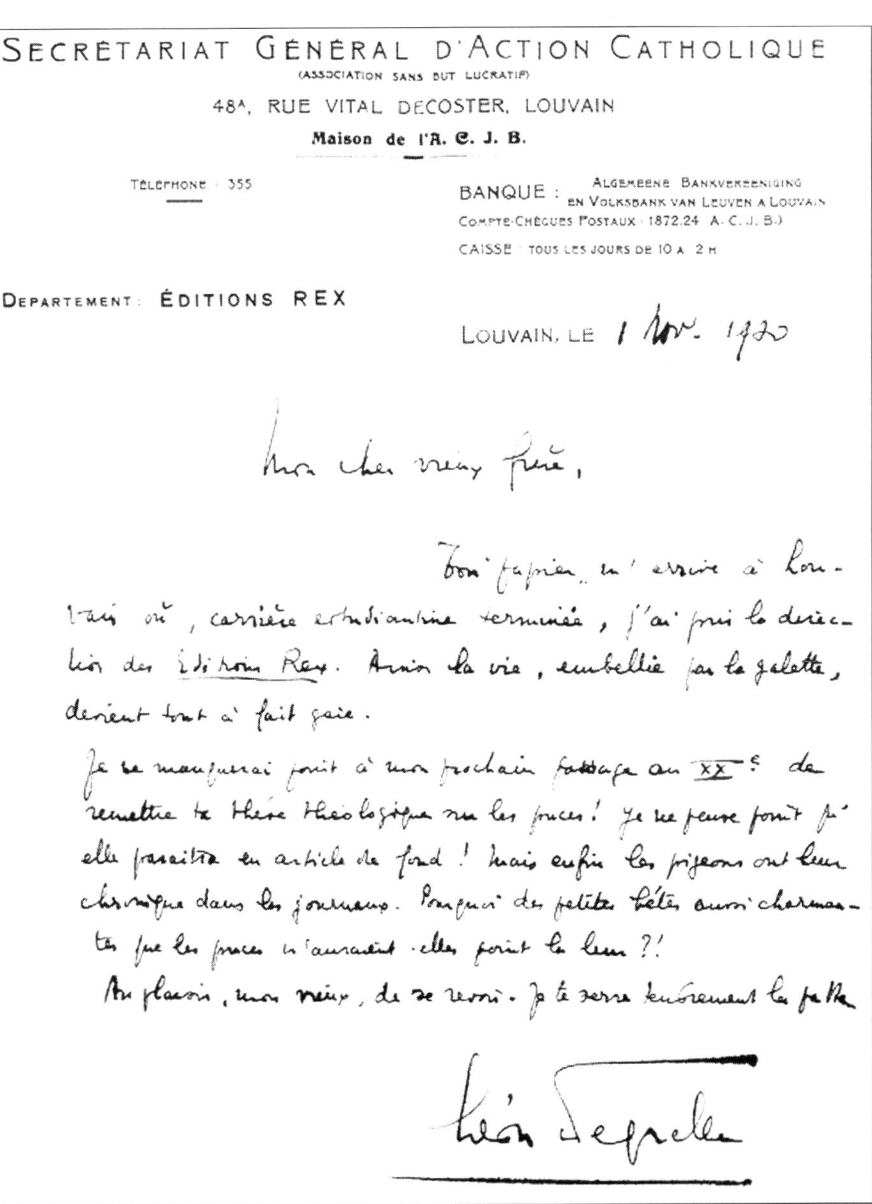

SECRÉTARIAT GÉNÉRAL D'ACTION CATHOLIQUE
(ASSOCIATION SANS BUT LUCRATIF)
48A, RUE VITAL DECOSTER, LOUVAIN
Maison de l'A. C. J. B.

TÉLÉPHONE : 355

BANQUE : ALGEMEENE BANKVEREENIGING EN VOLKSBANK VAN LEUVEN A LOUVAIN
COMPTE-CHÈQUES POSTAUX : 1872.24 (A. C. J. B.)
CAISSE : TOUS LES JOURS DE 10 A 2 H

DÉPARTEMENT : ÉDITIONS REX

LOUVAIN, LE 1 Nov. 1930

Mon cher vieux frère,

Ton papier m'arrive à Louvain où, carrière estudiantine terminée, j'ai pris la direction des Éditions Rex. Ainsi la vie, embellie par la galette, devient tout à fait gaie.

Je ne manquerai point à mon prochain passage au XXe de remettre ta thèse théologique sur les puces! Je ne pense point qu'elle paraîtra en article de fond! Mais enfin les pigeons ont leur chronique dans les journaux. Pourquoi des petites bêtes aussi charmantes que les puces n'auraient-elles point la leur?!

Au plaisir, mon vieux, de te revoir. Je te serre tendrement la patte

Léon Degrelle

Fig. 1.5. Letter dated 1 November 1930, in which Léon Degrelle announces to his brother Edouard he has turned his back on student life to take over control of the *Editions Rex* (*Private collection*).

him to become the director of the *Editions Rex*, the publishing house that produced pamphlets for the *Action Catholique* under the sign of *Christus Rex*.

As manager of the *Editions Rex*, Degrelle soon came to the attention of the Catholic Party, which badly needed a propaganda organizer. Through the *Editions Rex* Degrelle heavily got involved in the 1932 elections, too heavily for the liking of the (officially) non-political *A.C.J.B.*

The weekly papers he directed, such as *Vlan*, *Soirées* and *Rex*, soon upset the religious hierarchy because of the violent polemics against politicians and political programs. At the same time, they fascinated the whole Belgian society, young and old, scandalized as they were by the public disclosures of politico-financial scandals involving top government and banking officials.

In December 1933, the *A.C.J.B.*, through Monseigneur Picard, gave Degrelle an ultimatum to get rid of *Vlan* and to choose between his political interest and the *A.C.J.B.*, both being incompatible. From this point onwards, Degrelle, who did not finally break with the Catholic Party until February 1936, was determined to do away with the immobilism of the Catholic Party by replacing its leadership with a younger and more dynamic team.

Rex as a political movement started its activities on 2 November 1935, the very day when Degrelle and a handful young companions loudly interrupted

Fig. 1.6. Mgr Louis Picard, Degrelle's mentor.

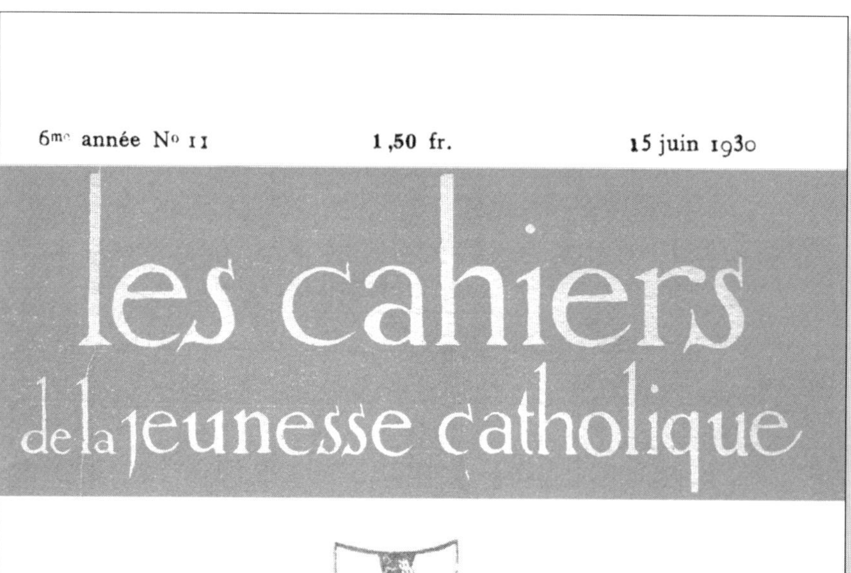

6me année No 11 — 1,50 fr. — 15 juin 1930

les cahiers de la jeunesse catholique

Giovanni Hoyois	**L'Action catholique et les intellectuels.**
Léon Degrelle	**La Belgique a deux ailes.**
José Streel	**Réponse à l'Etudiant Socialiste.**
Robert Haustrate	**Un poète symboliste**
André Vellut	**Poème.**

Notes

La vie Juciste. — Revue de la presse — Les livres.

LOUVAIN

48A, rue Vital Decoster — Bi-mensuel

Fig. 1.7. *Les Cahiers de la Jeunesse Catholique*. José Streel, author of an article in this issue, at first followed Degrelle in his collaborating policy but drifted apart in 1943 when Degrelle claimed the Walloons were of Germanic descent.

1.8. Young Degrelle

Above: **Fig. 1.9.** Degrelle liked to be depicted as the champion and (very popular) defender of the labouring class (*Collection E. De Bruyne*).

Right: **Fig. 1.10.** Léon Degrelle with daughter. Note Rex emblem armband (*Collection E. De Bruyne*).

Below: **Fig. 1.11.** Degrelle flaring up during one of his numerous speeches. Here he demands his opponent ... *to get lost* (*F ... le camp*)! (*Collection E. De Bruyne*).

Right: **Fig. 1.12** One of Léon Degrelle favourite poses.

Fig. 1.13 One of Léon Degrelle favourite poses.

the annual Congress of the *Fédération des Associations et Cercles Catholiques* (*Federation of Associations and Catholic Circles*) held at Courtray. The outcome was the founding of the Rex Movement.

From that moment on, his political action exploded into Barnumesque rallies where the eloquence of the *beau Léon* (handsome Léon) would rouse considerable crowds. In the atmosphere of the economic crisis-years of the depression, vehement attacks against socialism and hypercapitalism, the 'wall of money' raised by the so-called 'banksters', (a combination of bank and gangster) as Degrelle used to depict it, held a discontented middle class in suspense.

The *Pays Réel*, Degrelle's party newspaper, was published for the first time on 3 May 1936. During the same year, one of the most important leaders of the Catholic party sued Degrelle for having cast a slur on his reputation but lost the case in court.

The elections of 24 May 1936 were triumphant for Degrelle and his movement. However, less than two years later, the partial election of 11 November 1937, during which Degrelle competed alone against Prime Minister Paul Van Zeeland, associated to the three main democratic parties, proved to be a fiasco. And last but not least, the 2 April 1939 elections rang the death toll of Rexism.

2. 1940

There was no Nazi party movement as such in Wallonia before the outbreak of the war. Support for National Socialism in Wallonia was confined to groups of agitators in German pay and a handful of intellectuals. As for the Rex Movement, it only adhered to the Nazi cause after the occupation. In the end, it brought little weight to the cause of Collaboration as the mass of its members

Fig. 1.14. The public music stand at Abbeville where Degrelle and his companions were locked up in the vault under the platform.

Left: **Fig. 1.15.** Physically marked Léon Degrelle after his discharge from the Vernet camp (France) in July 1940 (*Collection E. De Bruyne*).

Right: **Fig. 1.16.** Otto Abetz, a personal friend of Degrelle, whom he relied upon for support from the Germans.

deserted the Movement during the war. Those who remained put themselves under the protection of the German occupier by entering one of their numerous services.

At dawn 10 May 1940, the Belgian authorities arrested Degrelle on grounds that his political activities, especially his growing affinities for Fascist Italy and Nazi Germany, had made him a potential enemy of Belgium. Also arrested were other Belgians, among them Communists, Rexists, German identified spies, European refugees, and Flemish Fascists, including *Verdinaso* Leader Joris van Severen and his companion Jan Rijckoort. In all 20 Belgians and 58 foreigners in his group were deported to France. In Abbéville Degrelle and his associates were locked up in the vault beneath the public bandstand. He miraculously escaped being killed when French soldiers shot 21 men of his group. Degrelle was finally freed from the Le Vernet camp near the Spanish border on 22 July 1940.

Eager to restart political activities, Degrelle looked for political support from King Leopold III, Cardinal Van Roey and the German ambassador Otto Abetz. However, his attempts to emerge as a central political figure in Occupied Belgium proved to be complete failure. Degrelle had no support from the German occupation administration. From the start the *Militärverwaltung* in Brussels had put the stress on the policy they had already adopted during WWI,

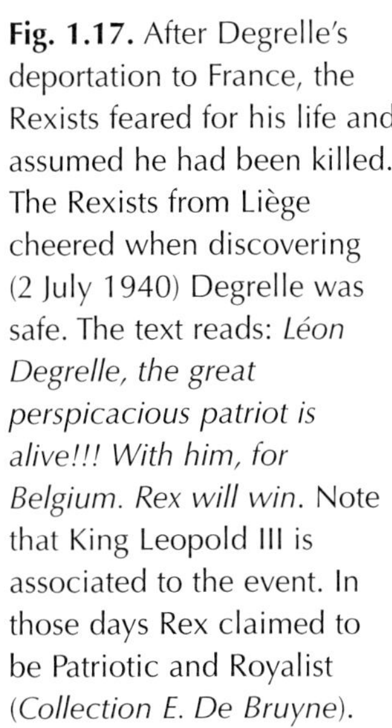

Fig. 1.17. After Degrelle's deportation to France, the Rexists feared for his life and assumed he had been killed. The Rexists from Liège cheered when discovering (2 July 1940) Degrelle was safe. The text reads: *Léon Degrelle, the great perspicacious patriot is alive!!! With him, for Belgium. Rex will win.* Note that King Leopold III is associated to the event. In those days Rex claimed to be Patriotic and Royalist (*Collection E. De Bruyne*).

Hebdomadaire Extrait du Numéro du 12 octobre 1934 3e année, n° 40

REX

Toute la Vie des Lettres

Léon DEGRELLE Directeur

Editions REX Louvain

AU SERVICE DE L'EGLISE

par Léon Degrelle

Fig. 1.18. Pre-war Rexist publication: the newspaper of the Rexist Movement.

Flamenpolitik: everything for the Flemings, nothing for the Walloons! On the other hand, Otto Abetz, whom Degrelle knew very well – for both their wives were very close friends as they had attended the same boarding school in France – could not get him the support of the Nazi leaders in Germany.

As soon as the *Pays Réel* was republished, Degrelle directed his attacks against the Church once again. By the end of the year, they had extended to the enemies of the New Order, Jews, Freemasons, and politicians. At the same time violence appeared. Politicians were assaulted in the streets. In Antwerp and Liège, units of the *Formations de Combat* – the Rex militia – attacked and sacked Jewish shops.

By the end of year it was quite clear that Degrelle had not been able to establish himself as the central political figure within Occupied Belgium, that he had not been able to gain the trust and support of the German authorities, and that to his great discontent he was destined to be overshadowed.

3. 1941

Since Degrelle was refused any participation in traditional politics there was nothing else to be done than look for another manner in which to elbow his way up to the top.

That is what he did at the National Rexist rally at Liège on 5 January 1941. That day, in presence of 5,000 Rexists, he concluded his speech with a vibrating *Heil Hitler*!

The profession of allegiance to Hitler split up the party. Close collaborators protested and many a Rexist resigned. A minority, however, thought they could accept the new orientation of the movement.

The major goal for Degrelle was to win the confidence of the Germans. Military collaboration was an excellent means to achieve this. And when in February 1941 the *Wehrmacht* authorities in Belgium decided to enrol local forces in their auxiliary transport corps, *Nationalsozialistisches Kraftfahrer-Korps* or *NSKK*, Degrelle immediately offered his assistance by creating a *Brigade Motorisée Rexiste*. He initially promised to recruit 1,000 drivers but could only find 300 of them.

While waiting for positive results Degrelle had started to reorganize the movement. A new *Etat-Major du Chef* was installed; the powers of the *Chefs de Région* (Wallonia, Brussels and Flanders for the Flemish Rexists) were extended.

Fig. 1.19. Pre-war Rexist publication: the periodical *Soirées*.

Top: **Fig. 1.20.** Fernand Rouleau (on the left)

Bottom: **Fig. 1.21.** By 1943, Rouleau had become the head of the recruiting service for the *Charlemagne* in Paris. Here he is (on the right) next to two officers of the Wlassow army. Rouleau fled to Switzerland in September 1944. Escaping the Belgian Justice, he managed to reach Spain, where he died in the course of 1984.

In September 1941, Degrelle, fearing Rouleau's influence and growing power, dismissed his Lieutenant from the *Légion Wallonie*. A few weeks later, he expelled him from the Rex Movement (*Arch. E. De Bruyne, via J. Mabire*).

On the other hand, the militia, the *Formations de Combat*, was deprived of much of its former autonomy. And last but not least, Degrelle succeeded in having francophone interests represented by two Rexists heading a *Cabinet wallon*, a department within the Ministry of the Interior.[5]

In fact, Degrelle was not getting any farther. He was despairingly waiting for an event to come, which would enable him to strike. The news of Hitler's attack on the Soviet Union was going to drag Degrelle out of inaction, and the new conflict was welcomed as an opportunity to escape from former isolation.

In early July 1941, Berlin gave the Rexists permission to create a unit – *Corps Franc Wallonie* or *Légion Wallonie* – composed of francophone Belgian volunteers.

The recruiting campaign received a boost when Degrelle announced his own enlistment on 20 July 1941. Degrelle was declared fit for armed service on 31 July 1941, his enrolment file bearing number 237.

As Léon Degrelle had no military experience,[6] he was refused the rank of Lieutenant when he discreetly expressed the idea an officer's rank would suit his political status better. The German verdict stood no appeal: lack of military and technical knowledge, it said.[7]

During the last days of the recruiting campaign, several hundred of the most experienced Rexist militants – including a number of *Chefs de Cercles* – joined the

Fig. 1.22. Degrelle wearing an *F.C.* uniform volunteers for the *Légion Wallonie*. Next to him (on his right) is Robert du Welz. He was the only Belgian who accompanied Degrelle on his escape flight to Spain from Oslo on 8 May 1945.

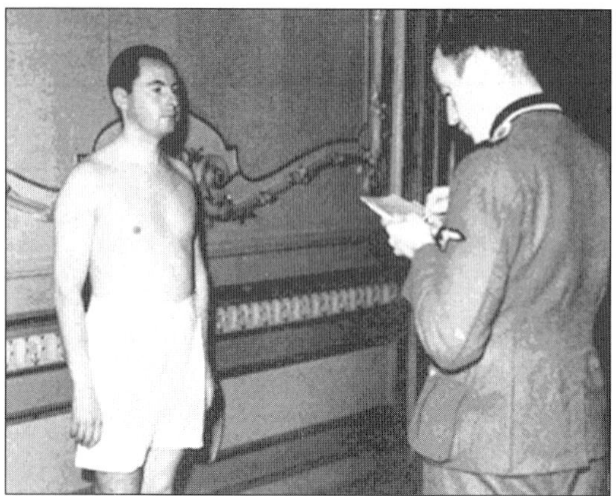

Fig. 1.23. Great publicity was given to Degrelle's volunteering for the Eastern front. Here he is being examined for physical fitness.

Légion with the consequence that on the appointed date of departure (8 August 1941) more or less 850 legionnaires gathered at *Place Royale*, Brussels. A majority of the volunteers were members of the *Formations de Combat* wearing their uniform. A small number of legionnaires belonged to the *AGRA*, *Les Amis du Grand Reich Allemand* (The Friends of the Greater German Reich), a Rex competing grouping, while others included Tsarist exiles, Catholic idealists, long-standing anti-Communists and a number of adventurers, who found in the *Légion* the opportunity to escape material or domestic difficulties.

Through the press the volunteers had been reassured that they would be back with their families before the end of the year after serving behind the front-lines, glorified with the prestige of participating in the defeat of Communism. At this point, Degrelle and his volunteers really feared one thing: that they would arrive on the front after the defeat of the Soviet armies.

Before leaving for the Eastern Front Degrelle appointed Victor Matthys, 27 years of age, his 'oldest and most loyal associate', to act as the *Chef ad interim* of the movement during his absence. Matthys had joined Degrelle in the early thirties and was known for his unflinching personal loyalty to Degrelle. Matthys, a journalist by profession, was appointed main editor of the *Pays Réel* although he hardly had any qualifications for his new post. Apart from the fact that he had been the chief of the propaganda department in May 1941, Matthys had no experience of administration. Degrelle, however, took care to surround him with more experienced men:

- Joseph Pévenasse, a lawyer from Charleroi, who would act as the *Inspecteur Fédéral du Mouvement* in charge of the Rexist local organization and the *Formations de Combat*. Pévenasse had formerly combined the position of *Chef de Rex-Wallonie* (chief of Rex in Wallonia) and *Chef de l'Ordre du Travail* (Labour Leader);
- Maurice Vandevelde retained control of the finances of the Movement;
- José Streel, a brilliant young journalist, was to become head of the political bureau of Rex and political director of the *Pays Réel*. He soon became Matthys' main advisor;

Fig. 1.24. After Léon Degrelle's departure for the Eastern Front, Victor Matthys was appointed Chief *a. i.* of the Rex Movement. (*Collection J.-L. Roba*).

Fig. 1.25. Joseph Pévenasse (centre) as an NCO of the *Légion Wallonie*. Lawyer by profession living in Charleroi, Pévenasse was an admirer of the Nazi system and used his authority ruthlessly in every field in which he was involved.

He successively became Chief of *Rex Wallonie* (early 1941), Chief of the Political Staff of Rex (1941), permanent Rex representative to the Province Governor, Federal Inspector of the Rex Movement (Spring 1941), non-commissioned officer in the *Légion Wallonie* (March 42–March 43), Inspector of the *F.C.* Militia (mid-1943), *SS-Ustuf.* of the *28.SS-Freiw.-Gren.Div.Wallonien*. Pévenasse disappeared after the German collapse. He was sentenced to death *in absentia*. (*Collection J.-L. Roba*).

- Jean Denis, former Rexist deputy, once reputed to be the most influential philosopher of the Movement. (He was later on relegated to the control of Rexist cultural activities).

By the end of the year Victor Matthys had created the *Solidarité Rexiste* (Rexist Solidarity), an organization meant to help those Rexists in need of assistance. The departure of the legionnaires – many of them were breadwinners – had put many a family in financial difficulties. A social service, the *Solidarité Légionnaire*, was created to care for the relatives of the absent soldiers.

During the winter of 1941, Victor Matthys had to face the first political murders committed on Rex Movement members. These acts of violence continued to grow exponentially until the end of the war.

During the autumn of 1941, Rex recruited a second military unit: the *Gardes Wallonnes* (Walloon Guards), which, like the *Légion Wallonie*, were to be part of the *Wehrmacht*. The *Gardes Wallonnes* were not to be used as front-line troops and would only operate within the jurisdiction of the *Militärverwaltung* (*i.e.* the Walloon provinces plus the French Departments *Pas de Calais* and *Nord*), where they would guard places of strategic importance such as airfields, bridges and railways lines. In France, they also guarded Soviet POW camps. These camps held many more nationalities than just Russians, for example Azerbaijanis, Georgians, Chechens, Uzbeks, Kazakhs, Ukrainians, and others.

Some weeks after the departure of the Legion, Streel suggested to Matthys that a *Service Politique* be created within the national Headquarters of Rex with responsibility for the political direction of the movement. Streel proposed himself for the political direction of the Movement.

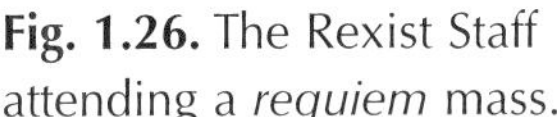

Fig. 1.26. The Rexist Staff attending a *requiem* mass.

Front row: left to right; Jean Denis, in 1943 chief of the Cultural Service; Victor Matthys, chief *a. i.* of Rex; José Streel, head of the Political Service.

Second row: André Derwael, deputy chief of the *Jeunesse Rexiste* in absence of John Hagemans at the Eastern Front; Marcel Dupont, Chief of the Territorial Services. (*CEGES*)

Top left: **Fig. 1.27.** Jean Denis – one of the ideologues of the Rex Movement wrote the Rexist doctrinal principles.

Top right: **Fig. 1.28.** *A man . . . A leader*. Léon Degrelle

Bottom left: **Fig. 1.29.** During the war Streel published *The Revolution of the XXth Century*, a basic work for the comprehension of his ideological engagement.

Bottom right: **Fig. 1.30.** During the pre-war period, Jean Denis, together with José Streel, had been one of the most prominent promoters of Rex. This is a copy having belonged to a former *F.C.* member of the town of Verviers.

In November 1941, Streel declared that "Rexist orthodoxy could only be measured by the degree of enthusiasm one showed for the *Feldgrau*" (German uniform).

Still in November 1941, the tandem Matthys-Streel was reinforced by the appointment of long-standing Rexist Marcel Dupont to the new post of *Chef des Cadres Territoriaux* in charge of the supervision of the activities of the local sections.

Matthys and Streel devoted the last months of the year to strengthening the bonds with the *Militärverwaltung* in Brussels. At the same time, they had to face dissident and Rex opposed movements such as the *MNPW – Mouvement National Populaire Wallon* – and the *AGRA – Les Amis du Grand Reich Allemand.*

4. 1942

While Degrelle was at the front during 1942 – he and his legionnaires would not be back for a first furlough until 18 December 1942 – Matthys and the Rexist front in Belgium were going to experience the cruel reality of being a collaborationist movement. The number of criminal assaults on and political murders of collaborationists grew increasingly. By the end of 1942, 67 criminal acts of violence involving Rexists had been committed. 60 of them had taken place in the second half of 1942. Between July and December 1942, 28 victims were killed in some way or another.

During February 1942, Rex had to face the Liège-based Rex dissident Antoine Leclercq in his efforts to meld Rex, *AGRA*, the *MNPW* (*Mouvement National Populaire Wallon* – Walloon National Popular Movement) and the *Défense du Peuple* (People's Defence) into one single collaborationist party. A soon as this danger was warded off, Matthys and his team started strengthening Rexist influence on all levels of public, cultural and political life. Four new, much larger (but Rex controlled) Greater-City administrations were established (*Grand-La Louvière, Grand-Charleroi, Grand-Liège* and *Grand-Bruxelles*). The advances within local government were accompanied by a similar expansion in its influence within the five provinces of francophone Belgium. In March 1942, the governors of Namur and Liège were replaced by two New Order nominees.[8]

However, the main public event by far was the announcement, in early April 1942, that the *Légion Wallonie* had been engaged in its first front-line battle at Gromowaja-Balka. From mid-February to 28 March 1942, the *Légion Wallonie* had suffered 55% losses. For the reward of 37 *EK II* (the German Iron Cross 2nd Class) awarded to the Walloon legionnaires, out

Fig. 1.31. Burial of a collaborationist. From 1942 onwards, the number of murders committed on Rexists and members of other collaborating groupings grew steadily (*Collection E. De Bruyne*).

Fig. 1.32. The 10 March 1942 contingent marching past the Grand Place, in front of the Brussels Town-Hall (*Arch. E. De Bruyne*).

Fig. 1.33. Members of the Rexist Youth present the new pennon and the four flags (one per company) of the *Légion Wallonie* (*R. Devresse; arch. E. De Bruyne*).

Fig. 1.34. A few weeks after enlistment Hagemans (centre) was back in Brussels to preside over a Rexist Youth ceremony held Place Rouppe, not far from the Rexist Headquarters. Left: Marie-Jeanne Larsimont heading the girls' section; right, Jean-Pierre Quoirin, Chief of the *Prévôté* (HQ) (*Arch E. De Bruyne*).

of total battle strength of 411 men, 71 had been killed and 155 suffered injuries.

A lot of fuss was made over Degrelle's immediate promotion to the rank of *Oberfeldwebel* on grounds of personal gallantry as, already very early during the battle, a shocked Degrelle had to be evacuated to the rear by his company commander, *Leutnant* Alfred Lisein, leaving *Oberfeldwebel* Jules Mathieu in charge of the battle positions of 1st Company.[9]

A second main event occurred 10 March 1942, with the departure of the second important contingent for the *Légion Wallonie*. The heavy losses within the unit jeopardized the existence of the *Légion*. Unless it was substantially reinforced, the *Légion Wallonie* would be disbanded.

A third even more important event intervened during October 1942. It was a highly confidential communication from Degrelle to Matthys that was going to change the face and the fate of Walloon collaboration in Belgium.

While fighting alongside the *Wiking* in the Caucasus, Degrelle had met with General Felix Steiner at Schadyschenskaja on 17 September 1942. Degrelle immediately understood the real long-term advantages he could get from leaving the reactionary *Werhmacht* to join a dynamic, revolution-thirsty *Waffen-SS* in the hands of which, one day or another, all power would be concentrated. The ethnic obstacle of the Walloons being listed as of non-Germanic lineage (and thus unfit for service within the *Waffen-SS*) would be no issue as Degrelle, to achieve his goal, was up to anything ... even to bring evidence that Walloons were American Indians, if this proved to be necessary![10]

Taking advantage of Prof. Dr Franz Petri's theory, initially exposed in a 1937 published thesis *Germanisches Volkserbe in Wallonien und Nordfrankreich* (Germanic Inheritance in Wallonia and northern France), Degrelle professed that the Walloons were a Germanic people ... speaking French. Of this Matthys was informed in a long letter sent from the Caucasus front and by which the *Chef* consequently ordered Matthys to announce the new orientation in the press. This is what Matthys did in his 25 October 1942 speech.

Fig. 1.35. Dr Franz Petri's thesis *Germanic heritage in Wallonia and northern France* allowed Degrelle to proclaim Walloons belonged to the Germanic community.

Germanisches Volkserbe in Wallonien und Nordfrankreich

Band 1

Ludwig Röhrscheid Verlag Bonn

5. 1943

Degrelle held a Rexist rally in the *Palais des Sports* in Brussels on 17 January 1943, during which he announced his acceptance that the future of the francophone Belgians lay within an expanded Germanic Empire. As the idea of a federation encompassing all of the German racial groups of Europe was the program of the *SS*, there could be no doubt that Degrelle, by giving that speech, deliberately proved his support to Himmler and associates. By presenting this new orientation, Degrelle officially abandoned his Royalist-Belgicist-unitarian attitude (opposed to a split up of Belgium) that he had been supporting for the last two years. Choosing openly for the *SS* policy meant that Degrelle was doing away with the idea of one undivided Belgium to start the promotion of a (Germanic) Wallonia to be annexed to the Third Reich. Many a Rexist did not agree with Degrelle's new anti-Belgian policy, and resigned. The most conspicuous Rexist to withdraw was José Streel. He resigned from both *Le Pays Réel* and the *Service Politique* of the Rexist Staff, on grounds that Degrelle, by proclaiming his unlimited reliance in a foreign chief of whom he had become the political soldier, had betrayed both Rex and his country.[11]

By mid-1943, General Eggert Reeder, chief of the German military administration in Brussels, reported in his monthly briefing that the Rexists had become an insignificant minority; that the total of its militants had fallen down to 8,000 members.

From now on only one thing mattered to Degrelle: the *Légion Wallonie* and its military exploits, the only way to political recognition and respect by the Germans. Knowing that the Rexist movement in Belgium would be more of a millstone round his neck than a support in the consolidation of his personal prestige within the Third Reich, Degrelle was to concentrate all his efforts on the *Légion*.

Since 1941, Degrelle had considerably strengthened his hold over the *Légion*. Many of those soldiers most opposed to him had died in battle or been demobilized. Those who replaced them were on the whole young with few political convictions or long-standing Rexist NCOs promoted to the rank of Company CO.

In the first category mention must be made of opponents such as:

- *Kdr* Pierre Pauly, who wanted the *Légion* to be a non-politically coloured military anti-Bolshevik unit, was forced to leave the *Légion* because he was a threat to Degrelle's ambition;
- Fernand Rouleau, whose ambition it was to achieve political leadership over the *Légion Wallonie*, was sent back to Belgium and expelled from the Rex Movement;
- Company CO Albert Van Damme was sent home because he did not accept the Rexist salute as a military one;
- the Catholic chaplain, Louis Fierens, who had been reluctant to join the *Waffen-SS* never showed up at the *Sturmbrigade* after the Cherkassy breakout;
- *AGRA* leader Dr Albert Miesse, after he had been dismissed from the *Légion* in March 1942 – in consequence of which he joined the

Fig. 1.36. Bearing spectacles and holding a document in his hands, General Eggert Reeder, chief of the Military Administration (*Arch. E. De Bruyne*).

Fig. 1.37. Left: *Leutnant* Albert Van Damme, CO/1Company. Next to him *Oberfeldwebel* Jules Mathieu, who was to become commanding officer of the 1st Company in April 1942. Marked with a cross: Léon Degrelle. (*J. Mathieu/Collection E. De Bruyne*).

Fig. 1.38. Second left: *Oberleutnant* Henri Derriks with *Spiess* Descamps (left) and three of his NCOs of 2nd Company near Pieske barracks. Note that Derriks wears the *Edelweiß* badge notwithstanding the fact that he did not participate in the Caucasus campaign (*Private Collection*).

> *Waffen-SS* – made vain efforts to be re-appointed to the Brigade as a doctor in charge of the medical service in June 1943.

In the end, Henri Derriks became the only opponent to Degrelle to be tolerated. The reason for this was that Degrelle was aware of the military value of this excellent front-line officer, and it was plainly clear to him that he needed Derriks' exploits for his personal prestige.

As to Lucien Lippert, Degrelle had found in him a military commander who, though not a member of Rex, could be relied upon to support most of his plans. Belonging to the second category mention must be made of Jules Mathieu, Georges Ruelle and Marcel Bonniver, all true Rexists and Degrelle followers.

6. 1944

Much of the Rex Movement's concern in 1944 was concentrated on the protection of its members. Special protection units, such as the *Formation B*, had been created. Their mission was to protect all Rexist militants and to act as a bodyguard protecting local Rexist politicians.

The *Département de Sécurité et d'Information – DSI*, a counter-terror organization headed by Charles Lambinon, gradually extended its activities to the main towns of Wallonia. That department operated on the fringes of the German police apparatus and carried out crude and violent interrogations on the suspects they had arrested. In February 1944, Matthys created the *Ordre du Sang* – Blood Order – to be awarded to those Rexists who had distinguished themselves in direct combat by killing the enemies of the Movement.

A last public ceremony was to be held on 1 and 2 April 1944 in Charleroi and Brussels, celebrating the so-called victorious return of the Cherkassy veterans.[12] It was as well a counter to Soviet propaganda claiming that the *Sturmbrigade* had been destroyed in the *Kessel*, and it was a

Fig. 1.39. The Cherkassy parade in Brussels: a triumphant, smiling Degrelle and two of his five children salute the crowd (*Collection J.-L. Roba*).

response to the BBC, which had announced Degrelle's death. To add to the effect, the column of legionnaires had been motorized for the occasion with vehicles borrowed from the *12. SS-Pz. Div. Hitlerjugend* stationed at Beverloo barracks at the time. A parade by a collaborationist military unit in full battle order through a capital city appears to have been a unique event in German-occupied Europe. It confirmed Degrelle's status as a leading figure in the Nazi propaganda system.[13] The Cherkassy parade was not only an important personal political victory, it also irritated the Flemish collaboration as they had been refused the favours granted to Degrelle. Despite the fact the *Sturmbrigade Langemarck* had been involved in comparably heavy fighting in the Jampol/Shitomir area in February 1944, the Flemish were refused the permission of organizing a similar parade. In the end, to calm things down and by way of compensation, Himmler promised the Flemish legionnaires would be granted the visit of their wives and fiancées in Germany …

In the course of the summer, as the Allied troops were approaching, the Resistance intensified its action. Terror called for counter-terror. During the night of 17–18 August 1944, the Rexists avenged the murder of the Rexist mayor of Charleroi, Oswald Englebin, by assassinating 27 innocent people.

A few days later, the Germans began to retreat from Belgium, evacuating their forces from nearly all of the country within a few days. The Rexists, together with other collaborators, were given the choice between accompanying the retreating German forces or to remain behind to face both the revenge of the Resistance and the military justice, promised by Prime Minister Pierlot in London.

7.1945

During the very first days of September 1944, about 5,000 Walloons fled to Germany, using all kinds of transport, railway, and motorized columns (by night). Those collaborators who were

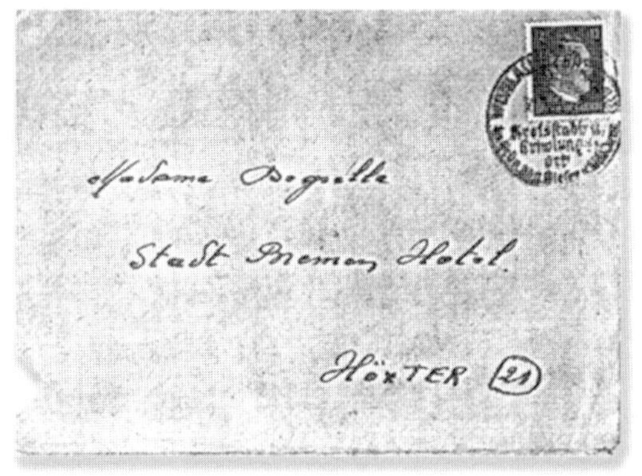

Fig. 1.40.

lucky enough to live near the German border in the eastern part of the country evacuated by tram to Aachen. This was the case in the Malmedy-Eupen and Verviers areas. Mrs. Degrelle and her children had already left Brussels on 31 August heading to Höxter, Hanover.

As the refugees had been directed to the southern part of the *Hannover-Gau*, a *Bureau Central d'Evacuation* was created at Springe and four Walloon *Kreisleiter* were appointed. Their task was to assist the German mayors of the different villages where the refugees had been housed.

The following towns had an administrative centre taking care of Walloon interests:

- Springe, headed by *Kreisleiter* Max Wefers, a Rexist from Brussels;
- Hildesheim, headed by *Kreisleiter* Maurice Bomans, former municipal magistrate of Grand-Liège;
- Alfeld, headed by *Kreisleiter* Albert Regnard, member of the *Département Politique de l'Etat-Major de Rex;*
- Hameln, headed by *Kreisleiter* Jean Villers, former chief of Rex-Namur.

When the Ardennes offensive was

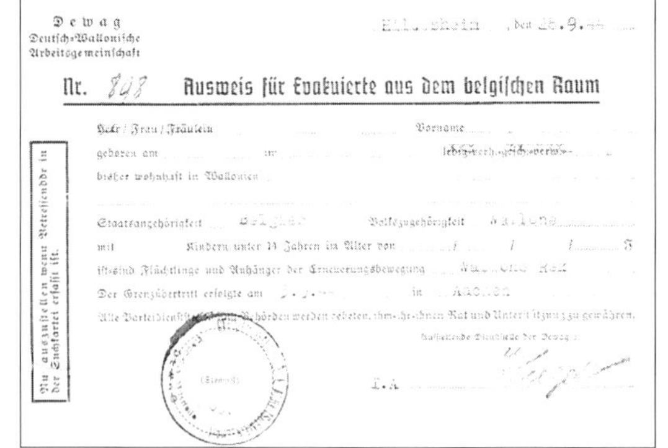

Dewag
Deutsch-Wallonische
Arbeitsgemeinschaft

Nr. 808 **Ausweis für Evakuierte aus dem belgischen Raum**

Herr / Frau / Fräulein ... Vorname ...
geboren am ... in ... ledig-verh.-gesch.-verw.
bisher wohnhaft in Wallonien ...
Staatsangehörigkeit ... Volkszugehörigkeit ...
mit ... Kindern unter 14 Jahren im Alter von ... / ... / ... J.
ist-sind Flüchtlinge und Anhänger der Erneuerungsbewegung ...
Der Grenzübertritt erfolgte am ... in ... AACHEN
Alle Parteidienststellen und Behörden werden gebeten, ihm-ihr-ihnen Rat und Unterstützung zu gewähren.

Nur auszustellen wenn Betreffende in der Suchkartei erfaßt ist.

Fig. 1.41. The *DeWag, i.e. Deutsch-Wallonische Arbeitsgemeinschaft* (German-Walloon Labour Community) was in charge of the evacuation of the Walloon refugees. It issued the necessary documents for housing and welfare care in Germany (*Collection E. De Bruyne*).

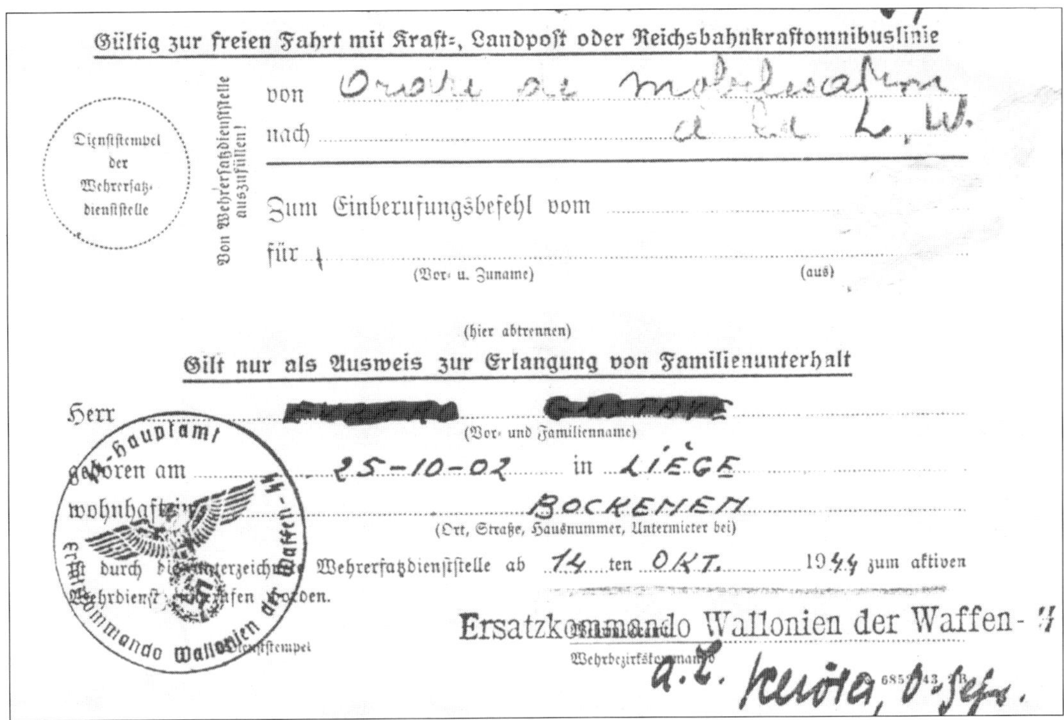

Gültig zur freien Fahrt mit Kraft-, Landpost oder Reichsbahnkraftomnibuslinie

Dienststempel der Wehrersatzdienststelle

Von Wehrersatzdienststelle auszufüllen!

von ...

nach ...

Zum Einberufungsbefehl vom ...

für ... (Vor- u. Zuname) ... (aus)

(hier abtrennen)

Gilt nur als Ausweis zur Erlangung von Familienunterhalt

Herr ... (Vor- und Familienname)

geboren am 25-10-02 in LIÈGE

wohnhaft in BOCKENEM (Ort, Straße, Hausnummer, Untermieter bei)

ist durch die unterzeichnete Wehrersatzdienststelle ab 14 ten OKT. 1944 zum aktiven Wehrdienst einberufen worden.

Ersatzkommando Wallonien der Waffen-SS

Wehrbezirkskommando

Fig. 1.42. October 1944, all Walloon refugees were called up for active military service by means of an *ad hoc* enlistment order (*Collection E. De Bruyne*).

launched, dozens of Rexist dignitaries, together with their administrative services, were transferred to Gummersbach with a view to return to Wallonia had the offensive been successful.

On 31 March 1945, in the absence of Léon Degrelle, Matthys and Collard dissolved the Rex Movement in the back-room of a pub at Bockenem/ Hanover.

During May 1945, the Belgian military and judicial authorities arrested most of the Rexists and their relatives.

Severe condemnation awaited them.

8. The *Mouvement Féminin Rexiste – M.F.R.* (Feminine Section of the Rex Movement)

Established at the end of the year 1942 by Marguerite Inghels, a journalist of the *Pays Réel*, the *M.F.R.* gave special attention to a section called *Faith in Life* (*Foi dans la Vie*), one of the three departments that had to develop a more specific training among the cadres of the feminine movement.

Inghels soon resigned and was replaced by Renée Bodart, bearing the title of General Delegate of the Feminine Rexist Movement. As such she was going to control and expand the section *Foi dans la Vie*, and she moulded it into the cradle of future feminine Rexist cadres.

On 9 February 1944, the feminine Rexist Movement was transformed into the Walloon Feminine Organizations (*Organisations féminines wallonnes – O.F.W.*) controlling the remainder of the old *M.F.R.* A new section, called *Specialized Services* (*Services Spécialisés*), was created. It was led by Jeanne Degrelle (one of Degrelle's sisters), who received the title of General Inspector of the *O.F.W.*, This reorganization was meant as a means to weaken Renée Bodart's power position as Victor Matthys suspected her of having too close contacts with the feminine leaders of the German *Frauenschaft*, eager to take control over all Walloon feminine organizations on the same pattern as achieved in Flanders. Renée Bodart kept the

Fig. 1.43. April 1941: Lowering of the colours ceremony at the training camp *Camp-Ecole Marguerite d'Autriche* at Uccle/Brussels (*Collection R. Devresse; arch. E. De Bruyne*).

Fig. 1.44. Foreground figures from left to right: Suzanne Lagneaux, Fernand Rouleau, Marguerite Inghels and John Hagemans (*Collection R. Devresse; – arch. E. De Bruyne*).

honorary title of Inspector of the *M.F.R.* while Huguette Defoiche became General Delegate to the Direction of the Specialized Services, grouping all matters pertaining to the *DRK* (*Deutsches Rotes Kreuz*), the feminine section of the *SVTW* (Labour Service) and the Walloon People's Welfare. She was also in charge of a school for Rexist girls (*Ecole Marie Bourgogne*), situated at Genval.

In September 1944, the feminine Rexist cadres also fled to Germany. Once Bodart had arrived in the *Hannover-Gau*, she tried to retake control over of the feminine movement thanks to the support of the German authorities. As a result of this, Victor Matthys, rather than see the movement fall into the hands of the Germans, dissolved the Feminine Rexist Movement in November 1944.

CHAPTER II

Rex Controlled Organizations

The Rex Militia

A. Pre-War Period

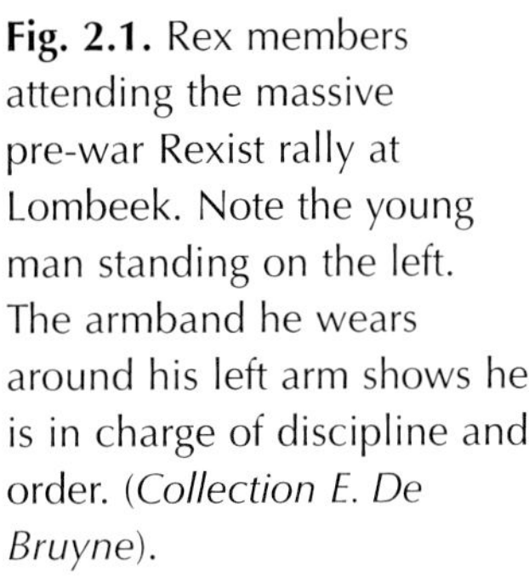

Fig. 2.1. Rex members attending the massive pre-war Rexist rally at Lombeek. Note the young man standing on the left. The armband he wears around his left arm shows he is in charge of discipline and order. (*Collection E. De Bruyne*).

1. The *Service d'Ordre et de Sécurité* (Order and Security Service)

One of the main characteristics of all authoritarian regimes during the *interbellum* period was the presence of uniformed paramilitary squads, also called stormtroopers. The mission of these militias was to protect the members at public meetings, to intimidate antagonists or even to crush any form of rebellion or opposition. The Rex Movement had its *Service d'Ordre et de Sécurité*, which, like any other uniformed grouping in Belgium, was forbidden by law on 4 May 1936.

B. War-time Period

1. The *Formations de Combat* – F.C.

On 9 July 1940, the General Council (*Conseil Général*) of the Rexist Movement decided to create a new paramilitary unit to be called the *Formation de Combat* – F.C. It rapidly expanded and by the end of the year they numbered more or less 4,000 members. The uniform was dark blue. The left breast pocket showed an embroidered red Burgundy Cross on black shield. The role of the F.C. was to be the shock troops and guardians of the Revolution.

The F.C. was divided into Banners; six in all, each Banner corresponding to a Rexist circle; a Banner being composed of several Flames.

The F.C. was successively commanded by:

1. Rutger Simoens (June 1940-February 1941);
2. Fernand Rouleau (February 1941-September 1941 – joined the *Légion Wallonie*);
3. Henri Brahy (September 1941-February 1942 – joined the *Légion Wallonie* for a very short time in March 1942);
4. Albert Constant (February 1942 – resigned in January 1943).

Trying to win the support of the Germans, Degrelle offered to raise the following paramilitary groupings:

Fig. 2.2. *Regenwurm* barracks, 12 August 41: four Rexist volunteers for the *Légion Wallonie* are still in their F.C. uniform. The young man on the right, Urbain Dodémont, was eventually killed in action on 28 February 1942. On the left is Jean Frisschen. (*J. Frisschen/Collection E. De Bruyne*).

- during October 1940, an Air Corps of Rexist aviators participating in the Battle of Britain and a regiment of Rexist colonial troops to be raised for freeing the Congo from the control of the Belgian government in London;
- during January 1941, a Rexist Motorized Brigade (*Brigade de Rex Motorisée*) with Rexist drivers assisting the newly introduced *Werhmacht-Luftwaffe* tutored *NSKK*.

In the course of 1942, many a member either had volunteered for the *Légion Wallonie*, for the *NSKK*, or had joined the *Garde Wallonne* with the result that, by mid-1943, the *F.C.* had shrunk to 14 officers, 46 NCOs and 726 men.

Now that the *F.C.* had almost bled to death, Matthys ordered (summer of 1942) a new élite unit be raised that would only operate on Belgian territory: the *Hilfsgendarmerie*, (auxiliary police force) a military trained unit intended to act as a German police reserve.

Training camps were organised near Antwerp (Kontich) but most Rexists were reluctant to join a service that was too closely linked with the German police services.

In the end, a moribund *F.C.* and the little success of the *Hilfsgendarmerie* left unsolved the problem of how the movement could raise and maintain a militia capable of protecting its militants and accomplish an eventual seizure of political power.[1]

Fig. 2.3. Léon Degrelle in his *F.C.* uniform. (*Collection E. De Bruyne*).

From now on, local Rexist authorities raised their own protection squads: the *Edgard Duquesne Squad*, (July 1943), also known as *Brigade A* in La Louvière; the *Bande Chéron* (Chéron gang) in the Borinage area; the *Brigade Funken-Fisette-Jadoul* in Liège, and the *Merlot Police* gang in Charleroi, all of which were going to be involved in bloody killings and arbitrary arrests.

2. The *Garde Wallonne – G.W.*

On 27 June 1941, Hitler approved the creation of national anti-Bolshevik legions for service on the Eastern Front.

In reality, German military authorities in Brussels were sceptical as to the success of raising volunteers for an anti-Bolshevik unit, and they demonstrated no particular enthusiasm in welcoming what in the end they thought would be nothing more than a handful men. Fearing a failure, they consequently demanded, by way of a test, the preliminary raising of a Walloon military formation that would assist the German occupying forces in keeping order in the country. Only if successful, would a recruiting campaign for an anti-Bolshevik legion be allowed. Yielding to the German wishes, in fact a disguised blackmail, Degrelle, speaking to the Brussels *Formations de Combat* on 6 July 1941, launched a vibrant call for the urgent raising – among the *F.C.* – of an armed paramilitary formation that he planned to christen *Garde Wallonne* in memory of the famous Walloon mercenaries who served in the Spanish armies in the 17th and 18th centuries. Party discipline ensured that *F.C.* militiamen rallied massively to the *Garde Wallonne*. Since the Rex Movement proved able to raise a pro-German military auxiliary formation in no time, the *Militärverwaltung* – confident in the positive outcome of a campaign in favour of an anti-Bolshevik legion – abandoned its initial reluctant attitude and authorized

Fig. 2.4. A member of the *Garde Wallonne*. (*Collection E. De Bruyne*).

the formation of the anti-Bolshevik *Corps Franc Wallonie*.

At its beginnings, recruitment for the *G.W.* was made essentially among WWI veterans who were members of the *F.C.*, but, as time went by, the newcomers – not all were Rexists or New Order sympathizers! – enlisted for reasons of personal interest, facility, necessity or just to escape forced labour service in Germany.

The first commander of the *Garde Wallonne* was the Belgian career officer, Major Torne. He was assisted by Captain of the Reserve Corps Jean Malherbe, who had been liberated for this purpose from *Oflag VIII C* (Juliusburg) on 2 January 1941. When Malherbe joined the *5. SS-Sturmbrigade Wallonien* in November 1943, Paul De Middeleer, former Staff officer of the *Formations de Combat*, replaced him.

In all three battalions were raised. Scattered in Wallonia (II Bn in Mons, III Bn in Liège) and in the north of France (I Bn in Douai), these *G.W.* battalions counted a variable number of companies.

Each company was attached to a German battalion. Operational orders were transmitted directly by the German authorities to the commanders of the various *G.W.* companies.

As the fortune of German armies turned, the *G.W.* extended its activities from simple surveillance of German military equipment or strategic places to the repression of black market activities. Later on, they even got involved in assisting the German *Feldgendarmerie* in tracking down and arresting young Belgian workers who had refused forced labour service in Germany.

Shortly before the liberation of Belgium, units of the *Garde Wallonne* helped elements of the *Wehrmacht* and

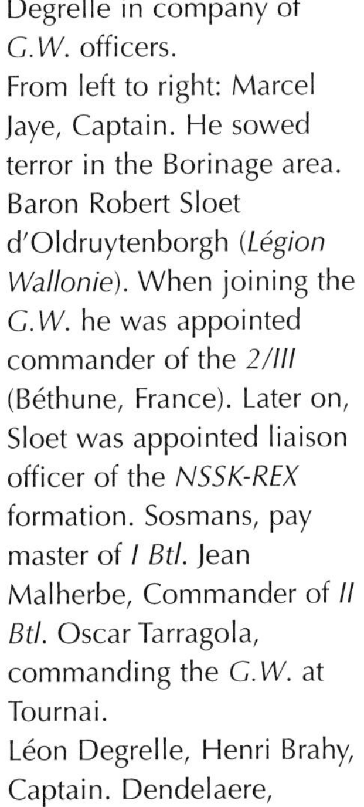

Fig. 2.5. 1943: Léon Degrelle in company of *G.W.* officers.
From left to right: Marcel Jaye, Captain. He sowed terror in the Borinage area. Baron Robert Sloet d'Oldruytenborgh (*Légion Wallonie*). When joining the *G.W.* he was appointed commander of the *2/III* (Béthune, France). Later on, Sloet was appointed liaison officer of the *NSSK-REX* formation. Sosmans, pay master of *I Btl*. Jean Malherbe, Commander of *II Btl*. Oscar Tarragola, commanding the *G.W.* at Tournai.
Léon Degrelle, Henri Brahy, Captain. Dendelaere, Georges Ruelle, (*Légion Wallonie*). Charles Herbecq, after Malherbe's departure, commander of *II Btl* at Mons. Provė , medical doctor *II Btl*. Jossart. (*Collection J.-L. Roba*).

Fig. 2.6. *G.W.* barracks at Namur. (*Collection J.-L. Roba*).

the *Waffen-SS*, in neutralizing partisan hide-aways.

In June 1944, after the landing of the Allied forces in Normandy, the *G.W.* was fully militarised and, by oath of allegiance to the *Führer*, assimilated to a German military unit.

On 1 September 1944, the *G.W.* gathered in the town of Liège and from there retreated to Germany. In October 1944, the *G.W.* members were forced to enrol in the *28.SS-Frw.Gren.Div.Wallonien* but a number of officers obstinately refused to join Degrelle's new formation because they were not granted the same rank in the *Waffen-SS* as the one they held in the *Garde Wallonne*.

The *G.W.* officers who had agreed to join the Walloon Division with a lower rank were sent to Sophienwalde Military Academy, where after a four-week training they were commissioned *SS-Untersturmführer*.

3. The *NSKK*

In February 1941, the *Wehrmacht* authorities in Belgium decided to enrol local men in their auxiliary transport corps, the *Nationalsozialistisches Kraftfahrer-Korps* or *NSKK*.

Two collaborationist groupings, *NSKK-REX* and *NSKK-AGRA*, committed themselves in the recruitment campaign and had their own sections. The *NSKK-REX* wore an arm-badge with the red Burgundy Cross on black. The Germans had their own services stationed at Forest, near Brussels.

The *NSKK-REX* was structured as follows:

Fig. 2.7. Walloon *G.W.* and German personnel. (*Collection J.-L. Roba*).

1. A reserve unit (*Ersatzabteilung*) stationed in Vilvorde. The centre of Vilvorde served as base for the volunteers enrolled by *AGRA* as well as for Flemish drivers enlisted by the *VNV* and the *DeVlag*, the two main collaborating groupings in Flanders;
2. Two brigades: the men in good health were sent to the 2nd Brigade stationed in Diest where the columns for the Eastern Front were formed. From 1942 onwards, the drivers leaving for Russia were armed. The men composing the 1st Brigade only operated in occupied Western Europe. After a short training session, they were sent to Clermont-sur-Oise, France.

Fig. 2.8. *NSKK-REX* liaison officer and *Staffelführer* Jacques Reylandt. He was dismissed in 1943. Note armshield bearing the Burgundy Cross. (*Collection J.-L. Roba*).

The *NSKK-REX* had a liaison staff with the German authorities in Brussels.

The first commander was the former Belgian career NCO Jacques Reyland. As a liaison officer, he held the rank of *Staffelführer* (Major). A former *Légion Wallonie* officer and nobleman, Baron Robert Sloet d'Oldruytenborgh, became his successor in 1943. The local liaison officer at Vilvorde was the long-time Rexist and anti-Communist specialist Charles Peters. An Antwerp-born individual by the name of Emile Weber operated in Diest as a representative of Rex.

In July 1943, *NSKK-REX* and *NSSK-AGRA* melded into a single entirely Rex-controlled unit.

Fig. 2.9. Left: Baron Robert Sloet d'Oldruytenborgh is shown documents. (*Collection J.-L. Roba*).

After the retreat of the German armies, the *NSKK* members who had fled to Germany were incorporated into the *28.SS-Freiw.Gr.Div.Wallonien* on 1 December 1944. From November 1944 onwards, the Walloon *NSKK Ers.Rgt.* was located at Wittenberghe, and it was headed by *Staffelführer* Baron Robert Sloet d'Oldruytenborgh.

Top photo: **Fig. 2.10.** Diest, 20 April 1942: departure for Chemnitz of the Walloon *NSKK Hauptkolonne II/Staffel I*. (*Private Collection*).

Poster: **Fig. 2.11.**

Middle photo: **Fig. 2.12.** Charles Peters (wearing glasses) is seated next to members of the feminine section of the Rex Movement. (*Private Collection*).

Bottom photo: **Fig. 2.13.** Charles Peters (centre) in company of Léon Degrelle (left). After WWI, as an intelligence officer, he actively participated in the occupation of the Ruhr by the Belgian troops. He was therefore listed in pre-war *Gestapo* files as an enemy of the Third Reich. Peters collaborated in order to protect himself from being arrested. (*Collection J.-L. Roba*).

Fig. 2.14. Léon Closset wearing the Rexist *SVTW* uniform (May–September 1944).

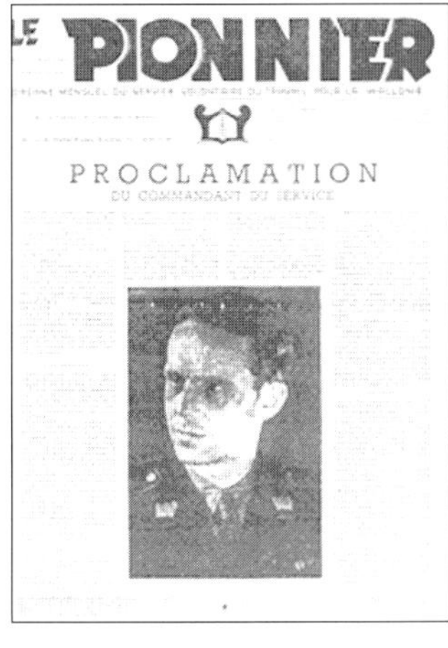

LE PIONNIER

PROCLAMATION

DU COMMANDANT DU SERVICE

Fig. 2.15. *Le Pionnier*, the mouthpiece of the Rexist Voluntary Labour Service in Wallonia.

4. The Voluntary Labour Service in Wallonia – *Service Volontaire du Travail pour la Wallonie – SVTW.*

a. Preliminaries

Responding to the King's rally-call of 28 May 1940, inviting the population to resume work, an organism inspired by circles eager to keep intact the royalist and patriotic spirit among young demobilized conscripts saw daylight in July 1940. Actually, the *SVTW* was initiated by the entourage of General Raoul Van Overstraeten, military adviser to King Léopold III, and with the help of officers of the Reserve Corps. The aim was to use demobilized soldiers for works of public use and national reconstruction. An officer of the Reserve Corps, Henri Bauchau, was assigned command. For some time he managed to preserve the association from Rexist influence. By mid-1941, however, the Rexist Movement got upset from being ignored, especially after it had in vain tried to make Bauchau espouse the Rexist cause. As Bauchau stubbornly continued to refuse Rexists in his cadres, Victor Matthys called on Léon Degrelle. By the end of December 1942, during the first furlough of the *Légion Wallonie*, Léon Degrelle and Victor Matthys had an interview in Berlin with Müller-Brandenburg, the representative for *R.A.D.* matters in occupied countries. As a result of this meeting, it was decided that Walloon Eastern Front legionnaires would be accepted into the *SVTW* after preliminary 6-week training in a German *R.A.D.* camp. Lucien Lippert was to detach the candidates, 50 in all. Two *R.A.D.* training sessions had been planned: the first at the *R.A.D. Arbeitsplatz Nr* 5 at Calw, near Stuttgart, from 15 April to 10 June 1943; the second at Miltenberg, in the Frankfurt-am-Main area, from 20 April to 15 July 1943.

On 29 June 1943, Henri Bauchau resigned from his post in protest against the Rexist intrusion.

A Walloon legionnaire officer, Léon Closset, was put in command of the new (Rexist) *SVTW* on 1 May 1944. A feminine section, under the supervision of Mrs De Harting was organized by the Rexist Movement.

The Closset *SVTW* had a newspaper: *Le Pionnier*, of which three issues were published between May and July 1944.

In September 1944, the *SVTW* evacuated to Germany and was billeted in four *R.A.D.* camps (Allerbüttel, Ohrum, Bodenstedt and Querum), all situated in the Hanover-Braunschweig area. At the same time, the *SVTW* changed its denomination into *Service du Travail Wallon – SVT*, which the German authorities translated as *Reichswallonischer Arbeitsdienst – RWAD.*

On 30 September 1944, Léon Degrelle, in his capacity of *Volksführer der Wallonen*, (Leader of the Walloon People) instituted the Walloon compulsory Labour Service for all Walloons (voluntary or deported) workers between 20 and 24 years of age residing on German territory. They were to be rounded up with a view to joining one of the Walloon *R.A.D.* camps for a three-month labour session. In all 500 young Walloons were concerned.

Fig. 2.16. August 1944: a last inspection before retreating to Germany. (*Private Collection*).

b. Organization of the *RWAD* (October 1944 – April 1945)

1. Headquarters housed at the R.A.D. camp of Querum (Braunschweig)

Chief	*Oberarbeitsführer* Léon Closset
Head of Staff	*Feldmeister* Paul Relick
Deputy Head of Staff	*Unterfeldmeister* Florent Lenoble
Division Education	*Feldmeister* Pierre Van Crean
Division Administration	*Feldmeister* Lucien Devaux
Division Instruction	*Unterfeldmeister* André Renotte
Judicial Division	*Unterfeldmeister* Louis Sartillot
Division Personnel	*Feldmeister* Paul Relick
Medical Division	*Feldmeister* Dr Gaston Haelbrecht

2. Cadre Camp at Querum (15.01.1945 – 1.04.1945)

Chief: *Unterfeldmeister* Raoul Verhiest assisted by Belgian instructors under the supervision of German cadres headed by *Oberfeldmeister* Pfaffenholz, representing *Generalarbeitsführer* Klausch (Chief of the Department *Organization of the R.A.D.)*

3. RWAD camp no. 01 (W1) of Allerbüttel (near Fallersleben)

(December 1944 – 15.02.1945 for the 1st session; from 15.02.1945 to 31.03.1945 for a second incomplete session)

Chief: 1. *Unterfeldmeister* Raymond Dreumont (Dec. 1944)

2. *Unterfeldmeister* Maurice Bourlet (Dec. 1944 – March 1945).

On 15 February 1945, two hundred conscripts were forced to join the *Ers. Btl. 36* with a view to being enrolled into the *28.SS-Frw.Gren.Div.Wallonien.*

4. RWAD camp nr 02 (W2) at Ohrum (near Wolfenbüttel) – End December 1944 – March 1945

Chief: *Unterfeldmeister* Albert Constant.

Informed of the forced enrolment into the *Waffen-SS* of the inmates of camp *W1*, in February 1945, the Walloon conscripts of *W2* burnt the flag of the *RWAD* in protest.

Degrelle himself paid a visit to the camp and in vain tried to convince the Walloon workers to join him. His visit being a complete failure, he consequently ordered all Walloon workers (more or less 200) be escorted under the threat of arms to the nearest by railway station with a view to sending them to the *Erst. Btl. 36* at Alfeld.

5. RWAD camp no. 03 (W3) at Bodentstedt (near Brunswick). November 1944 – March 1945

Chief: *Unterfeldmeister* Louis Dieu.

This camp never was fully operational (100 conscripts, the full capacity being 200) and only started its activities in February 1945.

In the course of the month of December 1944, two Walloon recruiting officers (Pierre Dengis and Charles Peters) visited the camps in the hope of enrolling volunteers for the *28. SS-Freiw. - Gren. Div. Wallonien*. Faced with bad results, Degrelle ordered forced enlistment in January-February 1945. The 'recruits' were sent to the *Ers. Btl. 36* and underwent military instruction at Grünenplan (commanding officer *SS-Ostuf.* Albert Lassois) and Dilligsen (commanding officer *SS-Ostuf.* Adrien Godsdeel) training camps. On 31 March 1945, two companies left for the Oder front. On 10 April 1945, a part of the *RWAD*-recruits was put in front-line duty between Passow and Schwedt, the remaining part joined the Walloon division at Bergholz (near Prenzlau), where it was placed under the command of *SS-Hstuf.* Jean Vermeire. The latter put the Walloons at work, digging antitank trenches at Plöne. The forced recruits were finally discharged from service at the end of April 1945.

A skeletal feminine *RWAD* section was operating at Bischofsrode camp under Mrs De Harting until February 1945.

Fig. 2.17. Léon Closset during an inspection tour in Belgium. (*Doc. P.R./ Collection E. De Bruyne*).

Fig. 2.18. The only known picture showing Léon Closset wearing the *R.A.D.* uniform with the rank of *Oberarbeitsführer*. (*Private Collection*).

CHAPTER III

Rexist Youth Movements

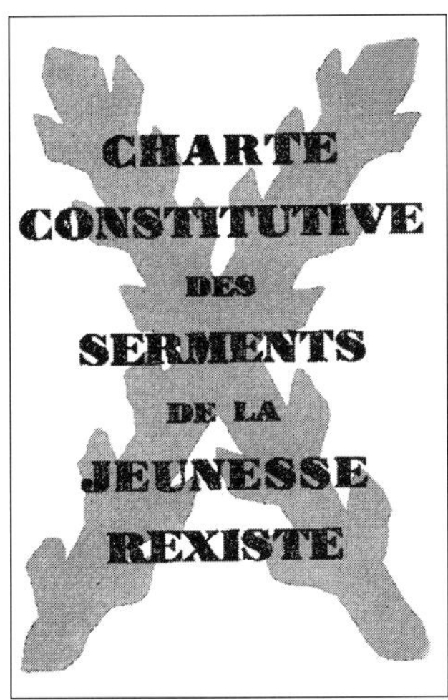

Fig. 3.1. The Charter of the Rexist Youth as established on 22 January 1941. (*Collection E. De Bruyne*).

Fig. 3.2. Service and membership record of the *J(eunesse) N(ationale)-S(ocialiste)*. (*Collection E. De Bruyne*).

A. The Jeunesse Rexiste

In 1935, the young Rexist Movement badly needed propaganda services that would take care of the spreading of propaganda material. The *CAP – Cadres Actifs de Propagande* – mainly composed of Rexist teenagers stepped forwards to fill that need. However, in the end their activity was judged too political for the liking of some leading Rexists, among them the influential Rexist senator Count Xavier de Grünne. By the end of 1936, the latter had founded the *Jeunesse Rexiste*, imposing its members to stand aside from any political activity whatsoever, the sole link with the Rex Movement being Léon Degrelle's recognition as chief.

During January 1937, in pursuance of the Law of 4 May 1936, (to the effect of prohibiting all uniformed organizations), the *Jeunesse Rexiste* was forbidden. In order to get around the law, the Rexist Youth movement was rechristened *ACT – Association pour le Campement et le Tourisme* (Association for Camping and Tourism). In the course of 1938, after experiencing a stay in a *R.A.D.* camp in Germany, the word *'Travail'* (Labour) replaced *'Tourist'*.

The breakout of the war scattered its members. In September 1940, John Hagemans, former Secretary of the Association of Communist Students (1933), but who had abandoned the Marxist ideology by 1936, was liberated from a *Stalag* (German POW camp). As he had become deputy chief in charge of the *ACT* when Count de Grünne quit the Rex Movement in December 1937, Degrelle appointed John Hagemans national chief of the masculine Rexist youth (*JRM*) on 20 December 1940. To head the feminine sections (*JRF*) he chose Suzanne Lagneaux.

In January 1941, Hagemans decided to structure his movement. The new appellation he had chosen for the youth movement was *Serments de la Jeunesse*. He himself was to be called *Prévôt de la Jeunesse*, his staff being the *Prévôté*. The catchy slogan of the *Serments* was *'Dur et Pur'* (Hard and Pure).

Three regions saw daylight, each headed by a *Chef de Région*:

Region I	(Brabant province and Brussels capital-city)
Region II	(Flanders – suppressed after May 1941)
Region III	(Wallonia)

As a former *Verdinaso* member striving for a greater Netherlands, John Hagemans was dreaming of re-establishing the *XVII Provinces* and changed the appellation of *Régions* into *Etendards*, the provinces into *Pays* and the departments into *Bannières*, vocabulary which recalled the glorious Burgundian administration of the lower Netherlands during the 15th Century.

In November 1941, the *Serments-écoles* (Cadre Schools) were formed and were intended to be the nucleus for future Rexist youth leaders. The *Serment-école* of the *Etendard I* was led by Hagemans himself, the one attached to the *Etendard II* was headed by his deputy chief André Derwael.

By the end of July 1941, Hagemans had established the first contacts with the *Hitler-Jugend*. In August 1941, John Hagemans, André Derwael and Suzanne Lagneaux were invited by the *Hitler-Jugend* to attend the Athletic Summer Games at Breslau, completing the trip with a visit to *Reichsjugendführer* Baldur von Schirach in Vienna.

Eager to be recognized as the unique

From top to bottom:

Fig. 3.3. July 1938: John Hagemans (seated) messing together with young *ACT* members.

Fig. 3.4. A meeting of the local *Jeunesse Rexiste* at Fléron, (near Liège), late 1940. Note Belgian (centre) and Rexist flags (foreground). (*Private Collection*).

Fig. 3.5 and Fig. 3.6. John Hagemans was a fervent adept of Order and Style. (*R. Devresse; arch. E. De Bruyne*).

From top to bottom:

Fig. 3.7. Suzanne Lagneaux (left), Head of the feminine section of the Rexist Youth, Victor Matthys (centre) and John Hagemans (right) a few minutes before attending the funeral of P. Gérard, Rex Cadre of the town of Tournai, shot by the Resistance on 17 September 1941. (*R. Devresse; arch. E. De Bruyne*).

Fig. 3.8. Breslau August 1941. From left to right: John Hagemans, Fernande Salmon, Suzanne Lagneaux, non-identified Germans. Right, deputy *Prévôt* André Derwael.

Fig. 3.9. and 3.10. March 1942: farewell ceremony for the departure of the John Hageman's contingent. (*R. Devresse; arch. E. De Bruyne*).

Top left: **Fig. 3.11.** Mrs Hagemans accompanied her husband to the train.

Middle left: **Fig. 3.12.** Member of the feminine branch of the pre-war Rexist Youth. The uniform is composed of a white shirt with red Burgundy Cross on black, a red tie and brown bonnet. The arm shield shows the arms of the Province of Liège. Note the early Rexist insignia on tie. (*Private Collection*).

Top right: **Fig. 3.13.** Member of the *Serment Notger* of Liège. (*Private Collection*).

Middle right: **Fig. 3.14.** John Hagemans in his uniform of *Prévôt* of the Rexist Youth Movement.

Bottom: **Fig. 3.15.** Youngsters of the *Jeunesse Rexiste Féminine* gather at Liège. (*Private Collection*).

Top: **Fig. 3.16.** Youngsters of the *Jeunesse Rexiste Féminine* gather at Liège. (*Private Collection*).

Middle: **Fig. 3.17.** Hageman's enrolment order was issued by the *Kommandostab Z* in Brussels, headed by Major Baumann. The *Kommandostab Z*, a section of the military administration, was responsible for the Belgian (collaborating) auxiliary armed forces. (*Devresse; arch. E. De Bruyne*).

Bottom: **Fig. 3.18.** NCO J. Hagemans (rank he held in the Belgian Army Reserve Corps). Hagemans was posthumously promoted to the rank of *Leutnant*.

301.-

Gestellungsbefehl
Ordre de Rappel

Der / *Le nommé* Hagemans John wohnhaft in / *domicilié à* Brüssel

geb. am / *né le* ... in / *à* ...

meldet sich am / *se présentera le* 9. 3. 1942 in Brüssel / *à Bruxelles*

Au Frontleitstelle Caserne S. Jean
Boul. Botanique à 9H du MATIN

Dieser Gestellungsbefehl gilt als Ausweis für die Einstellung. Ausserdem sind Kennkarte und Militärpapiere mitzubringen, um seinen Dienstgrad in der belgische-Armee nachzuweisen.

Cet ordre de rappel sert de pièce justificative pour l'engagement. En outre, il est nécessaire d'apporter la carte d'identité et les papiers militaires prouvant le grade acquis à l'armée belge.

Der Chef des Kommandostabes
Für den Militärbefehlshaber
in Belgien und Nordfrankreich,
I. A.
Baumann

Berechtigungsschein

zur einmaligen kostenfreien Benutzung der Eisenbahn in den besetzten Gebieten des Westens

für einmal in Buchstaben eine Personen in der 3. Klasse

von Bahnhof ...

nach Brüssel.

Name des Freiwilligen: Hagemans John

Zweck und Veranlassung der Reise: Einberufung zur « Legion Wallonie » (Wall. Inf. Bat. 373).

Ausgefertigt am ... 1942.

(Dienststempel)

chief of all New Order youth movements in the French speaking part of Belgium, Hagemans hoped to achieve his goal by turning towards military collaboration. In an ultimate attempt to draw the attention of the German authorities, he had changed the appellation of his troops into *Jeunesse Nationale-Socialiste* (National Socialist Youth).

On 10 March 1942, Hagemans left Brussels for Meseritz, the training centre of the *Légion Wallonie*. Seventy-five youngsters ranging from 16 to 18 years of age accompanied him. Most of his subaltern staff members (18 out of 22 *Chefs de Serment*) had volunteered, too. Only one *Chef de Pays* (out of a total of 5) had been allowed to leave, the others were ordered to stay in order to keep the movement organized.

On the day of the departure, a bomb exploded in Rexist Movement Headquarters in Brussels.

Hagemans was eventually killed in action in Tcherjakow (Caucasus) on 26 August 1942.

B. The Jeunesse Légionnaire

In January 1943, Degrelle informed the *JR* leaders that he intended to disband the Rexist Youth Movement and replace it by a new youth grouping, which would place the anti-Bolshevism struggle above the Party. Just to show that it was more legionnaire than Rexist-minded, this new grouping was to be named *Jeunesse Légionnaire* (Legionnaire Youth) As leader of the new *Jeunesse Légionnaire* Degrelle chose an Iron Cross II & I decorated legionnaire who had been badly wounded in the Caucasus, *Oberfeldwebel* Paul Mezzetta.

In April 1943, several Walloon New Order Youth Movements merged into the *Jeunesse Légionnaire*.

The *Jeunesse Légionnaire* was structured as follows:

- *Prévôt de la Jeunesse*, Paul Mezzetta, assisted by;
    a. Two general inspectors: Jean-Pierre Quoirin, in charge of the organization of the different services (5) and their departments (18); Gérard De Block, in charge of the *Services autonomes*, the later *Organismes connexes*.

Staff:

Albert Verpoorten
Pierre Malissart (October 1943)
Jean-Pierre Quoirin (May 1944)

The five services were:

General administration and Finance
Physical training
Education
Propaganda
Social affairs and welfare

In June 1943, the *Chevalerie*, a training centre for youth leaders, was formed. Located at Marcinelle, the school was under command of veteran legionnaire Max Havaux. After their instruction period at Marcinelle, the candidates spent two months within a section of the *Hitler-Jugend* in Germany.

A first session, the *Promotion Légion Wallonie*, started in September 1943 and numbered 38 candidates of whom 20 graduated. A second session, called *Promotion du Chef*, started in March 1944. The arrival of the Allied forces in August 1944 interrupted the session.

In October 1944, as the Flemish *Langemarck* managed to raise a youth battalion, Mezzetta desired the establishment of a Walloon counterpart within the *28.SS-Frw.Gren.Div.Wallonien*, and urged Havaux to enrol as many *JL* members as possible. In spite of Havaux's efforts, including moral and physical pressure (*i.e.* falsification of dates of birth, since the minimum age was 16) only 127 *JL* members were reported fit. Of the 127 initially enlisted youngsters, 62 could be retrieved *in extremis* by their parents.

After their instruction period, most *JL* members were incorporated in the *1/I/69Rgt* and participated in the Pomeranian campaign.

Paul Mezzetta was killed in action at Streesen on 4 March 1945.

Fig. 3.19. Paul Mezzetta seated next to Léon Degrelle after the Cherkassy breakout. Mezzetta wears the *JL* uniform with the *JL* insignia on left breast pocket. Above the *JL* insignia, the Iron Cross II ribbon, beneath it the Iron Cross I and the wounded badge. (*Collection E. De Bruyne*).

Fig. 3.20. Paul Mezzeta wears the twin braids of *Tressen* on the outer edges of his shoulder boards that show that he is an officer candidate. Since this photo was taken at the Sophienwalde Academy, which he attended between October and December 1944, he must be still in the early stages of his training. The shoulder boards would be exchanged for those of a *Standartenjunker* after he completed the first phase successfully (*Collection J.-L. Roba*).

Top left: **Fig. 3.21.** First version of the *JL* insignia.

Top right: **Fig. 3.22.** Second version of the *JL* insignia, which appeared in January 1944.

Below: **Fig. 3.23.** Members of the *Chevalerie* at Marcinelle. Turning his back: Georges Piessevaux, who, together with Jean-Pierre Quoirin, will be among the very few *JL* cadres to stay with their youngsters when enrolled within the *28.SS-Frw.Gren.Div.Wallonien* in October 1944. (*Private Collection*).

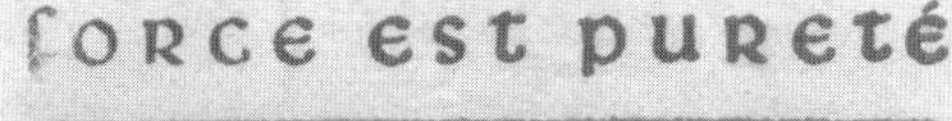

Top: **Fig. 3.24.** Max Havaux, the chief of the *JL* training centre *Chevalerie* at Marcinelle. The *Edelweiß* on his cap indicates that he participated in the Caucasus campaign. The Winter Campaign ribbon indicates that he participated in the first 1941–42 battles of the Legion. Note the *JL* insignia on left breast pocket. The three silver Burgundian Crosses on his shoulder strap indicate that Havaux holds the rank of *Chef d'Enseigne* of the *JL*. (Private Collection).

Middle: **Fig. 3.25.** June 1944: pupils of the *JL Chevalerie* posing in front of their training centre. Note that one member (sitting, first row) is wearing the Infantry Assault Badge, which indicates that he served at the Eastern Front (Hagemans contingent). (*Private Collection*).

Banner top: **Fig. 3.26.** The weekly of the *Jeunesse Légionnaire*.

Bottom two pictures: **Fig. 3.27. and Fig. 3.28.** The *Chevalerie* at Marcinelle celebrating the 24 June 1944 Solstice. (*Private Collection*).

Fig. 3.29. Departure for the Germanic Camp situated at Seeblick bei Seeboden.

C. The Jeunesse Légionnaire Controlled Oorganizations

1. Camps germaniques (Germanic Camps)

The *Camps Germaniques* or Germanic Camps was a section of the Department 'Physical training' within the Service of the same appellation.

The task of that department was to teach a pre-military formation consisting of basic manoeuvring, reading charts, orientation and signals. However, the main activity of this department was to send *JL* participants to Germanic Camps in Germany. There, the *Hitler-Jugend* organized pre-military training in their *Wehrertüchtigungslager* (self-defence training centres).

A first camp was organized in June 1943 with 30 Walloons participating. A second one involved 42 participants. The Germanic camp at Seeboden from 28 July to 29 August 1943, counted 140 young Walloons of whom 50 afterwards joined the *Waffen-SS*.

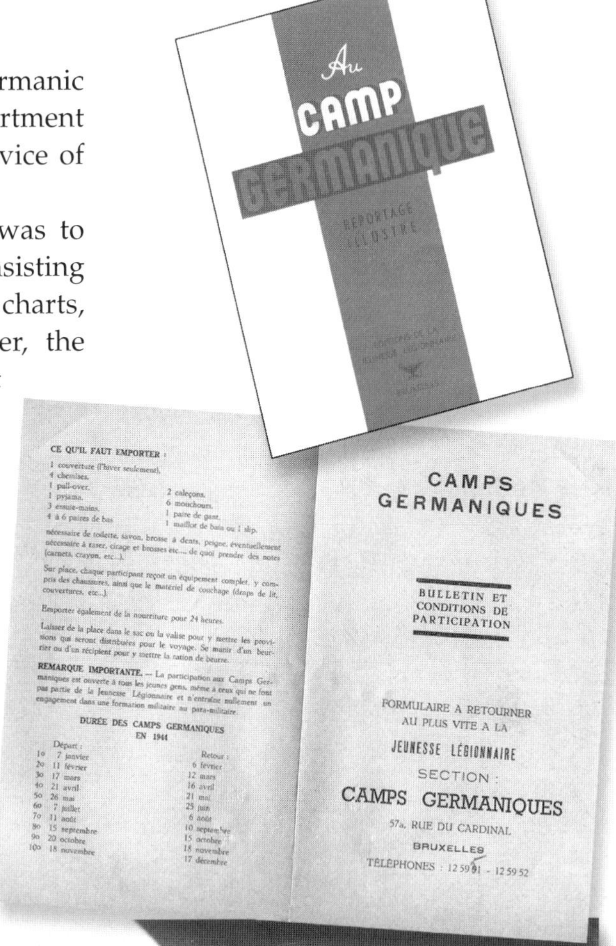

CE QU'IL FAUT EMPORTER :

1 couverture (l'hiver seulement),
4 chemises,
1 pull-over,
1 pyjama,
3 essuie-mains,
4 à 6 paires de bas
2 caleçons,
6 mouchoirs,
1 paire de gant,
1 maillot de bain ou 1 slip.

nécessaire de toilette, savon, brosse à dents, peigne, éventuellement nécessaire à raser, cirage et brosses etc.... de quoi prendre des notes (carnets, crayon, etc...).

Sur place, chaque participant reçoit un équipement complet, y compris des chaussures, ainsi que le matériel de couchage (draps de lit, couvertures, etc...).

Emporter également de la nourriture pour 24 heures.

Laisser de la place dans le sac ou la valise pour y mettre les provisions qui seront distribuées pour le voyage. Se munir d'un beurrier ou d'un récipient pour y mettre la ration de beurre.

REMARQUE IMPORTANTE. — La participation aux Camps Germaniques est ouverte à tous les jeunes gens, même à ceux qui ne font pas partie de la Jeunesse Légionnaire et n'entraîne nullement un engagement dans une formation militaire au para-militaire.

DURÉE DES CAMPS GERMANIQUES EN 1944

	Départ :	Retour :
1o	7 janvier	6 février
2o	11 février	12 mars
3o	17 mars	16 avril
4o	21 avril	21 mai
5o	26 mai	25 juin
6o	7 juillet	6 août
7o	11 août	10 septembre
8o	15 septembre	15 octobre
9o	20 octobre	18 novembre
10o	18 novembre	17 décembre

CAMPS GERMANIQUES

BULLETIN ET CONDITIONS DE PARTICIPATION

FORMULAIRE A RETOURNER AU PLUS VITE A LA

JEUNESSE LÉGIONNAIRE

SECTION :

CAMPS GERMANIQUES

57a, RUE DU CARDINAL

BRUXELLES

TÉLÉPHONES : 12 59 51 - 12 59 52

Top: **Fig. 3.30.**

Middle: **Fig. 2.31.**

Bottom: **Fig. 3.32.** 16 February 1944: high ranking *JL* cadre, René Coulon (second left, note the two sets of Burgundy Crosses of his shoulder strap) takes leave of a group of *JL* members leaving for a Germanic Camp in Germany. A very young Caucasus Campaign veteran, recognizable by the *Edelweiß* on his cap, is in charge of the group. (*Collection E. De Bruyne*).

2. *Kinderlandverschickung* – *KLV*

In order to protect children from air-raids, Baldur von Schirach was charged to save the German youth by sending the children to the countryside. This service was called *Kinderlandverschickung*. This service was extended to the occupied countries. The Walloon section started in 1942 with an evident goal of propaganda in order to attract parents concerned about the safety of their children.

The stay in Germany lasted six months. Teachers teaching the compulsory programmes as scheduled in Belgium accompanied the children.

The *JL* did not organize the first departures as, in 1943, it was still in the process of its own organization. In the autumn of 1943, taking advantage of the misfortune of the previous camps, the organization of the *KVL* came into the hands of the *JL*.

In all the *JL* sent more or less 600 children to different *KVL* camps in Germany.

The *KLV* department was headed by:

Max Léonard (25 September 1943 – August 1944).

3. The Agricultural Labour Service (*Service de la Terre – Landdienst*)

The Department of the *Service de la Terre*, a branch of the Service of Social Affairs, was also known under its German appellation of *Landdienst* since it was a copy of the German service.

The *Landdienst* welcomed girls and boys willing to help farmers with their crops and work on the fields.

The Walloon department was created mid-June 1943.

A first camp was organized on 27 June 1943, in Posen, and participated in the first Congress of the *Germanic Landdienst* organized by Artur Axmann.

The head of this department was:

Jules Delcomminette, for the masculine section;

Henriette Leuridan, for the feminine branch.

4. The Apprenticeship Centre (*Centre d'apprentissage professionnel – CAP*)

On 26 November 1943, the *Junkers* works opened a *Centre d'Apprentissage Professionnel – CAP –* at Morlenwelz. Rexist Edmond Nasy headed this Centre in liaison with Jacques Poels, a member of the Rexist Youth who had joined the *Légion Wallonie* on 10 March 1942.

After a 12 to 15-week training at Morlanwelz, the participants went to Germany where they worked at the Halberstadt *Junker* factory. They worked there as specialized millers for a scheduled period of 2 years, during which they were housed in a *JL* supervised home.

Plan sommaire
de
l'Enseignement Scolaire
dans les
Camps de la K. L. V.

Fig. 3.33. *KLV* propaganda brochure containing the official teaching programme as imposed by the Belgian Law. (*Collection E. De Bruyne*).

CHAPTER IV

Rexist Social and Welfare Organizations

A. The People's Welfare (The Bien-Etre du Peuple – B.E.P.)

New Order groupings planned social and welfare care, too. In addition, as they were interested in monopolizing these activities so as to strengthen their position on the collaborationist chess-board, they unavoidably came into association with the *Secours d'Hiver*, a non-Rexist governmental tutored welfare organization.

The *Bien-Etre du Peuple*, the counter-part of the *Volkswelzijn* in Flanders, was founded on 2 July 1943. These two organizations were exact blueprints of the German *Nationalsozialistische Volkswohlfahrt – NSV*.

The *B.E.P.* was a Rexist offshoot financed by the German *Westbank*. The aim of the *B.E.P.* was the regrouping of all social care organizations in the French-speaking part of Belgium. The first duty for the *B.E.P.* was the establishment of homes for mothers with young children; the main concern being a simulation of what life would be once the revolution had been achieved.

The *B.E.P.* was an organization established on behalf of the German authorities following a formula that had stood the test abroad, insisting on the fact that the existing non-New Order organizations – such as the *Secours d'Hiver* – were merely fostering misery.

The *B.E.P.* also favoured material, moral and social assistance to the relatives of enlisted men in paramilitary units. By doing so, the *B.E.P.* strove for political union of these families in order to convince them of the blessings of the New Order system.

B. Social Services of the Légion Wallonie

With a view to assisting the families of legionnaires deprived from income, the Rex Movement founded an organization for welfare and social assistance. First named *Solidarité Légionnaire* and stationed at Rue du Midi, Brussels, it was presided over by the previously-mentioned Mrs Jeanne Degrelle. Mrs du Welz, whose husband had also joined the first contingent of the *Légion Wallonie*, assisted her. This service was to function until 1943 when it was renamed *L'Honneur Légionnaire* (Rue du Congrès, 10, Brussels) with a Walloon legionnaire officer, Albert Lassois, to head it.

It had a department for *Social Affairs* headed by Raoul Colruyt and a department for *Press and Propaganda* directed by Albert Verpoorten. After the transfer of the *Légion Wallonie* to the *Waffen-SS*, in June 1943, the *Honneur Légionnaire* was absorbed by a single *SS*-organism for

Fig. 4.1. On the right, *SS-Ostuf.* Albert Lassois (*Arch. E. De Bruyne*).

Top: **Fig. 4.2.** *Nat. Soc. Voorzorg voor Waffen-SS in Vlaanderen en Wallonië*, being the Flemish/Dutch text for *Dienststelle Fürsorgeoffizier Flandern und Wallonien*. Note the rubber stamp mark *Deutsch-Vlämische Arbeitsgemeinschaft*, which is the Flemish counterpart of the Walloon *DeWag*. (*Deutsch-Wallonische Arbeitsgemeinschaft*) (*Private collection*).

Middle top: **Fig. 4.3.** (*Collection E. De Bruyne*)

Middle bottom: **Fig. 4.4.** Document forwarded by *SS-Ostuf.* Jensen to a Walloon volunteer for the Assault Brigade, informing them that a prior physical examination will take place at Brussels on 25 August 1943 (*Private Collection*).

Bottom right: **Fig. 4.5.**

Bottom left: **Fig. 4.6.** In order to raise money for welfare care, a local section of the *Solidarité Légionnaire* even composed a song (in Walloon dialect): *When you come back …* (*Collection E. De Bruyne*)

Nat. Soc. Voorzorg voor Waffen-SS
in Vlaanderen en Wallonie
quarante-cinq
Bon voor 45 kgr. aardapp.
pour kgr. de p. d. terre
Maison JOLLINGS
12, Quai de Maestricht
LIÉGE
18-7-44
Deutsch-Vlämische Arbeitsgemeinschaft
Vlaamsch-Duitsche Arbeitsgemeenschap

ENGAGEZ-VOUS A LA « ᛋᛋ-STURMBRIGADE WALLONIEN ». ERSATZKOMMANDO WALLONIEN DER WAFFEN-ᛋᛋ, BRUXELLES, RUE DU CONGRES, 10.

BRIGADE WALLONIE
Bureau de recrutement
de LA LOUVIÈRE
Place Maugrétout, 16 —
— Tél. La Louvière 1224

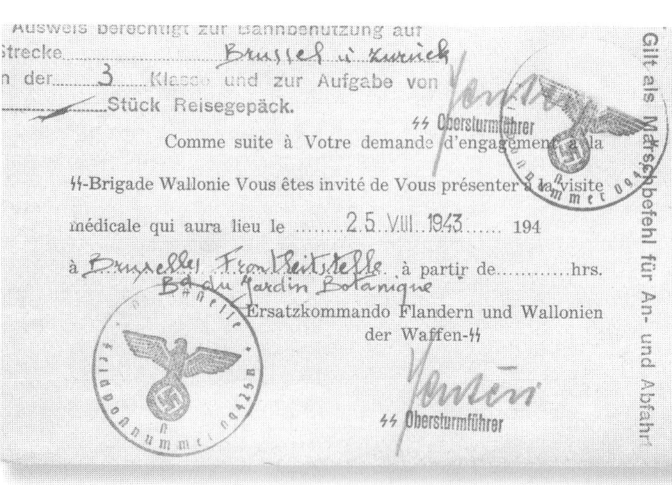

Ausweis berechtigt zur Bahnbenutzung auf
Strecke Brussel u. Zurück
in der 3 Klasse und zur Aufgabe von
Stück Reisegepäck.
ᛋᛋ Obersturmführer
Comme suite à Votre demande d'engagement à la ᛋᛋ-Brigade Wallonie Vous êtes invité de Vous présenter à la visite médicale qui aura lieu le 25.VIII.1943 194
à Bruxelles Frontleitstelle à partir de ....hrs.
Bd du Jardin Botanique
Ersatzkommando Flandern und Wallonien
der Waffen-ᛋᛋ
Jensen
ᛋᛋ Obersturmführer
Gilt als Marschbefehl für An- und Abfahrt

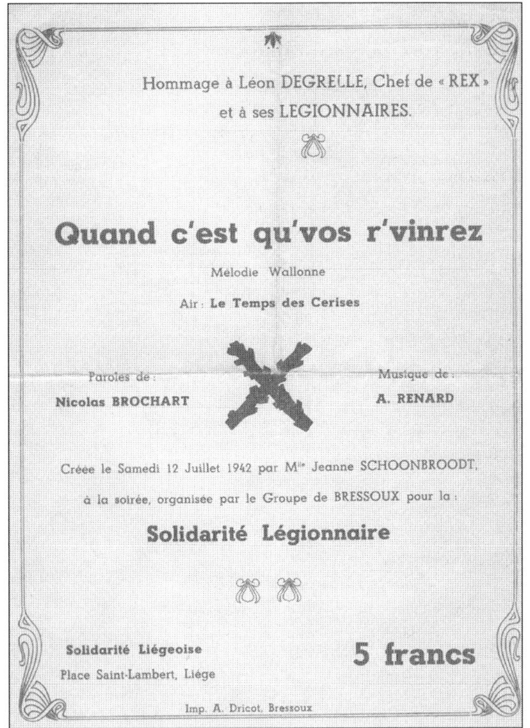

Fig. 4.7. In order to raise money for welfare care, a local section of the *Solidarité Légionnaire* even composed a song (in Walloon dialect): *When you come back . . .* (*Collection E. De Bruyne*)

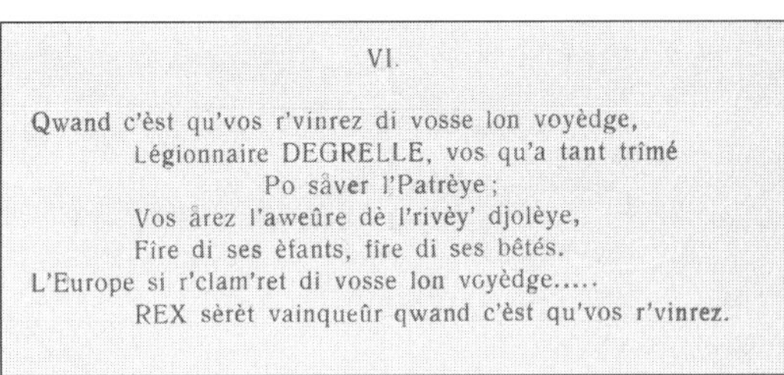

Fig. 4.8.

both the Walloon and Flemish communities: the *Ersatzkommando Flandern und Wallonien*, headed by *SS-Hstuf.* Adalbert Schindlmayr, and monitored by the *Dienststelle Jungclaus. SS-Ostuf.* Jensen, responsible for Walloon affairs, assisted Schindlmayr. Paul Suys,[1] a former member of *Rex-Vlaanderen* from Antwerp, was appointed *Fürsorgeoffizier* (Welfare Officer) for both the communities.

In July 1943, the service was divided into two distinct departments. The *Erstazkommando Wallonien der Waffen-SS* was put under command of *SS-Hstuf.* Karl-Theodor Moskopf,[2] replacing Jensen. The social department, the *Entr-aide nationale-socialiste*, was allotted to Albert Lassois, demobilized from the *Légion Wallonie* for that purpose. He was assisted by Raoul Colruyt and newcomer Julien Carlier (Press and Propaganda), replacing Albert Verpoorten, who had been called up to important functions within the *Jeunesse Légionnaire*.

At the end of August 1944, the *Erstazkommando* and all its services evacuated Belgium and settled in Hildesheim/Hanover. During the von Rundstedt offensive, it moved to Gummersbach, near Cologne. The whole service was placed under the command of *SS-Hstuf.* Moskopf. In January 1945, the *Entr-aide nationale-socialiste* was established at Springe and placed at the disposal of the department *Rasse und Siedlungsamt Hauptamt-Fürsorge und Versorgungsamt der Waffen-SS*. A savings bank and pension fund was established in Praque and run by *SS-Ustuf.* Valère Roemaet.

CHAPTER V

Non-Rexist New Order Youth Movements

A. The Roman Youth (*Jeunesse Romane*)

During June 1941, and while Raymond De Becker, chief editor of *Le Soir* (*The Evening*), a German censored newspaper, and Robert Poulet, his counterpart from the *Nouveau Journal*, were considering the founding of a unique political party comprising the Belgian roman provinces, – dissident members of the *Légion Nationale* established the *Jeunesse Romane*. The reason for this was without any doubt motivated by the desire of its promoters to oppose Rexist Youth leader John Hagemans, who planned a unique Walloon New Order Youth Movement under his control.

The ideology of the *Jeunesse Romane* consisted of grouping the French-speaking youth of the country into a more or less neutral organization favouring physical training and moral standards thanks to discipline, social dedication and work, its slogan being: *People, Youth and King*. The common ideal was the uprising of the Fatherland and the establishment of a royalist and populist state.

The *Jeunesse Romane* was against the idea of a racial community as claimed by the *AGRA* and desired a kind of *Dietschland* that would be under royal power. It rejected the idea of a youth committed to National Socialism.

Even if the *Jeunesse Romane* was catalogued as a New Order organization, it was by no means pro-German and therefore hardly had any chance of survival. In January 1942, a first schism appeared within the organization and led to the new grouping *Jeunesse Wallonne* that adopted a diametrically opposed orientation than the one displayed by the *Jeunesse Romane*.

Finally, in March 1943, leaders of the *Jeunesse Romane* pronounced the dissolution of their organization and accepted cooperation with the establishment of a unique Youth Movement under the aegis of the *Jeunesse Légionnaire*. Gérard Deblock, the leader of the *Jeunesse Romane*, joined the *Jeunesse Légionaire* and was given authority over the *Services Connexes*, a department within the *JL*, fostering Youth Hostels. Gérard Deblock was mysteriously assassinated on 28 June 1944.

B. The Walloon Youth (*Jeunesse Wallonne*)

The *Jeunesse Wallonne* is born from dissensions that appeared between leaders of the *Jeunesse Romane* during January 1942. The discord resulted from incidents of personal and ideological order, the misinterpretation by non-Walloon leaders from Brussels of the Walloon myth being the main stumbling block.

The *Jeunesse Wallonne* extolled a racial ideal and claimed the existence of a homogeneous Walloon community of Nordic extraction. It proclaimed that Wallonia, including the francophone

Fig. 5.1. (*Coll. E. De Bruyne*)

part of Brussels, belonged to the Walloons. The Brussels leaders, on the contrary, maintained with vehemence that Wallonia was by no means a populist and racial community based on racial homogeneity and trends as expressed in the German words *Volk* and *Volkstümlich*.

The *Jeunesse Wallonne* was in favour of a popular community with strong Germano-Walloon nationalism. These views were diametrically opposed to the Belgian unitarian ideas professed by Léon Degrelle at that time.

Leaders:

Robert Radelet(January 1942 – May 1942),

V. Habrant (May 1942 – April 1943).

Like most of the other youth movements, the *Jeunesse Wallonne* was caught up in the spiral of the unification of all New Order Youth movements in April 1943.

C. The Students' New Order Movements

1. The *Amitiés Culturelles Estudiantines Germano-Wallonnes – AEGW* (Germano-Walloon Cultural Students' Friendship)

This New Order student circle was founded at the university of Liège on 18 March 1941, due to the instigation of the local *Oberfeldkommandantur*, and with the help of Dr Strieffler of the

Fig. 5.2. (*Coll. E. De Bruyne*)

Studentenführung, a section within the Youth Department of the *Jugendführung* in Brussels. The first leader was the academic assistant in medicine Fernand Brickus. René Goffaux succeeded him in May 1942.

The goal of the movement was to achieve the cultural community of mutual feelings with German students, so as to obtain a counterbalance in the cultural work performed by Germanophobe students of the University of Liège. The recruiting terrain being too narrow, Brickus sought to extend his activities among non-university level students. By doing this, he overstepped Dr Franz Petri's (in charge of the cultural direction in Wallonia) directives in the matter of student organizations.

In March 1942, the German Lieutenant Rudolf Hemesath, head of the youth groupings in Belgium, ordered Brickus not to accept as members students other than those attending a university and ordered all students belonging to other levels of education to leave the movement.

By May 1942 the *AEGW* did not number more than twenty members. The organization was dismantled and its chief F. Brickus resigned.

2. The Walloon Students' Youth (*Jeunnesses Estudiantines Wallonnes – JEW*)

The *Jeunesses Estudiantines Wallonnes* were the Students' Youth Movement of the *Communauté Culturelle Wallonne* (*CCW*) and was founded early June 1942. This initiative was taken by a Christian Despretz, a science student from Brussels, whose father was in charge of the organization and direction of the German language courses within the *CCW*.

The grouping wanted to level up Walloon culture. Its aims consisted in gathering students of all schools and publicly demonstrating the spirit of Wallonia. Subjects dealing with Walloon literature, music, architecture, sculpture and sciences were part of the program that had to be studied thoroughly. The results were to be published in the magazine *Wallonie*, organ of the *CCW*. After the study of Wallonia's cultural treasures, the association planned to study the great neighbouring cultures and make sure Wallonia deserved its place in a New Europe.

The *JEW* had only a short existence. Established in the beginning of June 1942, it was incorporated into the *Association of Walloon Students – ADEW –* on 12 June 1942.

3. The Association of Walloon Students (*Association des Etudiants Wallons – AEDW*)

The Association of Walloon Students is born from the fusion of the *AEGW* and the *Gildes Estudiantines*.[1] The German authorities recognized it as the sole New Order Student Organization for Wallonia in June 1942. Léon Debotte, a Germanic languages teacher from Liège, became the head of the Association bearing the impressive title of *Wallonischer Studentenführer* (Walloon Students Leader).

There was a close collaboration between the *ADEW*, Rex and the *Jeunesse Nationale Socialiste*. The *ADEW* had links with the *Deutscher Akademischer Austauschdienst* and the *Deutsches Institut*. These institutions organized inter-university student exchanges and granted scholarships to students willing to take courses at a German university, especially at Marburg University where a lecture in Walloon Studies had been created. The *ADEW* also had connections with the Berlin-based *Deutsch-Belgische Gesellschaft*.

Léon Van Huffel, a journalist close to *SS* circles, created a *European Study Circle* (*Europa Studienkreis*). This section intended to explore and promote the idea of a New Europe in history and literature by means of conferences, to which German personalities, such as the *Gastprofessoren* Drs Münsch, F. Textor, Kraus and others, would be invited. The *ADEW* was still operational in 1944.

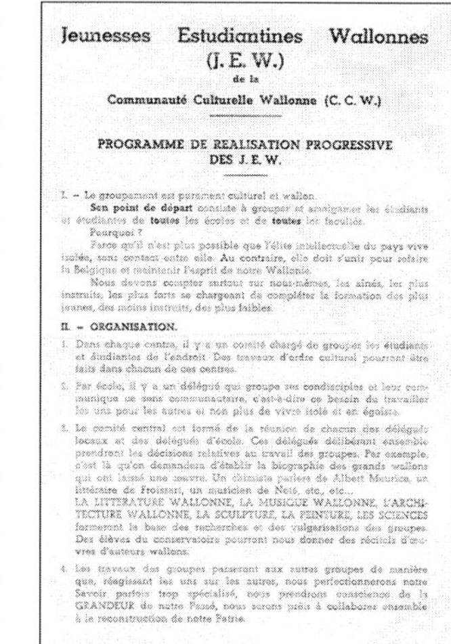

Jeunesses Estudiantines Wallonnes
(J. E. W.)
de la
Communauté Culturelle Wallonne (C. C. W.)

PROGRAMME DE REALISATION PROGRESSIVE DES J. E. W.

I. – Le groupement est purement culturel et wallon.

Son point de départ consiste à grouper et amalgamer les étudiants et étudiantes de **toutes** les écoles et de **toutes** les facultés.

Pourquoi ?

Parce qu'il n'est plus possible que l'élite intellectuelle du pays vive isolée, sans contact entre elle. Au contraire, elle doit s'unir pour refaire la Belgique et maintenir l'esprit de notre Wallonie.

Nous devons compter surtout sur nous-mêmes, les aînés, les plus instruits, les plus forts se chargeant de compléter la formation des plus jeunes, des moins instruits, des plus faibles.

II. – ORGANISATION.

1. Dans chaque centre, il y a un comité chargé de grouper les étudiants et étudiantes de l'endroit. Des travaux d'ordre culturel pourront être faits dans chacun de ces centres.
2. Par école, il y a un délégué qui groupe ses condisciples et leur communique ce sens communautaire, c'est-à-dire ce besoin de travailler les uns pour les autres et non plus de vivre isolé et en égoïste.
3. Le comité central est formé de la réunion de chacun des délégués locaux et des délégués d'école. Ces délégués délibérant ensemble prendront les décisions relatives au travail des groupes. Par exemple, c'est là qu'on demandera d'établir la biographie des grands wallons qui ont laissé une oeuvre. Un chimiste parlera de Albert Maurice, un littéraire de Froissart, un musicien de Noté, etc., etc...
LA LITTERATURE WALLONNE, LA MUSIQUE WALLONNE, L'ARCHITECTURE WALLONNE, LA SCULPTURE, LA PEINTURE, LES SCIENCES formeront la base des recherches et des vulgarisations des groupes. Des élèves du conservatoire pourront nous donner des récitals d'oeuvres d'auteurs wallons.
4. Les travaux des groupes passeront aux autres groupes de manière que, réagissant les uns sur les autres, nous perfectionnerons notre Savoir parfois trop spécialisé, nous prendrons conscience de la GRANDEUR de notre Passé, nous serons prêts à collaborer ensemble à la reconstruction de notre Patrie.

Fig. 5.3. (*Coll. E. De Bruyne*)

Fig. 5.4. (*Coll. E. De Bruyne*)

Fig. 5.5. (*Coll. E. De Bruyne*)

CHAPTER VI

Rex-Opposed Collaborating Movements

A. The Agra – The Friends of the Greater German Reich

A. G. R. A.
MOUVEMENT SOCIALISTE WALLON
TRÉSORERIE GÉNÉRALE
C. C. P. 2165.86 - J. ISTAZ, Liége
Téléphone 260.11

Fig. 6.1. (*Collection E. De Bruyne*)

The *Amis du Grand Reich Allemand* – or *AGRA* for short – was founded in Liège on 13 March 1941, by Rexist dissidents, unconditional sympathizers of Nazi Germany. Unlike other Walloon New Order groupings, such as the *Communauté Culturelle Wallonne – CCW*, it had not been initiated by the *Militärverwaltung* but was confidentially supported and backed by the *SS*. These first interferences of the *SS* into internal politics inaugurated a long struggle between Heinrich Himmler and Eggert Reeder, the competent head of the *Militärverwaltung* in Brussels. In the end, the *SS* won the battle as a civil administration replaced von Falkenhausen in July 1944.

AGRA members did not recognize Degrelle's authority; only Hitler was the undisputed leader of the New Europe. The *AGRA* movement was in favour of creating a racial state and claimed Wallonia belonged to the Nordic vital space, in which Nazi Germany was the shining light. Its program was violently anti-Semitic, despised Communism, proposed the dissolution of Freemasonry as well as seeking sterilization of the incurable, mentally and physically disabled people.

As this program was printed and spread without the knowledge of the *Militärverwaltung*, Brussels forbid it in December 1941. However, permission was given to be operational under the banner of *Mouvement Socialiste Wallon – MSW*, in September 1941 provided it strictly stuck to cultural activities without overlapping the Rexist movement's monopoly.

Although *AGRA* had far less members than Rex, it was the second New Order grouping in importance in Wallonia and the Rex Movement's most dangerous opponent. At the end of the war, however, the number of its members had dramatically declined from several thousands in 1941–42, to 1,500 in 1943, and to just 21 in spring 1944.

Les Amis du Grand Reich Allemand
AGRA
MOUVEMENT DE CULTURE POLITIQUE
Fondé à Liége, le 13 Mars 1941
Die Freunde des Gross - Deutschen Reiches
POLITISCHES KULTURBEWEGUNG
Am 13en März 1941 in Lüttich gegründet
MITGLIEDSBUCH

Fig. 6.2. (*Collection E. De Bruyne*)

AGRA was headed by:

Alfons De Boungne

Julien Velut (January 1941)

Georges Scaillet (January 1942),

Jean Gerits (1943 – 44).

AGRA had its own newspaper, *Notre Combat* (*Our Struggle* – a broad hint at Hitler's *Mein Kampf*) founded by Scaillet and Gerits in September 1942. *Notre Combat* made intensive recruitment propaganda in favour of the:

Organization Todt – O.T. (from 1941 to 1943, *AGRA* claimed to have recruited 2,000 men);

NSKK (1,850 men by 1943);

the *Waffen-SS*, more particularly the *Wiking* (305 men by 1943).

As for its structure, *AGRA* was based upon the *Führerprinzip*, *i.e.* one single person controlling the whole organization. The *Chef* was assisted by a:

Conseil des Référendaires (Councellors);

Département des Relations extérieures (Department of Exterior Relations) that was to establish friendly contact with German administrative services and with New Order groupings (except Rex);

Département des Renseignements politiques (Department of Political Intelligence);

Département du Service de Protection (Department of the Protection Service);

Sécretariat administratif (Administration);

covering a Region (Wallonia), itself divided into 7 *Cercles*, the *Cercles* covering groups, and the groups cells.

The *Département des Renseignements Politiques* collected all kind of political information, including investigating the political reliability of its own members. The *Département du Service de Protection* disposed of a close protection squad of 140 uniformed (black uniform with khaki shirt) men headed by Willy Cremer, a former member of the *Légion Nationale*, who had been expelled for his pro-German ideas. Its job was to secure meetings organized by *AGRA*.

AGRA had its own Youth movement and its own *NSKK* section.

Although *AGRA* applauded Degrelle's public statement of Walloons being of Germanic essence in 1943, rivalry between the two groupings would never cease. The *SS*, in their efforts to counter the *Militärverwaltung*, made any endeavour to encourage it.

In the end, *AGRA* lost the battle, and it was to be slowly absorbed by Rex from September 1943 onwards.

The *AGRA* program contained 22 points, of which following excerpts speak for themselves:

Article 2. The members recognize in the person of the *Führer* and Chancellor of the German Reich, Adolf Hitler, the undisputed Leader of New Europe. They adhere wholeheartedly and without reserve to the doctrines of National Socialism.

Article 3. The aims of *AGRA* are:

to advertise, to expand, and to defend the ideas of National Socialism by all means within its power and in every stratum of society;

to establish and to

Fig. 6.3. *AGRA* Membership card (*Private Collection*).

develop cultural links with the German Reich in the realm of politics, social affairs and art;

to encourage opinions among the Belgians combating the conceptions of democracy, liberalism, Jewry and Freemasonry.

Article 12. The leader of the party will maintain constant contact with the German National Socialist authorities as to what the detailed activities of the association Should be.

According to *AGRA*, the Belgium of 1830 was a mistake due to the liberal politics of that time. This mistake was to be corrected in the New Europe.

In its propaganda, *AGRA* made no reference to Belgian patriotism, but tried to create a Walloon nationalism within a Germanic framework. When addressing Walloon labourers, *AGRA* laid the stress on the social achievements of National Socialism. *AGRA* loudly claimed that the Walloons were Germans. Therefore, according to *AGRA*, Hitler was the first statesman to achieve socialism, and he was consequently the undisputed leader of the Germanic peoples.

B. The Agra Youth Movement

A first attempt to establish an *AGRA* Youth Movement was made by the 20 year old Liège chemistry student Raphael Lenne in December 1941. The number of members adhering to the Youth Movement did not exceed a few dozen. A second centre of activity with better results took place at Charleroi, where chemist Joseph Archambeau and his wife managed to create a girls and boys section. By April 1942, Archambeau had taken over command of the whole organization.

From the start, the *AGRA* youth tried to arrange closer links with the *Hitler-Jugend* sections in Belgium, more particularly at Liège.

In March 1942, the *AGRA* youth had its own periodical, *Le Pionnier* (*The Pioneer*) financed by the *Ligue de la Défense du Peuple*, one hundred being the number of issues printed.

In Wallonia, the number of adhering members never exceeded a maximum of one hundred.

C. The Agra Controlled NSKK

From the start, *AGRA* recruited for the

Fig. 6.4. Raphaël Lenne, first Chief of the *AGRA* Youth Movement. In the course of 1942, he became one of the main leaders of the *Association des Etudiants Wallons*, a New Order Students' Organization. After a short passage within the *NSKK* (March-April, 1942), he was called back to Liège, where his presence was necessary. In December 1943, Lenne married a German native and left for Berlin. While attending Marburg University, he became a part-time correspondent of the Liège New Order newspaper *La Légia* (*Private Collection*).

Fig. 6.5. *NSKK-AGRA* officer. Note the *Sonnenrad* swastika on cap and left breast pocket (*Private Collection*).

NSKK. However, by doing so it faced the hostility of Rex, which intended to keep a monopoly in the field of political, cultural and military collaboration with the Germans. In 1943, *AGRA* lost a foothold. The agreement between Degrelle and Himmler (May 1943) with a view to joining the *Waffen-SS* not only resulted in the integration of the *AGRA* recruited *Waffen-SS* volunteers into the 5th Assault Brigade *Wallonien*, it also deprived *AGRA* from the support of its main German protector.

Jean Gerits, who had taken over from Scaillet as the formal leader of the *AGRA*, understood that the only way of surviving was to seek for an agreement with Rex. In July 1943, he accepted that the *NSSK-AGRA* recruited drivers should be integrated together with the *NSKK-REX* volunteers into a larger *NSKK-Wallonie* unit. The fusion took place during a ceremony attended by Degrelle and Gerits in a barracks in northern France.

Until the fusion of 1943, the *NSKK-AGRA* was headed by Gerits'

Fig. 6.6. and 6.7. (*inset*) *NSKK-AGRA* driver recognizable by the yellow-blue arm badge showing the yellow *Sonnenrad* swastika on blue (*Collection E. De Bruyne*).

brother-in-law, liaison *Staffelführer* (Major) Joseph Augustin. Two *Sturmführer*, José Manguette and Jean Wauthy, assisted him.

D. The Cercle Wallon (CW) and Maisons Wallonnes (MW)

Following an agreement passed between the *Deutsche Belgische Gesellschaft* (Belgo-German Association) and Dr Robert Ley's *Deutsche Arbeitsfront – D.A.F.*, the *Walloon Circle* was installed in Germany by the *UTMI* (*Union of Manuel and Intellectual Labourers*) in 1941 for the purpose of assisting Walloon voluntary labourers in Germany, who had been tutored until then by the *Foyers français*, a French organization. The *Cercle Wallon* implanted cells in the main cities of the Reich and named them *Maison Wallonne*. The *UTMI* chose and appointed the leaders of these cells among its members. At the same time, these delegated Walloons were under control of the *D.A.F.*, omnipotent in social matters.

So as to overrule *UTMI* and *CCW*

Fig. 6.8. *The* Maison Wallonne *of Liège* (*Collection E. De Bruyne*).

(*Walloon Cultural Community*) activities in the social area, extremist collaborationist groupings, more or less Rex dissident, started to implant, this time in Belgium, on 5 April 1943, a second *Cercle Wallon*, which, despite its identical appellation, was fundamentally different from its homonym covering Germany. The former, showing social aspirations, was in the hands of the *UTMI* and had *Maisons Wallonnes* all over the Reich. Maurice Pirson ran the organization from his Berlin office. The latter was openly National Socialist coloured. Fernand-Marie Collard, a journalist and resolute opponent of Léon Degrelle, had taken the direction of the Cercle, whilst management of the *Maisons Wallonnes* scattered all over Wallonia was in the hands of Paul Garain.

Under the impetus of its leader Collard, the action of this new *CW* in Belgium was to undermine the *UTMI* Walloon Circle in Germany, and to trace a line of conduct where the social would yield to an unconditional collaboration policy.

Soon after their establishment in the Reich, the Collard-Garain version of the *Maisons Wallonnes* managed to monopolize the social welfare taking care of Walloon labourers' interest in Germany in a clearly National Socialist spirit. Encouraged by this success, they soon interfered in the organization of social assistance to be provided for the families of workers in Belgium, a strictly *UTMI* matter by virtue of a mutual agreement.

In the meantime, the Collard version of the *Cercle Wallon* went on proclaiming that it favoured the creation of the European National Socialist Order and that this would be achieved thanks to the victory of the German armies.

As the *UTMI* and its cells escaped control by the *SS*, the latter did not rest until they had their own social policy-controlling organ. The establishment, in the premises of the *SS-Hauptamt* in Berlin, 3 April 1944, of the *DeWag – Deutsch-Walllonische Arbeitsgemeinschaf*[1] bridged this gap. The *DeWag* was meant to absorb the *DWAK* (*Deutsch-Wallonische Arbeitskreis*) or German-Walloon Work Circle,[2] which was controlled by the Ministry of Foreign Affairs.

The *DeWag* was supposed to be in Wallonia what *DeVlag* (*De Vlaamsch – Duitsche Arbeidsgemeenschap*) was in Flanders: an instrument in the hands of the *SS* with a view to destroying the monopoly of Rex in social and cultural matters.

CHAPTER VII

Rexist Dissident Movements

A. The Walloon National Popular Movement (Mouvement National Populaire Wallon – MNPW)

Antoine Leclercq, a dissident of the Rexist Party, founded the *MNPW* – Walloon National Populist Movement – in April 1941. Until then, Leclercq had been assigned as Chief of Rex for both the province of Liège and the rest of Wallonia. During May 1941, he obtained the support of the Liège *Propaganda Abteilung* for the publication of his program: *Wallons, Réveillez-vous!* (*Walloons, wake up!* A remake of *Deutschland, Erwache!*). The German occupying authorities recognized the movement in June 1941.

The *MNPW* thundered against Jews, Freemasons, Communists, Parliamentarianism and Capitalism. However, *MNPW* penetration was local and hardly went beyond the province of Liège, where it was born.

Its organic structure was as follows:

Supreme direction of the movement and responsible chief: Antoine Leclercq.

The Chief was assisted by a *Conseil Supérieur du Mouvement* (Superior Council of the Movement) composed of three members:

Auguste Defraigne
Raymond Lacroix
François Doutreloux

Themselves assisted by a set of five counselors, the whole forming the *Conseil Général* (General Council).

Fig. 7.1.

MOUVEMENT NATIONAL POPULAIRE WALLON
WALLON TOUJOURS

In the area of social work, activities of the *MNPW* covered moral and financial assistance to the families of the workers volunteering for labour in Germany. The *MNPW* was also involved in the preparation of an anti-Bolshevik exhibition held in Brussels in March 1942. With regard to political activities, Leclercq in vain attempted to create a unique New Order Party in Wallonia that would have merged all existing collaborationist groupings, including Rex.

During April 1942, the *MNPW* passed an agreement with the anti-Semitic movement *La Défense du Peuple* (The People's Defence).

During November 1942, Leclercq ceased all activity within the *MNPW* to devote himself to the organization of the *Maison Wallonne*, a New Order social care grouping, financed by the local Liège *Werbestelle*. At the end of the year 1943, Leclercq left the *Maison Wallonne* because, in the meantime, it had been taken over by Rex with which Leclercq was still at loggerheads.

In the last month of the occupation, Leclercq worked for the local Liège *Werbestelle* rounding up workers to be sent to forced labour in Nazi Germany. He ended the war working for the *Propaganda Staffel*. During the last weeks of the war, he contributed to the drawing up of a brochure featuring soldiers having been awarded the Knight's Cross.

Before the *MNPW* merged with the League for the People's Defence, it had no newspaper. In April 1942, the *L'Ami du Peuple*, – the bimonthly of the People's Defence, became the newspaper of the two movements.

The *MNPW* also had a Youth movement. Even skeletal, (staffs being reduced to some children officered by an older adolescent), it had a chief for the masculine section, Roger Schmit, and a female captain, Jeanine Defraigne, for the girls' section.

Fig. 7.2.

B. The League of the People's Defence (Ligue de la Défense du Peuple – D.P.)

The League for the People's Defence was the French-speaking section of the Flemish Movement *Volksverweering*, founded by the Antwerp attorney René Lambrichts in January 1937.

Violently anti-Semitic, the movement propagated the idea of the race and combated all ideas opposed to its stance. It railed against Jews and all those who adopted an ideology contrary to the interests of the People. It strove against Jesuitism and the influence of both Jewry and Freemasonry. As an emblem the movement chose the rune on a white background, representing the race and the soil.

Late in 1940, French-speaking sections of the *Volksverweering* implanted in Charleroi and Liège. In the latter city, under the impetus of Dr Sylvère Miesse, who was to join the *Légion Wallonie* together with 26 members of the grouping in July 1941, the Movement boomed. As most of the *D.P.* members adhered to the *AGRA*, meetings were held in the local *AGRA* quarters.

The Liège *D.P.* section had its own protection squad, the *Garde de la Défense du Peuple*, headed by René Masson, a

Fig. 7.3. Propaganda leaflet issued by the *D.P.* promoting the anti-Semitic film *The Eternal Jew* (*Collection E. De Bruyne*).

Fig. 7.4. The *D.P.* rune symbol and contribution fee affixed to what seems to be a membership card (*Collection E. De Bruyne*).

Rexist librarian, who was shot by the Resistance later on.

Besides protecting prominent members and assuring order at public rallies, the protection squad also served to escort Jews to the Liège railway station with a view to their transfer to Malines, last halting-place before their transfer to Germany.

The fusion of the *D.P.* with the *MNPW* signalled the end of the presence of a specific anti-Jewish movement in Wallonia. As most members had strong links with Rex, it fell apart when Leclercq and his anti-Rex staff took over the administration of the Liège cell. There only remained followers of the *AGRA* movement and the unconditional Jew-haters. The situation in Charleroi and Brussels was hardly different.

Newspaper: *L'Ami du Peuple* – (*The People's friend*), Bimonthly for the Defence of Race and Soil.

CHAPTER VIII

Rex Connected Movements

A. The Walloon Cultural Comunity (Communauté Culturelle Wallonne – CCW)

In May 1941, Wilhelm Kemp, collaborator of Dr Brahn from the German Foreign Office, was transferred to the *Propaganda Abteilung* of Brussels. He was to become the person in charge of Walloon propaganda affairs and thereby called upon to work in close collaboration with Dr Franz Petri, attaché to the *Gruppe Kultur* within the Military Administration.

The Walloon Cultural Community was established at the instigation and under the impetus of the *Propaganda Abteilung*. The apparent goal of the *CCW* was to favour the progress of Walloon culture in general but, under the impulse of its first Secretary General, René Simar, it stimulated a narrow and direct collaboration between Walloons and Germany. The real goal was to wake up Walloon conscience in the cultural, economic and social fields so as to integrate Wallonia into the framework of a German dominated New Europe. At the same time, the *CCW* endeavoured to develop a cultural

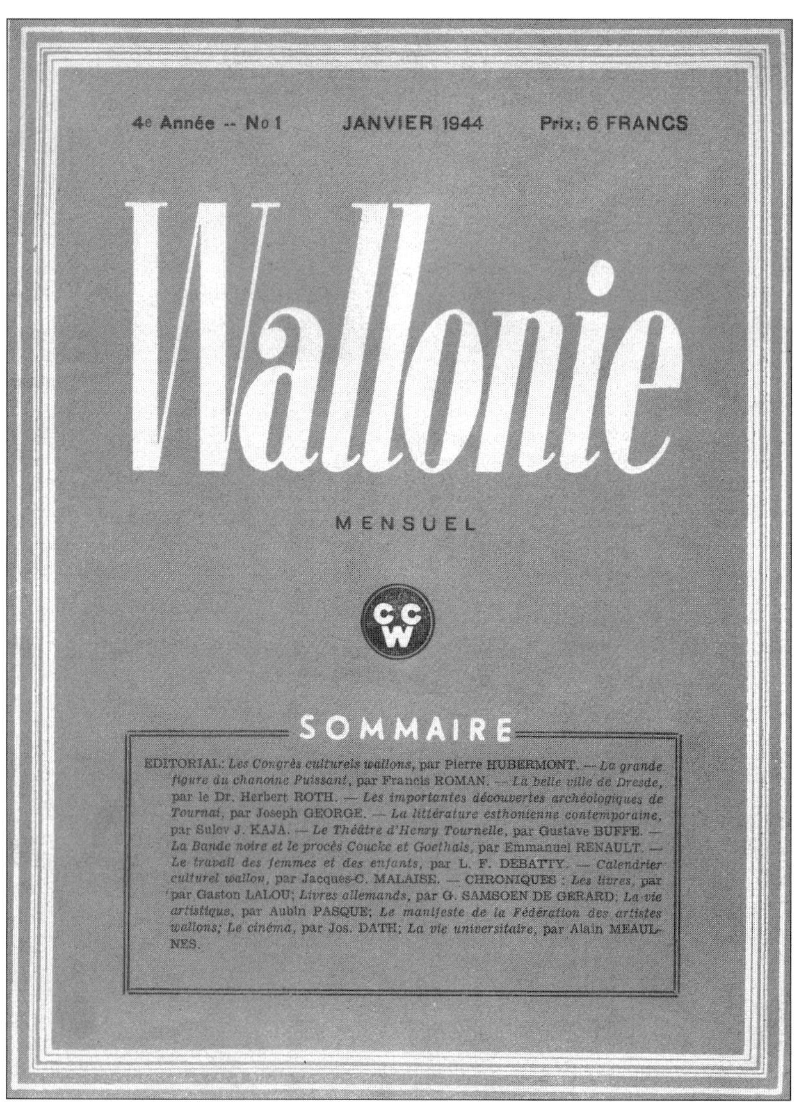

4e Année -- No 1 JANVIER 1944 Prix: 6 FRANCS

Wallonie

MENSUEL

CCW

SOMMAIRE

EDITORIAL: *Les Congrès culturels wallons*, par Pierre HUBERMONT. — *La grande figure du chanoine Puissant*, par Francis ROMAN. — *La belle ville de Dresde*, par le Dr. Herbert ROTH. — *Les importantes découvertes archéologiques de Tournai*, par Joseph GEORGE. — *La littérature esthonienne contemporaine*, par Sulev J. KAJA. — *Le Théâtre d'Henry Tournelle*, par Gustave BUFFE. — *La Bande noire et le procès Coucke et Goethals*, par Emmanuel RENAULT. — *Le travail des femmes et des enfants*, par L. F. DEBATTY. — *Calendrier culturel wallon*, par Jacques-C. MALAISE. — CHRONIQUES : *Les livres*, par par Gaston LALOU; *Livres allemands*, par G. SAMSOEN DE GERARD; *La vie artistique*, par Aubin PASQUE; *Le manifeste de la Fédération des artistes wallons; Le cinéma*, par Jos. DATH; *La vie universitaire*, par Alain MEAULNES.

Fig. 8.1. The monthly bulletin of the *CCW*

activity with a view to favouring the junction between Walloon nationalism and pro-German feelings.

The German authorities, however, fearing an uprising in Wallonia might occur if true intentions were to be known, were opposed to a public political union between Walloons and the Reich. They estimated that such a project had to be processed with more diplomacy and discretion.

During the spring of 1941, René Simar and his direct collaborator Martin Gaillard, who had proved themselves too 'political' and not 'cultural' enough, were dismissed in order not to shock public opinion. Simar and Gaillard were then championed by Dr Rolf Wilkening, head of the Cultural Group within the Brussels *Propaganda Abteilung* and were given a mission that put them at a distance from the great public. A few months later both leaders were replaced by Pierre Hubermont, a journalist and author, who, according to appearances, wanted to make the *CCW* look like a purely Walloon cultural institution showing friendly ties with Germanic culture.

With this purpose in mind, Hubermont organized cultural trips in Germany. During the spring of 1942, he organized a Walloon Congress at Liège. Promoters of the *CCW* wanted to make this town the centre of the movement, from where political culture would radiate.

In 1944, *HSSPF* Richard Jungclaus, Himmler's deputy in Belgium, ordered the taking over by the Rex Movement and invited the different New Order groupings to gather around Victor Matthys. Hubermont, who until then had hardly displayed Rexist feelings, imitated the other organizations in joining Rex. Despite the opposition of some members, he then agreed to transform the *CCW* into an out-and-out German propaganda instrument.

During its existence, the *CCW* counted more or less 500 members spread around in various *Chambers* (one per great city) throughout Wallonia.

Newspapers:

- *Notre Terre Wallonne*, weekly, that became *Terre Wallonne* in 1942;
- *Chez Nous*, published for the first time on 2 August 1941;
- *Wallonie*, monthly.

In the area of social care, the *CCW* intended to create a Walloon Social Service in charge of the cultural and moral assistance to children of Walloon Eastern Front legionnaires, providing them with summer holidays in Germany.

A relief fund for artists and intellectuals was also scheduled.

CHAPTER IX

Governmental Organizations

Introduction[1]

After the Belgian government had fled to Great Britain, the administration of the country was taken over by the *Secrétaires-Généraux* (General Secretaries), the highest ranked civil servants heading each of the ministerial departments. During the war, they acted collectively as a Cabinet, assuming many of the powers formerly exercised by the Ministers.

The *Secrétaires-Généraux* were assigned the difficult task to act as executors of German orders and, at the same time, be the guardians of the interests of the Belgian population during the absence of the Government.

Apart from a skeletal Walloon Cabinet within the Department of the Interior, Rex was not represented in the higher spheres of political structure. (See shaded box opposite.)

A. The Secours d'Hiver (Winter Help)

In the first weeks of the occupation, the necessity of creating a widespread welfare system was commonly accepted. Occupied Belgium badly needed a similar service to the *National Relief Fund* that had been created during WWI.

However, when the creation of such

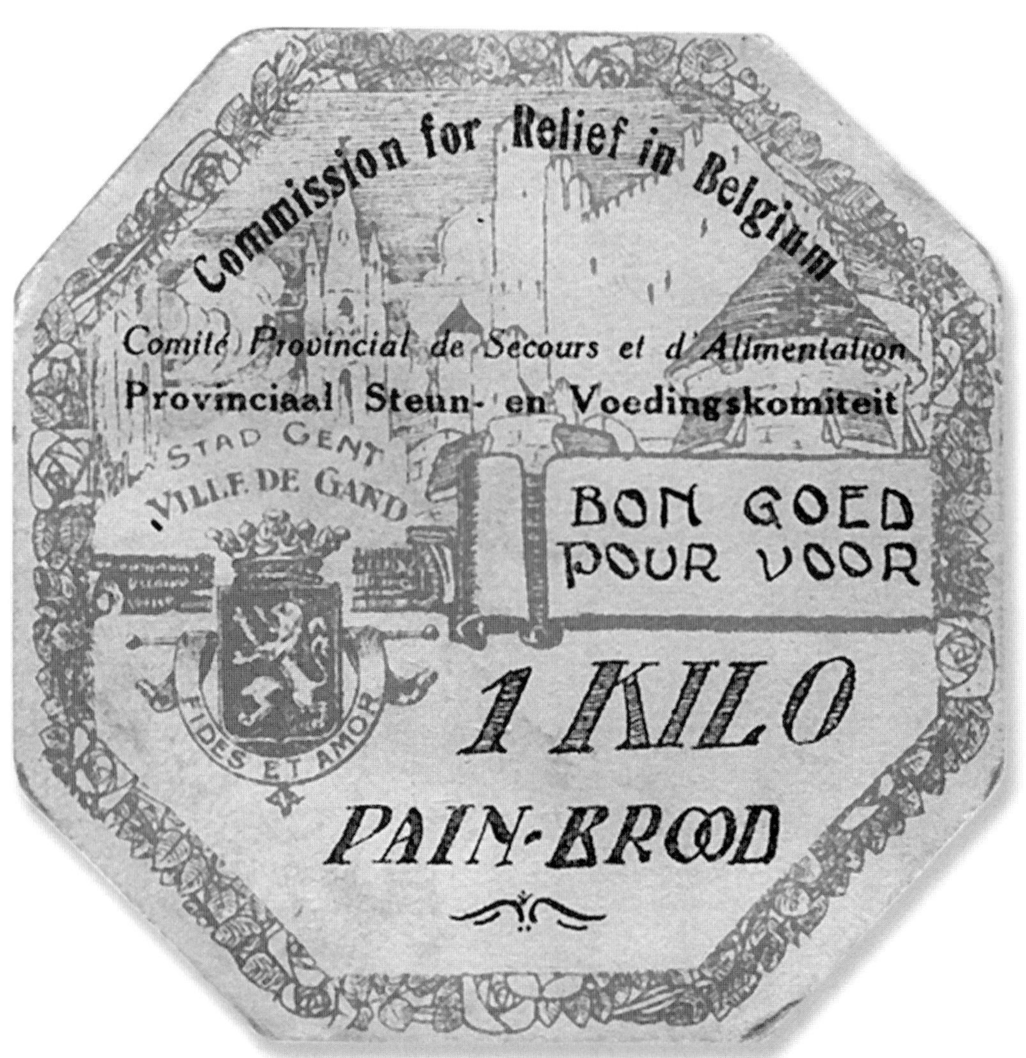

Fig. 9.1. Contrary to what happened during WWII, the Belgian population could benefit from the US sponsored WWI *Commission for Relief in Belgium* from 1914 to 1918 (*Collection E. De Bruyne*).

President of the body of Secretaries General:

1. A. Delmer (16.05.1940 – 02.09.1940)
2. A. Ernst de Brunswyck – (03.09.1940 – 31.01.1941)
3. A. Delmer (03.02.1941 – 31.02.1941)
4. O. Plisnier (04.04.1941 – September 1944)

Department of Justice:

1. J. Hubrecht (16.05.1940 – 01.08.1940)
2. A. Ernst de Brunswyck – (02.08.1940- 31.01.1941)
3. E. Wauters (03.02.1941 – 31.03.1941)
4. G. Schuind (04.04.1941 – 17.09.1943)
5. R. De Foy (01.10.1943 – September 1944)

Department of Agriculture and Food Supply:

1. E. De Winter (29.07.1940 – September 1944).

Department of Public Health (attached to the Ministry of the Interior on 24.09.1940):

1. R. Delhaye

Department of Economic Affairs:

1. G. Raven (16.05.1940 – 14.08.1940)
2. V. Leemans (04.04.1941 – September 1944)

Department of Communications:

1. Van Overstraeten (16.05.1940 – 03.08.1940)
2. Castiau (03.08.1940 – 31.03.1941)
3. G. Claes (04.04.1941 – September 1944)

Department of Colonies:

1. M. Van Hecke (16.05.1940 – 16.08.1940)
2. E. Dejonghe (17.08.1940 – 31.03.1941)
3. M. Van Hecke (04.04.1941 – 30.04.1943)
4. Van Den Abeele (07.05.1943 – September 1944)

Department of the Interior:

1. J. Vossen (16.05.1940 –21.02.1941)
2. Bajard (05.03.1941 – 21.03.1941)
3. Librecht (24.03.1941 – 31.03.1941)
4. G. Romsée (04.04.1941 – 01.09.1944 – fled to Germany on 1 September 1944)

Department of Public Instruction:

1. M. NYS (16.05.1940 – September 1944)

Department of Finances:

1. O. Plisnier (16.05.1940 – September 1944)

Department of Public Works:

1. A. Delmer (16.05.1940 – 31.03.1941)
2. De Cock (04.04.1941 – 14.08.1942)
3. De Meyer (28.08.1942 – September 1944)

Department of Labour and Social Welfare:

1. C. Verwilghen (16.05.1940 – 20.03.1942)
2. J. De Voghel (03.04. – 22.05.1942)
3. Vervaeck (29.05.1942 – 27.11.1942)
4. L. Bisqueret (04.12.1942 – 19.02.1943)
5. Olbrechts (26.02.1943 – 25.02.1944)
6. Nys (01.03.1944 – September 1944)

Fig. 9.2.

an organization came up for discussion a new tendency appeared: some circles wanted to unify the already existing welfare services and combine all resources and allowances into a new organism. This centralization seemed to smell of the New Order and was combated by the leaders of secular and religious charitable institutions. Promoters of this new tendency considered that coordination was necessary. Consequently, their main goal was to subordinate the numerous public and private relief and welfare services into a unique direction.

This controversy was not entirely settled when the *Secours d'Hiver* was installed by decree of 20 October 1940.

From the start, the newly created institution had to face a serious prejudice: German authorities imposed the appellation *Secours d'Hiver* (Winter Help) in Wallonia and *Winterhulp* in Flanders, which obviously recalled the German Nazi *Winterhilfe*. Moreover, some appointments, imposed by the German authorities, led to discontent among the population. However, in spite of all obstacles, the *Secours d'Hiver* was going to create and develop a vast national solidarity movement.

The *Secours d'Hiver* could have become a political machine in the hands of pro-German collaborationist groupings but, apart from a few local

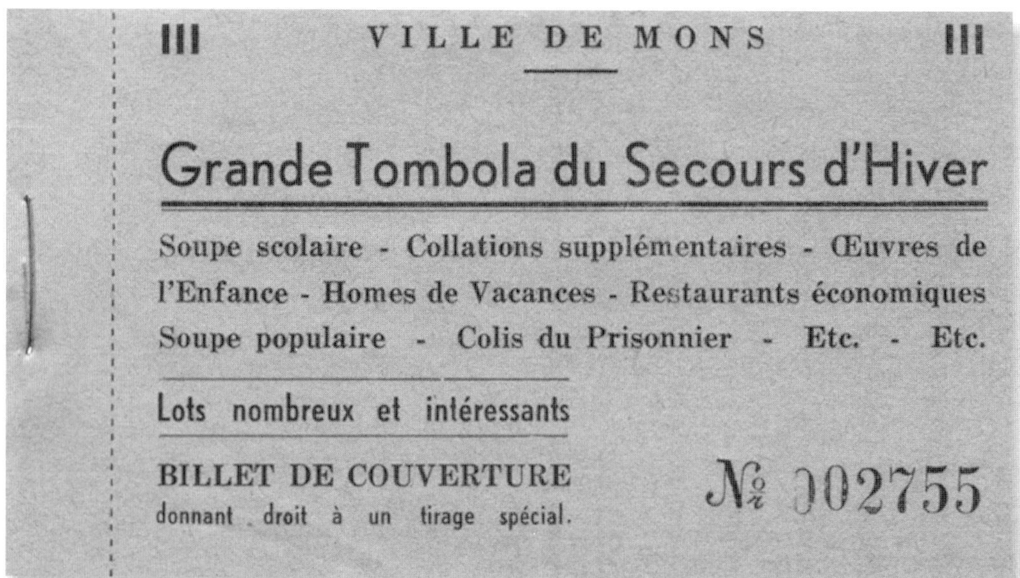

Fig. 9.3. Organising weekly lotteries was a way of raising the necessary funds to operate (*Collection E. De Bruyne*).

exceptions, the President and the executive Committee managed to avoid the danger and were successful in setting up a true movement of Belgian national solidarity.

Although its creation had been strongly criticized, nobody thought of incriminating the *Secours d'Hiver* after the liberation of the territory. This is because President Paul Heymans had been cautious enough as to surround himself with persons whose moral integrity and patriotism were above all suspicion. In addition, the highest moral authorities of the country had, by their financial support (such as important gifts in money by King Léopold III and the mother Queen Elisabeth) or by the presence during public meetings of respected personalities (among others Cardinal Van Roey), contributed to a moral caution that calmed the conscience of the population.

This Belgian way of conducting ticklish affairs frustrated New Order supporters. In 1942, the censored press started a campaign against the *Secours d'Hiver* ... calling it "a nest of anglophiles and opportunistic till-the-end-of-the-war-waiters sticking to the old political regime". The collaborationist newspaper *Cassandre*, directed by Paul Colin, used to call *Secours d'Hivers* ... *Secours divers* (a phonetic pun), whereas the Resistance referred to *Secours d'Hiver* as *Secours d'Hitler*, *hiver* rhyming with *Hitler*.

B. The Union of Manual and Intellectual Workers (Union des Travailleurs Manuels et Intellectuels – UTMI)

The *UTMI* (Union of Manual and Intellectual Workers) was established in 1940. This Union resulted from the agreement convened between leading members of the socialist General Confederation of Belgian Workers (*C.G.T.B.*), the Catholic Union Confederation (*C.G.S.*), the liberal Unions and the Flemish *Arbeidsorde*, a

Fig. 9.4.

Fig. 9.5.

copy of the German Labour Service (*Deutsche Arbeitsfront – D.A.F.*), jointly set up by the Flemish *VNV*, the *Verdinaso* and a few Catholic Union leaders showing Flemish nationalistic trends.

Long negotiations preceded the formation of the *UTMI*. A first agreement had been settled between Socialists, Catholics and Liberals, while the *Arbeidsorde* (Labour Order) boasted it could take control over all the Union organizations, first in Flanders and later all over the country. This was the moment (October 1940) when Dr Voss from the *Dienststelle Hellwig* and German auditor to the Belgian Unions, chose to interfere. He summoned various Union organization leaders, including representatives of the *Arbeidsrorde*, and urged them to find a solution for Belgium's future social status, it being understood that the new Union to be worked out would be the only one to be recognized by the German authorities.

In June 1940, two crucial events were to hasten the forming of the *UTMI*. First was the manifest by the influential Henri De Man, President of the Belgian Labour Party. The proclamation announced the dissolution of the Belgian Socialist Party (*Parti Ouvrier Belge*) stating that the political role of this Party had come to an end. De Man urged the comrade workers to rally to a single party. The second event was a circular by Arthur Juniaux, President of the powerful Socialist Health and Sick Fund. This letter referred to the resolution of a session (21 August 1940) in the course of which the National Committee had opted for a vast economic reorganization plan, inviting both patrons and workers to set up joint work and social welfare communities liberated from the ancient customs barriers. A clearer call for joining a New Order social organization was hardly possible.

On 22 November 1940, the press announced the constitution of the *UTMI*. The same day Victor Grauls, president of the new Union, pronounced a long expatiate asserting that a revolutionary spirit was blowing over Europe, and that the *UTMI* had to take a hint from the same model.

There were frequent contacts between the *UTMI* representatives and New Order organizations. The *UTMI* ideology was in concordance with the ideas professed by the various collaborating groupings such as *REX*, *AGRA* or the *DeVlag*. The Union was in contact with the League of the People's Defence and the *Cercle Wallon*. Cooperation with the Walloon Cultural Community (*CCW*) was particularly spectacular since both instances organized holiday trips in Germany for Walloon children.

C. The National Corporation of Agriculture and Alimentation – Corporation Nationale de l'Agriculture et de l'Alimentation – CNAA, or Food Estate

The *CNAA* was established by a statutory order of the Secretary-General of the Ministry of Agriculture and Supply on 27 August 1940 as an organization striving after:

- increasing agricultural production;
- mobilizing this production to the benefit of the State;
- storing the products under the exclusive control of the State and to distribute them.

D. The National Office of Goods – Offices Centraux de Marchandises – or Raw-material Allocating Offices

The German occupying authorities wished to create in Belgium the equivalent of the *Warenstellen* in the Reich, *i.e.* structures meant to organize the production and the distribution of essential goods.

They were established by the statuary order of 2 September 1940. Their mission was to observe the rational use of raw materials. The staff of the Central Offices – a blueprint of a Department of the *Wirtschaftsabteilung* (Economic Section) – was composed of Belgian personnel supervised by a German representative of the economic section within the Military Administration.

E. The National Work Office and Emplyment Agencies Office National du Travail and Werbestellen

The civilian *Werbestelle* (as opposed to the military recruitment centres, also called *Werbestellen*), in this case *Werbestellen des Arbeitseinsatz* or employment agencies, was a German recruitment organization of manpower to be sent to Germany and controlled by the local *Oberfeldkommandanturen*.

The *Office National du Travail* (established on 10 April 1941) was a Belgian service supplying manpower in Belgium. These two agencies worked hand in hand and were housed in the same building.

The task of the *Werbestellen* was to send to Germany as many Belgian workers as possible and make them take part in the German war industry effort. Upon their activity depended the solution of the alarming problem of replacement of German manpower that the campaign in the East had drained (almost all valid Germans had been called up for military service).

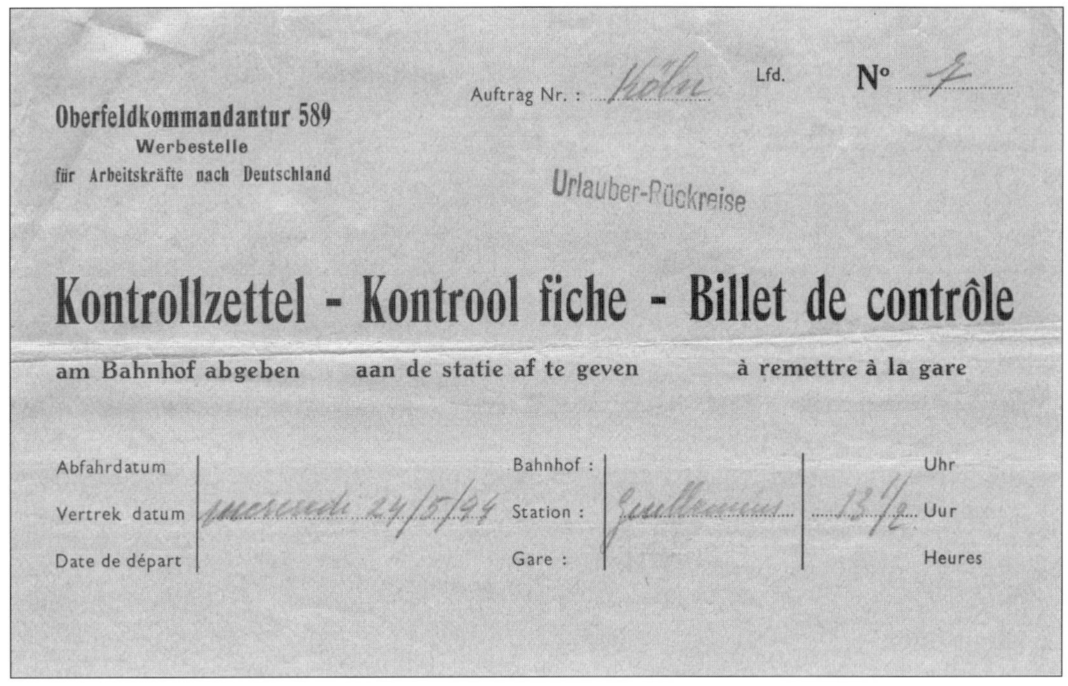

Oberfeldkommandantur 589
Werbestelle
für Arbeitskräfte nach Deutschland

Auftrag Nr. : Köln Lfd. N° 4

Urlauber-Rückreise

Kontrollzettel - Kontrool fiche - Billet de contrôle

am Bahnhof abgeben aan de statie af te geven à remettre à la gare

Abfahrdatum / Vertrek datum / Date de départ	Bahnhof : / Station : / Gare :	Uhr / Uur / Heures
mercredi 24/5/44	Guillemins	13½

Fig. 9.6. Document issued by the Liège *Oberfeldkommandantur 589* to a Walloon forced labour worker indicating that he had to check in at the local *Guillemins* railway station on Wednesday 24 May 1944, at 1:30 p.m. Destination: Cologne (*Private Collection*).

Until 1942, the *Werbestellen*, in association with the *Office National du Travail*, made every endeavour to accelerate the departure for Germany of the voluntary workers.

In March 1942, forced labour in Germany was set up, giving birth to a new category of citizens: the *réfractaires*, the fugitives from forced labour.

F. The Rural Guard – Garde Rurale

On the initiative of the *CNAA* (*Corporation Nationale d'Agriculture et d'Alimentation*) and the Secretaries-General, this rural police force was established in Wallonia on 19 April 1941. Their duty was not only to ensure the safety of agricultural property, fields and crops against theft and acts of sabotage; it also relieved the German *Feldgendarmerie* (Field Police), who previously fulfilled these tasks.

Its members were expected to be recruited by the Belgian provincial and local authorities. Enlistment was voluntary but in those villages where the number of volunteers did not reach the figure of one man for every 10 hectares, the mayor (most pre-war mayors had been replaced by Rexists) had the right to conscript up to the required quota among men between 18 and 50 years.

At the beginning of the summer of 1942, thirty-eight thousand peasants had been enrolled in the *Garde Rurale*. However, the collaborationist press complained that many *Garde Rurale* members were not doing their work properly, and that local authorities (fearing revenge and acts) were protecting offenders.

Actually, the Rural Guard was composed to a great extent of agricultural workers, patrolling at night in the agricultural properties in their area. The guards had no uniform but wore a special arm-badge instead. At first, they were not armed but as they were frequently assaulted, the Germans took the decision to issue a limited number of rifles in July 1942.

CORPORATION NATIONALE
DE L'AGRICULTURE
ET
DE L'ALIMENTATION

GARDE RURALE

RÉF. :

PRIÈRE DE RAPPELER DANS LA RÉPONSE
LES RÉFÉRENCES CI-DESSUS

Fig. 9.7.

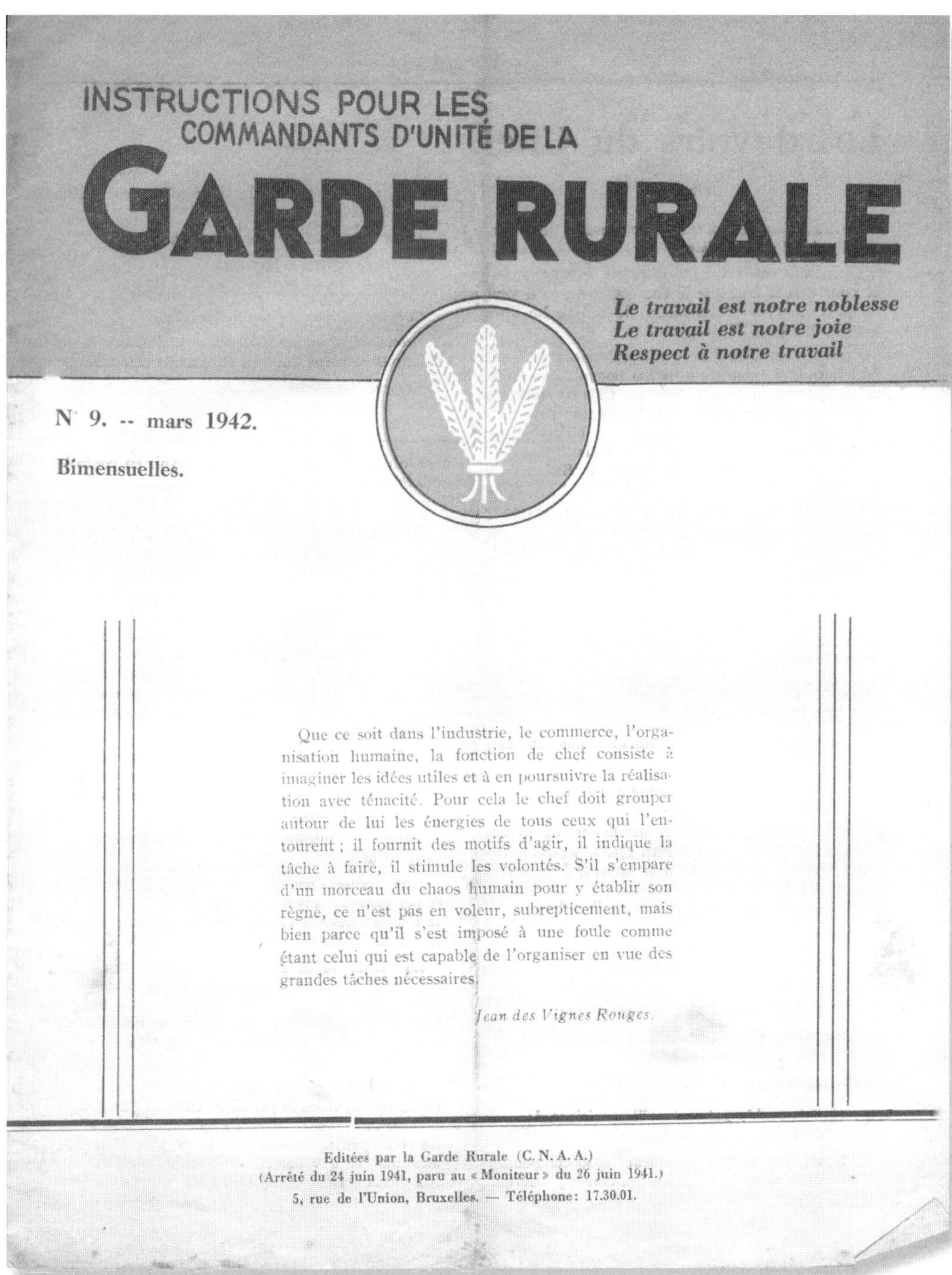

INSTRUCTIONS POUR LES COMMANDANTS D'UNITÉ DE LA

GARDE RURALE

Le travail est notre noblesse
Le travail est notre joie
Respect à notre travail

N° 9. -- mars 1942.

Bimensuelles.

Que ce soit dans l'industrie, le commerce, l'organisation humaine, la fonction de chef consiste à imaginer les idées utiles et à en poursuivre la réalisation avec ténacité. Pour cela le chef doit grouper autour de lui les énergies de tous ceux qui l'entourent ; il fournit des motifs d'agir, il indique la tâche à faire, il stimule les volontés. S'il s'empare d'un morceau du chaos humain pour y établir son règne, ce n'est pas en voleur, subrepticement, mais bien parce qu'il s'est imposé à une foule comme étant celui qui est capable de l'organiser en vue des grandes tâches nécessaires.

Jean des Vignes Rouges.

Editées par la Garde Rurale (C. N. A. A.)
(Arrêté du 24 juin 1941, paru au « Moniteur » du 26 juin 1941.)
5, rue de l'Union, Bruxelles. — Téléphone: 17.30.01.

Fig. 9.8. (*Collection E. De Bruyne*)

Headquarter of the Walloon Rural Guard was in Brussels, the chief being Gottfried Dalle. His deputy chief P. Vandersypen replaced him on 28 September 1943.

If the cadres of the Walloon Rural Guard were in sympathy with the New Order, the majority of the guards themselves, even those who had joined voluntarily, performed their duties with reluctance or did not perform them at all. All they were interested in was to protect their produce and doing such was not considered a pro-Rexist activity.

CHAPTER X

The Auxiliary Police Forces

A. The Zivilfahndungsdienst (Secret Police Service Tracking Unwilling Workers)

By the end of 1943, German authorities got alarmed by the ever increasing number of defections among workers called up for forced labour in Germany. The number of disobedient labourers grew day by day and a lot of them, in an attempt to avoid arrest, joined the Resistance. The German occupying authorities then decided to call upon Rex and other New Order-minded organizations with a view to recruiting Belgians who would accept to be part of a German police service within the *Feldgendarmerie* (Field Police), and whose job it would be to track down absentee workers. The Rex Movement responded to the German wish and created the *Formation A* that was to be the antechamber of the *Zivilfahndungsdienst*.

The *Werhmacht* supervised the *Formation A* as the latter was meant to be a special assistant body helping the *Feldgendarmerie*. In reality, enlistment within the *Formation A* had proved disappointing and forced the Germans to tutor the *Zivilfahndungsdienst* themselves.

The first contingent was incorporated on 11 April 1944 and sent to the training camp of Zellik, near Brussels. The local *Werbestellen* directly activated the following contingents. The candidates accomplished a preliminary period of probation within the *Ermittlungsdienst* (see below) and were then sent to a 6 days military instruction period at Zellik.

The aim of the *Zivilfahndungsdienst* was to assist the *Feldgendarmerie* in tracking down persons assigned to forced labour in Germany, in arresting those who had not showed up when summoned and those workers who were in breach of contract. The Belgian *Zivilfahnder* often acted on their own initiative and operated arrests to their

Fig. 10.1. Identification card of Section *A* of the *Feldgendarmerie* (*Private Collection*).

own benefit; others were active in (lucrative) special sections: research of raw materials, repression of the fraud or again infiltration of the Resistance.

Enlistment terms were as follows:

- to defend the cause in the New Order in Europe under the direction of the German Reich;
- to possess the necessary physical requirements;
- to have no criminal record (*sic*) and to be politically reliable;
- to serve at least a period of six months.

Tracking down refractory workers became frantic as soon as the Allied forces had landed in Normandy. A last convoy of arrested absentee workers left Liège for Germany on 1 September 1944 (Liège was liberated on 7 September 1944).

B. The Ermittlungsdienst

This service was manned with Belgian employees. They dealt with workers who had not returned to Germany after their leaves had expired. They also summoned the workers who had failed to appear in the *Werbestelle*. Whenever an infringement was discovered the service informed the *Arbeitseinsatz*, which was qualified for the mobilisation of Labour Force policy. This service then requested the *Feldgendarmerie* to execute an arrest in collaboration with the *Zivilfahnder*.

Individuals serving within the *Ermittlungsdienst* also had to visit the different local civil administrations with a view to identifying and listing the young men (age-group 1920–24) submitted for compulsory labour in Germany.

A small number of Walloons belonged to sections which were either secret or more or less confidential. This was the case of people who had entered the *AST/Abwehrstelle* – the service of the military counterespionage of the German army, or those who had joined the department of political information of the various collaborationist groupings. The *V-männer* (agents) of the *Sipo-Sd* and the *Feldgendarmerie* also belonged to that category. The latter operated in mufti and were specialized in tracking down and arresting shot down Allied pilots. They were also active in dismantling Resistance groupings and the clandestine press. Others worked in the economic area and had joined services in charge of (profitable) purchases of raw material. Others again were specialized in tracking down Jews, Freemasons and so-called 'asocials'.

C. The Formation B

By the end of 1943, Victor Matthys, who had been alarmed by the growing number of assaults committed against Rexists – the murder of Paul Colin, director of the collaborating *Nouveau Journal* on 7 April 1943, being decisive, asked *HSSPF* Richard Jungclaus that Rex be permitted to form a Wallonia-wide spread armed security squad.

On 15 February 1944, the *National-Socialist*, the internal organ of the Rex Movement, officially announced the establishment of the *Formation B*. The *Etendard de Protection Paul Colin* was the generic name given to this direct intervention troop. The German authorities recorded it under the appellation of *Rexistisches Schutzkorps* (Rexist Protection Corps).

The *Formation B* appeared as a special unit of the *Formation de Combat*, and its members were paid in their capacity as volunteers. Headquarters were located in Brussels, first Place Rouppe, later at the Avenue du Midi, 165.

Formation B sections were active in the main cities of Wallonia. Training took place at Namur, in the barracks occupied by the *Gardes Wallonnes*. Half a dozen training sessions were organized, the first on 17 January 1944. Eight weeks after its creation, the *Formations B* numbered 460 men so that an NCO training centre became necessary (12 July 1944).

In the beginning, the *Formation B* was meant to be a protection squad to be integrated into the local police force, its main mission being the protection of local or national Rexist VIPs. This formula was

Fig. 10.2. 1 April 1944: *HSSPF* Richard Jungclaus (centre) in company of Léon Degrelle (left) and Sepp Dietrich (right) during the Cherkassy parade at Charleroi (*Collection J.-L. Roba*).

rapidly replaced by what was to become a unit of bodyguards, whose mission it was to closely guard threatened Rexists VIPs.

The members of the *Formations B* executed their missions under the jurisdiction and cover of the Brussels section of the *SS-und Polizeigericht X*, in The Hague, (the Netherlands), their acts and missions escaping control and application of the Belgian law.

But little by little the *Formation B* was to adopt the methods of the French *Milice*. Its members were informed that they would have to carry out numerous summary executions as a response to terrorist assaults, and that they had to act brutally.

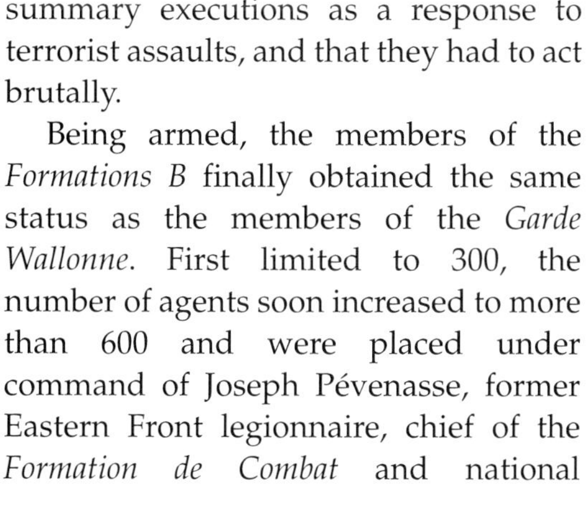

Being armed, the members of the *Formations B* finally obtained the same status as the members of the *Garde Wallonne*. First limited to 300, the number of agents soon increased to more than 600 and were placed under command of Joseph Pévenasse, former Eastern Front legionnaire, chief of the *Formation de Combat* and national commander of the *Rex Milice*. The technical and military direction of the *Formation B* lay in the hands of the second Commander of the *Légion Wallonie*, Captain B.E.M. Pierre Pauly, who had been dismissed from his command in March 1942.

Fig. 10.3. Joseph Pévenasse, chief of the Rexist Milice here as an NCO of the *Légion Wallonie* (*Collection J.-L. Roba*).

Members of the *Formation B* were recruited among all the New Order groupings: *NSKK, Garde Wallonne, Jeunesse Légionnaire*, agents of the *Sipo-Sd*, or demobilized legionnaires from the Eastern front.

D. The D.S.I. – Security and Intelligence Department (Département de Sécurité et d'Information)

The Security and Intelligence Department was created in March 1943 with an obvious view to protecting the members or sympathizers of the Rex Movement. Charles Lambinon was appointed head of this organization. Previously he had directed the service *B.I.R.D.* (Bureau of Intelligence, Investigation and Documentation).

In the beginning, the *D.S.I.* was only operational in Brussels. Later, Lambinon installed Brigades in the main cities of Wallonia. Their mission was to collect information and to take suspects into custody, for this Lambinon was given a free hand.

The missions executed by these Brigades were put down in a special confidential record (*Bulletin de police*) that mentioned the people involved: members of the Resistance, enemies of the Rex Movement, unwilling workers, printers or clandestine newspaper distributors, persons bearing a false identity card, deserters of collaborationist paramilitary formations, Jews, workers in breach of labour contract in the Reich, shot down Allied pilots, etc.

The *D.S.I.* was divided into 8 Brigades, each covering a major town in Wallonia:

- the *Brigade Z* was operational in Brussels – capital city and numbered 15 agents;
- the *Brigade A*; operated in La Louvière, counting 18 to 20 agents;
- the *Brigade B*; operational in Charleroi, counting 18 agents;
- the *Brigade C*; operational in Huy, 5 agents;
- the *Brigade D*, operational in Liège with 12 agents;
- the *Brigade E*, operational in Braine-L'Alleud;
- the *Brigade F*, operational in Mons with 5 agents.

During June 1944, a *Brigade H* was in the process of being installed in Namur.

All agents carried an identification number unknown to the other members. In the first semester of 1944, the *D.S.I.* Brigades carried out 492 arrests in Wallonia (106 'terrorists', 64 members of the *Front of Independence*, 71 members of the *White Army*, 6 hired killers, 23 authors and clandestine pamphlet distributors, 31 traffickers of arms, 32 unwilling workers for forced labour in Germany, 4 spies, 43 assumed identity bearers, 13 authors of armed robberies, 34 Jews, 21 people having given shelter to absentee workers, 4 escaped prisoners, etc.)

Fig. 10.4. *Kommandeur* Pierre Pauly (right) in company of Léon Degrelle at the time he was serving in the *Légion Wallonie* (picture taken during the winter 1941–42) (*Collection J.-L Roba*).

Fig. 10.5. This poor picture is probably the only photograph available of Paul Lambinon. In May 1945, Lambinon disappeared. The Belgian authorities never did seize him (*Arch. E. De Bruyne*).

CHAPTER XI

The Anti-Freemason League (Ligue Anti-Maçonnique)

Docteur Paul OUWERX

Prix : 25 francs

Les Précurseurs du Communisme

LA FRANC-MAÇONNERIE PEINTE PAR ELLE-MÊME

TEXTES DES SERMENTS, ETC., ETC.

1° Répertoire des FF∴ MM∴;
2° Répertoire des satellites des loges;
3° Répertoire des dirigeants et du corps enseignant de l'U∴ L∴ B∴ (Fondation maçonnique)

1940

Reproduction interdite

Fig. 11.1.

Anti-freemason action is as old as the existence of the Lodges. In pre-WWII years, opponents of Freemasonry were numerous. Most of the time, they belonged to fascist-minded right wing groups, to the extreme right, occasionally to the left, more particularly Communists. Rex was not absent from the struggle and took advantage of the politico-financial scandals to denounce what it called the Judeo-Freemasonry collusion.

In the pre-war period two personalities known for their orthodox anti-Communist feelings had been very active in combating freemasonry: Commander de Launoy and the Brussels lawyer Marcel Dessy. In 1932, they had founded the *Action and Civilization*. In 1937, two other dedicated anti-Communists joined the team: Dr Paul Ouwerx and Léopold Flament.

After the occupation of Belgium by the German armies, Ouwerx, Flament,

PREMIERE ANNEE. – N° 9.
Abonnement : 25 francs par an.

30 NOVEMBRE 1941.
Le numéro : 2 fr. 50.

LE REMPART

Organe officiel de « L'EPURATION », Ligue anti-maçonnique belge

Fac-simile du journal juif « Pour Tous », paru six mois avant la guerre, en mars 1939.

Fig. 11.2. *Le Rempart*. Official organ of the *Ligue antimaçonnique Belge-Epuration* (Collection E. De Bruyne).

and newcomer André de Harting decided to create an anti-Freemasonry movement: the *Ligue antimaçonnique Belge-Epuration*, which saw daylight on 14 December 1940. It had a newspaper called *Le Rempart*, the first issue being published on 1 February 1941.

During August 1940, the *Sipo-Sd* had already forbidden the Lodges, and their premises were occupied either by German services or by collaborationist groupings. By prescription of 20 August 1941, the German authorities imposed the dissolution of Freemasonry.

During the war, the sole noteworthy activity of the League was the organization of an itinerant anti-freemasonry exhibition.

CHAPTER XII

Belgian German-Speaking Pro-Nazi Groupings

A. The Heimattreue Front – H.F.

The rise of National Socialism in Germany and the assumption of power by Adolf Hitler considerately strengthened the already existing pro-German spirit in the so-called *'Eastern Cantons'*, comprising the districts of Malmedy-Eupen-St Vith, formerly German territory that had been allotted to Belgium as a reparation at the 1919 Versailles Treaty. The active local pro-German press was financially supported by the *Verband für Deutschtum im Ausland – V.A.D.* – (League for Germandom in foreign countries), an agency promoting Germanism and striving to maintain the German language, customs and culture among those of German extraction outside the German borders.

In 1936, several pro-German autonomist groupings unified to give birth to the *Heimattreue Front*.

The internal organization was a copy of the *NSDAP*. Thanks to substantial Nazi financial support, the *H.F.* deeply rooted into the German speaking part of Belgium.

Wilhelm Bührke, a renegade of the Socialist Party, became the chief of the *H.F.* in Malmédy. Stefan Gierets[1] was in office in Eupen, while St-Vith was under the authority of Franz Genten.

After the invasion of 1940, on the suggestion of Josef Grohe, (*Gauleiter* of Aachen-Cologne), Stefan Gierets became *Kreisleiter* of Eupen, while Gabriel Saal (*Kreisleiter* of Monschau since 1934) was invested in Malmédy on 22 May 1940.

On 11 June 1940, Walter Rexroth, the new mayor of Eupen and local *H.F. Ortsgruppenleiter*, proclaimed the *Heim ins Reich* – back to the Reich – of the *'Eastern Cantons'*.

The incorporation into the *Reich* of districts bordering Germany implied *ipso facto* the enrolment of its male

Fig. 12.1. Members of the *Heimattreue Front* marching through La Calamine/ Malmédy (*Private Collection*).

inhabitants into the German army. Members of paramilitary groupings such as the *Heimat SS* or the *Allgemeine SS* automatically joined the ranks of the *Waffen-SS* after successful racial and medical examination.

During the 1939 mobilization of the Belgian army a number of pro-Nazi inhabitants of the German speaking districts deserted and crossed the Belgian-German Border. These young men were then transferred either to the *Baulehr Regiment zbV 800 Brandenburg*, a unit specialized in carrying out special missions, or joined the *SD*. On 10 May 1940, a number of Belgian deserters accompanied the German spearhead units carrying out scouting and sabotage missions. Belgian deserters were also involved in the attack on the Eben-Emael fortress.

B. The German Language Association (Deutcher Sprachverein – DSV)

In 1938, Rexist dissidents from Arlon (south-eastern Belgium) quit the Rexist Movement. They regrouped in 1941 to found a new pro-German political party, the *Deutscher Sprachverein*, which was immediately forbidden by the local *Kommandantur* of Arlon. In March 1941, the group called in the arbitration of Franz Petri, head of the Department of Culture within the Brussels *Militärverwaltung*. Petri's views were that the region was not important enough to justify the creation of a new political party. But, the linguistic problem – its

Fig. 12.2. Stefan Gierets, *Kreisleiter* of Eupen. The *Kreis* was a subdivision of the *Gau*.

Left: **Fig. 12.3.** *H.T.* official at La Calamine/Malmédy (*Private Collection*).

Above: **Fig. 12.4.** Josef Grohe in his formal uniform of *Gauleiter*. He was to become head of the Civil Administration, replacing General von Falkenhausen in July 1944.

Fig. 12.5. Leo Maas, leader of the *Deutcher Sprachverein*.

population spoke a German dialect – could encourage the start-up of a German popular grouping, which, under cover of cultural activities, would satisfy the political ambition of the group.

The establishment of the *Deutscher Sprachverein – DSV* – took place on 19 April 1941.

- President: Léopold Maas
- General Secretary: Jean-Pierre Majeres
- Treasurer: Joseph Hieronimus

The *DSV* was active in the area of cultural and social issues. Politically, it favoured the annexation to the *Reich* of a small strip of land along the German border of the German (dialect) speaking part of the province Luxemburg.

The *DSV* had its own sections:

- the *Frauenschaft*, the female section;
- the *Lektorat*, or *Deutsche Akademie*, a

Fig. 12.6. *Gauleiter* Josef Grohe greeting the local *HJ* section at Eupen. Standing next to him, in plain clothes, Stefan Gierets (*Private Collection*).

school where German was taught and exhibitions held (92 members in 1943);

- a boys' youth movement copied from the *Hitler-Jugend*, the *Areler Volksjugend* founded by Paul Lespagnard, notorious *Sipo-Sd* agent, and later (October 1944) head of the *Leitstelle Siegfried*, an espionage training centre based in Marburg-an-der-Lahn;
- the *Arlerer Jung-Mädel*, (a copy of the *BDM – Bund Deutscher Mädel*), the girls' section;
- the *Kindergruppen*. (Young children's section).

The *DSV* also had a protection squad, the *Schutzgruppe*, instituted in April 1943.

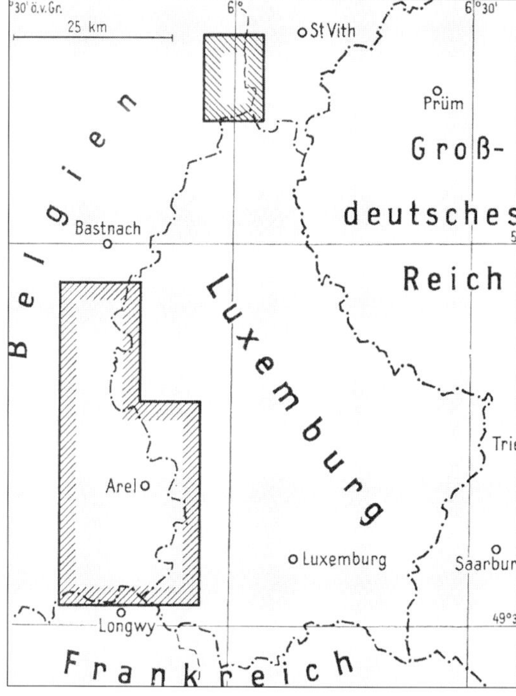

Fig. 12.7. Geographical situation of Arlon, Arlon being the French for Arel. The German-speaking parts of the Provinces of Luxemburg and Liège cover a strip of territory situated along the border with Germany and the Grand Duchy of Luxemburg.

CHAPTER XIII

Flemish Pro-Nazi Groupings in Wallonia

A. The Algemeene SS (Flemish General SS)

Unlike the *Waffen-SS*, which was a combat unit, the *Algemeene SS-Vlaanderen*, founded in September 1940 by the Antwerp lawyer René Lagrou, was an organization seeking to gather the elite among the Flemish National Socialists. Its goal: the integration of Flanders into the *Third Reich*.

A militia saw daylight. Originally, it adopted the name of *SS-Vlaanderen*, *Germaanse SS* becoming its definitive appellation in October 1942. The *Algemeene SS* and the *Germaanse SS* (Germanic *SS*) was subdivided into *Stormbanen*. *Stormbaan V* included the Flemish speaking province of Limburg, and comprised the French speaking cells in Wallonia. Since the *DeVlag* (a small Flemish ultra Nazi extremist faction led by Jef van de Wiele opposed to the moderate *VNV*) had no militia of its own, it soon penetrated the *Allgemeene SS*. As, geographically speaking, recruitment was limited, the *DeVlag* sounded out Wallonia, hoping to win over to their cause the numerous Flemings that had settled in the French speaking part of Belgium.

By the end of 1941, the *DeVlag* direction in Brussels had convinced the cultural and political branch of the *SD* that public meetings be authorized in Liège. However, it was not before 1943 that an official subdivision of the *Algemeene SS* was established in Wallonia.

Its structure was articulated as follows:

- head of the movement: François Haesevoets, chief of the Namur Cell;
- chief of organization and propaganda: Victor Bracke from Charleroi;
- chief of social service: Antoon Lint from Liège;
- chief of finances: Bosmans.

As membership was very limited, the *Algemeene SS* in Wallonia never was more than an insignificant lilliputian grouping.

B. The Vlaams Nationaal Verbond – VNV

Founded in 1933, the *VNV* was organized after a number of Flemish nationalist groupings had banded together. Under their leader, Staf De Clercq, the *VNV* advocated the splitting up of Belgium and the establishment of *Dietschland*, in fact a Greater Netherlands, which would comprise all peoples of Dutch/Flemish extract living in the Delta between Rhine–Meuse and Scheldt.

Unlike the *DeVlag*, the *VNV* was more a Flemish nationalist grouping striving

Fig. 13.1.

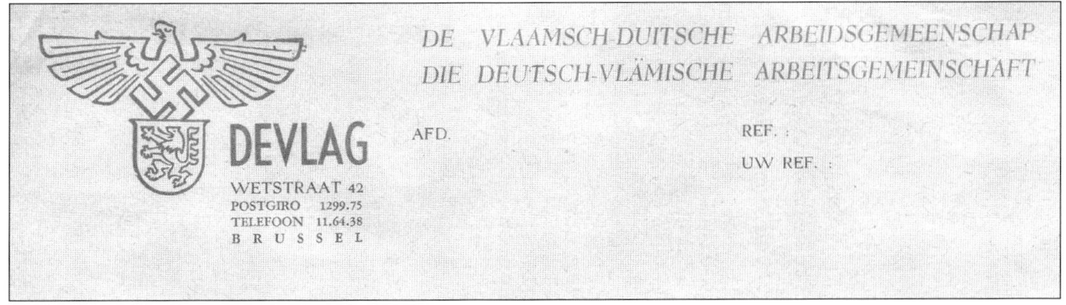

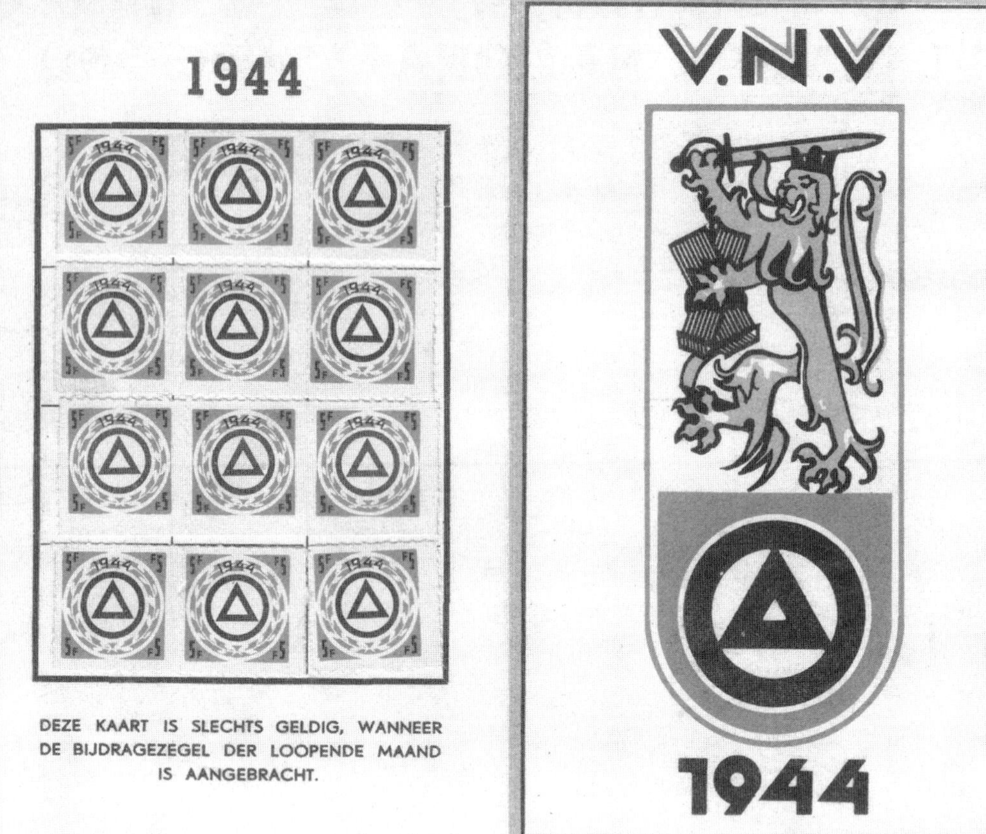

Fig. 13.2. The Delta sign symbolized the *Dietschland* (*Collection E. De Bruyne*).

Fig. 13.3. *VNV* publication issued for the Flemish families having settled in Wallonia.

for cultural and political independence that it hoped to acquire thanks to the presence of the Germans. When it became clear that Nazi Germany would never agree to an independent Flanders, the VNV officials put a serious curb on their collaborating with the Germans, eventually discouraging their members from enrolling into the *Waffen-SS* and *Langemarck* (Brigade and Division).

Forty cells of the Flemish communities in the French-speaking part of Belgium represented the *VNV* in Wallonia.

CHAPTER XIV

The German Military Administration

A. The Military Administration (Militärverwaltung)

Following order 12771/40 of the *O.K.H.*, General Walter von Brauchitsch appointed 62 years old reactivated General Alexander *Freiherr* von Falkenhausen[1] as Military Governor in Belgium and northern France (*Militärbefehlshaber in Belgien u. Nordfrankreich*) on 31 May 1940.

In his capacity of *Befehlshaber* (Commanding officer), he was not only assigned military command, it was also his responsibility to take care of the civil administration. This is why he was assisted by two general staffs, one military (*Militärverwaltung*), the second being civil/administrative (*Verwaltung*).

A: The military *Kommandostab* under Colonel of the Reserve Corps von Harbou[2] until December 1943, then Heider, dealt with military matters pertaining to the occupying military forces only.

b: The *Militärverwaltungstab* under Chief of the Military administration (*Militärverwaltungschef*) general Eggert Reeder,[3] honorary *SS-Gruppenführer*, dealt with all political, economic and cultural matters.

As Reeder's office covered all aspects of life in Belgium, next to the *Präsidentbüro*, two other important departments were operational: the Economic Department (*Wirtschafts-Abteilung*) under Colonel Nagel and the Department Administration (*Verwaltungs-Abteilung*) under H. von Craushaar.

Von Falkenhausen's position as military governor did not protect him from interference from outside, which made his task very difficult. For example von Bargen, Ambassador to Brussels, also took orders from von Ribbentrop's Office (*Auswärtiges Amt*); the Equipment Inspection Belgium (*Rüstungs Inspection Belgien*) reported to Thomas, head of the *O.K.W. Wi-Rü Amt*; Vogel, chief of the Secret Field Police (*Geheime Feldpolizei*)

Fig. 14.1. March 1942. Members of the Military Administration are attending an exhibition. From left to right: *General der Flieger* Wilhelm Wimmer, CO of the *Luftgau Belgien u. Nordfrankreich*, *Oberfeldkommandant* General Harry von Craushaar, General Baron Günther von Hammerstein-Equord, Dr Hagemayer (Rosenberg's representative), General Eggert Reeder and General *Freiherr* Alexander von Falkenshausen (*CEGES*).

obeyed to Schmidt, Chief of the Army Field Police (*Heeresfeldpolizeichef*); the *Abwehr* (Military Intelligence – *Abwehrstelle – AST* – Belgien) under Dr Dischler obeyed the *O.K.W. Abwehr* ruled by Admiral Canaris; the *Propaganda Abteilung* under Major Gerhardus reported to Goebbel's *Reichsministerium für Volksaufklärung und Propaganda – Promi -*; Dr Voss, the representative in Belgium of the German Labour Front (*Deutsche Arbeitsfront – D.A.F.*) reported to Dr Robert Ley; Dr Schultze responsible for Employment (*Arbeitszeinsatz*) took orders from Goering's Four-Year Economic Plan and last but not least *Sipo-Sd* chief Constantin Canaris obeyed Himmler's *RSHA*.

Under von Falkenhausen's administration Belgium was divided into four *Oberfeldkommandanturen – O.F.K.*, two of which covered Wallonia.[4] The four *O.F.K.* were divided into ten *Feldkommandanturen – F.K.*, the latter into 33 *Ortskommandanturen*.

As maintaining order was important, the German occupying forces immediately put the country under control of different police forces.

B. The Feldgendarmerie (Field Police)

They had to assure peace and order in the country. Notwithstanding the fact that the *Feldgendarmerie* was primarily a military police force for the members of the *Wehrmacht*, they also fulfilled surveillance missions among the population.

C. The Geheime Feldpolizei – G.F.P. (Secret Field Police)

On 14 June 1940, Berlin appointed a Leading Field Police Director (*Leitender Feldpolizeidirektor*) chief of the *G.F.P.* in Belgium and northern France. The *G.F.P.* operated as the secret military police and their tasks were multiple: execution of inquiries issued by the courts of the *Kommandantur*; surveillance of the members of the *Wehrmacht* and their families; tracking shot down Allied pilots, dismantling Secret Army hide-outs, protection against espionage and sabotage. Being an executive police force, the *G.F.P.* undertook arrests.

D. SIPO-SD Sicherheitspolizei-Sicherheitsdienst)

Located at Brussels, Avenue Louise, 543, the *Sipo-Sd* took care of all security matters.

Dr Karl Hasselbacher[5] was appointed head of the *Sipo-Sd* in July 1940. Up to this point *SS-Brigadeführer* Thomas, residing in Paris, had been the acting chief of the *Sipo-Sd* for Belgium and northern France (*Beauftragte des Chefs der Sicherheitspolizei und des SD in Belgien und Nordfrankreich*).

Two main outposts (*Außentstellen*) were operational in the Walloon part of the country: Liège (under *SS-Ostuf.* Georg Graff) and Charleroi (successively under *SS-Hstuf.* Willy Müller and Walter Michelsen). In the course of August 1943, Brussels HQ ordered the Liège *Sipo-Sd* to transfer a number of their men in order to establish a *Sipo-Sd* local station (*Nebenstelle*) in Arlon. *SS-Ustuf.* Heinz Böttcher, former head of the Liège *IV.E* section (counter-espionage) was assigned command. Dinant, a local outpost situated in the middle of the Ardennes Maquis, was manned with *Sipo-Sd* personnel in June 1944, first under Fritz Habbricht, former *Kriminal Sekeretär* in Dresden until his death on 29 June 1944 in a clash with the Resistance, later under Georg Graff, coming from Liège. On 2 September 1944, *SS-Ostuf.* Willy Asthalter, last chief of the Liège *IV.B.C.D.* section (Jews-Sects-Churches) was assigned command. The Dinant outpost received the appellation *Sonderkommado Ardennes*.

On 25 May 1944, the *Sipo-Sd* offices scattered all over Wallonia were merged into the Liège-located *Sipo-Sd Wallonien*, headed by *SS-Ostubaf.* Eduard Strauch.[6]

Fig. 14.2. General Eggert Reeder, chief of the Department Administration of the Military Government headed by Gen. Alexander von Falkenhausen. Although honorary General of the *SS*, he opposed himself to *SS* interference in military administration in Belgium until July 1944.

Fig. 14.3. The *Sipo-Sd* Liège out-station in full strength. The mascot is in front of *SS-Ostuf.* Georg Graff (*Collection J.-L. Roba*).

E. The Abwehr

Military intelligence service of the Army, the Belgian section of the *Abwehrstelle Belgien* or *AST-Belgien* – was placed under the authority of Dr Dischler,[7] and had its headquarters in Brussels.

Fig. 14.4. Eduard Strauch (left) and Wilhelm 'Willy' Asthalter (right) during their post-war trial (*Collection J.-L. Roba*).

Outposts (*AST-Außenstellen*) operated in Liège (*Dienststelle Otto* or *Bureau III. F* under Josef-Paul Schellewald, alias Dr Schubert[8]) and Charleroi, first under Dr Stubbe, alias Stahmer, later *Rittmeister* Nölle. The out-station Charleroi ceased its activities in August 1943, and was transferred to Mons under Wilhelm Baake. The latter was to play an important role in the organization and the implantation of *stay-behind* teams in September 1944.

Fig. 14.5. Snapshot by the Resistance of Wilhelm Baake on the streets of Charleroi (*Collection J.-L. Roba*).

The task of the *Abwehr* was to infiltrate agents into Allied spying groups, and to mislead Allied intelligence by all sorts of means. The arrest of agents was conducted through the *Amt-IV.Sipo-Sd* and with the help of the *G.F.P.*

In the beginning of 1944, fierce rivalry had arisen between the intelligence services of the army, the *Abwehr*, and those controlled by the *Amt VI* of the *RSHA*. In February 1944, Hitler dismissed Admiral Wilhelm Canaris in his capacity of Chief of the *Abwehr*. Consequently, most branches of the military services were transferred to the *RSHA*. In order to protect the headquarters of the armies a *Militärisches Amt* (Military Office) was established within the *RSHA* on 14 May 1944. Henceforth, every larger combat unit disposed of special intelligence sections with a view to detecting and countering subversive actions. The *Abwehrstelle Belgien* ceased to exist and was replaced by a Reconnaissance (Scouting) Commanding Post – *Aufklärungskommando*, composed of several *Frontaufklärungstrupps*, among which the *FAK 123* located at Brussels and the Liège-located *FAK* 363 (codename *Allasch*), regrouping the former *Abwehr* personnel of the Mons, Charleroi and Liège outposts; in all 25 agents, placed under the command of the already mentioned Schellewald.

In early September 1944, *FAT 123* and *363* retreated to Gmund-Eiffel and Bad-Godesberg and became involved in training Walloon sabotage squads to be dropped behind the Allied lines, on Belgian territory.

On 18 July 1944, the *Militärverwaltung* was replaced by a Civil Administration (*Zivilverwaltung*) headed by Joseph Grohe, *Gauleiter* of Aachen-Cologne. At the same time, General Grase was appointed as General of the armed forces in Belgium (*Wehrmachtsbefehlshaber in Belgien*).

CHAPTER XV

German Services

Fig. 15.1.

Nationalsozialistische Deutsche Arbeiterpartei
Auslands-Organisation
Landesgruppe in Belgien

Bankkonto :
Konto 602 bei der Westbank, Brüssel

Postanschrift :
Brüssel, Handelsstraat, 112

Fernsprecher : Brüssel 11.81.01

A. The Auslands-Organisation – A.O.

After the 1930 elections, the *NSDAP* decided to create Party sections abroad for the *Reichsdeutschen* living outside the German borders. Ernst Wilhelm Bohle was appointed leader and *Gauleiter* of the *A.O.*, with seat in Berlin.

In 1934, Belgium covered two *Kreise* (districts): *Kreis Belgien I* (Brussels) under *Kreisleiter* Ebenfeld, and *Kreis Belgien II* (Antwerp) under Dr Werner Hellwig. On 1 January 1937, the two *Kreise* were suppressed and all local sections (*Ortsgruppen*), among which Liège and Eupen-Malmédy-St-Vith – as far as the Walloon part is concerned, became a *Landesgruppe* under *Landesgruppenführer* Adolf Schulze.

Officially, the *O.A.* had to take care of *NSDAP* propaganda matters but it was also secretly given other tasks such as scouting and tracking the enemies of the regime among the German refugees, and last but not least espionage duties.

Fig. 15.2.

Volksdeutsche Bewegung Luxemburg in Belgi

BRUSSEL - 23, REGENTLAAN -- BOUL. DU RÉGENT, 23 - BRUXELLES

TEL. : 11.86.31 - 11.84.79

B. The Volksdeutsche Bewegung – VDB

Under the slogan *Heim ins Reich*, Dr Damien Kratzenberg from Luxemburg city founded the *Volksdeutsche Bewegung*, a pro-Nazi movement favouring the annexation of the Grand Duchy into the Reich on 13 July 1940.

On 2 August 1940, *Gauleiter* Gustav Simon of Moselland with seat in Koblenz became the head of the civil administration of the Grand Duchy of Luxemburg. By the end of the month of October 1941, the *VdB* numbered 71,768 members, of whom more than 1,500 had volunteered for service in the *Wehrmacht*.

During September 1941, cells abroad

Fig. 15.3.

were created, more particularly in France and Belgium. Belgian sections numbered 23 in total spread all over the country with strong representation in Brussels, Liège, Antwerp and Charleroi. These sections were centralized in Brussels in a *Landesgruppe der VdB* under Nicoals Pünnel, assisted by Jean-Henri Brincourt as chief of the Propaganda Department, and J. Deesen as *Organisationsleiter*.

In the course of November 1941, the *Auslands-Organisation* absorbed the *VdB Landesgruppe Belgien*, which by then counted more than 2,000 members.

Fig. 15.4.

Heil Hitler!

L. Pünnel

Leiter der VDB. in Belgien

C. The Deutsches Rotes Kreuz – DRK[1]

Fig. 15.5.

Health matters for all personnel of the German military or civil services fell to the *DRK*. The *DRK* had its own representative in Belgium and northern France.

D. The Organisation Todt – OT

Named after its founder Fritz Todt, the *OT* supervised the realization of the works of military engineering: fortifications, repairing of roads, building shelters and airfields, etc. It therefore hired local manpower.

For the missions and the works to be undertaken in combat zones or places exposed to armed partisan actions, the *OT* disposed of an armed protection squad – *Schutzkommando*. Also, note that the *OT* had a *Fahndungsdienst*, a special service that tracked workers in breach of contract.

E. The Lebensborn (Maternity Homes)

Right-hand column: Fig. 15.6.

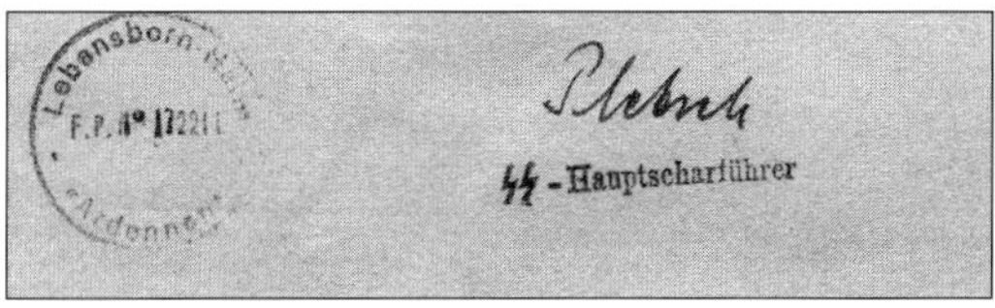

The sole home in Belgium for (Walloon and Flemish) women pregnant from racially pure Germans was housed in the castle of Wégimont-Soumange, near Liège, in 1943.

The official appellation was *Lebensbornheim 'Ardennen', Feldpostnummer* 17 221 L.

The service *Lebensborn* was administrated by the *Dienststelle Jungclaus* (*Abteilung VII*), and the department was headed by *SS-Stubaf.* Lang. This centre evacuated to Wiesbaden in September 1944.

F. The Economic Investigation Service (Witschaflichter Fahndungsdienst)

Headed by *SS-Surmbannfüher* Alfred Naujocks (the very man who played a major role in the phony Gleiwitz radio station attack, prelude to the invasion of

Poland), this service replaced (May 1944) the old *Überwachungsstelle* and dealt with the repression of the black market, on the one hand, and the acquisition of goods to the benefit of the Germans, on the other hand.

G. The Dienststelle Rosenberg Belgien

Created in July 1940, the *Dienststelle Rosenberg Belgien* was headed by Dr Müchow as a department of the *Einsatzstab Reichsleiter Rosenberg für den besetzten Gebieten* (Operational Staff Rosenberg for the Occupied Countries) and was entrusted with *'securing'* (*Sicherstellung*) works of arts or valuables belonging to Jews. It also seized documents and books of the *'ideological enemies'* such as: Freemasons, Communists, etc. The most significant among the seized items disappeared. The surplus was then sent to Germany for victims of the Allied bombings.

The Service also inspected libraries, archives and every other kind of cultural esablishment and confiscated their contents for the achievement of the aims of National Socialism.

H. The Dienststelle Jungclaus (Feldpostnummer 07515 CB)

Named after its Chief *SS-Gruppenführer u. Generalleutant der Polizei* Richard Jungclaus,[2] this department was part of the *Germanische Leitstelle* (Germanic Liaison Office within the *RSHA*) in charge of every matter pertaining to the Germanic volunteers. Its appellation in Belgium was *Germanische Leitstelle – Außentstelle Flandern u. Wallonien*, and covered the outposts Flanders and Wallonia.

By the turn of 1943–44, 289 men were detached from the *5. Sturmbrigade Wallonien* to form the *6/Stabsabteilung der Waffen-SS beim SS-Hauptamt* within the *Dienststelle Jungclaus.*

During the evacuation in September 1944, this company was integrated into the *Kampfgruppe Jungclaus.*

The *Dienststelle Jungclaus* comprised following departments:

I Adjutantur:

SS-Adjutantur / Personal (*SS-Ostuf.* Stöhr)

Polizei Adjantur (*SS-Ostuf.* Eckert)

Persönl. Referent (*SS-Ostuf.* Dr Grabs)

Sekretär D. Grupp. F. Fr (Deege)

Persönl. Büro (Mrs. Bode)

Stabsführer (*SS-Stubaf.* Schleich)

Höhere Nachrichten Führ Vertr. (*SS-Ostuf.* Wolf)

Let. San. Führ. (*SS-Stand. Fhr* Dr Hördemann)

II SS-Departments:

Ersatz Kommando Flandern (*SS-Stubaf.* Schünemann)

Ersatz Kommando Wallonien (*SS-Hstuf.* Moskopf)

SS-Fürsorge Kommando (Welfare) (*SS-Hstuf.* Strate)

SS Polizei Gericht XXXII (Justice) (*SS-Hstuf.* Seifert)

Verwaltung der Waffen-SS (Administration) (*SS-Hstuf.* Neubauer)

Zentralbauleitung d. Waffen-SS (Central Construction Office) (*SS-Ostuf.* Appelt)

Auftragsverlagerung d. Waffen SS (Order Office) (*SS-Ostuf.* Scheibe)

Standarte Kurt Eggers d. Waffen-SS (*SS-St.O.Ju.* Vierbücher)

SS-Ausbildungslager Schoten (Flanders) (*SS-Stubaf.* Lindeman)

SS-Ausbildungslager Namur (Wallonia) (*SS-Ostuf.* Lassois)

Lebensborn E. V. Wégimont (*SS-Stubaf.* Lang)

Germanische Leitstelle (*SS-Grup. Fhr* Jungclaus)

- *Referat Flandern* (*SS-Stubaf.* Schleich)
- *Referat Wallonien* (*SS-Hstuf.* Moskopf)
- *Kultur – Politischer Referat*

(*SS-Ostuf.* Dr Augustin)

- *Reichsschule Flandern/Heimschule Schoten* (*SS-Ostuf.* Dr Steck)

G. L. Verwaltung NSKK (*Stand-Fhr* Pape)

SS-Abschnitt Flandern (*SS-Stubaf.* Höffler)

Volksdeutsche Mittelstelle (*SS-Hstuf.* Lackmann)

III Police Departments:

Befehlshaber der Sipo-Sd (*SS-Stand. Fhr* Dr Canaris)

Befehlshaber der Orpo (Chief of the Police Forces)

Stab. Chef Bandenbekämpfung (HQ/anti-Partisan struggle)

Polizeiverwaltung (Administration of the Police Forces)

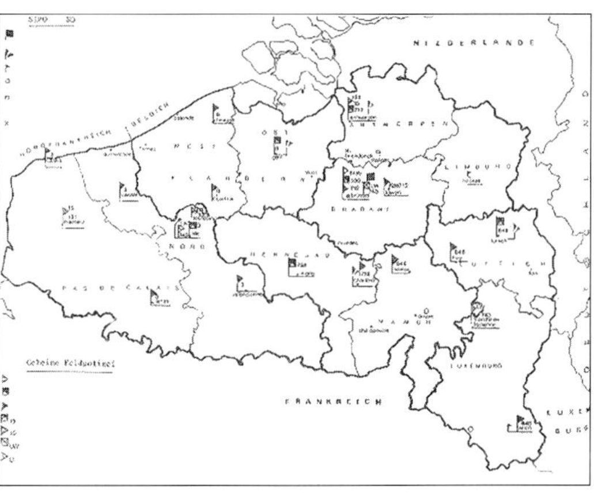

Fig. 15.7. *Sipo-Sd* and *Geheime Feldpolizei* offices in occupied Belgium and northern France. Until 24 May 1944, *Sipo-Sd* headquarters for Belgium were centralized in Brussels. From that date onwards, a *Kommandeur der Sipo-Sd Wallonien* was appointed (*SS-Ostubaf.* Eduard Strauch) with HQ at Liège, exercising full authority on the outposts of Arlon, Dinant (housing the *Sonderkommando Ardennen*) and Charleroi, while *HSSPF* Richard Jungclaus was in charge of the whole organization (*Arch. E. De Bruyne*).

I. The Ahnenerbe – Germanische Wissenschafteinsatz Flandern U. Wallonien

As a section of the *Rasse und Siedlungsamt – RuSA –* (Race and Resettlement Department), the Belgian department was headed by *SS-Ustuf.* Dr Augustin, his task being to advocate the Germanization of culture and scientific life in Wallonia and Flanders, and to study the Germanic inheritance, more particularly in Wallonia. In Flanders, Dr Augustin headed the *Germaanse Werkgemeenschap Vlaanderen*. Both of the Walloon and Flemsih departments also issued the marriage authorizations and genealogical certificates for *SS* men.

J. The Ersatzkommando Flandern U. Wallonien Der Waffen-SS (Summer 1943 – June 1944)

When the Walloon Legion was transferred to the *Waffen-SS* in June 1943, all matters pertaining to the administration of Walloon military and paramilitary units were transferred from the *Wehrmacht*-run *Kommandostab Z* to the joint *Ersatzkommando Flandern u. Wallonien* (*Dienststelle Jungclaus*) under *SS-Hstuf.* Bernt Schindlmayr.

When the Walloon *Ersatzkommando* became autonomous in July 1944, *SS-Hstuf.* Karl-Theodor Moskopf became the head of the Walloon section.

K. The Kommandostab Z

This department (the *Z* standing for *Zeppelin*) within the *Militärverwaltung* was headed by Major Baumann. The latter was in charge of the liaison between the German authorities and the units that it was sponsoring, such as the *Legion Wallonie, Garde Wallonne, Garde des Chemins de Fer*, and the Speer drivers (which became the *NSKK* later on). The goal of the *Kommandostab Z* was the recruitment for all these paramilitary groupings as well as the social and financial assistance to the members' relatives.

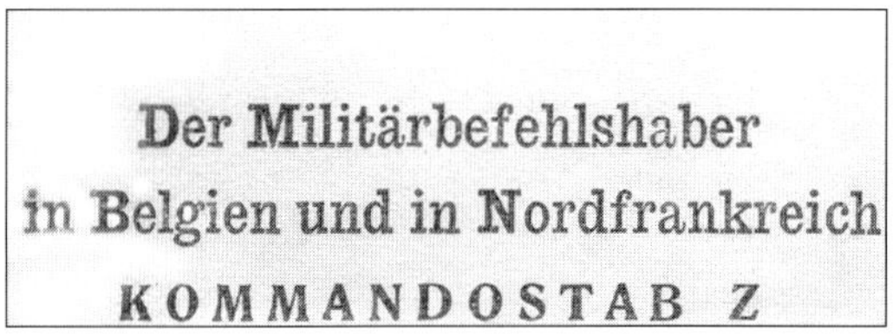

Fig. 15.8.

Der Militärbefehlshaber
in Belgien und in Nordfrankreich
KOMMANDOSTAB Z

The *Kommandostab Z* also served as a mobilization and demobilization centre, and assigned demobilized people to New Order services or Rexist organizations. Major Baumann was replaced by *SS-Hstuf.* Adalbert Schindelmayer in June 1943, with headquarters at Brussels, rue de Namur, 3.

indemnité de 150 francs mensuellement (+ 20 à 50 %).

Par suite d'arrangements spéciaux, les ayants droit de la candidate sont affiliés à la Krankenkasse. Les primes d'assurance vie et dommages de guerre peuvent être remboursées.

L'engagement se fait pour la durée de la guerre et tout au moins pour un an.

Les prestations se font dans des hôpitaux du front ou auprès d'autres services de la Croix Rouge Allemande.

Toutes les candidates, sauf les infirmières diplômées sont astreintes à un cours préparatoire qui se donne à Bruxelles.

Chaque candidate doit avoir des notions de langue allemande. Lors de l'engagement, les documents suivants sont exigés :

1) Curriculum vitae indiquant : nom, prénoms, date et lieu de naissance, domicile, études faites, emplois occupés (éventuellement domicile des parents).
2) Trois photos.
3) Certificat de bonne vie et mœurs.
4) Déclaration d'engagement.
5) Questionnaire dûment rempli.
6) Eventuellement diplôme d'infirmière (traduction légalisée).

JEUNES FILLES DE WALLONIE
Soyez dignes de nos Légionnaires

Servez la Patrie et l'Europe
dans la
DEUTSCHES ROTE KREUZ

Above: **Fig. 15.9.** Propaganda leaflet for enlistment in the Walloon section of the *DRK* (*Coll. E. De Bruyne*).

Left: **Fig. 15.10.** Two Walloon *Schwestern* (nurses) of the *DRK* (*Private Coll.*).

CHAPTER XVI

Hitler-Jugend Sections in Wallonia

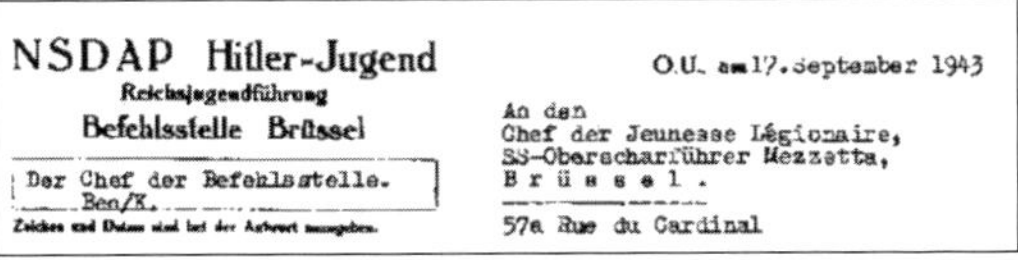

NSDAP Hitler-Jugend
Reichsjugendführung
Befehlsstelle Brüssel

Der Chef der Befehlsstelle.
Ben/K.
Zeichen und Datum sind bei der Antwort anzugeben.

O.U. am 17. September 1943

An den
Chef der Jeunesse Légionaire,
SS-Oberscharführer Mezzetta,
Brüssel.

57a Rue du Cardinal

Fig. 16.1.

There were *HJ* sections in Liège and Charleroi, the two main Walloon cities, and in Brussels. They were subordinated to the German *Reichsjugendführung*,[1] represented in Brussels by *HJ-Oberbannführer* Rudolf Hemesath who took office in February 1941 with the title of Delegate of the Reich's Youth Direction in Belgium and northern France (*Beauftragter der Reichsjugendführung in Belgien und Nordfrankreich*). The Antwerp native Frans-Lodewijk Weyler assisted him. Hemesath and his staff (as well as his successor *HJ-Hauptbannführer* Gerhardt Bennewitz[2] later on), was competent for both Flanders and Wallonia. The main task consisted of trying to unify all New Order Youth Movements in Belgium into one grouping, which would then be an exact blueprint of the *Hitler-Jugend*.

The *HJ* in the French-speaking part of Wallonia recruited their members among the children of the German occupation personnel, also among the *Volksdeutschen* and people of German antecedence living in Wallonia. The *HJ* was strongly represented in the German-speaking parts of Belgium (Eupen-Malmédy-St-Vith).

Fig. 16.2. The local Liège *HJ* section (*Collection E. De Bruyne*).

Fig. 16.3. The Liège born *Volksdeutscher* Maurice Pauss held the rank of *HJ-Oberscharführer*. In September 1944 he joined Oberhof-Schweiterhof where he was appointed *Lager-Mannschaftsführer* for the local *KLV-Lager*. He finally joined the ranks of the *Waffen-SS* (Private Collection).

Johann Orpel, a Belgium-born *Volksdeutscher* of Polish origin, established the Liège section in December 1941. In the end, it numbered 32 male members and 29 girls, not all of German extraction.

The *Hitler-Jugend* in Belgium was divided into banners or *Standorte*, headed by a *Standortführer* for the male section, and a *Mädelführerin* for the girls' section.

CHAPTER XVII

Final Assessment

After the retreat of the German forces, the judicial machine set to work immediately. From September 1944 to December 1949, 346,283 records involving collaboration with the Germans during WWII had been numbered nation-wide. The general activity of the military prosecutor's department (including all matters other than collaboration) reached the level of 728,850 files. This number of 728,850 included numerous cases that had been entered several times or dispatched to other jurisdictions, in all 167,520 files. From the 561,346 remaining files 156,279 were put aside on grounds of non-suit or extinction through decease, etc., so that, in end, 405,067 files dealing with collaboration were to be examined. As the judicial authorities finally decided that the voluntary workers (58,784) for Germany would not be prosecuted, only 346,283 records were taken into account.

For the French-speaking part of Belgium (38.53% of the population, that

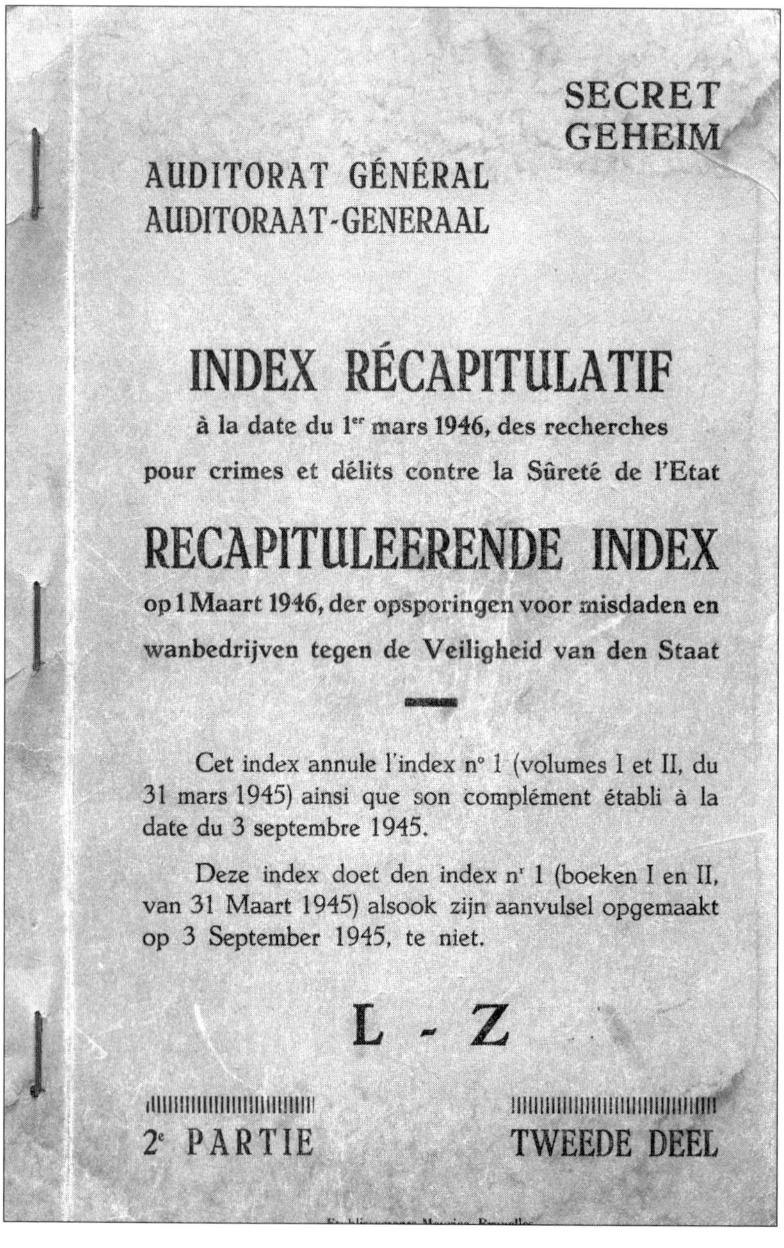

SECRET
GEHEIM

AUDITORAT GÉNÉRAL
AUDITORAAT-GENERAAL

INDEX RÉCAPITULATIF
à la date du 1er mars 1946, des recherches
pour crimes et délits contre la Sûreté de l'Etat

RECAPITULEERENDE INDEX
op 1 Maart 1946, der opsporingen voor misdaden en
wanbedrijven tegen de Veiligheid van den Staat

Cet index annule l'index n° 1 (volumes I et II, du 31 mars 1945) ainsi que son complément établi à la date du 3 septembre 1945.

Deze index doet den index nr 1 (boeken I en II, van 31 Maart 1945) alsook zijn aanvulsel opgemaakt op 3 September 1945, te niet.

L - Z

2e PARTIE — TWEEDE DEEL

Fig. 17.1.. By the end of the war, the Belgian government in exile in London had elaborated the numbering of all collaborators. Every police station in Belgium was given such an index as this one. It allowed police forces to execute the arrests (*Private Collection*).

Table 1

art.	113 (military collaboration)	24,317
art.	118 (political collaboration)	29,016
art.	121bis (press, radio, cinema)	17,066
art.	115 (economic collaboration)	17,454
art.	114,116,119 (espionage)	502
	various	2,388
Total		**110,803**

is 3.5 million inhabitants), the investigated cases numbered 110,803, and are shown on Table 1.

In Wallonia, statistics show that 0.52% of the Walloon population (and 0.56% of Brussels capital city) were convicted, to various degrees and under various forms, of having collaborated with the enemy.

119 out of the 242 capital punishments by firing squad took place in Wallonia.[1]

Léon Degrelle was condemned *in abstentia* on 27 December 1944.

In order to avoid prescription after 30 years, the Belgian Parliament voted a special law, the *Lex Degrelliana*, allowing Degrelle to be arrested and condemned if ever he entered Belgian territory.

PART II

Military Collaboration in Wallonia, 1941–1945: Légion Wallonie, 5th Assault Brigade, 28th 'Wallonien' Division

CHAPTER XVIII

The Wehrmacht Period

Preliminaries

Article 113 of the Belgian Penal Code punishes military collaboration with the enemy. Wearing an enemy's uniform was an important factor that constituted the offense.

Enforcement of art. 113 concerned the following categories: all Belgians, (in this case all Walloons) having belonged to the:

- *Waffen-SS,*
- *Légion Wallonie,*

Fig. 18. Brussels, 8 August 1941: the colour-bearer is Liège born Joseph Fauconnier, WWI veterans René Verdeur (left) and Pagnoul (right) stand next to him.

- *Hilfsgendarmerie* (Auxiliary Police Force),
- *Fahndungsdienst* (Service tracking unwilling workers),
- *Sipo-Sd*,
- *Feldgendarmerie* (Field Police),
- *Kriegsmarine*,
- *Geheime Feldpolizei* (Secret Field Police),
- *Garde Wallonne*,
- *NSKK* (Rex and *AGRA*),
- *Schutzgruppe* of the *Organisation Todt* (Protection Squad of the *OT*),
- Eisenbahnwache *(Railway Guard)*,
- *Jeunesse Legionnaire* (Feminine and male sections for members older than the legal age of 21).

When speaking of military collaboration with Germany during WWII, the *Légion Wallonie* immediately comes to one's mind.

Tackling the subject of the *Légion Wallonie* is not possible without mentioning Léon Degrelle, both being inextricably linked. The Legion identified itself with Léon Degrelle and the latter subjugated the former. The former could not exist, nay survive, without the presence of the latter, hand in glove together, so to speak.

Contrarily to what is commonly accepted (and to what has been written so often), Degrelle never held military command over the *Légion Wallonie*. In compensation, he was the undisputed political leader of the Walloon formation. And if later, in September 1944, he was finally assigned command of the *28.SS-Frw.Gren.Div.Wallonien*, Degrelle, unfit for any military command, left military matters to Frans Hellebaut, his competent *Ia* (operations officer).

A. The Légion Wallonie (August 1941 – May 1943)

1. Introduction

On 27 June 1941, Hitler approved national legions to be raised as anti-Bolshevist units participating in the struggle against Communism from each country of occupied Western Europe as well as among the populations of the Axis allies such as Croatia, Spain and Italy.

Belgium was to raise two such legions on ethnic grounds: one Flemish, the *Waffen-SS* controlled *Vlaams Legioen*; the other being the *Wehrmacht*-tutored *Légion Wallonie*.

A special section within the Brussels *Militärverwaltung*, the *Kommandostab Z* under *Hptm* Baumann, was to act as an intermediary agency between Fernand Rouleau, Degrelle's ambitious deputy and head of the *Formations de Combat* (militia of the Rexist Movement). Taking advantage of Degrelle's departure for Paris (where he was to have talks with ambassador Otto Abetz), Rouleau started negotiations on his own with a view to raising a *Corps Franc Wallonie* (Walloon *Freikorps*) to be sent to the Eastern Front under his command.

Following order no. 3680/41 of the *gKdos*, the Walloon volunteers had to be grouped into the *Wall(onische) Inf. Btl. 373* (*Feldp. Nr 38918*) and sent to *Regenwumlager* training camp at Meseritz, near the Polish border. Simultaneously, the Legion was allotted the replacement battalion identity *Ers. Btl. 36;* while the *Ers. Btl 477*, under Major Bode, was put in charge of the military and technical training.

On 8 August 1941, 860 Walloon volunteers embarked at the Brussels *Gare du Nord* railway station. Among the legionnaires was eye-catching volunteer number 237, Léon Degrelle, acting as political leader. And even if Degrelle was lucky enough to enrol a dozen Rexist officers of the Reserve Corps, enlisting career officers proved to be a major stumbling-block despite the Rexist Leader's repeated statements that serving at the Eastern Front was in no way incompatible with an officer's oath of allegiance to King Léopold III.[1]

Although Degrelle's main goal had been to remain in Belgium where he hoped to play a major political role, Rouleau's manoeuvring had left him no other choice but volunteer too lest his

Fig. 18.1. Identification disk of the *Inf. Ers. Btl. 477*, the training centre of the *Légion Wallonie*. (*Collection E. De Bruyne*).

deputy should take over command, and derive personal prestige and benefit from the operation. Whether he liked it or not, Degrelle announced his departure for the front during a Rex meeting at Liège on 20 July 1941.

Known appellations from 8 July 1941 onwards:

- *Corps Franc Wallonie*, used at the very beginning of the recruitment campaign as a reference to the post-WWI *Freikorps* operating in the Baltic countries;
- *Légion Belge Wallonie*, used for a very short time in a vain attempt to impose a sole Belgian Legion advocating a unitarian Belgicist spirit as opposed to the Flemish separatist aspirations;
- *Légion Wallonie*, which was the final appellation.

Fig. 18.2. A few hours before leaving Brussels for the Meseritz training camp, Léon Degrelle and Fernand Rouleau as they are leaving the *Palais des Arts* at Brussels. Behind Degrelle is Victor Matthys, the freshly appointed chief deputy of the Rexist Movement. (*J. Mathieu/Collection E. De Bruyne*).

Above: **Fig. 18.3.** Just after leaving the *Palais des Arts*, the companies were formed. Fernand Rouleau is marching in front of the companies, just behind the Rexist colours. Note the stripes on René Verdeur's (left) upper sleeve, each stripe representing 6 months of frontline presence during WWI. (*Collection E. De Bruyne*).

Right: **Fig. 18.4.** Centre: Major Bode, commander of the *Inf. Ers. Btl. 477*. *Left*: Georges Tchekhoff (*J. Mathieu/Collection E. De Bruyne*).

Fig. 18.5. 8 August 1941: the Walloon volunteers are making their way towards the Brussels *Gare du Nord* railway station on a drizzling day. Again, note the stripes on the upper left sleeves of the two Walloons marching next to the colour-bearer indicating that they are WWI veterans with impressive frontline service. (*J. Mathieu/Collection E. De Bruyne*).

Top: **Fig. 18.6.** Marching ahead is a German band. The Walloon volunteers for *the Légion Wallonie* are marching in front of King's Palace in Brussels. Note the lack of public interest. Moreover, in order not to have to salute, two policemen (with white helmet) are openly turning their backs on the Walloon volunteers.
(*J. Mathieu/Collection E. De Bruyne*).

Above: **Fig. 18.7.** Departure for Meseritz is imminent. Jules Mathieu (*left*), Léon Degrelle and F. Foulon (*right*).
(*J. Mathieu/Collection E. De Bruyne*).

Right: **Fig. 18.8.** Summer 1941: in this group of Walloon legionnaires, only one (second right) is wearing the regular *Wallonische Btl 373* numeral on his shoulder-straps. Also note that not all legionnaires wear the regular Walloon armshield. (Private Collection).

Dates

12 August 1941: arrival at Meseritz.

22 August 1941: oath of allegiance to Hitler as Chief of the *Wehrmacht*.

28 August 1941: oath of allegiance to Léon Degrelle.

Strength

20 officers and 850 legionnaires (including three members of the Belgian nobility and a handful White Soviets, veterans of the Wrangel and Denikin armies).

Note that apart from the professional soldiers Lucien Lippert, Adolphe Renier, René Duprés and Jacques de ***de ***, all cadre officers belonged to the Reserve Corps of the Belgian army, most of them being experienced WWI veterans.

Also note that unlike some other foreign volunteers, Walloon officers kept the rank they held in the Belgian army when joining the *Wehrmacht* (and later on the *Waffen-SS*).

Fig. 18.9. Gen. *Freiherr* von Dalwigk zu Lichtenfels, the local *Wehrkreisbefehlshaber* presided over the oath-taking ceremony of allegiance to Hitler. From left to right: Lt Jean Vermeire, *Schütze* Degrelle, Lt Fernand Rouleau, 1st Company/CO *Htpm* Albert Van Damme. Jules Mathieu is next in line. (*Collection J. Mathieu/ Collection E. De Bruyne*).

Mission

It was understood that the Legion was to be employed as a light infantry unit after having undergone a few weeks of military training. Besides, it was clearly laid down that the Walloon unit would have no front-line duties and would only be engaged in mopping-up operations behind the main frontlines.

Since the German armies were victorious on all fronts at that time, Degrelle promised his men that they would be back before Christmas. At the same time, he secretly endeavoured to reach the front as soon as possible for fear he would arrive too late, after the collapse of the Soviet armies when ... *everything would be over, without having drawn the attention of the Germans ...*

The *Légion Wallonie* was officered as

Fig. 18.10. A few days later the legionnaires swore allegiance to Léon Degrelle. (*J. Mathieu/Collection E. De Bruyne*)

follows:

Commander:

Capt-Cdt (rank between Captain and Major) Georges Jacobs,[2] a reactivated retired career officer.

Staff:

Lt Lucien Lippert (†13.02.1944, Novo-Buda/Cherkassy).

Lt Fernand Rouleau (dismissed and expelled from the Rexist Movement in September 1941 as a result of personal conflict with Léon Degrelle. In 1943, Rouleau was in charge of the recruitment in favour of the French *Waffen-SS Charlemagne* at Versailles-Paris).[3]

Health Service:

1Lt Dr Pierre Jacquemin.

Sonderführer Dr Sylvère Miesse (a prominent *AGRA* member opposed to Degrelle and as such expelled from the Legion in March 1942. He then joined the *Waffen-SS*).

Pharmacist:

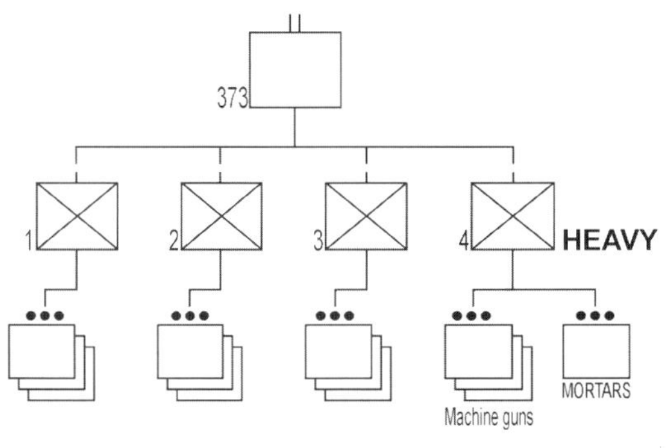

Fig. 18.11. The *Wallonische Inf. Btl 373* was composed of three infantry companies with 3 platoons each and one heavy weapons company with 4 platoons.[3] (*Ph. Heinderyckx*).

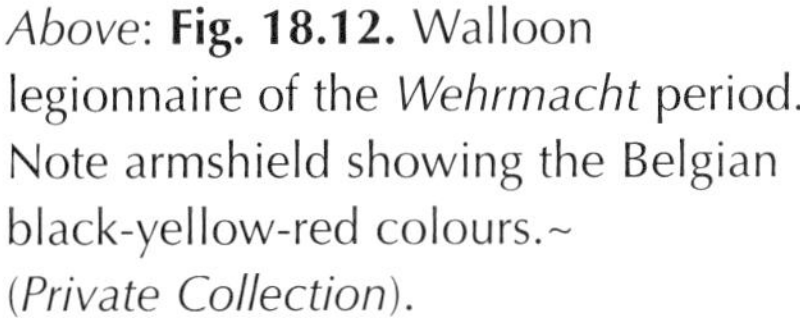

Above: **Fig. 18.12.** Walloon legionnaire of the *Wehrmacht* period. Note armshield showing the Belgian black-yellow-red colours.~ (*Private Collection*).

Top right: **Fig. 18.13.** 2nd platoon of 4th Company (heavy weapons). Note that Walloon armshields were not yet available on 14 September 1941. Second row, second right: André Régibeau, future CO of *1/I/69Rgt*. (*A. Régibeau/Collection E. De Bruyne*).

Middle right: **Fig. 18.14.** Standing on the foreground between the two German officers is Jules Mathieu, high ranking *Formation de Combat* cadre. Note the presence of L. Degrelle behind J. Mathieu (*left*). (*J. Mathieu/Collection E. De Bruyne*).

Bottom right: **Fig. 18.15.** Standing on Degrelle's left hand side is Félix Frank, Degrelle's personal secretary. (*J. Mathieu/J. Mathieu/ Collection E. De Bruyne*).

Fig. 18.16. Waiting for Léon Degrelle to join the ranks.~ (*J. Mathieu/Collection E. De Bruyne*).

Oberfeldwebel Camille Pêtre.

Veterinary:
Captain (Chemist) Victor Boullienne (August 1941-December 1941). At the age of 60 (born in 1881), Boullienne was the oldest volunteer of the first contingent.

Roman Catholic chaplain:
Georges Sales, from the abbey of Clervaux.

German liaison officer:
Lt Leppin.

Commanding frontline officers (period November—December 1941):

1st Company:
Capt-Cdt Albert Van Damme (August 1941 – January 1942).[4]

2nd Company:
Hptm Willy Heyvaert (August 1941 – January 1942).

3rd Company:
Hptm Georges Tchekhoff, former naval officer of the Tsar's Imperial Marine and future *Kdr* of the *Légion Wallonie* in April 1942.

4th Company:
Hptm René Duprés (†Grischino 01.12.1941).

Olt Baron Robert Sloet d'Oldruytenborgh (04 December 1941–11 January 1942).

Olt Arthur Buydts (January – †28.02.1942).

As Léon Degrelle had no military experience (as eldest son of a large family he had not been drafted like any other young Belgian), he was refused the rank of Lieutenant when he expressed in vain the idea an officer's rank would suit his political status better.[5]

Waiting for better times (which weren't long to come), Léon Degrelle served as a *Schütze* in the 1st group of the 1st platoon, of the 1st Company. Degrelle's platoon commander was *Oberfeldwebel* (and high-ranking officer of the *Formations de Combat*) Jules Mathieu. The latter was to become *SS-Sturmbannführer* (20.04.45) and *Kommandeur* of the *69Rgt* in September 1944.

Armament

- *Walther P38* (Company and platoon COs)
- *9mm Lüger Parabellum P08* (*idem*)

Fig. 18.17. Jules Mathieu leads the way. (*J. Mathieu/Collection E. De Bruyne*)

- *98K* (*Mauser Karabine*) rifle
- *MP 38* submachine gun
- *MG 34* (*Maschinengewehr*) machine gun
- *Panzerbüchse 39* (anti-tank rifle – allotted in March 1942)
- *l Gr.W.36* (50mm light mortar)
- *8cm s Gr.W.* (81mm heavy mortar)
- *Stielhandgrenate* (stick grenade) – *Eiergrenate* (hand grenade)
- *37mm PAK* (*Panzerabwehrkanone* / anti-tank gun).

B. Departure For The Front (October 1941)

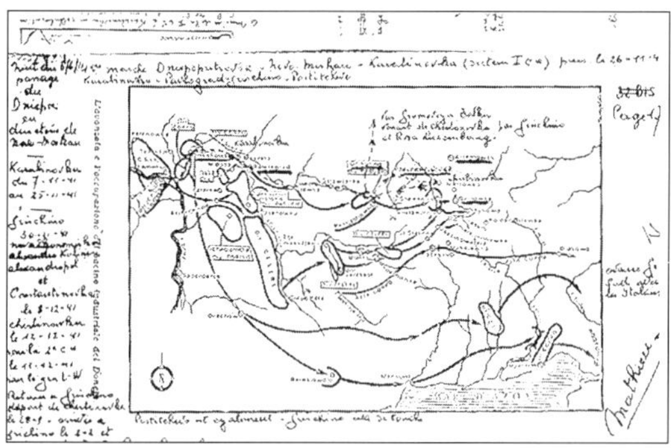

Fig. 18.18. Chart of operations. Note the post-war handwritten comments by Jules Mathieu. (*J. Mathieu/Collection E. De Bruyne*).

Battle strength: 16 officers and 776 legionnaires.

On 15 October 1941, the *Légion Wallonie* moved eastwards and disembarked at Dniepropetrovsk on 2 November 1941. A first contact was made with the local Italian expeditionary forces (under General Luigi di Micheli) rather than with the Germans as the Walloon battalion was to be dispatched to the Samara area held by the Italian 9th (Pasubio) and 52nd (Torino) divisions.

The Italian forces were part of the *C.S.I.R.*[6] under General Giovanni Messe, which had conquered the western part of the Donets Basin. Together with the Rumanian armies, the Italian forces operated within the *Heeresgruppe Süd* under Field-Marshal Gerd von Rundstedt.[7]

Leaving Dniepropetrovsk, the Walloon battalion marched eastwards and made its first contact with Soviet partisans on 19 November. Between mid-November 1941 and 17 February 1942, the Legion was employed behind the main frontline. Its task was to clear the Samara region of Soviet units that had been overrun by the German divisions driving eastwards.

A landmine mortally wounded *Hptm* René Duprés, commanding officer of 4th Company, on his way to Grichino-Selo on 1 December 1941. He was the first of a very long list of KIA legionnaires.

On 10 December the Legion was attached to the *101. Jäger Division* and was integrated into the defence system of the *III A.K.*, at Atemosk-Gorlowka (Gen. Ott).

Fig. 18.19. The winter of 1941–42 was exceptionally cold. Apart from Jules Mathieu, wearing his *F.C.* uniform boots, the other legionnaires had to do with the laced boots they had been equipped with at *Regenwurmlager*. (*J. Mathieu/Collection E. De Bruyne*).

In the meantime, extreme weather conditions, inadequate training as well as lack of proper clothing had contributed to decimating the Legion. Older legionnaires, about fifty in all, including the *Kommandeur* himself and three company commanders, were demobilized and sent back to Belgium.

Internal cohesion of the Walloon battalion also suffered from continuous quarrels between Rexists, non-Rexists and supporters of the anti-Semitic *Ligue de la Défense du Peuple* (League of People's Defence). Legionnaires belonging to the numerically smaller *Ligue de la Défense du Peuple* accused their Rexist comrades of having embraced Italian Fascism, and in consequence betrayed National Socialism by their rejectionist attitude towards Germany. Degrelle and his followers, on the other hand, considered the members of the *League* as traitors as they favoured splitting up Belgium, while non-Rexists accused both parties of advocating a politically inspired formation instead of uniting all efforts into a military unit combating Communism.

On 1 January 1942, Captain B. E. M.[8] Pierre Pauly, a career officer released from Lückenwalde *Oflag* after he had volunteered for the Eastern Front, was appointed *Kommandeur* of the *Légion Wallonie* in replacement of Georges Jacobs.

Battle force: more or less 600 legionnaires (see Table 2).

Fig. 18.20. Pierre Pauly thought he could ignore Degrelle's presence and mould a *Legion* in accordance to his own military conceptions without Rexist intervention. However, it did not take long before Degrelle sacked him. (On 21 June 1948, Pierre Pauly was executed by firing squad for his participation in the Courcelles massacre of 17–18 August 1944).

In the course of January 1942, the *Légion Wallonie*, together with 237 Croats[9] from the Croatian *Inf. Regt. 369* under Colonel Ivan Markulj,[10] formed a column charged with mopping-up duties in the area south of the Samara River.

By mid-January 1942, the battle strength of the Walloon battalion had dropped to 320 legionnaires, and it had been integrated into the *Kampfgruppe Tröger*.[11]

On 15 January 1942, Degrelle suffered

Table 2

Commander:	Hptm Pierre Pauly (January-March 1942)
Staff/Headquaters:	Olt Lucien Lippert (†13.02.1944)
	Lt Thys (January 1942 – †28.02.1942)
Medical Service:	Olt Dr Sylvère Miesse. (AGRA)
	Lt Dr Albert
Roman Catholic chaplain:	Georges Sales.
German liaison officer:	Hptm Dr Erich von Lehe.
1st Company:	Lt Alfred Lisein, (Rexist), lawyer by profession
2nd Company:	Lt Joseph Daulne, (dismissed on grounds of conflict with Degrelle in March 1942)
3rd Company:	Hptm Georges Tchekhoff, (replaced by Léopold Thys on 24 February 1942).
4th Company:	Olt Arthur Buydts, (Rexist), († 28.02.1942).

Fig. 18.21. (*right*) and **18.22.** (*below*) In a book published in January 1944, Degrelle, mainly for propaganda purposes, gave an idyllic and often exaggerated account of the November 1941-March 1942 events, which Jules Mathieu, in post-war comments, reduced to a more realistic scale. Note that the French words *'faux'* and *'exagéré'* mentioned by J. Mathieu mean 'false' and 'exaggerated'. (*J. Mathieu/Collection E. De Bruyne*).

128 FELDPOST

de la vie. On voudrait être Dieu soi-même, pour reprendre ce jour, lui rendre la fraîcheur de l'aube et le garder contre son cœur avec crainte, jusqu'à la nuit. Dès le premier péché, nous savons que nous n'aimerons plus jamais autant que nous aurions pu le faire. Et c'est ce qui rend si déchirant — parce que sans solution — le repentir...

Quand on a connu cette douleur de l'irréparable, on voudrait dépasser les possibilités du cœur pour que quelques gouttes d'amour, arrachées au maximum, puissent compenser ce qui tomba dans les ombres...

Sans doute est-ce cela que donne le baiser de l'agonie ? La paix ? La paix qui met fin aux regrets, au désespoir d'avoir mal aimé, d'avoir trop peu aimé, ou d'avoir sali l'amour que l'on avait pourtant donné d'abord avec un cœur si aimant et si vif ? ...

* *

8 janvier 1942.

C'est la nuit.

Je viens de rentrer, glacé, momifié, d'une mission le long du front. Ce voyage avait quelque chose d'extraordinaire, car la piste, dégagée seulement depuis quelques jours longe les lignes russes, à la portée des fusils.

his first wound at Nikolewskaja, a sleigh loaded with ammunition having crushed his foot and strained his ankle.

On 17 February 1942, the *Kampfgruppe Tröger* reinforced the *100.le.I.D.* (Gen. Sanne) positioned at Stepanowka. The Walloon battalion was charged with the mission of occupying the village of Gromowaja-Balka in liaison with the *1Btl SS-Rgt Germania* under *SS-Stubaf.* August Dieckmann.

C. Gromowaja-Balka

1. General situation at the front

On 18 January 1942, while the German armies were overcome by the rigours of the winter and supply difficulties, Timochenko launched a powerful offensive at the junction of the 6th and 17th German armies. Supported by very aggressive airpower, some 12 tank divisions, – backed up by specially trained and equipped Cossack cavalry units, – opened an 80 km wide breach between Slaviansk and the right flank of the 6th Army.

From 23 January onwards, Soviet spearhead troops overpowered Barwenkowo. Two days later they occupied Losowaja, supply centre of the 17th Army, driving towards Poltava, Pawlograd and the Dnepr River.

In spite of heavy snowstorms, light sledge-carried combat units and Cossack mounted troops infiltrated the whole region south of the Samara River, outflanking the weak German garrisons, notwithstanding the desperate defence of the numerous improvised strong points.

As a result of this, the whole 17th Army was exposed to being overrun from the west, thrown back southward and finally cut off from its supply bases. The German command had no strategic reserve to face this worrisome situation since the *1 Pz. Armee* was involved in resisting powerful attacks on the Mius and at Taganrog. In order to avoid a disaster there was nothing else to be done but remove a part of the armoured units and engage them in an energetic counterattack in the Grischino area so as to throw the Soviets beyond the Samara River.

The whole operation depended on the resistance of the *III A.K.* around the town of Slavianks, that Koniev had to conquer at all costs since the railroad, which bypassed the south of the city, was the only possible means of supplying his troops from Barwenkowo and Losowaja. At the same time the *XLIV A.K.* immediately removed a part of the *97. Jäger Div.* from the Artemosk area and dispatched it to the south-west of Slaviansk in order to seal the breach, which had been opened south of Barwenkowo.

Such was the military situation when on 26 January 1942, the Walloon battalion was ordered to move towards the Samara River.

2. Walloon intervention

On 18 February 1942, the Walloons approached and occupied Gromowaja-Balka under heavy Soviet artillery fire.

The battle positions were as follows:

- 1st Company organized the defence of the eastern approaches;
- 2nd Company defended the northwest outlet and the *Kolkhoz* (collective farm);
- 3rd Company was in position at the southwest outlet of the village
- 4th Company were held in reinforcement of the three infantry companies.

A Croatian *Art. Abt.* under Lt. Col.

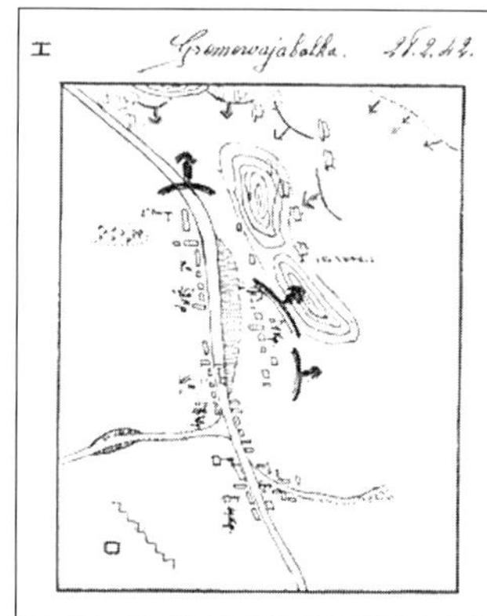

Fig. 18.23. The positions held by the Walloon battalion as mentioned in a post-war document drawn up by Frans Hellebaut during his captivity. (Arch. E. De Bruyne).

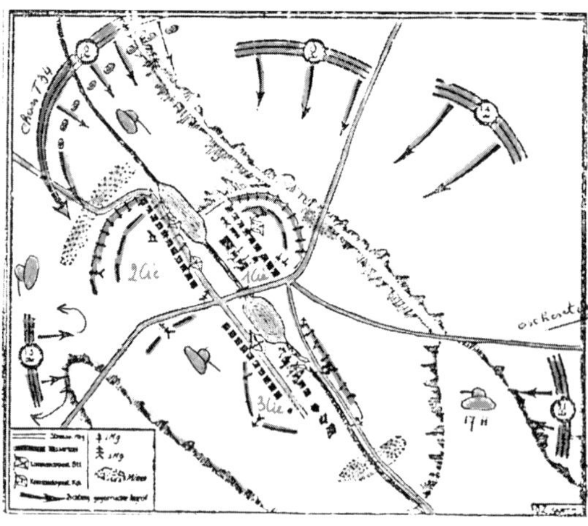

Fig. 18.24. The same battle positions as published in the Rexist press during the war. (*Arch. E. De Bruyne*).

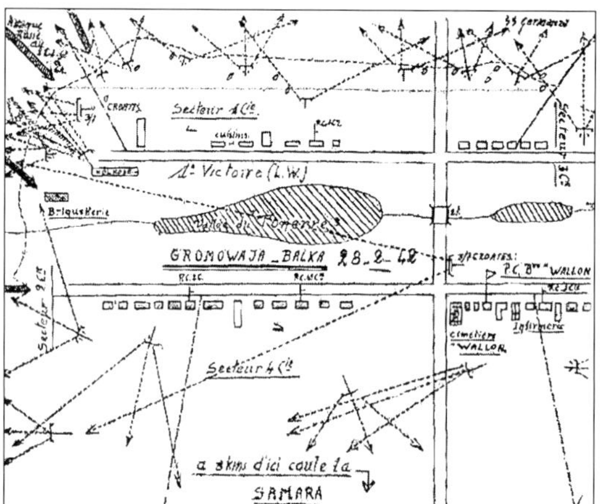

Fig. 18.25. A more complete chart shows the firing positions. (*Arch. E. De Bruyne*).

Marko Mesic[12] operated from the south-eastern portion in direct support of the Walloon positions, while the Croatian Bn and the rest of the Tröger Group occupied Golubowka strong point (3 km S.E. of Gromowaja-Balka), the whole battle formation being completed by mine fields.

An already disseminated unit of the *SS-Rgt Germania* held a 2 km distant strongpoint at Ortscheterino, to the south-east. A Walloon platoon under *Oberfeldwebel* Georges Ruelle posted halfway acted as liaison between the German strongpoint and the Walloon positions at Gromowaja-Balka.

On 28 February, after ten days of ceaseless artillery shelling causing the death of 9 Walloons and 45 other casualties, the Soviets attacked with two infantry regiments supported by tanks.

The Ortcheterino stronghold and the tiny Walloon liaison platoon were overrun in no time. As the presence of the minefield jeopardized a frontal attack from the east, the main effort of the Soviets was launched from the north in direction of the 2nd Company. For a while firing from the 2nd platoon/2nd Company prevented the first Soviet assault wave from advancing. In spite of the energetic intervention of a *s. Mi* platoon (heavy machine guns – *Oberfeldwebel* Camille Bosquion/4th Company), 2nd Company hardly contained the impact of the Soviet forces.

At 7:30 *a.m. Feldwebel* Brasseur, commanding the 3rd platoon/2nd Company, which defended the northwest salient, was killed. The subsequent wavering permitted the Soviets to overrun the position.

The approaches of the *Kolkhoz* were bitterly defended by 3rd Platoon /1st Company (commander *Oberfeldwebel* Léon Closset) and by an improvised counter-attack led by Dr S. Miesse. The rest of the 2nd Company gradually withdrew to the centre of the village after *Oberfeldwebel* Nicolas, commanding the 2nd platoon, had also been killed.

At 8:00 a.m. the situation of the left wing had become critical. 20 legionnaires had been killed, a further 20 suffered wounds and the *Kolkhoz* had fallen into Soviet hands. *Olt* Buydts, WWI veteran and commanding officer of 4th Company, was killed next to his field guns[13] while close combat actions were developing in the centre of the village.

As 2nd Company had been swept from its battle positions, 1st Compnay was attacked from the rear and soon showed signs of weakness. A spontaneous counter-attack led by *Feldwebel* Hubert Van Eyzer,[14] the determination of Léon Closset's platoon (1st Company), and Dr S. Miesse's (Headquarters) spontaneous action restored the situation.

A first counter-attack backed up by the Bosquion (4th Company) *s. Mi* platoon resulted in momentary reoccupation of some *isbas*. However, due to the continuous pressure of the Soviets, the Walloons were soon thrown back towards the centre of the village, in front of the combat post of 4th Company.

At 11:00 a.m., the whole Walloon defence system had shrunk to a very small perimeter around the Battalion strong point, behind the central crossroads. While being under direct fire from a heavy tank, Drs Jacquemin and Albert continued to dress the wounded. A desperate counter-attack led by *Kdr* Pauly himself with elements of the 3rd Company reconquered for a short time the lost terrain as far as the combat post of 4th Company, while Lt Thys was killed by a high-explosive shell in front of the battalion command post.

At 1:00 p.m. as both 1st Company and 2nd Company had lost all battle positions, and after evacuation of the wounded, the command post of the Battalion was forced to retreat as well.

One hour later, the remainder of the Walloons regrouped in front of the artillery positions in the south-eastern part of the village. Taking advantage of a dive-bombing intervention of 3 *Stukas* at 3:00 p.m., *Kdr* Pauly personally launched a second decisive counter-attack that liberated the south-eastern bottom part of the village. The arrival of a German

Fig. 18.26. General Werner Sanne, commanding the *100. le. Inf. Div.* congratulates Léon Degrelle after presenting him with the Iron Cross II. *Hptm* Pauly is standing in the background. (*Collection J.-L. Roba*).

Left: **Fig. 18.27.** 1901 born Laurent Wollacher, one of the 71 Walloons (1Co) killed in action on 28 February 1942. (*Collection E. De Bruyne*)

Right: **Fig. 18.29.** Weather conditions were extreme during the 1941–42 winter campaign. This photo, taken by Jules Mathieu at Cherbinowka, shows an unrecognizable Léon Degrelle. (French text says: *'picture taken by me (Mathieu) at the Cherbinowka collective farm'*). (*J. Mathieu/Col. E. De Bruyne*).

battalion, accompanied by 10 tanks dispatched by the *100. le. Inf. Div.*, forced the Soviets to evacuate Growowajabalka.

In blocking the passage of Gromowaja-Balka for more than 10 hours without any assistance, the *Légion Wallonie* had achieved its first battle honour, and was mentioned in the dispatches of the *100. le Inf. Div.*

Léon Degrelle, who had been appointed *Gefreiter* on 11 February, was promoted *Oberfeldwebel* on the spot. He and Pauly were presented with the *EK II* by General Sanne himself during a ceremony at Stepanowka (command post of the *100. le. Inf. Div.*) on 2 March 1942.[15]

The losses suffered during the Gromowaja-Balka battle were severe:

- of a total battle strength of 411 men (another 150 men had stayed with the train at Grischino), 71 were killed and 155 wounded, representing 55% of the total strength.
- two of the four company commanders were killed, *Olt* Adolphe Renier was badly wounded from a shot in the left lung. *Lt* Daulne was wounded, too.
- 2nd Company had to be disbanded as only 12 fit men were left.

On 13 March 1942, a parade was organized during which 35 Walloons were awarded the Iron Cross II.

The severe losses resulted in a reorganization in the command of the companies. While waiting for commission to the rank of *Leutnant*, *Oberfeldwebel* Jules Mathieu, Georges Ruelle[16] and Camille Bosquion took over command of respectively 1st, 3rd and 4th Companies.

A la suite des combats du 28 février 1942, la Croix de Fer de deuxième classe a été décernée aux Légionnaires dont les noms suivent :

de la Compagnie E. M.
Lippert, Lucien
Renier, Adolphe
Jacquemin, Pierre
Hermans, André
Winandy, André

de la 1re Compagnie :
Lisein, Alfred
Closset, Léon
Mathieu, Jules
Van Eyser, Hubert
Laruelle, René
Stregier, Frédéric
Steenbruggen, Alphonse
Gilis, Léon
Reickmans, Henri
Bayart, Georges

de la 2me Compagnie :
Vanderstappen, Edouard
Dupont, Léon
Jehay, Albert
Renotte, André
Feldbusch, Henri

de la 3me Compagnie :
Miesse, Sylvère
Crépin, Léon
Descamps, Walter
Mezzetta, Paul
Dohet, Carlos

de la 4me Compagnie :
Bosquion, Camille
Brossel, Mathias
Cosyns, Alfred
Genin, Robert
Daras, Emile
Regnard, Albert
Lodrière, René
Nile, Ernest

Deuxième promotion (à la suite des combats livrés sur la rivière Samara)
Lombars, Pierre
Léonard, Charles
Baujot, Joseph

Troisième promotion (à la suite de la bataille de Kharkov)
Tcheckoff, Georges
Lassois, Albert
Nortier, Albert
Nollet, Jules
Van Lierde, Maurice
Lecomte, Fernand
Jaucot, Aimé
Quadbach, Gérard
Badot, Théo
Ruelle, Georges
Henry, Marcel
Bonniver, Marcel

A la suite de ces derniers combats, la Croix de Fer de première classe a été accordée au lieutenant Léon DEGRELLE.

Fig. 18.28. (List of recipients of the Iron Cross II). The Rexist press set great value on the Walloons being awarded a German decoration for gallantry.

D. Isjum (May – June 1942)

1. Nowo-Jablenskaja (May 1942)

Due to a personal conflict with Léon Degrelle, Pierre Pauly was relieved from his command and temporarily replaced by *Hptm* Georges Tchekhoff on 1 April 1942.[17]

On 1 May, Degrelle was commissioned to the rank of *Leutnant* and immediately joined the Staff.

On 5 May the *Légion Wallonie* was attached to the *97. Jäger Div.* under General Ernst Rupp and would remain so until after the Caucasus campaign.[18]

Order of battle: 450 men (see Table 3).

The resistance of the *III A.K.* around Slaviansks had allowed the *III.Pz Korps* (Gruppe *von Mackensen*) and the *17. Armee* (Hoth) to restore a defensive front on the heights of the Samara, between the Donets River and Losowaja.

Table 3

Kommandeur:	Hptm Georges Tchekhoff (01.04.1942–04.06.1942)
HQ:	Olt Lucien Lippert
1st Company:	Lt (01.06.42) Jules Mathieu
3rd Company:	Lt (01.06.42) Georges Ruelle
4th Company:	Lt (01.06.42) Camille Bosquion
Engineers:	Oberfeldwebel Joseph Mirgain

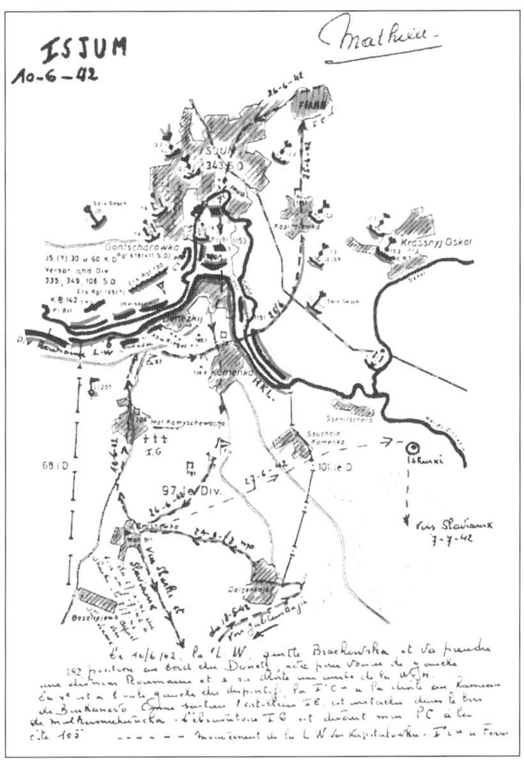

Fig. 18.30. General view of the Isjum operations, in which the 3 companies of the *Légion Wallonie* took part, 1Co (Mathieu) pushing towards Ferma. (*J. Mathieu/Collection E. De Bruyne*).

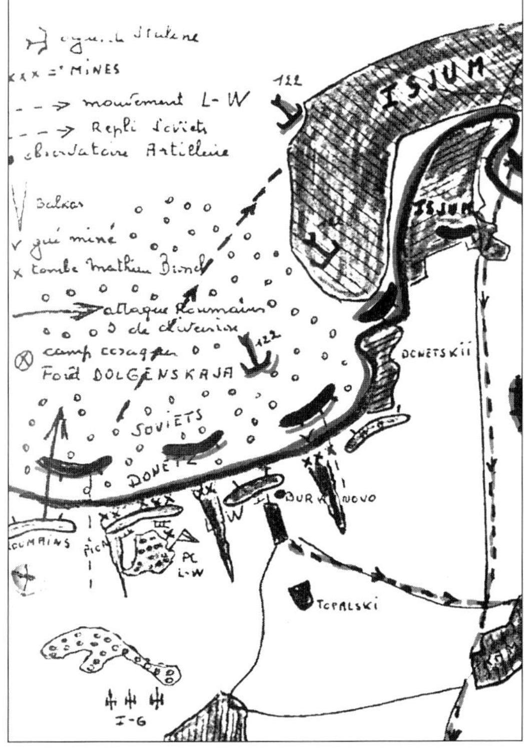

Fig. 18.31. Hand-drawn chart by J. Mathieu showing the *Légion Wallonie* positions in front of the Donets River mid-June 1942. Elements of the 4th Rumanian Div. are operating on the left wing of the Walloons. (*J. Mathieu/ Collection E. De Bruyne*).

The German command intended to resume the initiative as soon as weather conditions would allow it, but Timochenko, anticipating the Germans, launched a new offensive on 9 May 1942. It broke through the frontlines of the *6. Armee* (Paulus) at Woltschank and crossed the Donets River north of Kharkow. At the same time, Koniev's tank army, emerging from the Alexandrovka area, threw back the German *VIII A.K.* northwards, overpowering Taranowka and Krasnograd, at about 40 km from Poltowa, and approached the Merefa railway junction south of Charkow, the main supply link of the *6. Armee* with Kiev. Farther southwards, IV Rumanian Corps and *XI A.K.* hastily retreated westwards, north of Poltawa.

All of a sudden the German command had to face a desperate situation: the *6 Armee*, which had been sustaining heavy fighting around Charkow and Merefa, had lost contact with the virtually encircled *LI A.K.* near Liman and Balakleja. Only an offensive to the north of Barwenkowo could save the situation.

Taking part in this counter-offensive, the Walloon battalion left Blagodatch on 11 May 1942, and headed for Alexandrowka and Marvarowka in order to relieve elements of the *101. le. Div*[19] in position north of the Nowo-Jablenskaja village.

On the other side of the river, Soviet troops had dug in and were occupying Jablenskaja and Nikolajewka. A Walloon assault group composed of the following:

- one platoon engineers under *Feldwebel* Joseph Mirgain, comprising;
- section Nortier
- section Damiani
- section Van Haeren

- one platoon under *Oberfeldwebel* Marcel Bonniver (4th Company), comprising
- 1 section *s.MG34*
- 1 section *le.Gr.W.* (5cm mortar)
- 1 section *s.Gr.W.* (8.1cm mortar) under *Feldwebel* Minet,

... was to a clear a passage through the minefields in front of the Soviet positions, while a Walloon artillery liaison observation team under *Oberfeldwebel* Albert Lassois was attached to the *101. Jäg. Div.* A heavy Soviet bombardment caused the death of 12 Walloons and other 17 casualties, which represented 6% losses. After bitter defensive combat, the Soviets abandoned the place, a German *Pz. Gren.* group occupied Jablenskaja while the Walloon 3rd Company cleared Nikolajewka.

After the military operations another 12 Walloons were awarded the Iron Cross II, among them *Kommandeur* Tchekhoff.

Degrelle was presented with the Iron Cross I on 21 May 1942.

The German counter-offensive had completely surprised the Soviet command, which continued to believe in its victory without caring about the risks that were threatening its troops. Koniev thought he could persist in exploiting his success in the direction of Merefa, Poltawa and the Dnepr, quite unaware of what was to become the Charkow encirclement.

On 1 June 1942, five *Oberfeldwebel*, Jules Mathieu, Georges Ruelle, Camille Bosquion, Albert Lassois and Léon Closset, were commissioned to the rank of *Leutnant* as a result of their meritorious conduct in frontline duties (*Frontbewährungsoffizier*, *i.e.* officer having sufficient front-line experience).

2. Spaschowska (June 1942)

The second important contingent that had left Brussels on 10 March 1942 for military training at *Regenwurmlager*/ Meseritz, disembarked at Slavianks on 4 June. Composed of two companies, the 6th under *Leutnant* Jean Vermeire[20] and the 7th under *Leutnant* Henri Thyssen,[21] numerical battle strength amounting to 3 officers, 23 NCOs and 308 men. 76 sixteen to eighteen year old members of the *O.J.N.S.*, led by their *Prévôt* John Hagemans, had been integrated into the 6th Company. Older recruits (mainly volunteers coming from the *Garde Wallonne*) as well as the recovered legionnaires from the Gromowaja-Balka battle were part of the 7th Company. The detachment was led by *Rittmeister* von Rabenau, who had been in charge of the military training at *Regenwurmlager*. He was to replace *Hptm* Dietzl as a liaison officer.

On 6 June 1942, *Hptm* Georges Tchekhoff was transferred to the Meseritz *Erst. Btl. 36. Olt* Lucien Lippert succeeded him as fourth *Kommandeur* of the *Légion Wallonie*.

On the same day 1st, 3rd and 4th companies relieved a German battalion at Spaschowka-Burchonowo on the Donets River, on the right flank of the Rumanian 4th Division.[22] The sector was relatively quiet but subjected to irregular harassing shelling. Snipers posted on the other side of the bank caused the death of two Walloons.

The arrival of the second contingent allowed the refitting of the 2nd Company shattered at Gromowaja-Balka. A towed *I.G.* section was being formed and 15 Soviet *Hiwis* had been enrolled to take care of the horse teams.

Thanks to this reinforcement the battle force of the Walloon battalion was boosted up to 850 volunteers:

Kommandeur:	*Olt* Lucien Lippert
Headquarters:	*Lt* Albert Lassois *Lt* Léon Degrelle *Lt* Jean Vermeire (pending assignment within the 2nd Company)
Health Service:	*Olt* Dr Jacquemin *Lt* Dr Albert
1st Company:	*Lt* Jules Mathieu
2nd Company:	*Lt* Jean Vermeire
3rd Company:	*Lt* Georges Ruelle
4th Company:	*Lt* Camille Bosquion

Fig. 18.32. Left: Léon Closset. Right, Camille Bosquion, two former NCOs who were commissioned *Frontbewährungsoffizier* in June 1942. (*J. Mathieu/Collection E. De Bruyne*).

Fig. 18.33. The picture on the right shows *Kdr* Georges Tchekhoff. (*J. Mathieu/Collection E. De Bruyne*).

Left: **Fig. 18.34.** The *Légion Wallonie* was transferred to the *97. Jäg. Div.* in May 1942. Here General Ernst Rupp makes acquaintance with his new troops. *Kommandeur* Lucien Lippert is standing on the right while Lt Henri Thyssen is the Rex Colour-bearer. Note the 2nd Co flag in the foreground. (*Collection J.-L. Roba*).

Below: **Fig. 18.35.** 23 July 1942: *Leutnant* Léon Degrelle with Rumanian officers of the 4th Rumanian Div. (VI Army Corps *Dragalina*). Note the presence of John Hagemans (left). (*Collection J.-L. Roba*).

Bottom left: **Fig. 18.36.** *Rittmeister* von Rabenau. (*J. Mathieu/Collection E. De Bruyne*).

Bottom right: **Fig. 18.37.** *Regenwurmlager*, 2 April 1942. *Second* left is *Leutnant* Henri Thyssen taking the oath of allegiance on behalf of the 7th Company. (*Arch. E. De Bruyne*).

In the middle of June, *1. Pz. Armee* had been given the task of a preliminary attack, which was to ensure a more favourable assembly position for the offensive planned to follow. It had to overpower the last bridgehead in Soviet hands at Isjum and throw back Soviet forces north-east as far as Kupjanks, on the eastern bank of the Oskol River.

The operation was not easy because the Soviets were solidly entrenched on both sides of the Isjum River. A wide envelopment movement was the sole chance of success that von Kleist imparted to the excellent 14th, 16th and 22nd *Pz Div* of the *III Pz. K* (von Mackensen). The main attack was to be carried out in the direction of Kupjanks with the support of the 60th *Mot. Div.* and the *LI A.K.* of the *6. Armee*. The Rumanian divisions (*XI A.K.* Strecker) and those of the *XLIV A.K.* participated in this operation on both sides of the Isjum River so as to pin as many Soviet reserves as possible onto the Donets.

The attack was launched after a violent artillery preparation on June 24. The Walloon Bn participated in the operation as a part of the *97. le. Div.*, leaving its positions at Spachowka to occupy a waiting position at Kamenka.

Emerging south of Kharkow, von Mackensen's *Panzer* divisions managed to drive deeply into the Soviet positions north of Balakleja, in spite of very strong resistance. The Rumanian forces crossed the Donets and progressed slowly southwest of Isjum with a view to attacking the city from the rear.

The Walloon battalion crossed the Donets River at Kamenka. It progressed through forest paths in direction of Krasnyi-Liman, reaching without any major difficulties the railway line Kransyi-Liman-Isjum, 2 km farther to the north.

In the afternoon, the Walloons were at Kapitanowska, 3 km east of Isjum, restoring contact with elements of the *97. le. Div*. Only 1st Company (Mathieu) was to move as far as Ferma with a view to securing the road coming from the north.

The Walloon battalion had accomplished its mission and was sent back to Brachowka on 25 June, having suffered no losses.

The following day, the Walloon formation reached Shurki, northwest of Slawjanks, where it underwent complementary training under the supervision of *Rittmeister* von Rabenau.

On 4 July 1942, General Ernst Rupp inspected the unit. On that occasion, a handful Walloons received the Iron Cross II.

E. The Vormarsch (June–August 1942)

After the hardships of winter and Timochenko's offensive, the battle south of Charkow and the destruction of Koniev's armies allowed 6th and 17th armies to resume the initiative.

In the meantime, Hitler envisaged a vast offensive by the Army Group von Bock with the intention of conquering the Kuban and the Caucasus, south-eastern oil regions that the German armies had not been able to reach in 1941. Field-Marshals von Rundstedt, von Bock and List uttered numerous objections, considering that their armies were no longer able to sustain operations on such a large scale. Hitler stuck to his idea and as a result relieved from their commands the generals who did not share his views.

In the first days of June 1942, the *Armee Gruppe Süd* split up into two army groups, Army Group B (von Weichs) and Army Group A under direct orders of the *O.K.W.* with headquarters at Winniza (Ukraine), comprising *1. Pz Armee* (von Kleist), the 17th Army (Ruoff) and the 3rd Rumanian Army, having for its objective Rostov, the Kuban and the oilfields of the Maïkop-Tiflis area.

On 7 July 1942, the Walloon battalion, part of the *97. Jäg. Div., XXXXIV A.K.* (Gen. Dengelis), left Shurki and crossed the Donets River at Slawjanks three days later.

Marching side by side with the *97. Jäg. Div.*, the *Légion Wallonie* crossed the sandy region of Krasni-Liman, heading for Novo Astrakhan. The Walloons continued their march along the left bank of the Aïdar and the Donets Rivers, heading toward Kamensk.

Coming back on the right bank of the

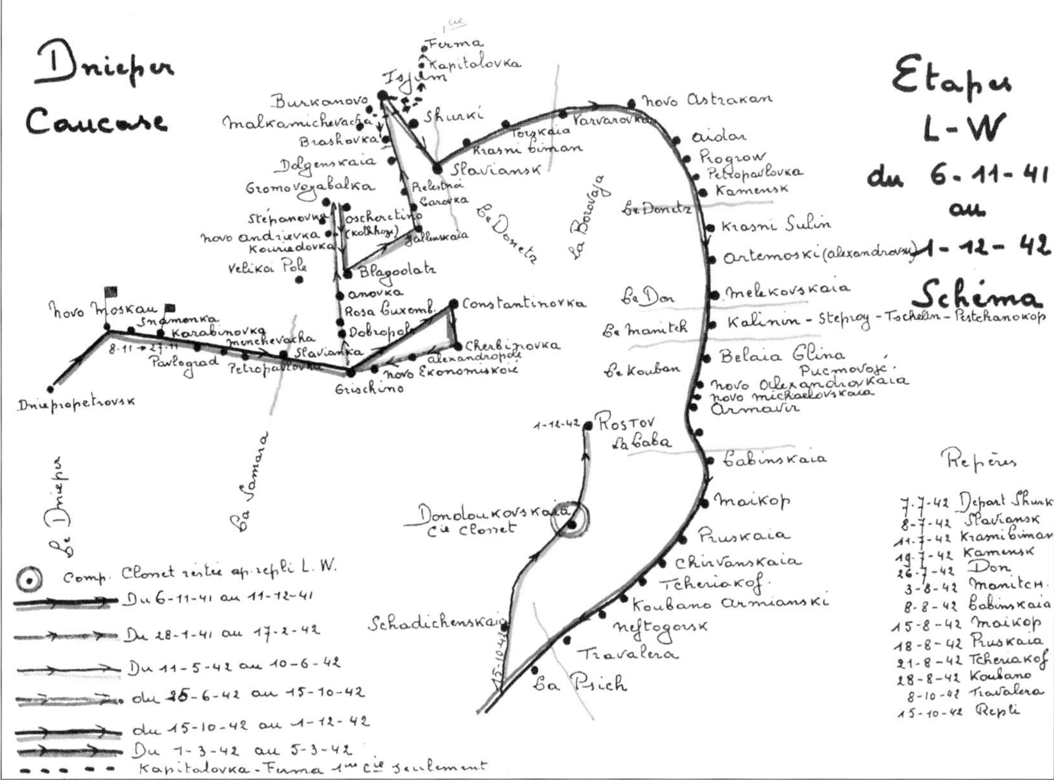

Fig. 18.38. Route followed by the *Légion Wallonie* during the Spring 1942 *Vormarsch*. (*Doc. J. Mathieu/ Collection E. De Bruyne*).

Fig. 18.39. This postcard taken for propaganda purposes shows Léon Degrelle marching ahead of his men during the *Vormarsch*. Unlike his men, Degrelle, like any other officer of the *Légion Wallonie*, did not cover the 800 km between Shurki and Maïkop on foot . . . but on horseback. (*Collection E. De Bruyne*).

Donets at Kamensk, the column edged southwards, crossed the Kraniss-Soulin-Artmeski plateau and reached the lower Don, 65 km north-east of Rostov.

On 24 July 1942, the Walloon battalion crossed the Don River at Melekhov Skaja. Two days later, the Walloons arrived in sight of the Manitsch River, the frontier between Europe and Asia.

On 4 August, the Walloons reached the Kuban River.

On 13 August 1942, after 38 days of forced marches, the main body of the *Légion Wallonie* entered Maïkop.

The battalion had covered 800 kms through hot temperatures. Although the unit did not see combat, its battle strength, due to extreme fatigue and

Fig. 18.40. During the *Vormarsch*: two Walloon legionnaires have a cup of water from a bucket. (*Collection E. De Bruyne*).

Fig. 18.41. Dust, heat, blisters and thirst accompanied the Walloon legionnaires during the 800km long *Vormarsch*. (*Collection J.-L. Roba*).

illness, had melted away like snow in the sun.

F. The Caucaus Campaign (August–November 1942)

Illness and fatigue caused by the exhausting *Vormarsch* had reduced the battle strength of the *Légion Wallonie* to less than 500 men. It then constituted a battle group of the *97. Jäg. Div*,[23] itself part of the *XXXII A.K.* of the *1. Pz. Armee*, whose mission it was to rush through the solidly-defended Pschisch River front.

All through the months of August-September 1942, the Walloons were engaged in several skirmishes.

In mid-August 1942, a ten-day Soviet bombardment of the vicinity of Chirvanskaja caused the death of 15 legionnaires, while 41 others were injured and 1 legionnaire reported missing in action.

On 26 August 1942, the Rexist Youth

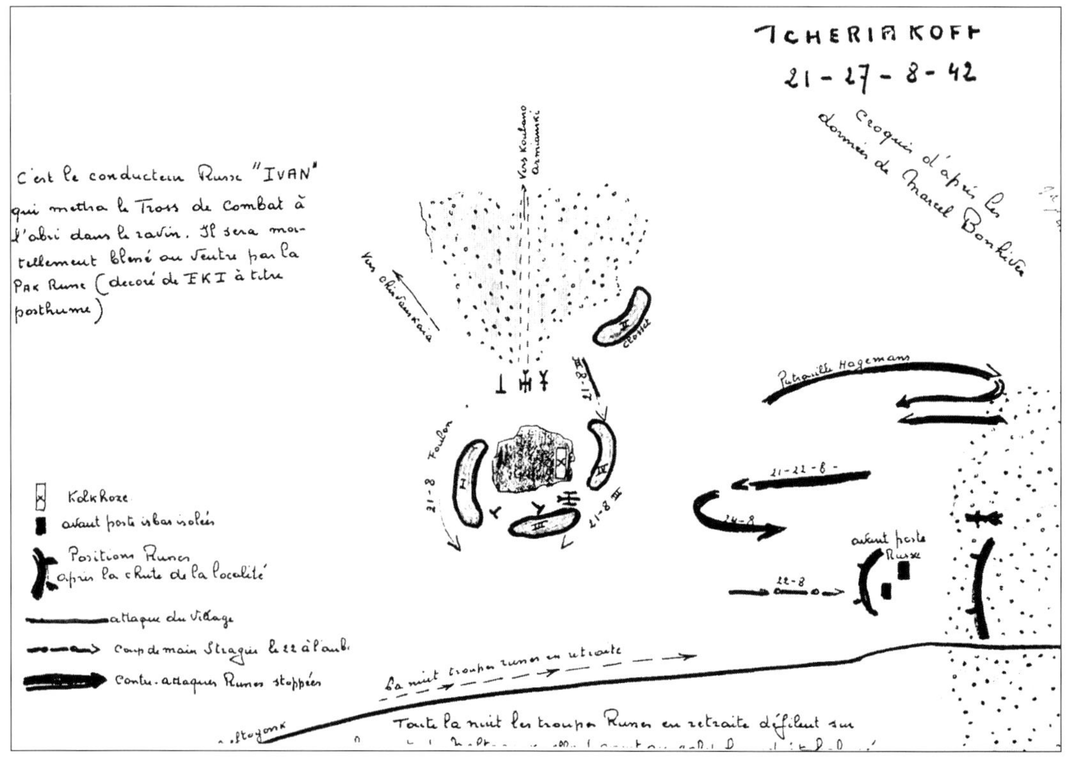

Fig. 18.42. Hand-drawn chart by J. Mathieu (thanks to indications provided by Marcel Bonniver) showing the Cherjakow operations late August 1942. French text on the top right says: *Hiwi Ivan sheltered the Tross in a ravine. He was eventually mortally wounded in the belly. He was awarded the EK I posthumously*. Text below says: *Retreating Russian troop during the night*. (*J. Mathieu/ Collection E. De Bruyne*).

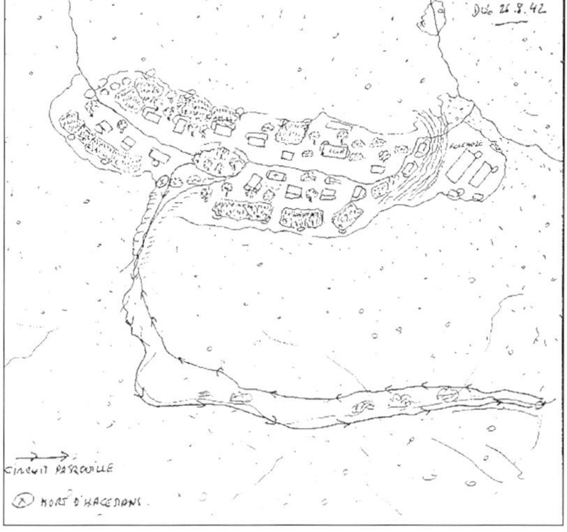

Fig. 18.43. The X marked spot indicates the place where Hagemans was killed. (*R. Devresse; arch. E. De Bruyne*).

leader (John Hagemans) was mortally wounded at Tcherjakow.

On Wednesday 26 August, orders from the Division prescribed patrol duties in order to dislodge a Soviet company hidden in the surrounding hills, whose mortar shelling had caused severe losses among the Walloons (4 deaths and 9 other casualties, among the latter Lts Bosquion (4th Company), Dumont (1st Company) and three other platoon commanders). As a first unsuccessful patrol had not been able to locate the Soviet forces, *Kommandeur* Lippert decided to launch a second more important one early in the afternoon. Taking part were three platoons from 1st Company and 3rd Company, whose mission it was to comb the south-western flank of the mountain hiding the Soviet forces. Just as the patrol was ready to start, and while elements of 3rd Company were already climbing the first slopes, a Soviet mortar shell exploded among the commanding group of the patrol, still gathered at the outskirts of the village, killing three people, including John Hagemans, and injuring another nine.

John Hageman's death not only caused a great stir, but it also relieved Degrelle of a political opponent, since Hagemans, like Degrelle, had chosen military collaboration as an unavoidable transition prior to any political activity, which, no doubt, would have discontented Degrelle.[24]

Hagemans was promoted to *Leutnant* posthumously.

At the end of the Tcherjakow battle, Commander Lucien Lippert was awarded the *EK I*. Léon Degrelle obtained the *Allgemeine Inf. Sturmabzeichen* (General Infantry Assault Badge). Another 11 legionnaires were presented with the Iron Cross II.

From 28 August until 2 September, the Legion was again engaged in fighting around Kubano-Armiansk (1 death and 1 other casualty). A few days later, two motorized companies of the *SS Wiking* relieved the Walloons.

Fig. 18.44. John Hagemans mortally wounded. (*R. Devresse; arch. E. De Bruyne*).

Fig. 18.45. Léon Degrelle and General Ernst Rupp, CO/97. *Jäg. Div.* (*Collection J.-L. Roba*).

Throughout September and October 1942, the Legion progressed along the Pschish River, in the direction of Touapse, which was never to be reached.

On 11 November 1942, Degrelle and his men were withdrawn from the front-line. At that time, their battle strength had fallen to a minimum.[25]

A first furlough was granted to 180 legionnaires of the first contingent. A rear-guard (the 10 March 1942 contingent), under Lt Léon Closset, participated in the evacuation of the Terek and Kuban area and eventually was evacuated to the Crimea by aircraft in February 1943. The train (under *Feldwebel* Generet) reached Kherson by road, where it arrived on 15 March 1943.

The Legion was then mustered at Mesertiz barracks for refitting. Its

Fig. 18.46. Brussels railway station, 18 December 1942: a first furlough awaits 180 veterans of the first contingent after an absence of 17 months. Paul Schreiber (foreground left), future instructor at Kienschlag *Panzergenadier Schule*; second right, Henri Philippet. The latter was to attend one of the last Bad-Tölz courses in March-April 1945. Next in line is legionnaire J. Charbonnier (with black bag) He was eventually killed in the ranks of the French Foreign Legion in Indo-China. (*H. Philippet*).

A LA GLORIEUSE MEMOIRE
de
Gérard MARQUEBREUCQ
Volontaire
de la Légion Belge « Wallonie »
Né à Mons, le 30 juin 1921, tombé héroïquement
au front de l'Est (dans le Caucase)
le 22 août 1942,
pour Dieu, la Belgique et l'Europe

Fig. 18.47. Obituary of Walloon legionnaire killed on 22 August 1942. Text says: *Fallen for God, Belgium and Europe.* (*Collection E. De Bruyne*).

Right column top: **Fig. 18.48.** May 1943, on the stairs of the Casino at Wildflecken barracks. From left to right: Lt Joseph Dumont, who replaced Jules Mathieu (evacuated during the *Vormarsch*) as CO/1st Company; Lt Josy Graff, former career NCO of the Belgian army and nephew of General Graff, co-founder of the *Légion Nationale*; Lt Louis Calonne and Lt Dr Albert Jacquemin. (*J. Mathieu/Collection E. De Bruyne*).

Right column bottom: **Fig. 18.49.** Wildflecken 1943. From left to right: Lt Hannicq, unknown, Catholic chaplain Louis Fierens and Lt Camille Bosquion.

Commander, Lucien Lippert, was promoted to the rank of *Hauptmann*.

As a sign of recognition of outstanding service within the *97. Jäg. Div.*, the Walloon Caucasian campaign veterans were given the privilege of wearing the mountain troops insignia, the *Edelweiß*, a metal clasp on the left side of their caps and an embroidered insignia on their right arm sleeves.[26]

CHAPTER XIX

The Waffen-SS Period

A. Transfer to the Waffen-SS (June 1943)

Fig. 19.1. Pieske barracks, May 1943: two members of the Hagemans contingent, veterans of the Caucasus campaign (note the *Edelweiß*). From left to right: Georges Thonon, Jacques Leroy. Note that both men wear the standard outfit of the Mountain troops including the mountain boots (*Schnürschuhe*), cap (*Jägermütze*) and typical trousers. (*G.Thonon, via R. Devresse*).

During April 1943, a general concentration took place at Pieske barracks, 8 km from Meseritz. By June 1943, battle strength was to reach 2,048 men and the Walloon formation, thanks to fresh enlisting, quickly reached infantry regimental strength at two battalions.

Fig. 19.2. Wildflecken, summer 1943. From left to right: Dentist R. Lejeune, *Sonderführer* R. Zavadsky (White-Russian), J. Mathieu, Winterscheidt (German Liaison Staff) and Ch. Generet. (*J. Mathieu/ Collection E. De Bruyne*).

Since the departure of the 10 March 1942 contingent, Rexist recruitment in Belgium had almost run out and new horizons were to be explored. Prisoners of war (more or less 80,0000 Francophone soldiers) and Belgian labourers in Germany (more or less 200,000 Walloons and Flemings in May 1942) were a reservoir of potential candidates, which Degrelle hoped to place in his hands.

Joseph Pévenasse (NCO since 10 March 1942) was charged with coordinating a propaganda tour in the different *Stalags* scattered all over the Reich. Results proved to be disappointing. From June 1942 to May 1943, twenty-six camps had been visited resulting in 192 recruits. *Stalag IA* at Stablack, by far the most important in number of POWs, released 40 candidates, of whom 6 deserted.[1] Those from Alten-Grabow (*XI.A*) and Sandbostel (*XI.B*) followed respectively with 26 and 20 enlistments.

By extending his recruiting to non-Rexist circles Degrelle took the risk of dragging into the Legion individuals whose motivation was other than that of anti-Bolshevism: domestic problems, the desire to escape the dull environment of a POW camp and the hope for a furlough in Belgium in case of enlistment (as promised), being the main ones. As a result of this, transfer to the *Waffen-SS*, on 1 June 1943, showed a spectacular impoverishment of the ideological commitment and led to a disastrous increase of desertions among the newly enlisted men.

For the whole year of 1942, recruitment levels for the Legion had reached the figure of 1,834 volunteers.[2] During that year, the Walloon Court Martial only investigated 28 cases of desertion. As of 31 May 1943, among the 192 POWs the

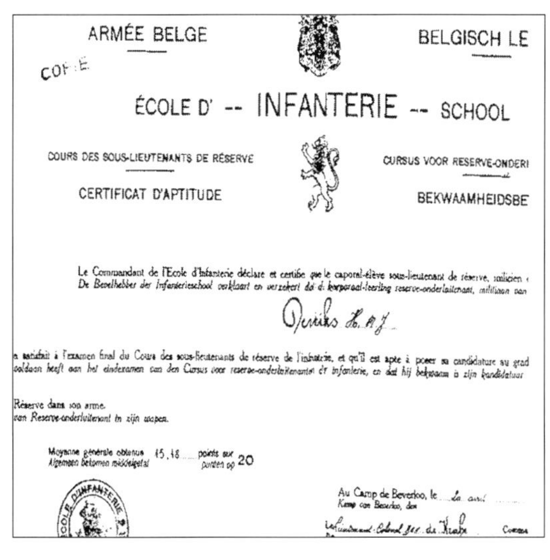

ARMÉE BELGE — BELGISCH LE

COPIE

ÉCOLE D' -- INFANTERIE -- SCHOOL

COURS DES SOUS-LIEUTENANTS DE RÉSERVE — CURSUS VOOR RESERVE-ONDERI

CERTIFICAT D'APTITUDE — BEKWAAMHEIDSBE

Le Commandant de l'Ecole d'Infanterie déclare et certifie que le caporal-élève sous-lieutenant de réserve, milicien
De Bevelhebber der Infanterieschool verklaart en verzekert dat de korporaal-leerling reserve-onderluitenant, militiaan van

Derriks H. A. J.

a satisfait à l'examen final du Cours des sous-lieutenants de réserve de l'infanterie, et qu'il est apte à poser sa candidature au grad
voldaan heeft aan het eindexamen van den Cursus voor reserve-onderluitenanten der infanterie, en dat hij bekwaam is zijn kandidatuur

Réserve dans son arme.
van Reserve-onderluitenant in zijn wapen.

Moyenne générale obtenue 15,18 points sur 20
Algemeen bekomen middelgetal punten op

ÉCOLE D'INFANTERIE

Au Camp de Beverloo, le
Kamp van Beverloo, den

Fig. 19.3. H. Derriks' certificate (20.04.1936) of promotion to the rank of Lieutenant of the Reserve Corps with the excellent note of 15,18/20. (*Arch. E. De Bruyne*).

recruiting teams had enlisted, 34 deserters were still on the run![3] A more meticulous study reveals that the recruitment in the *Stalags* remained small and represented, in most of the cases, less than 10% of the men recruited elsewhere. On 31 December 1942, the number of POWs released for recruitment into the *Légion Wallonie* amounted to 136, while in Belgium 1,310 civilians had volunteered and another 388 members of the *Gardes Wallonnes* had enlisted. The rest of the 1st June 1943 battle strength was provided by men enrolled in the workers' camps.

Among the 1942 recruits was non-Rexist Henri Derriks.[4] As an officer of the Belgian Reserve Corps, he intended to play a major military role within the *Légion Wallonie*, and it was not long before he actually did.

On 24 May 1943, *Reichsführer-SS* Heinrich Himmler inspected Pieske barracks and announced the passage of the Legion to the *Waffen-SS*, scheduled for 1 June 1943.[5]

From June until October 1943, the new *SS-Sturmbrigade Wallonien* underwent its military instruction at Wildflecken training camp.

The organization of the unit was based on the classic pattern of a battalion comprising 4 companies of motorized infantry, plus sections of motorcyclists and pioneers, heavy weapons, train and services.

The cadre of the unit was to be completed by sending 53 Walloon legionnaires and non-commissioned officers to the *11. Kriegslehrgang* at Bad-Tölz, of whom 23 graduated. NCO courses were organized at Posen while infantry tactics were taught at Wildflecken. *PAK* instruction took place at Arys, *FLAK* at München, *I.G.* at Breslau-Lissa. Pioneer training was at Dresden while radio transmission courses were organized at Nürnberg.

A German liaison and instruction officer joined the Walloon unit, *SS-Obersturmbannführer* Albert Wegener.[6]

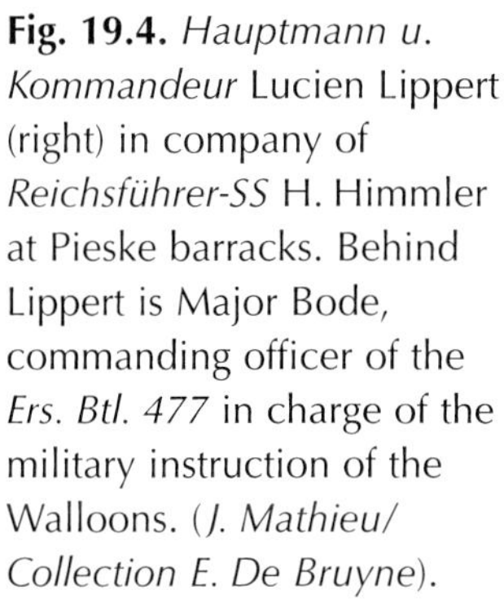

Fig. 19.4. *Hauptmann u. Kommandeur* Lucien Lippert (right) in company of *Reichsführer-SS* H. Himmler at Pieske barracks. Behind Lippert is Major Bode, commanding officer of the *Ers. Btl. 477* in charge of the military instruction of the Walloons. (*J. Mathieu/ Collection E. De Bruyne*).

1. Tactical Organization

Staff Company:

- 1 platoon of 30 motorized scouts with three light machine guns (*M.G.42*);
- 1 *Pi* platoon (5 submachine guns *M.P.38/40* (*Schmeißer*), 6 flamethrowers);
- 1 platoon of telephone and radio operators (1 light machine gun).

One motorized inf. battalion comprising:

- 3 motorized rifle companies each comprising:
- 3 platoons of riflemen, that is 9 groups equipped with 21 light machine guns (*le.M.G.42*) and 1 platoon of heavy weapons composed of:
- 2 sections of 4 heavy machine guns (*s.M.G.42*);
- 2 sections of 4 mortars (*m Gr.W.8cm*);
- 24 motor vehicles per company (Ford V 3000/2.5 tons) and 4 motorcycles (*BMW R 75*);
- 1 company heavy weapons composed of:
- 2 platoons with 4 sections of 2 heavy machine guns (*sM.G.42*);
- 1 platoon with 3 sections of 2 mortars (*m Gr.W.42*), 26 Ford 2-ton vans and 9 motorcycles.

Heavy weapons:
5th company (*PAK*)

- 3 platoons with 9 anti-tank guns (7.5cm *PAK*), Maultière half- track lorries, 10 light machine guns

6th company (*FLAK* 2cm)

- 3 platoons with 12 heavy auto cannon (*FLAK* 2 cm, 1938 model), *K52* or Ford trailers, 3 light machine guns, 45 motor vehicles, 9 motorcycles

7th company (*FLAK 88*)

- 1 battery of 4 towed guns (*FLAK 8.8cm*) with ranging fire system, 3 heavy auto cannon (*FLAK* 2 cm)

8th company (*I.G.*)

- 2 platoons of 4 towed howitzers (*I.G.* 7,5cm); 1 platoon of 2 towed howitzers (*I.G.* 15 cm), 2 light machine guns

9th company (*StuG*)

- 3 platoons: 10 7.5cm armoured assault guns, 9 machine guns.[7]

10th train

- 25 to 50 light or medium/heavy lorries (supplies and evacuation), 3 light machine guns

  Services (supply, medical service, repair shop

Total: 1,850 legionnaires and more or less 250 vehicles of all kinds.[8]

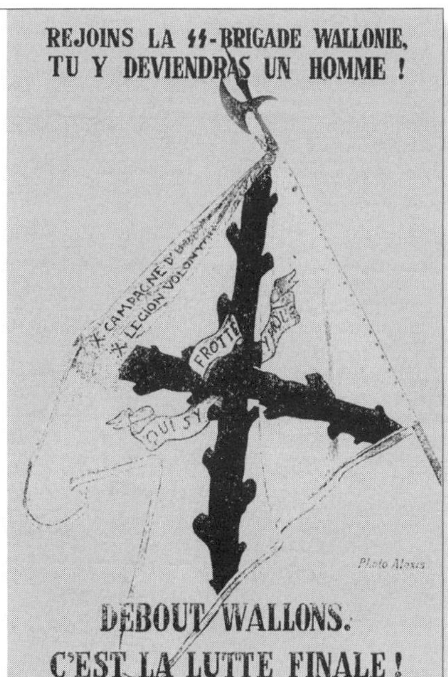

Pour gagner il faut se donner.
L. Degrelle

LA OU LES WALLONS SE TROUVENT, NOUS POUVONS ETRE TRANQUILLES,

déclarait au Donetz un général allemand.

N'est-ce pas le plus bel éloge que puissent mériter des soldats?

Et, lorsque cet éloge émane d'un des Chefs de la meilleure armée du monde, il prend une signification toute particulière.

LA ϟϟ SERA L'ELITE DE LA PATRIE DE DEMAIN.

La ϟϟ imposera à tous les parasites qui vivent de la sueur du peuple, le RESPECT DU TRAVAIL ET DES TRAVAILLEURS.

Nous luttons pour le nom et l'honneur de la Patrie. ***L. Degrelle***

REJOINS LA ϟϟ-BRIGADE WALLONIE, TU Y DEVIENDRAS UN HOMME !

DEBOUT WALLONS. C'EST LA LUTTE FINALE !

Above: **Fig. 19.5.** Summer 1943 at Wildflecken: *SS-Ostubaf.* Albert Wegener (middle) and *SS-Ostuf.* Léon Degrelle. (*Collection J.-L. Roba*).

Top right: **Fig. 19.6.** The transfer to the *Waffen-SS* intensified the propaganda effort considerably. Shown here is one of the numerous leaflets inviting the Walloons to join the brand new Brigade. (*Collection E. De Bruyne*).

Middle right: **Fig. 19.7.** Before the war, Jules Mathieu participated in several motorcycle rallies. Since the Brigade was mechanised, he could not help testing the new equipment. (*J. Mathieu/Collection E. De Bruyne*).

Fig. 19.8

2. Order of Battle

Kommandeur	*SS-Stubaf.* Lucien Lippert (†13.02.1944)
Ia:	*SS-Oscha.* Roger Wastiau (until 01.11.1943, when sent to Bad-Tölz) *SS-Ustuf.* Albert Lassois (until mid-December 1943, when sent back to Belgium) *SS-Hstuf.* François Anthonissen (†10.02.1944)
Ib	?
Ic	*SS-Ustuf.* Dr Heinz Forsteneichner (German)
IV a	*SS-Ustuf.* Schluck (German)
IVb	*SS-Hstuf.* Dr Schultz (German) *SS-Ustuf.* Dr Stahl (Alsatian) *SS-Stand. O.Ju.* Dr P. Roekens *SS-Ustuf.* Lejeune (dentist) *SS-Hscha.* Camille Petre (chemist)
Aide-de-Camp	*SS-Ostuf.* Nicolas Kamsky *SS-Ostuf.* Léon Degrelle
Judicial Service	*SS-Hstuf.* Dr Fleichsig (German) *SS-Ustuf.* Adrien Godsdeel
Catholic Chaplain	Louis Fierens.
Social Service	*SS-Hstuf.* Reinfahrt (German)
Technical Service	*SS-Ustuf.* Stéphane Devrees
Liaison officer	*SS-Ostubaf.* Albert Wegener (German) *SS-Ustuf.* Winterscheid (German,from 14.01.1944 on *SS-Ostuf.* Hans-Karl Drexler (detached from the *II/SS Pz. Gr. Rgt Westland*)[9]
Staff Company	*SS-Ostuf.* Robert Sloet d'Oldruytenborgh (01.10.1943) *SS-Hstuf.* F. Anthonnissen (†10.02.1944)
Moto platoon	*SS-Hscha.* Maurice Deravet *SS-Ostuf.* Adolphe Renier (after 01.10.1943)
Signals	*SS-Ostuf.* Adolphe Renier (until 01.10.1943) *SS-Hscha.* Jean-Marie Lantiez
Pioneer	*SS-Ustuf.* Joseph Mirgain
Field music	*SS-Hscha.* Deltenre
1st Company	*SS-Ustuf.* Jules Mathieu *SS-Ustuf.* Hubert Van Eyzer (†13.12.1943)
2nd Company	*SS-Ostuf.* Henri Derriks *SS-Ustuf.* Albert Wéhinger
3rd Company	*SS-Ustuf.* Robert Denie *SS-Ostuf.* Léon Degrelle (holding an honorary command)
4th Company	*SS-Ustuf.* Marcel Bonniver *Sonderführer* Rotislav Zavadsky
5th Company	*SS-Ustuf.* Marcel Lamproye *SS-Ustuf.* François Daras (†17.02.1944)
6th Company	*SS-Ostuf.* Louis Calonne *SS-Ustuf.* Henri Thyssen
7th Company	*SS-Ustuf.* Joseph Dumont *SS-Ustuf.* Fernand Foulon

8th Company	*SS-Ustuf.* Josy Graff
9th Company	*SS-Ustuf.* Pierre Dengis *SS-Hscha.* Thirionnet *SS-Hscha.* Smets *SS-Hscha.* Moland *Spieß: Oscha.* Dohet
Train *SS-Ustuf.*	Georges Ruelle

3. General enrolment terms

Age:	17 to 45
Minimum height	1.60 m
Enrolment time	duration of the war.

ALLOCATIONS FAMILIALES

L'allocation est calculée sur la base du revenu net du volontaire. En outre il sera payé une indemnité de vie chère de 20 % ainsi que le loyer pour les volontaires mariés.

Exemples :

1. Un père de famille s'engage :

Composition de la famille : épouse et 3 enfants. Revenu avant l'engagement du volontaire : fr. 1800.—. Loyer mensuel : fr. 200.—.

Il sera payé :

Allocation pour l'épouse . . . . . fr.	1200.—
3 enfants (2 fils et une fille en dessous de 16 ans) chacun fr. 250.—	750.—
	1950.—
+ 20 % de majoration pour vie chère .	390.—
+ loyer	200.—
Total. . . fr.	2540.—

2. Un fils s'engage :

a) Composition de la famille :

Père et mère, 3 frères et sœurs en dessous de 16 ans.

Revenu du fils avant son engagement ... Il remettait à ses parents son salaire total ... famille). Le revenue total du ménage av... ment du fils s'élevait à fr. 3000.— par m...

Les 2/3 du revenu du volontaire (800... pour le moins atteindre 1/4 du reve... ménage (750.—).

Il sera payé :

Allocation pour les parents . . . .
3 frères et sœurs en dessous de 16 ... (150.—) . . . .
+ 20 % d'indemnité pour vie chère .

Total. . .

Les membres des familles jouissent du RA... MENT SPECIAL des Allemands habitan... outre elles sont ASSUREES GRATUITE... DEUTSCHE KRANKENKASSE.

Pour tous renseignements s'adres... l'Ers.-Kdo. WALLONIEN DER ... ᛋᛋ. RUE DE LA LOI. 44. A BRU... SOIT DANS UN BUREAU DE... TEMENT.

Fig. 19.9. Particular stress was laid upon the social advantages, such as extra income, free health insurance and German food and coal supply. (*Collection E. De Bruyne*).

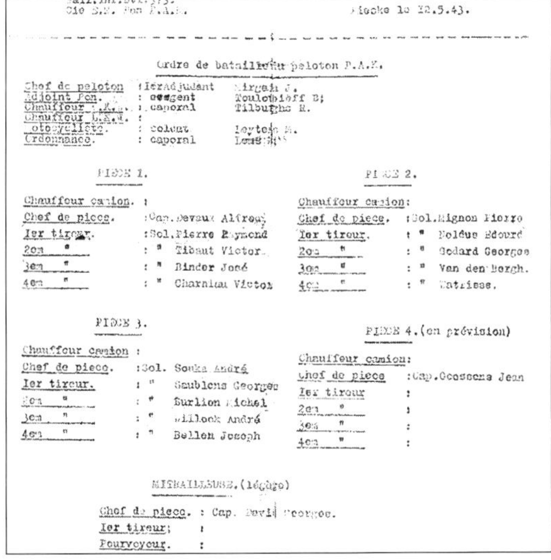

Cie S.W. Pon P.A.K. — Mecke le 22.5.43.

Ordre de bataillon peloton P.A.K.

Chef de peloton	: 1erAdjudant	Mirgain J.
Adjoint Pon.	: sergent	Toulotbioff B.
Chauffeur	: caporal	Tilburghs R.
Chauffeur	:	
Motocycliste.	: soldat	Leyten M.
Ordonnance.	: caporal	

PIECE 1.

Chauffeur camion.	:
Chef de piece.	: Cap. Devaux Alfred
1er tireur.	: Sol. Pierre Raymond
2em "	: " Tibaut Victor
3em "	: " Binder José
4em "	: " Charnieau Victor

PIECE 2.

Chauffeur camion:	
Chef de piece.	: Sol. Mignon Pierre
1er tireur.	: " Noldus Edouard
2em "	: " Godard Georges
3em "	: " Van den Borgh.
4em "	: " Catrisse.

PIECE 3.

Chauffeur camion	:
Chef de piece.	: Sol. Souka André
1er tireur.	: " Saublens Georges
2em "	: " Surlion Michel
3em "	: " Willock André
4em "	: " Bellen Joseph

PIECE 4. (en prévision)

Chauffeur camion:	
Chef de piece	: Cap. Goossens Jean
1er tireur	:
2em "	:
3em "	:
4em "	:

MITRAILLEUSE. (légère)

Chef de piece.	: Cap. Devil Georges.
1er tireur;	:
Pourvoyeur.	:

Fig. 19.10. May 1943: the *PAK* platoon was in the process of being completed. (*Arch. E. De Bruyne*).

B. The Cherkassy Campaign (November 1943-FEBRUARY 1944)

1. General situation

During the autumn of 1943, the general situation of the frontline along the middle Dnepr was precarious. A powerful Soviet army, after crossing the river in the region of Kiev and driving back the German forces to the outskirts of Zhitomir (130 km west of Kiev), pushed southwards and threatened Uman, Ukraine. This situation threatened the German divisions with encirclement. It obliged the Germans to abandon a part of their established positions downstream from the breach, along the river, forcing them to establish a holding position between Berditchev, Bielaja Tserkow and Kanev. About ten more or less fatigued divisions were engaged in this operation.

Farther south, the German command, taking advantage of the small possibilities of clearing the Dnepr, tried hard to retain the advantageous strongpoints on the river so as to prevent the Soviet armies from driving into central Ukraine, in the direction of the Bug, the Dnestr and Rumania.

Among these strongpoints, about 160 km downstream from Kiev, the Cherkassy industrial area, and strategic penetration route towards western Ukraine, constituted a very exposed but fiercely defended German salient.

The *5. SS-Pz. Div. Wiking* (regiments *Germania* and *Westland*, reinforced with the Estonian *Freiw. -Pz. -Gren. Btl Narva*) under the command of *SS-Gruppenführer* Herbert-Otto Gille was assigned the important mission to push back or at least contain the Soviet forces which had concentrated in the region.

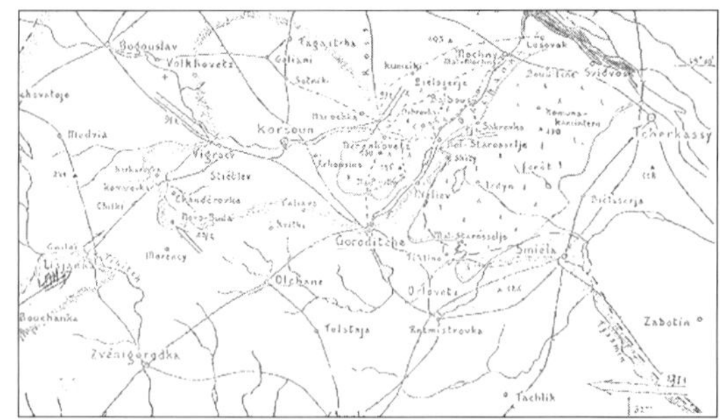

Fig. 19.11. Walloon strong points were positioned along the Olschanka River, facing the Cherkassy forest. *(Doc. F. Hellebaut/ Arch. E. De Bruyne).*

Fig. 19.12. Typical Russian winter landscape: Mochny near the Olschanka River and command post of the 1st Company (*SS-Ustuf.* J. Mathieu). (*J. Mathieu/ Collection E. De Bruyne*).

The Cherkassy area was a vast swampy forest, spreading out over about 20 km as far as the confluence of the Olschanka River. Fierce battles had been fought for the protection of the only two supply roads towards Cherkassy via Chpola and Gorodichtche-Korsun.

2. The Olschanka River front-line

On 11 November 1943, the Walloon mechanized brigade left Gersfeld/ Wildflecken railway station in the direction of the Ukraine, where it arrived at Korsun on 19 and 20 November. The Walloons were put at the disposal of the *5. SS-Pz. Gren. Div. Wiking*, as a tactical reserve.

On 26 November the Brigade was deployed on a 25 km long frontline sector along the Olschanka River. The 2nd Company, under *SS-Obersturmführer* Henri Derriks, was temporarily detached to reinforce the *Westland* Regiment at Bolstaro-Sesselia.

During December 1943, the Walloons participated in several assault actions. On the 12th, the 1st Company undertook a surprise attack on an armed partisan camp of the Gorodok District. The following day *SS-Ustuf.* Hubert Van Eyzer and 27 men (1st Company) crossed the Olschanka on a battle reconnaissance mission at Sakaloroskaja. Trapped in an ambush, the whole patrol (except 6 men) was decimated.

On 22 December 1943, the 2nd and 3rd companies executed another surprise attack at Irdynn, which cost the death of 3 Walloons together with 7 other casualties. At the same time, the remainder of the Soviet volunteers (*Hiwis* – about 50 men forming a platoon of mortars within 4th Company under *Sonderführer*. R. Zavadsky), who had joined the *Légion Wallonie* in 1942, became a constant source of concern since the contacts some of them had secretly established with the Soviet partisans had put the Walloon command in fear of betrayal.

In the course of January 1944, the Walloons were to particularly distin-

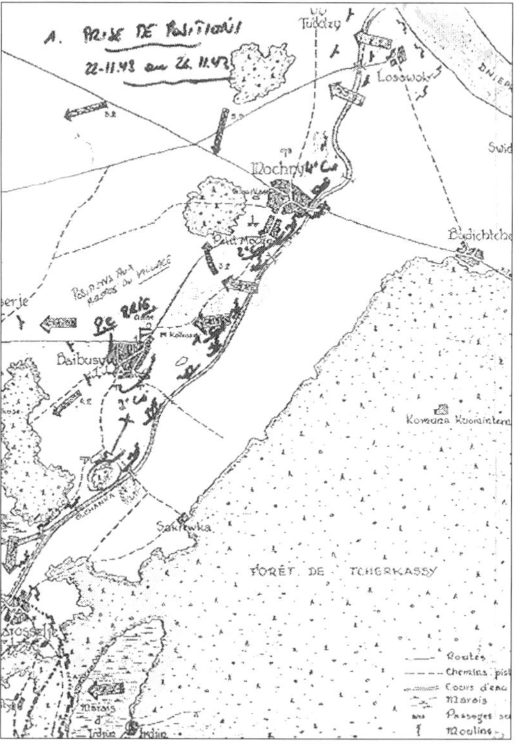

Fig. 19.13. (*Doc. F. Hellebaut with post-war comments by R. Devresse; arch. E. De Bruyne*)

Fig. 19.14. Chaplain Louis Fierens' masses were well attended, especially before action. Note that the Walloon Catholic chaplain is wearing a *Wehrmacht* uniform. (*Collection J.-L. Roba*).

guish themselves. On 4 January 1944, an assault group (*Stoßtrupp*) under *SS-Ostuf.* Derriks and a similar unit under *SS-Ustuf.* Denie executed a successful

Fig. 19.15. The Soviet *Hiwis* who joined the Walloon Brigade during the Caucasus Campaign, stuck to the Soviet way of drill. (*Collection J.-L. Roba*).

pincer movement around the strongpoint of Sakrewka. However, the most sensational action was to take place in mid-January 44.

3. Teklino

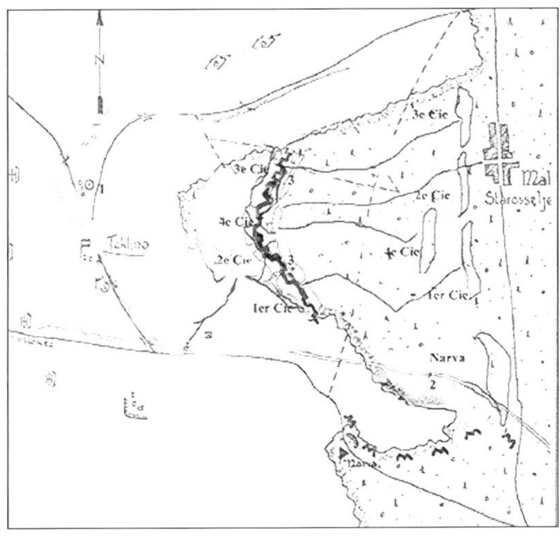

Fig. 19.16. (*Doc. F. Hellebaut/ Arch. E. De Bruyne*).

In the first days of January 1944, considerable Soviet forces started a new offensive in the direction of Boguslav. Powerful armoured columns advanced from the north (Buki area) with the obvious intention of bringing down the whole defence of the Dnepr sector. In the southern sector of the Soviet penetration, the offensive activity of entrenched forces hidden in the forest of Cherkassy led to numerous local actions, with a view to gaining new and better attacking positions.

Meanwhile, two regiments of Soviet engineers had overpowered a place of great strategic importance: the triangular-shaped forest salient east of Teklino.

As this situation was a direct threat to the supply route between Korsun and Cherkassy, on 8 January 1944, the German command, after a strong artillery preparation, engaged in a series of counter-attacks in order to retake this position.

Since Soviet engineers had established solid defences, the counter-attacks were thrown back and the forces suffered severe losses.

On 11 and 12 January, the *5. SS-Pz. Div. Wiking* took over and in vain engaged *Germania* and *Narva*. The German élite forces having failed, General Gille accepted Degrelle's most astonishing proposal that the Walloon Brigade be assigned the task of launching a new counter-attack![10]

With a view to storming the position, the four infantry companies of the Brigade were temporarily relieved from their positions (Mochny and Starosleje sub-sectors) by two companies of the *Feld-Ers. Btl Narva* stationed at Stieblev.

After the unsuccessful German counter-attacks the arrival of the Walloons on the spot at Orlowez aroused sceptic and often ironic comments among the experienced *Wikinger*. A show-card with the inscription *Hier Zirkus Wallonien. Morgen Vorstellung ab 6 Uhr bis 8 Uhr. Eintritt frei* (Circus Wallonia – Performance tomorrow – Entrance free) was placed so that it was impossible not to notice it.

On 14 January, at 06:05 a.m., after an artillery preparation of 800 shells, the Walloon battalion attacked under violent Soviet counter-fire, the four companies being deployed in a rhombus pattern, 1st Company (*SS-Ostuf.* Mathieu) marching ahead.

Fig. 19.17. Walloons in action in the Teklino forest. (*J. Mathieu/Collection E. De Bruyne*).

Fig. 19.18. After the Teklino attack, a ceremony was held at Beloserje on 21 January 1944. General Herbert Otto Gille himself presented the Walloon participants in the attack with awards. Here he congratulates men from the 3rd Company. From left to right: Jean Moreau, Georges Thonon, Jean-Pierre Quoirin – high ranking cadre of the *Jeunesse Légionnaire* (note the *JL* badge) – shaking hands with Gille, and Roland Devresse. The latter was to become *SS-Ustuf.* He was the highest ranked of the second Kienschlag session in 1945. (*Collection G. Thonon via R. Devresse*).

A few *Sturmgeschütze* backed up the attack along the forest edge. The Walloons easily reached the western corner of the forest. After penetrating into the forest, however, their progression quickly slowed down, due to close combat actions, ambushes and well-camouflaged fortifications. In the end it took the Walloons three days to invest the Teklino forest. The price they had to pay was high.[11]

Two days later, the Walloon battalion was relieved by *Narva*. A few days later, the Germans lost the bitterly conquered terrain again.

4. The Encirclement

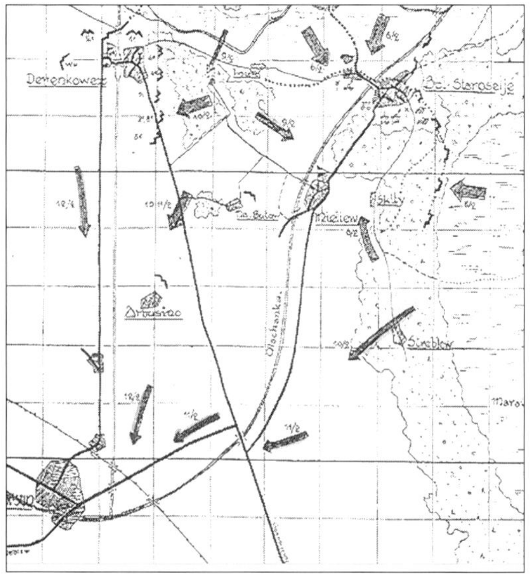

Fig. 19.19. After retreating from the Olschanka River positions, the Walloon Brigade was given the mission to secure the north-eastern area around Korsun, especially the Goroditche-Korsun axis in order to allow German forces fighting east of Korsun to retreat. (*Doc. F. Hellebaut. Arch. E. De Bruyne*).

By 20 January 1944, the situation had become very critical on the central Dnepr River frontline. The Soviet offensive had outflanked most of the solidly defended German strong points and had begun a vast envelopment movement towards Svenigorodka, southwards.

At the same time, the westward thrust had also reached such a depth that the whole German Dnepr Army was cut off from its essential communications.

The German High Command still had important and mobile reserves. As usual, they were determined to throw them into the battle only at the best moment. Their intention was to offer a firm resistance to the Soviets by immobilizing or wearing down their manoeuvring abilities. Orders were given to the divisions to remain in their previous positions and to cover the jeopardized flanks. The *Luftwaffe* was to ensure supply and urgent evacuations. By 21 January 1944, the Soviets had encircled the German forces, trapping 56,000 men and perhaps 10,000 vehicles into a space of 40 km x 60 km.

Covering a north-eastern salient position, Lippert and his men were doomed to executing a most delicate rearguard mission. As soon as the German command had decided to attempt a breakout operation, the Brigade was entrusted with the protection of the retreat in dramatic conditions. By using a firm but very well coordinated defence the Walloons were to save time for the troops to move westward by blocking any dangerous penetration likely to disrupt the defence or cut off the main retreating routes.

At the beginning of February 1944, the different companies abandoned their battle positions in good order and started a well-coordinated retrograde movement with significant rearguard engagements at Starosselje and Derenkowetz. As soon as the remainder of the Brigade had reached the vicinity of Stieblev, south of Korsun, Gille ordered Lucien Lippert to perform a final precarious effort: to cover the concentration of the breakout forces by defending Novo-Buda village at all costs.

5. Novo-Buda

Having severely suffered during 14 days of fighting and marching in snow and mud, almost without any rest or supply, the Brigade had shrunk to 250 Walloons capable of offering battle. The rest had been killed, wounded, captured or evacuated.

In the morning of 13 February 1944, twenty-two T–34 tanks and accompanying infantry attacked the positions of 1st and 2nd companies, and it was not long before they had broken through 3rd Company. In the middle of *PAK* firing at point-blank range and engagements with *Panzerfäuste*, *Kommandeur* Lucien Lippert wanted to scout out the situation

Fig. 19.20. Walloon legionnaires getting into position at Nowo-Buda. (*Collection J. Matthieu/ Collection E. De Bruyne*).

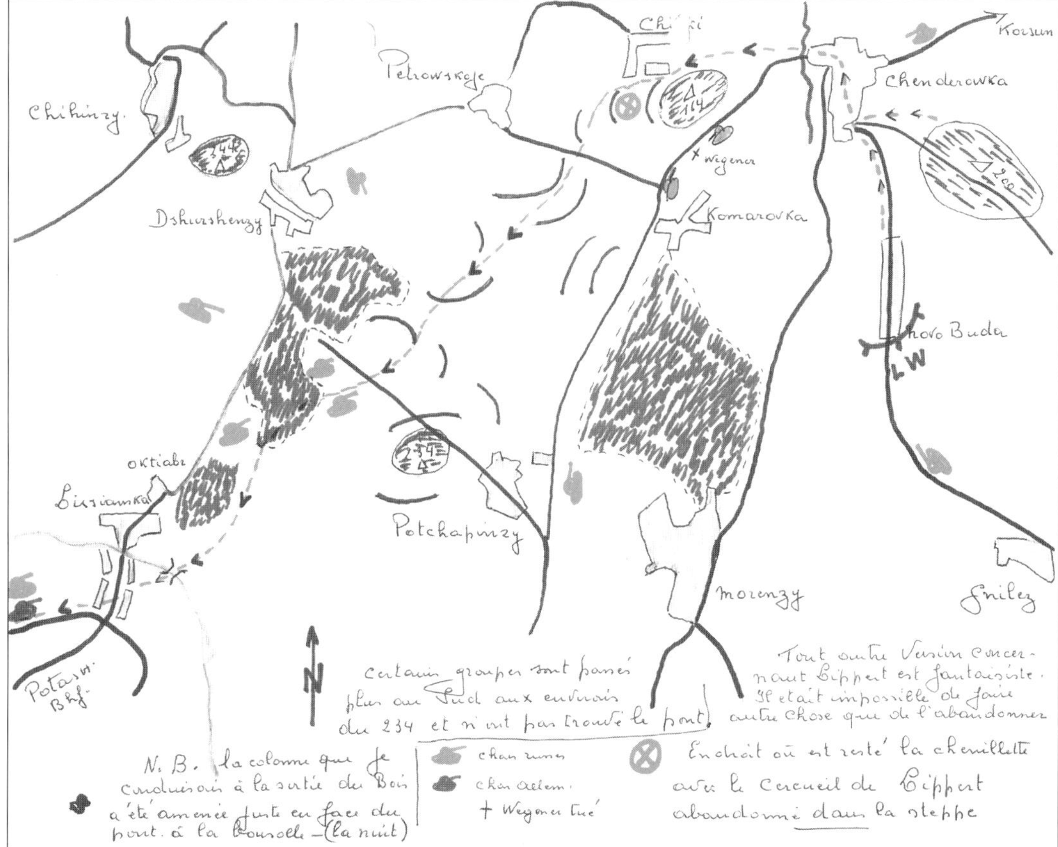

Fig. 19.21. Post-war chart drawn by Jules Mathieu showing the breakout route on 17 February 1944. The cross in red circle indicates where Lucien Lippert had to be left behind. Mathieu, leading a column of Walloons among whom was Degrelle, reached the bridge over the Gniloï-Tikisch River at night. Those who retreated south of Hill 234 were less lucky. (*Doc. J. Mathieu/Collection E. De Bruyne*).

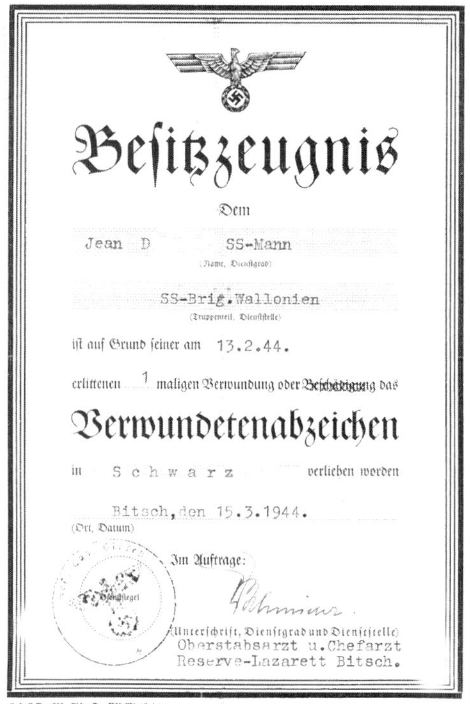

Besitzzeugnis

Dem

Jean D SS-Mann
(Name, Dienstgrad)

SS-Brig.Wallonien
(Truppenteil, Dienststelle)

ist auf Grund seiner am 13.2.44.

erlittenen 1 maligen Verwundung oder Beschädigung das

Verwundetenabzeichen

in Schwarz verliehen worden

Bitsch, den 15.3.1944.
(Ort, Datum)

Im Auftrage:

(Unterschrift, Dienstgrad und Dienststelle)
Oberstabsarzt u.Chefarzt
Reserve-Lazarett Bitsch.

Top left: **Fig. 19.22.** 40 years later! Jules Mathieu is posing in a self-made re-enactment uniform. (*Private Collection*).

Middle left: **Fig. 19.23.** December 1943 at Mochny, Command Post of 1Co. From left to right. *SS-Ustuf.* H. Van Eyzer, CO/1Plt/1Co/ and two of his men, Husson and Paillez. A few days later, the whole platoon (27 men) was ambushed at Komunam – Kommintern (13.12.43). Only 6 men would escape. (*J. Mathieu/Collection E. De Bruyne*).

Top right: **Fig. 19.24.** Date of injury shows that Walloon *SS-Mann* Jean D . . . was wounded at Novo-Buda. (*Private Collection*)

Bottom left: **Fig. 19.25.** Despite Degrelle and Derriks (right) both smiling and seeming to get along very well, dissension between the two men was real. This picture was taken in the Cherkassy pocket on 19 January 1944. A few moments before taking the picture Degrelle said to Derriks: *'let us smile so that people think we are not at loggerheads'.* (*Private Collection Arch. E. De Bruyne*).

on the spot, but was shot by a sniper as he tried to cross an exposed area.

Meanwhile, Degrelle had been wounded and evacuated to Schanderowka.[12] During a dramatic meeting of the remaining Walloon officers, *SS-Ostuf.* Jules Mathieu was unanimously (save for one dissenting vote) designated to take over command. At 5 o'clock in the morning of 17 February, in the absence of Degrelle, Mathieu ordered his men to get ready for the breakout. Mention must be made that the Walloon Brigade was the last unit to evacuate the area.

A last obstacle, the Gniloï-Tikitsch River, had to be overcome. Dramatic scenes occurred on the frozen banks of the 8 metre wide river. Men and horses jumped into the ice-cold water hoping to reach the other side. This was usually a small stream, but melting snow from recent storms had turned it into a torrent.

Mathieu, Degrelle and a group of Walloons were luckier.[13] During the breakout, Mathieu could check the topographical map he had been given as a commanding officer and made his way to a small wooden bridge he had located over the Gniloï-Tikitsch. The group he was leading could cross it without any difficulty.

The Brigade *Wallonie* was mentioned in dispatches (the *Wehrmachtbericht*). Degrelle was awarded the *Ritterkreuz* while Lucien Lippert received the German Cross in Gold posthumously as well as a promotion to the rank of *SS-Obersturmbannführer*.[14]

From the 1,850 men initially engaged in the Cherkassy campaign in November 1943, 632 escaped encirclement without becoming casualties.[15]

Fig. 19.26. On Monday February 20 1944, a funeral service in memory of Lucien Lippert was held in Brussels. Note the Rexist colours on the coffin. (*Collection E. De Bruyne*).

Fig. 19.27. Degrelle's proudest moment, the second day of the Cherkassy parades, 2 April 1944. His armoured half-track, borrowed for the occasion from the *12. SS-Panzer Division* has just pulled up in front of the *Bourse*, the Belgian stock exchange in Brussels. Degrelle happily poses for press photographers. Rexist officials from the Movement, the *G.W.* and the *J.L.* can be seen lined up to the left rear. (*Collection J.-L. Roba*).

Fig. 19.28.

C. The impact of Cherkassy

The Cherkassy breakout was exploited in a masterly manner. Degrelle even performed the amazing feat of turning a hurtful defeat into a sensational victory, as attention was only focused on his successful escape from the encirclement.[16]

Backed up by the exploits of his men and the impact caused by the *Tcherkassykämpfer* all over the Reich and occupied Europe – to such an extent that Degrelle was featured on the cover of the May 1944 issue of the periodical *Signal* – the *Chef* felt that the moment had come to step forward and impose himself as the sole recognized interlocutor of the Germans in Belgium.

The parade Degrelle organized on 1 April 1944 in Charleroi, and in Brussels on the following day, not only proved to be an important personal political victory, it also had the side-effect of dissatisfying the Flemish collaboration deeply because they had been refused the favours granted to Degrelle. Contrary to Degrelle, the Flemish were not allowed to organize a similar public demonstration although the *Sturmbrigade Langemarck* had faced – around Zhitomir/February 1944 – as hard combat as that fought by the *Wallonie* during the breakout.[17]

Degrelle obviously intended to use to the utmost the publicity made around the 'victorious' return of the Walloon legionnaires. The post-Cherkassy period was consequently very fertile in political steps, speeches and spreading of the political ideas so dear to Degrelle, more particularly the Burgundy myth.

On 5 March 1944, Degrelle gave a speech in Paris, at the *Palais de Chaillot*. On that occasion, addressing the cream of French collaboration, he glorified the common commitment in the East.

Fig. 19.29. Degrelle even involved his children in the show. Note that Degrelle had been promoted twice in a short time and is now *SS-Sturmbannführer*.

Fig. 19.30. Léon Degrelle leaving the *Palais de Chaillot* in March 1944. Next to him is Fernand de Brinon. Behind de Brinon (second row on the left) is Victor Matthys. The man wearing a cap and a German uniform is Gaston Chavanne, Rexist deputy for the constituency of Liège. Both his sons were serving in the *Sturmbrigade Wallonien*. (*Ach. E. De Bruyne*).

Degrelle's public activities were only interrupted by the unexpected departure for Estonia – at the end of the month of July 1944 – of a combat group (*Kampfgruppe*) under *SS-Ostuf.* Georges Ruelle.

Meanwhile, Degrelle was facing several attempted military takeovers by the Germans.

At the beginning of 1944, Gottlob Berger, chief of the *SS-Hauptamt*, had clearly set down that he intended to abolish the national character of all foreign legions and place them under German command.

The Germans were perfectly aware of the weakness of the beheaded brigade. During the Cherkassy campaign, Degrelle had not held any specific military command. He had only acted as an officer without a clearly defined responsibility within 3rd Company.

Fig. 19.32. A cheerful Himmler receiving Herbert Otto Gille and Léon Degrelle after the dramatic Cherkassy breakout where the Walloon leader lost two-thirds of his men.

By chance, after Lippert's death, Degrelle happened to be the highest ranked officer within the Brigade.[18] Normally Lippert's succession should have fallen into his hands. Nothing of the kind happened. Of course, Degrelle, as a political leader, acted in full authority on the legion. Onto this authority he now wanted to graft military command, to the great despair of some of his officers, more realistic about Degrelle's military abilities.

During his lifetime, Lippert had been the sole officer capable of holding an important military command. One can expect that that he would have risen in rank, too. In the same way, it is quite evident that Degrelle, even promoted successively *SS-Hauptsturmführer* (01.12.1943) and *SS-Sturmbannführer* (20.04.44), would not have been in a position to compete with Lucien Lippert's military command if the latter had survived.

Moreover, it was clear that Degrelle was not to be entrusted with functions and duties for which he did not have the slightest competence. The young Major's death and later developments ensured that Degrelle could combine political and military directions even if he had to elbow his way through numerous obstacles.

PROMOTION D'OFFICIERS AU SEIN DE LA SS-BRIGADE

A l'occasion du retour glorieux de la SS Brigade d'Assaut « Wallonie », le Führer a promu à des grades supérieurs les officiers wallons qui s'étaient le plus distingués à Tcherkassy.

A été promu au grade de Major (SS-Sturmbannführer)

Le Capitaine Léon DEGRELLE.

Ont été promus au grade de Capitaine (SS-Hauptsturmführer)

Les premiers Lieutenants MATHIEU Jules et RENIER Adolphe.

Ont été promus au grade de premier Lieutenant (SS-Obersturmführer)

Les Lieutenants DUMONT Joseph, THYSSEN Henry, LAMPROYE Marcel, BONNIVER Marcel, DENIS Robert, GRAFF Jean, DENGIS Pierre et MIRGAIN Joseph.

Ont été promus au grade de Lieutenant (SS-Untersturmführer)

Les aspirants-officiers GENERET Charles, SERLET Edouard, [illegible]ERENNE Jacques, WASTIAU Roger, GILLIS Léon, LANTIEZ Jean-Marie, SAPIN Albert, PAQUOT Gustave, RUE Henri, WARNIER Guy, ROMAN Jean, GRAIDE Willy, NORTIER Albert, CHOME François, BAL Rodolphe, MONFILS Charles, CAMBY Raymond, STEIVER Albert, DE GOY Roger, WILHELM Marc, CAPELLE Jacques, THOMAS Marcel, CAPOEN Marcel, SCHUMACHER Charles, SANDRON Jules, THEATRE Jean, WAUTELET Jacques, DECOSTER Martin, VAN EESBEECK Georges et SCHREIBER Paul.

Fig. 19.31. After the Cherkassy outbreak promotions awaited a number of Walloon legionnaires. Note that apart from Albert Sapin, Léon Gillis and Jean-Marie Lantiez, all the other *SS-Ustuf.* had just graduated from Bad-Tölz.

Fig. 19.33. Degrelle and his officers are celebrating the Cherkassy breakout in the restaurant *L'Horloge* in Brussels on 11 April (Saint Léon) 1944. Note the unorthodox position of the *'Wallonie'* armshield on the lower sleeve of the third Walloon officer, Marcel Thomas (first row, 3rd from the right). Note that all Walloon graduates of the Bad-Tölz *11. Kriegslehrgang* were given permission to wear their *SS-Ustuf.* insignia from 1 April 1944 onwards. This was a favour obtained by Degrelle as a direct result of the Cherkassy breakout. (Promotion was scheduled for 21 June 1944). (*Doc. J. Mathieu/Collection E. De Bruyne*).

Fig. 19.34. The Cherkassy parade at Charleroi. From left to right: *Adjutant* Roger Wastiau, Sepp Dietrich, Léon Degrelle shaking hands with *SS-Ostuf.* Marcel Lamproye. Behind Marcel Lamproye is *SS-Hscha.* Pascal Bovy; *Spiess* of 1Co and eventually, in 1945, head of the Walloon *Feldgendarmerie* (Military Police) of the *28. SS-Freiw.-Gren. Div. Wallonien*; next to Marcel Lamproye is *SS-Ostuf.* Marcel Bonniver. *SS-Ustuf.* J.-M. Lantiez (hidden) is next in line. (*Arch. E. De Bruyne*).

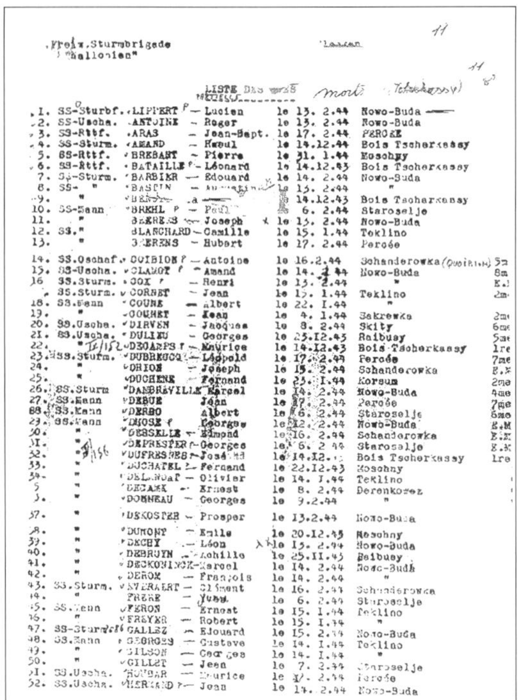

Freiw. Sturmbrigade "Wallonien"

LISTE DES [illegible] mort (Tcherkassy)

No.	Rank	Name	First name	Date	Place
1.	SS-Sturbf.	LIPPERT	Lucien	le 13. 2.44	Nowo-Buda
2.	SS-Uscha.	ANTOINE	Roger	le 13. 2.44	Nowo-Buda
3.	SS-Rttf.	ARAS	Jean-Bapt.	le 17. 2.44	PERCEE
4.	SS-Sturm.	AMAND	Raoul	le 14.12.44	Bois Tscherkassy
5.	SS-Rttf.	BREBANT	Pierre	le 31. 1.44	Moschny
6.	SS-Rttf.	BATAILLE	Léonard	le 14.12.43	Bois Tscherkassy
7.	SS-Sturm.	BARBIER	Edouard	le 14. 2.44	Nowo-Buda
8.	SS- "	BASTIN	[illegible]	le 13. 2.44	"
9.	"	[illegible]	[illegible]	[illegible] 14.12.43	Bois Tscherkassy
10.	SS-Mann	BREHL	Paul	[illegible] 6. 2.44	Staroselje
11.	"	BEERENS	Joseph	le 13. 2.44	Nowo-Buda
12.	SS."	BLANCHARD	Camille	le 15. 1.44	Teklino
13.	"	BEERENS	Hubert	le 17. 2.44	Percée
14.	SS.Oschaf.	COIBION	Antoine	le 16.2.44	Schanderowka (Quoibion)
15.	SS-Uscha.	CLAMOT	Amand	le 14. 2.44	Nowo-Buda
16	SS.Sturm.	COX	Henri	le 13. 2.44	"
[illegible]	SS.Sturm.	CORNET	Jean	le 15. 1.44	Teklino
18.	SS.Mann	COUNE	Albert	le 22. 1.44	"
19.	"	COURET	Jean	le 4. 1.44	Sakrewka
20.	SS.Uscha.	DIRVEN	Jacques	le 8. 2.44	Skity
21.	SS.Uscha.	DULIEU	Georges	le 25.12.43	Raibusy
22.	"	DEOARPS	Maurice	le 14.12.43	Bois Tscherkassy
23.	SS.Sturm.	DUBREUCQ	Léopold	le 17. 2.44	Percée
24.	"	DRION	Joseph	le 15. 2.44	Schanderowka
25.	"	DUCHENE	Fernand	le 25. 1.44	Korsum
26.	SS.Sturm	DAMBREVILLE	Marcel	le 14. 2.44	Nowo-Buda
27.	SS.Mann	DEBUE	Jean	le 17. 2.44	Percée
28.	SS.Mann	DERBO	Albert	le 6. 2.44	Staroselje
29.	SS.Mann	DHOSE	Georges	le 12. 2.44	Nowo-Buda
30.	"	DESSELLE	Edmond	le 16. 2.44	Schanderowka
31.	"	DEPRESTER	Georges	le 6. 2.44	Staroselje
32.	"	DUFRESNES	José	le 14.12.[illegible]	Bois Tscherkassy
33.	"	DUCHATEL	Fernand	le 22.12.43	Moschny
34.	"	DEL.NOAF	Olivier	le 14. 1.44	Teklino
[illegible]	"	DECAMK	Ernest	le 8. 2.44	Derenkowez
[illegible]	"	DONNEAU	Georges	le 9.2.44	"
37.	"	DEKOSTER	Prosper	le 13.2.44	Nowo-Buda
38.	"	DUMONT	Emile	le 20.12.43	Moschny
39.	"	DECHY	Léon	le 13. 2.44	Nowo-Buda
40.	"	DEBRUYN	Achille	le 25.11.43	Raibusy
41.	"	DECKONINCK	Marcel	le 14. 2.44	Nowo-Buda
42.	"	DEROM	François	le 14. 2.44	"
43.	SS.Sturm.	EVERAERT	Clément	le 16. 2.44	Schanderowka
44.	"	FRERE	Yves	le 6. 2.44	Staroselje
45.	SS.Mann	FERON	Ernest	le 15. 1.44	Teklino
46.	"	FREYER	Robert	le 15. 1.44	"
47.	SS-Sturm.	GALLEZ	Edouard	le 15. 2.44	Nowo-Buda
48.	SS.Mann	GEORGES	Gustave	le 14. 1.44	Teklino
49.	"	GILSON	Georges	le 14. 1.44	"
50.	"	GILLET	Jean	le 7. 2.44	Staroselje
51.	SS.Uscha.	HOUBAR	Maurice	le 17. 2.44	Percée
52.	SS.Uscha.	[illegible]	Jean	le 14. 2.44	Nowo-Buda

Fig. 19.35. First page of the list mentioning the Cherkassy deaths. (The French word *'percée'* means breakout). (*Arch. E. De Bruyne*).

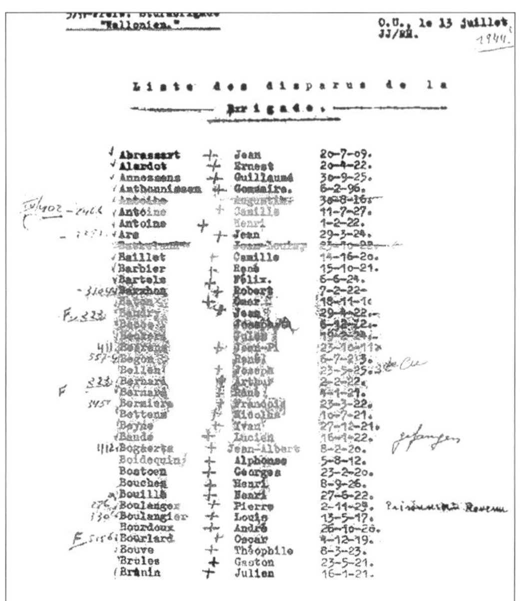

SS-Freiw. Sturmbrigade "Wallonien."

O.U., le 13 Juillet 1944. JJ/RM.

Liste des disparus de la Brigade.

Name	First name	Date of birth
Abrassart	Jean	20-7-09.
Alardot	Ernest	20-4-22.
Annezaens	Guillaume	30-9-25.
Anthonnissen	Gommaire.	6-2-96.
[illegible]	Augustin	30-8-16.
Antoine	Camille	11-7-27.
Antoine	Henri	1-2-22.
Are	Jean	29-3-24.
[illegible]	Jean-Louis	[illegible]
Baillet	Camille	14-10-20.
Barbier	René	15-10-21.
Bartels	Félix.	6-6-24.
Barzhon	Robert	7-2-22.
[illegible]	Omer	18-11-1[illegible]
[illegible]	Jean	29-4-22.
[illegible]	Joseph	6-12-22.
[illegible]	Julien	[illegible]
[illegible]	Jean-Pi[illegible]	23-10-11.
Begon	René	6-7-23.
Bellen	Joseph	23-5-25.
Bernard	Arthur	2-2-22.
Bernard	René	4-1-21.
Bernier	François	23-3-22.
Bettens	Nicolas	10-7-21.
Beyne	Ivan	27-12-21.
Bande	Lucien	16-1-22.
Bogaerts	Jean-Albert	8-2-20.
Boidequin	Alphonse	5-8-12.
Bostoen	Georges	23-2-20.
Bouches	Henri	8-9-26.
Bouillé	Henri	27-6-22.
Boulanger	Pierre	2-11-23.
Boulangier	Louis	13-5-17.
Bourdoux	André	26-10-26.
Bourlard	Oscar	4-12-19.
Bouve	Théophile	8-3-23.
Brules	Gaston	23-5-21.
Brunin	Julien	16-1-21.

Fig. 19.36. First page of the list mentioning the Walloons missing following the Cherkassy outbreak. The post-war added text *'prisonnier revenu'* means prisoner (sent) back home. (*Arch. E. De Bruyne*).

After the Cherkassy breakout, Degrelle developed the ambition to extend the Brigade to a full division under his command. However, as no Walloon officer held a rank high enough to command such a unit, Berlin dispatched *SS-Oberführer* Karl Burk (June 1944) to take command over the Walloons.[19]

In the end, Degrelle succeeded in thwarting the plans of the Germans. Just in the same way the designation of *Leader of the Walloons* (*Führer der Wallonen*) had not been sanctioned by an official signature, the one of *Kommandeur* made its appearance in a spontaneous way.[20] This is due to the fact that thanks to the new military exploits in Estonia, Degrelle had the privilege to penetrate the higher spheres of the National Socialist leadership, more particularly Hitler, who received him for the second time during this war to present him with the Oakleaves.

Thus, on 3 September 1944, for the very first time, Degrelle was officially designated as *SS-Sturmbannführer u. Kdr der SS-Frw. Brig. Wallonien*, a function that he would keep when the Brigade became a Division.

By July 1944, the Brigade had drawn up lists of the Cherkassy losses.

D. Estonian Campaign (August 1944)

1. General military situation

The III Germanic SS Armoured Corps (*III (germ.) SS-Panzerkorps*) under *SS-Obergruppenführer* Felix Steiner, including a Flemish battle group of reduced battalion size from the *Langemarck* Brigade, held the corridor between the bay of Finland and Lake Peipus. It was threatened by Soviet forces progressing in two directions: towards Tallinn and between the lakes Peipus and Pskow, in the south.

The rearguard combats in Estonia were intended to allow a methodical

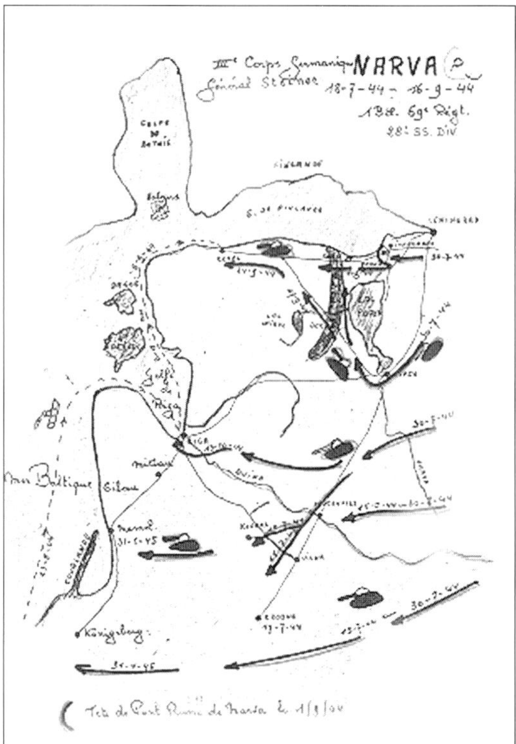

Fig. 19.37. Post-war chart and comments by Jules Mathieu. (*J. Mathieu/Collection E. De Bruyne*).

evacuation by sea from Reval (Tallinn) of the troops, armament, rolling stock and supplies of Army Group North.

In reality, the III Germanic *Panzerkorps* was retreating from Estonia south to the Riga area where it set up a screen to allow the infantry of Army Group North to withdraw to a defensive line across the base of the Courland peninsula, the last bastion before East Prussia, fighting with bitter determination.

Fig. 19.38. Bad-Tölz promoted *SS-Ustuf.* Marcel Thomas was severely wounded during the Estonia campaign, but survived the war. (*Private Collection*).

2. Internal situation of the *5.SS-Freiw.-Sturmbrigade Wallonien*

In the summer of 1944, the Walloon formation was in the middle of refitting after the Cherkassy outbreak when it received the order to send a battalion to Estonia. The bulk of the Legion was stationed at Heidelager (Debica) training barracks, but numerous contingents were scattered all over the Reich attending various specialized weapons schools.[21]

As *SS-Hstuf.* Jules Mathieu was commissioned to command this battalion, he and his Adjutant, *SS-Ustuf.* Jules Sandron, were summoned to the *SS-Führungshauptamt* at Bad Sarau where they were to meet *SS-Standartenführer* Weber, in charge of supplying the different theatres of operations with troops. The latter desired to question Mathieu on the battle readiness of the Walloon unit and the requirements in weapons and different equipments.

As the reduced battalion consisted for the greater part of fresh recruits, some of them had spent hardly one week with the Brigade, Mathieu obtained from *SS-Standartenführer* Weber a promise that the recruits would be trained in Estonia before being thrown into action ...

On 21 July 1944, an urgent oath-taking ceremony had even been organized at Heidelager barracks by *SS-Stubaf.* Tchekhoff (Degrelle was in Belgium for his brother's burial – he had been shot by the Resistance) for a number of latecomers who were then sent to Estonia with a second convoy.

The cadre, on the other hand, consisted of frontline battle-experienced NCOs, while the officers were either veterans who had survived the previous battles or freshly promoted *SS-Ustuf.* from the *SS-Junker Schule* Bad-Tölz.[22]

In the meantime, Mathieu had been sent to Putlos military academy where he was to attend preparatory courses for a future regimental command. *SS-Ostuf.* Georges Ruelle was then designated to command what was going to be known as the *Kampfgruppe Ruelle.*[23]

On 25 July 1944, 452 officers, NCOs and legionnaires disembarked at Johvi, 45 km west of Narwa.

According to the promise made by

Fig. 19.39. *SS-Oberscharführer* Henri Philippet joined the *Legion* in August 1941 at the age of 17. Veteran of all previous campaigns without suffering any injuries, he was wounded while attacking the Patska positions on 19 August 1944. (*Doc. H. Philippet*).

SS-Standartenführer Weber the battalion started basic military training at Voka on 28 July 1944.

On arrival, the battalion comprised two companies (*Einsatzkompanien*) ready for immediate action and one reserve company (*Feldersatzkompanie*) under *SS-Ustuf.* Jacques Capelle, based at Weissenstein, that still needed military instruction!

On 29 July 1944, *SS-Obergruppenführer* Felix Steiner inspected the Walloon battalion, which was organised as shown in the grey box below.

I./SS-Freiw. Sturmbrigade "Wallonien"
Kampfgruppe Ruelle

En train, le 23.7.1944

Détail de la force embarquée

	Off.	Adj.	Sgt.	Sdts.	Totaux
Cie.E.M. :	3	3	6	13	25
Pon.T.Tr. :	-	-	1	19	20
Pon.Pak. :	1	1	4	21	27
1. Cie. :	2	1	7	88	98
2. Cie. :	2	3	7	79	91
4. Cie. :	2	4	12	107	125
Total de la force embarquée. le 22.7.44.	10	12	37	327	386

J. Wastiau

Lieutenant et Adjudant-Major.

Fig. 19.40. Document signed by *SS-Ustuf.* Roger Wastiau showing the original battle strength of the *Kampfgruppe Ruelle*. Among the 386 men, there were 19 Frenchmen. In the end, the full force was 452 men.[23] (*Arch. E. De Bruyne*).

SS-Stubaf. Léon Degrelle with no specific military command.

Orderly	*SS-Ustuf.* Robert du Welz
Team of War Correspondents	*SS-Ustuf.* F. Chomé
Kommandeur	*SS-Ostuf.* Georges Ruelle
Adjutant-Major	*SS-Ustuf.* Jacques Wautelet
HQ/Company	*SS-Ustuf.* Schebella (German)
Liaison officer	*SS-Ostuf.* Karl Schaeffer (German)
Interpreter	*Waffen SS-Ustuf.* Georg von Schafroff (White Soviet)
Signals	*SS-Uscha.* Kaison
1st Company (*Feldersatz*):	*SS-Ustuf.* Jacques Capelle *SS-Hscha.* Paul Chenut, Lamboray and Dohlen, 98 men in all
2nd Company (*Einsatzkompanie*):	*SS-Ustuf.* Marc Willem (†Patska 19.08.1944) *SS-Ustuf.* Marcel Thomas *SS-Ustuf.* Marcel Capoen (†Patska 19.08.1944) *SS-Oscha.* Cabaret, Foucart, Philippet.
4th Company (heavy weapons):	*SS-Ostuf.* Marcel Bonniver. *SS-Ustuf.* René Verenne (†Liiva 14.08.1944). *SS-Oscha.* Lempereur, Guyot, Liebart, Deschrijver, in all 125 men.

A *PAK* platoon (under *SS-Ustuf.* Léon Gillis assisted by *SS-Oscha.* Tilburgs and 9 NCOs, in all 27 men) was attached to 4th Company.

In fact, the Walloon formation was a much reduced battalion with only one rifle infantry company (2nd Company) with incomplete numerical strength and a strong 4th Company (heavy weapons), backed up by a *PAK* platoon.

In the course of the month of July 1944, Degrelle had been called back to Belgium to attend his brother's funeral, killed by the Resistance in his Bouillon hometown (14 July 1944). Informed of the unexpected departure of the reduced battalion for Estonia, Degrelle, rather than join the unit in Germany, where he refused to appear as long as the Germans had not clarified *SS-Oberführer* Burk's

Fig. 19.41. *SS-Ustuf.* Léon Gillis, together with Léon Degrelle and Marcel Bonniver, was one of the three survivors of the 1st contingent of August 1941 (860 men) having participated in all the battles and campaigns from 1941 to 1945. (*Collection J.-L. Roba*).

situation, travelled to Estonia, where he arrived on 8 August 1944.

Degrelle immediately sought contacts with Steiner. Far from requiring a longer delay for the instruction of his men and referring to Cherkassy, he guaranteed the combat value of the battalion.

On 10 August 1944, the Walloon battalion left Voka for Maarja-Magdaleine, north of Dorpat (known as Tartu in Estonian).

The Walloon formation was sent as a reinforcement to *Kampfgruppe* Wagner (elements of the III Germanic *SS-Panzerkorps* detached from the Tannenberg front to the north, and led by Brigade *Nederland* commander Jürgen Wagner) and occupied a number of strongpoints (*Stützpunkte*) on a 30 km long frontline, covering the southern area of Dorpat (Elva, Liiva, Patska). A few days later, *SS-Ustuf.* Verenne was ambushed while executing a reconnaissance mission at Liiava. Of the 30-man group only 2 or 3 men escaped the deadly trap.

In the afternoon of 19 August, most of the battalion was dispatched near Patska, with the mission to dislodge a solidly held Soviet position. The objective was reached at the cost of very heavy losses (65 killed and wounded) at the end of the afternoon but the Walloons could not even spend the night on the conquered position as Soviet spearheads were already driving in the direction of Dorpat.

The next day the frontline blazed up again. The Soviets attacked from all directions and the Germans and Walloons had to yield ground. *In extremis* the Walloons succeeded in joining the lorries which had carried them to Patska the day before, and were driven back the other way round to Kambja. There, they found an even more disastrous situation than the one they had faced when leaving for Patska. 1st Company was called in as reinforcements to fill up the losses incurred at Patska.

The Walloons remained in direct and uninterrupted contact with the Soviets from August 20th to the evening of the 23rd, between Kambja and Nôo, about 30 km from Dorpat. This strip of frontline was also the target of Soviet attacks which had been launched simultaneously from the south and the west.

This is the very moment when *SS-Ustuf.* Gillis confirmed the outstanding combat qualities of the Walloon legionnaire as revealed in the press all over occupied Europe.

From 19 until 22 August 1944, Gillis took over command of 2nd Company,

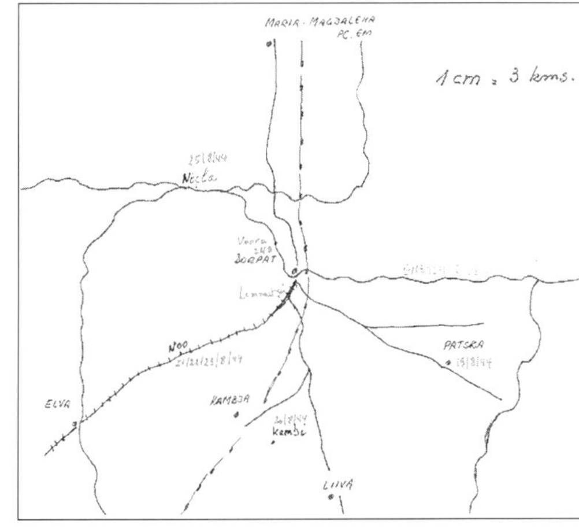

Fig. 19.42. Doc. Ph. Canva, former *Gefechtsschreiber* (combat secretary) of the *Kampfgruppe Ruelle*. (*Arch. E. De Bruyne*).

whose commander had been killed in action that day, and he immediately became involved in the fierce defensive battles around Kambja.

By 00:30 a.m., on 23 August 1944, Gillis had positioned his three *PAK* guns, his mortars and his men. At first daylight, his surprise was great when he noticed that the surrounding Estonian forces had retreated during the night without any notice. Meanwhile, the Soviet forces had passed by Gillis' positions and were driving north-eastwards toward Lemmatsi, 10 kms from Dorpat, cutting off the Walloons.

Only by decisive and daring individual actions by his men – as they were continuously in direct contact with Soviet tanks – could Gillis break through the encirclement, suffering the loss of one *PAK* gun due to a direct hit.

On 22 August, this time as commanding officer of the *PAK* platoon, Gillis was given the urgent mission to hold the Riga-Dorpat road at Nôo, the triangle Elva-Kambja-Nôo area having fallen into the hands of the Soviets. To accomplish this mission, the Walloon officer disposed of three anti-tank guns, of a platoon of mortars (under *SS-Hscha.* Liebart) and about twenty riflemen. He and his men were to be integrated into an Estonian border guard regiment (grouped into *Division zbV 300*) that was defending the place. In reality, Soviet forces had already by-passed Nôo and were on their way to Dorpat!

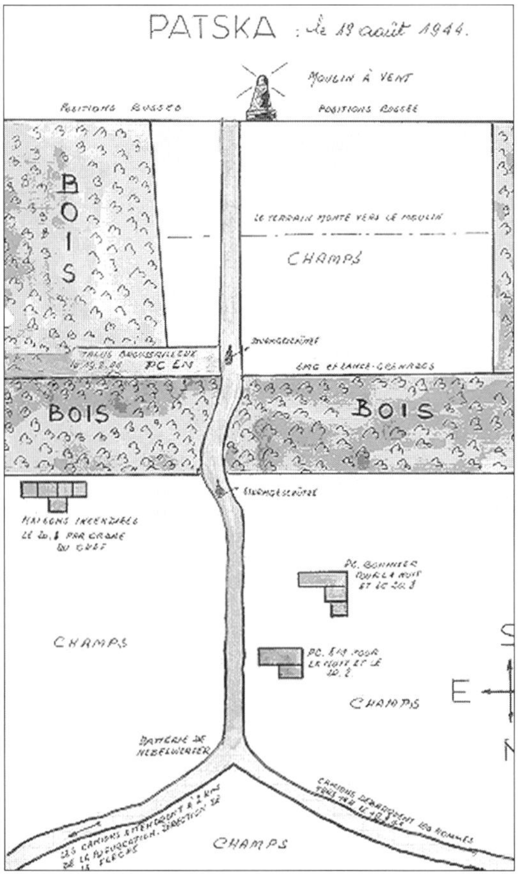

Farther northwards, the Soviets had arrived as far as the north-western area of Dorpat and threatened to cross the Lembach River at Voora so as to achieve their pincer movement. In the meantime, Gillis, fighting his way through, had reached Voora bridge and faced 10 Stalin tanks ready to attack. At the sight of the Soviet forces the local Estonian border guards withdrew hastily, abandoning Gillis to his fate. At 2:00 p.m., the Soviets launched their attack. Gillis, serving himself one of two remaining *PAK*, let the first tank approach within 30 meters before firing and hitting it. As he had just accomplished this second hit his *PAK* gun was lifted into the air by counter-fire and he himself was seriously wounded in the eyes. For this action Degrelle recommended Gillis for the *Ritterkreuz*.

On the morning of Wednesday 23 August, Degrelle left Dorpat with a view to visiting the *PAK* platoon he assumed to be at Nôo. But he was soon blocked at Lemmatsi by the Soviet spearheads that were rushing from the south-west. The weak second-rate Estonian local forces could not stand the shock, broke up, and fled in disorder. The frontline was about to be overrun definitively when Degrelle showed up in his *Kubelwagen*. He himself rounded up all men within reach, Walloons, Germans and Estonians, and established a line of resistance that held the positions for the rest of the day. Degrelle's determined intervention had prevented the German command from facing a disastrous situation, as Dorpat would have been conquered the same day had Degrelle not displayed personal courage and determination.

For this action both *Kdr. Heeres Gruppe Nord* General Schörner and General Grasser, in charge of *the Armee-Abt. Narwa* recommended Léon Degrelle for the Oakleaves in a cable they sent to the *O.K.H* on 25 August. Two days later,

Fig. 19.43. (*Doc. Ph. Canva; arch. E. De Bruyne.*)

Degrelle was awarded the Oakleaves to his Knight's Cross. At the same time, he received the *Nahkampfspange in Gold* (Close Combat Clasp in Gold) and the *Deutsches Kreuz in Gold* (German Cross in Gold). The former award indicated that he had surpassed his 50th day of hand-to-hand combat with the enemy.

The very next day, 24 August, while the Soviets were temporarily stopped 20 km south of Dorpat, General Wagner was informed that a sudden Soviet strike had taken the bridge over the Ema river at Nöela, 15 kms south-west of Dorpat, threatening the town with encirclement. Once again the Walloons would be thrown into the battle.

From the original battle strength of 452 men only about 150 legionnaires could still be counted on. As to the command, *SS-Ustuf.* Verenne, Willem and Capoen had been killed, *SS-Ustuf.* Thomas was seriously wounded and so was *SS-Ustuf.* Gillis. There remained: *SS-Stubaf.* Degrelle, *SS-Ostuf.* Bonniver and *SS-Ustuf.* Capelle (*Kommandeur* Ruelle was to be injured on the 25th) surrounded by a handful of NCOs. Embarked on a few lorries, the Walloon legionnaires were transported towards Nöela where they were immediately put into contact with the enemy. The whole night and the next day of August 25th the Walloons participated in actions to retake the lost terrain, which seemed to progress well for a moment but in the end failed due to the lack of numerical strength.

At the end of the 25th, only 90 legionnaires were fit and ready for action. For a while, the positions seemed stabilized but soon the staff of the Wagner Group mentioned a new breakthrough and ordered the Walloons to stop it at Lombi-Keerdu. 70 legionnaires were left at Nöela as reinforcement to two German companies. The others returned to Maarja-Magdalena to be merged into various services and into what remained of the HQ Company to form a mixed troop under the command of *SS-Ostuf.* Bonniver. *SS-Oscha.* Paul Mezzetta, head of the *Jeunesse Légionnaire*, who had left Breslau a week before, arrived just in time to join Bonniver. Along with some isolated Germans, they were to fight without any orders, liaison or supply for 3 days and 3 nights. When the group was finally relieved on 31 August there were only 20 Walloons left! All 20 were awarded the Iron Cross I at Maarja-Magdalena.

After a brief stay at Maarja-Magdalena, the debris of the battalion *Wallonie* was put in reserve at Gut-Toila, near the bay of Finland, before sailing to Germany in the first days of September 1944.

The Walloon battalion had lost 50% of its battle strength and was mentioned in the *Wehrmachtbericht*. On 6 September 1944, Degrelle recommended *SS-Ustuf.* Léon Gillis for the *Ritterkreuz* (recommendation No. 3666), which was awarded on 30 September 1944, for particular gallantry at Nôo and Voora.[24]

On recommendation by Degrelle, the following frontline officers were promoted one rank higher: Georges Ruelle and Marcel Bonniver, promoted to *SS-Hstuf.*; Jacques Capelle, Marcel Thomas, Jacques Wautelet, Georg von Schafroff and Léon Gillis were awarded the rank of *SS-Ostuf.* Marc Willem (†) Marcel Capoen (†), René Verenne (†) were awarded the same rank posthumously.

E. Command crisis

Between February and September 1944, Degrelle, to his great discontent, was not recognized as *Kommandeur* of the Brigade in spite of a written request to Himmler. The *Reichsführer*'s orders were without appeal: Degrelle was only to be tolerated and referred to as *Führer der Wallonen* (Leader of the Walloons).

After the Cherkassy breakout, Degrelle developed the ambition to build up a much larger unit. This also meant that the commander of that formation could not possibly be a (too low-ranked) *SS-Sturmbannführer* (Degrelle) without military academic training!

Unless a Belgian (professional) senior officer were ready to serve in the *Wallonie*, both Berger and Jüttner made clear to Léon Degrelle that the Germans would take over command as, in the meantime, Berlin had decided that all

Le général-major Chardome

rejoint la SS-Division Wallonie

de former une petite [illegible]vision. En 1934, d'ailleurs, le général-major Chardome eut l'insigne honneur de présenter cet immense régiment à S. Majesté le Roi Léopold III, au cours d'une cérémonie qui se déroula aux environs d'Arlon.

Une fois son organisation achevée, le Régiment de Chasseurs Ardennais fut dénommé Corps de Chasseurs Ardennais et fut placé sous le commandement d'un lieutenant-général auquel Chardome fut adjoint comme chef d'État-Major. A cette occasion, le général-major Chardome reçut du Roi la Commanderie de l'Ordre de la Couronne pour services exceptionnels rendus au pays.

•

Fin 1936, le général-major Chardome fut versé au IIIe Chasseurs à Pied à Tournai. Il convient de noter qu'il avait été nommé colonel au début de la même année. En juin 1937, il prit le commandement officiel du IIIe Régiment à Pied dans la même ville de Tournai et lors de la mobilisation de 1939 il reçut le commandement d'un groupement — appelé groupement Chardome — à qui était dévolu la tâche de surveiller un secteur de la frontière sud.

Nommé général-major en mars 1940, il rejoignit au Canal Albert la Ve Division comme commandant de l'infanterie. Et il venait d'être désigné pour diriger à la tête des [illegible] de tir quand la guerre éclata.

Immédiatement, sa division fut regroupée et elle prit possession de la ligne de défense prévue entre Malines et Louvain. On sait qu'à la suite de la retraite des troupes anglaises, l'armée belge fut amenée à se replier successivement sur différentes positions jusqu'au moment où elle arriva au canal de dérivation de la Lys. Au cours de cette retraite, le général-major Chardome fit personnellement sauter dix ponts après s'être assuré cha-

[illegible]ral-major Chardome (Exclusivité Eil Wail.)

Fig. 19.44. On 26 May 1944, the Belgian General-Major Lambert Chardome was released from *Oflag II A* (Prenzlau) with a view to enrolling in the Walloon Assault Brigade. Note that the press referred to the Assault Brigade as a *SS Division*!

Fig. 19.45. After the war, General-Major Lambert Chardome was sentenced to 15 years imprisonment. (*Doc. Prof. Francis Balace*).

foreign legions were to be placed under German control, including the *Wallonie*. This attitude was in flagrant opposition with what had been agreed upon in June 1943, when joining the *Waffen-SS*: military command in Belgian hands. That is why Degrelle hurried to *Prenzlau-OflagII A* in May 1944, in the hope of finding a commanding senior officer who would protect the unit from German interference.

At the same time, the Germans, convinced that Degrelle was trapped, prepared the take over by sending *SS-Oberführer* Karl Burk from *SS u. Pol Fhr Ost-Krakau* to the Walloon Assault Brigade. By secret letter from Himmler, dated 8 July 1944, Burk was retroactively appointed *Kommandeur* of the *Brigade Wallonie* from 21 June 1944 onwards.

Burk's secret appointment as Commander of the Walloon Assault Brigade resulted from Degrelle's failure to recruit a Belgian senior officer at *Prenzlau Oflag II A*. General Chardome's defection, and those of colonels Frankignoul and Long, caused the problem of the rank of the officer called for taking command of a future division to resurface. As a senior officer, Degrelle had only managed to recruit Frans Hellebaut, a career B.E.M. Major (Staff College Certificate) of the Belgian Royal Army, an insufficiently high rank to aspire to command a division.

Meanwhile, Degrelle had been informed that there was mischief afoot in Berlin. In order to show his discontent, Degrelle, who by that time had returned to Belgium to attend his brother's funeral, refused to show up among his men in Germany as long as Burk had not been removed from his command.

The unexpected departure for Estonia of a Walloon battalion proved to be a unique opportunity to face Berger and Jüttner.

By repeating the Cherkassy scenario

Fig. 19.46. Frans Hellebaut as a Major B.E.M. of the Belgian Royal Army. (*F. Hellebaut; arch. E. De Bruyne*).

Antwort-Postkarte
Carte postale de réponse
An den Kriegsgefangenen
Au prisonnier
Major BEM HELLEBAUT

Oflag II A
Geprüft

Gebührenfrei! Franc de port!

Absender:
Expéditeur:
Vor- und Zuname:
Nom et prénom
Ort:
Lieu
Straße:
Rue
Kreis:
Département

Gefangenennummer: 655
No. du prisonnier
Lager-Bezeichnung:
Nom du camp
Kriegsgef.-Offizierlager II A
Prenzlau
Deutschland (Allemagne)

Fig. 19.47. From the five *Prenzlau Oflag II A* POW officers, – General Chardome, Colonels Long and Frankignoul, Maj. BEM Hellebaut and Cpt-Cdt Lakaie, – who had accepted to join the Walloon Assault Brigade by the end of the month of May 1944, only Frans Hellebaut and Léon Lakaie persisted. Note that the postcard is directed to Lucien Lippert. *(Arch. E. De Bruyne via J.-L. Roba).*

in Estonia, Degrelle overthrew Berger's plans. Thanks to outstanding deeds of derring-do by his men, and his personal involvement as well, Degrelle finally got access to the higher spheres of the National Socialist apparatus, more particularly to Hitler. This strengthened Degrelle's position ahead of the group favouring an immediate German take-over of the foreign legions.

Being the only non-German with such impressive records, admired by New Order sympathizers all over occupied Europe, Degrelle had finally pushed himself up into a privileged position.

Édition spéciale
L'EFFORT WALLON

DEGRELLE CHEZ NOS OUVRIERS

A Berlin, près de 2.000 travailleurs l'acclament

Fig. 19.48. During an imposing meeting held at the *Reichssportfeld* in Berlin on 25 June 1944, Degrelle announced that General Chardome had volunteered for the Assault Brigade. A later change in attitude decided otherwise.

CHAPTER XX

The Last Months of the War

A. Establishment of the 28.SS Freiw.-Gren.Div.Wallonien

1. Preliminaries

On 23 September 1944, Degrelle announced that the Brigade had become a Division since the 17th and that the *Reichsführer-SS* had appointed him as *Kommandeur*.[1]

Thanks to the arrival in the Reich of thousands of Rexist refugees and a number of paramilitary groupings, Degrelle made so bold as to claim he would in less than no time command a 8,000 men strong unit, which would have comprised these sections (see grey box opposite).

By November 1944, expectations showed the figures shown in Table 4.

Fig. 20.1. Identification disk of the *28. SS-Freiw. -Gren Div. Wallonien* (*Private Collection*).

Table 4

Remnants of the Brigade	1200
Garde Wallonne	400
NSKK	600
Jeunesse légionnaire	1264
Rexist refugees	900
Kriegsmarine	150
Ers. Btl. 36.	800

A total of more or less 4,000 men[5] that SS-Sturmbannführer Frans Hellebaut[6] was ordered to mould into a combat unit.

Headquarters with 3 sections:

Ia (operations)

Ib (equipment-supplies)

Ic (intelligence) and an *Adjutantur* (administration)

Three infantry regiments with 2 battalions plus 2 mechanized companies:

69 Rgt ('t Serclaes de Tilly)[2]

70 Rgt (Bucquoy)[3]

71 Rgt (never raised)

Panzer Jäger Abteilung 28.

Fusilier Btl 28.

Artillerie Rgt 28.

Pionier Btl 28 (2 Companies)

Nachrichten Abteilung 28 (2 Companies)

Train, repair shops, supply, medical and social services

The organization of an infantry regiment (on a 1,850 men basis) was scheduled as shown in the following shaded box:

1 HQ Company
2 Inf. Battalions (*Inf. Btl*)
1 Field Artillery Company (*s I.G.* – 15cm)
1 Anti-tank Company (72 *Panzerschreck*).

Each Battalion (615 men in total) comprised:

1 HQ Company
3 Assault Companies (*Sturmkompanie* – 115 men) armed with 50 *MP 44;* 21 *M.G.42;* 6 rifles with telescopic sights
1 Heavy Company (*Schwere Kompanie* – 142 men) armed with 8 *s.M.G.42;* 8 *m Gr.W.* – 8 cm and 4 *le. I.G.* (7,5 cm).

The Anti-Tank Battalion was supposed to comprise:

1 Anti-tank Company (*PAK*- 7.5 cm)
1 Company equipped with twelve 2.36cm self-propelled anti-aircraft guns (*sfl FLAK*)
1 Company with 14 self-propelled anti-tank guns (*Stu. Ges.*).

Expected organisation for the Artillery Regiment was as follows:

3 battalions with one battery anti-tank guns (*s PAK* – 7.5 cm)
2 Companies equipped with light field howitzers (*leichte Feldhaubitze – le.F.H.* – 10.5 cm field howitzers)
1 battalion of 3 batteries of heavy field howitzers (*schwere Feldhaubitze – s.F.H.* – 15 cm).

The Pioneer Battalion with two companies was to be raised and trained as an elite unit specialized in positional warfare operations and close-quarters anti-tank combat.

In October-November 1944, the organization of the future division allowed the forming of:

- 1 reduced divisional headquarter group
- 2 headquarters at the regimental level
- 3 infantry battalions
- 1 each *PAK* and *Flak* companies
- 1 group of signals troops (sent to Sterzing/ Vipiteno (Italy) for training – (5 officers and more or less 100 men)
- 1 pioneer battalion (instruction at Hradischko – 4 officers and 400 men)
- Incomplete train and auxiliary services.

From the military point of view, the situation presented the following characteristics:

- profusion of older volunteers without the required physical fitness
- shortfall of Belgian officers and specialists[7]
- scattered billeting
- comfortable situation as far as small arms, light material and signals was concerned;
- great difficulties in procuring heavy armour and horses; large deficit and delays with regard to motor vehicles and fuel[8]
- irregular and deficient individual winter clothing
- normal but very monotonous food supply (common civil rations in times of military training)
- volunteers with poor morale due to the situation, more particularly among the Rexist refugees having fled Belgium, of leaving their homes (and sometimes relatives) behind.

On 30 November 1944, St André's Day – patron Saint of the *Légion Wallonie* – Léon Gillis, recently promoted to *SS-Ostuf.* and wearing the *Ritterkreuz*, was paraded in front of the mustered troops at Gronau barracks in the presence of the whole Rexist colony.

On 12 December 1944, a new German liaison officer was appointed: *SS-Oberführer* Johan Nikolaus Heilmann.[9]

By mid-December 1944, the general mobilization ordered by Degrelle was completed. The Division had reached a strength of more or less 4,300 men, allowing the forming of *II/69Rgt* and completion of the regimental headquarters (*69* and *70 Rgt*).

Glossary (for following shaded pages)

m.	*mittler*	medium
le.	*leicht*	light
s.	*schwer*	heavy
le. MG	*leichtes Maschinengewehr*	machine gun on bipod (light machine gun)
s. MG	*schweres Maschinengewehr*	machine gun on tripod (heavy machine gun)
m. Gr. W.	*mittlerer Granatwerfer*	medium mortar (being the new classification for the 8.1cm mortar. This weapon had previously been known as the *schwerer Granatwerfer* (*s. Gr. W.*) when the 12cm mortar appeared)
PAK	*Panzerabwehrkanone*	anti-tank gun
FLAK	*Fliegerabwehrkanone*	anti-aircraft artillery gun
Stu. Ges.	*Sturmgeschütz*	self-propelled assault-gun

2. Order of Battle

Kommandeur	*SS-Sturmbannführer u. Ritterkreuzträger mit Eichenlaub* Léon Degrelle[10]
Aides	*SS-Hstuf.* Karl Schaeffer[11] *SS-Ustuf.* Tony Gombert (Flemish Rexist coming from the *Langemarck*) *SS-Ustuf.* Raymond Camby
Deputy *Kommandeur* and *Ia*	*SS-Stubaf.* Frans Hellebaut
Headquarters	
First Ordinance Officer	O1 *SS-Ustuf.* A. Nortier (assisting the *Ia*)
Quarter-Master *Ib*	*SS-Ostuf.* Hermann (German)
Intelligence *Ic*	*SS-Ustuf.* A. Vinckenbosch (reported missing 09.02.1945 Müscherin area)[12]
Equipment (*Wa. G*)	*SS-Ostuf.* Thiemann (German)
Adjutantur (*II*)	*SS-Stubaf.* Jacobs (former *Kommandeur* of the *L.W.*)
Judicial Serv. (*III*)	*SS-Hstuf.* Flechsig (German)
Supply (*IVa*)	*SS-Hstuf.* Jehn (German)
Health Service (*IVb*)	*SS-Stubaf.* Dr Becker (German), heading a company with 2 platoons each comprising 1 officer (medical doctor), 1 *SS-Hscha*, 6 NCO ambulance orderlies, 36 stretcher bearers.
Veterinary	*SS-Hstuf.* Dr Bedercke (German)
Tech. Serv. (*V*)	*SS-Ustuf.* S. Devrees
Feldgendarmerie	*SS-Ostuf.* Bachinger (German) *SS-Hscha.* Pascal Bovy
Welfare Service	*SS-Ostuf.* Dr Oetzmann (German)
Catholic Chaplain	*Padre Gérard* (L. Stockman), with the divisional rank of a *SS-Sturmbannführer.*
69 Rgt/' t Serclaes de Tilly	
Kommandeur-SS-Stubaf.	J. Mathieu[13]
Adjutant	*SS-Ostuf.* J. Sandron
Aide	*SS-Ustuf.* F. Grube
Equipment	*SS-Ustuf.* H. Guillemont
Judicial Serv (*III*)	*SS-Ustuf.* J. Pévenasse
Hq Company	*SS-Ustuf.* J. Galère
Supply (*IV a*)	*SS-Ustuf.* J. Schebella (German)
Tech. Serv. (*V*)	*SS-Ustuf.* J. Ducate
Signals	*SS-Ustuf.* L. Cremers
I/69Rgt	
Kommandeur	*SS-Stubaf.* H. Derriks[14]
Adjutant	*SS-Ustuf.* R. DeGoy

(continued overleaf)

Aide	*SS-Oscha* (later *SS-Ustuf.*) J. Leroy[15]
SS-Hscha.	Paul Mezzetta (†04.03.1945)
Supply (*IVa*)	*SS-Ustuf.* Walter Zaplethal (German)
Health Service	*SS-Ostuf.* R. Buy (Frenchman)
1st Company	*SS-Ustuf.* A. Régibeau *SS-Ustuf.* D. Wouters (†20.04.1945) *SS-Ustuf.* J. Leroy (March 1945) *SS-Oscha.* P. Hancisse *SS-Oscha.* M. Havet (†20.04.1945)
2nd Company	*SS-Ostuf.* M. De Coster *SS-Ustuf.* J. Piron *SS-Ustuf.* M. Deravet
3rd Company	*SS-Ustuf.* E. Serlet *SS-Ustuf.* H. Nizet (†Krüssow 01.03.1945) *SS-Ustuf.* J. Hallebardier[16]
4th Company	*SS-Hstuf.* M. Bonniver *SS-Ustuf.* R. Serlet. (†Altdamm 18.03.1945) *SS-Ustuf.* L. Bervaes[17]

II/69 Rgt

Kommandeur	SS-Hstuf. H. Lakaie
Adjutant	*SS-Ustuf.* J. Théâtre
Aide	*SS-Ustuf.* J. Liènart
Supply	*SS-Ustuf.* Wanka (German)
Med. Service	*SS-St.O.Ju.* Dr Roekens
Signals	*SS-Ustuf.* Rusinger (German)
5th Company	*SS-Ustuf.* H. Rue (†Krüssow, 12.02.1945) *SS-Ustuf.* P. Della Faille d'Huyse
6th Company	*SS-Ustuf.* R. Rooryck *SS-Ustuf.* Méan
7th Company	*SS-Ustuf.* J. Capelle (†Lindenberg, 17.02.1945)
8th Company	*SS-Ustuf.* C. Monfils *SS-Ustuf.* H. Lovinfosse *SS-Ustuf.* R. Jourdain

Regimental I.G. Company (in the process of forming)

SS-Ustuf. G. Dupire (†Breslau-Brissa, January 1945)

Regimental Anti-tank Company (not established).

(continued opposite)

70 Rgt – Bucquoi

Kommandeur	*SS-Stubaf.* G. Tchekhoff
Aide	*SS-Ostuf.* G. von Schafroff (White Russian)

I/70 Rgt

Kommandeur	*SS-Hstuf.* G. Ruelle
Aide	*SS-Ostuf.* R. Denie
Adjutant	*SS-Ustuf.* G. De Bongnie
Supply (*IVa*)	*SS-Ostuf.* Lochann (German)
Med. Serv.	*SS-Ostuf.* Dr Metzger (German) *SS-Ostuf.* Dr Griesmann (German) *SS-Ustuf.* Dr Baanante (Spaniard)
Signals	*SS-Ustuf.* J. De Heug
1st Company	*SS-Ustuf.* D. Lecoq (†Lübov, 06.03.1945) *SS-Ustuf.* Van Gysegem *SS-Ustuf.* R. Foulon *SS-Ustuf.* F. Caudron
2nd Company	(not raised)
3rd Company	*SS-Ostuf.* Valdajos (Spaniard) *a. i. SS-Ustuf.* R. Bal (†Lübov, 06.03.1945)
4th Company	*SS-Ustuf.* H. Schumacher *SS-Ustuf.* A. Delannoy *SS-Ustuf.* G. Suain.

Pioneer Battalion (2 companies in the process of training):

Kommandeur	*SS-Ostuf.* J. Mirgain *SS-Ustuf.* A. Sapin *SS-Ustuf.* P. Mignon *SS-Ustuf.* L. Collard

Signals Battalion (1 Company):

CO	*SS-Ostuf.* R. Wastiau *SS-Ustuf.* J. M. Lantiez *SS-Ustuf.* A. Winandy *SS-Ustuf.* V. Smets *SS-Ustuf.* N. Vachaudez

Artillery Battalion (4 batteries in the process of training – in all 12 officers and more or less 400 men):

Kommandeur	*SS-Hstuf.* J. Malherbe
Adjutant	*SS-Ustuf.* G. Soenen
Aide	*SS-Ustuf.* Winterscheidt (German) *SS-Ustuf.* A. Devaux

(continued overleaf)

1st Battery	*SS-Ustuf.* J. Dumont *SS-Ustuf.* Destatte
2nd Battery	*SS-Ustuf.* F. Foulon
3rd Battery	*SS-Ustuf.* M. C. Grisay *SS-Ustuf.* Count de Backer de Réville (†Schönwerder, 27.04.1945)
4th Battery	*SS-Hstuf.* A. Dumont *SS-Ustuf.* L. Bourdouxhe

Anti-tank Battalion (s. PAK):

1. PAK Company

CO	*SS-Ostuf.* M. Lamproye *SS-Ostuf.* L. Gillis *SS-Ustuf.* Gé. Pé ... (later SS-*Ostuf.*) *SS-Ustuf.* J. Mahieu

2. FLAK Company (2 cm)

CO	*SS-Hstuf.* H. Thyssen (†Schillersdorf, 20.04.1945) *SS-Ustuf.* R. Gondry

3. Stu. Gesch. Company (not created)

B. A SS-WEST CORPS FOR DEGRELLE?

On 13 November 1944, Léon Degrelle and Lt Dr Heinz Forsteneichner[18] were on their way to Sigmaringen, a small town in Baden-Württemberg, not far from Lake Constance, seat of the French *Délégation française pour la défense des intérêts français,*[19] presided over by Fernand de Brinon.

The presence at Sigmaringen, next to Degrelle, of a representative of the *Auswärtiges Amt* (Ministry of Foreign Affairs) is not surprising, as the town had been housing a restricted diplomatic corps since September 1944. This diplomatic corps was formed by the remainder of the Vichy government,[20] German embassy personnel from Paris,[21] Italians with a consul general acting as a plenipotentiary minister representing the Saló republic and by the Japanese ambassador. As to Degrelle, he disposed of a more or less confidential *bureau.*

Degrelle's political services at Hildesheim,[22] more particularly the Staff of the *Jeunesse Légionnaire,* had regular

Fig. 20.2. Sigmaringen castle, seat of the French puppet government.

Fig. 20.3. Jacques Doriot, former Communist and Leader of the *Parti Populaire Français*.

contacts with Sigmaringen. However, its task proved to be touchy, as those undercover contacts required tact in order not to hurt the susceptibility of the various competing French groups. Indeed, the Governmental Committee headed by Fernand de Brinon stood out strongly against the *PPF* (*Parti Populaire Français*) clan led Jacques Doriot. Besides, the latter was to create the *Comité de Libération*[23] and definitively put an end to the aspirations of the Governmental Committee to emerge as the sole interlocutor of the French Collaboration with the *Reich*. To achieve this, Doriot could count on the friendly support of both *Gauleiter* Josef Bürckel and Gottlob Berger, chief of the *SS-Hauptamt*, omnipresent whenever it came to curbing Léon Degrelle's political, military and territorial ambitions. Of course, the *Gestapo* was keeping a close watch on all these people.

As a man of letters, Degrelle was most interested in the journalistic activities of the Frenchmen. In Sigmaringen, two French newspapers were available: *La France,* the organ of the *Comité Gouvernemental* and the *Petit Parisien,* (from January 1945 onwards), published by the Doriot group in Mainau/ Constance. Degrelle had been particularly flattered by Jean Luchaire's laudatory comments on the *La Toison d'Or* published in Berlin by the Rex Movement and of which Degrelle was very proud. As soon as he took the floor Luchaire faced questions about this first-rate weekly. He bitterly regretted he was not allotted as much money as the Belgians, so as to publish something similar. In the small Sigmaringen enclave, the French newspapers could in no way compete with this unequalled *Toison d'Or.*[24]

The arrival of the commander of the Division *Wallonie* at Sigmaringen on 13 November 1944 was for reasons other than just to pay respects to Marshal Philippe Pétain. Of course, Degrelle requested he be granted a meeting with the leader of the French state. He was politely dismissed. However, Degrelle did not care a fig. As a matter of fact, he had other more interesting things in mind than to greet this old man. He was more absorbed by the idea of examining the chances of forming and controlling a *Corps Occidental* (Corps West) to be established with the Belgian divisions *Langemarck* and *Wallonie,* and the French division *Charlemagne.* These plans, which had met the approval of his friend Otto Abetz, were to be discussed in the presence of Fernand de Brinon, General Eugène-Marie Bridoux and Jean Luchaire. General Gustav Krukenberg, Inspector of *Charlemagne,* and the pro-Nazi collaborationist wing represented by the *PPF* were hostile to this project.

The French collaboration still had in mind Degrelle's visit to Paris and his famous speech at the *Palais de Chaillot* on 5 March 1944. On that occasion, his territorial claims on Burgundy and other parts of eastern France had irritated the French collaboration. This romantico-historic delusion, once encouraged by Himmler himself, seemed as dangerous as it was irrelevant. To some it was even ridiculous.[25]

Seven months later the cards were shuffled differently, this time in favour of an outsider since wrangling, feuds and dissension had split the French collaboration in exile. Degrelle thought he could take advantage of this situation. Within the *Charlemagne,* Darnand's militiamen maintained constant domestic quarrels with Doriot's dedicated followers. *LVF* veterans did not get along with the *légionnaires* belonging to the French *SS* Assault Brigade. In addition, the latter could not bear the sight of officers coming from Darnand's *Milice* who, despite a lack of frontline experience, were given command duties. In a word, Degrelle felt that the fruit was ripe and ready to be plucked.

Joseph Darnand and Jacques Doriot both longed for a dominating and preponderant role. The former was seeking the command of the division *Charlemagne.* The latter was aiming at political power but this obviously implied control of the French unit. But in the meantime, the Germans had developed other views when it came to military command of non-German forces. These views had been clearly defined in a speech that Gottlob Berger gave in the Casino of the Ministry of Air in March 1944: foreign legions and non-German units were to be commanded by German officers only.[26] The Germans did everything they could to muzzle the two protagonists. This is exactly the moment that Degrelle chose to make his appearance.

The sectarianism and particularism that had been raging within the *Charlemagne* made an excellent pretext for Degrelle's personal interference in French affairs. Tired of sterile intrigues, which had been paralyzing the French unit since their arrival in Germany, whole barrack-rooms of French *légionnaires* deserted to join the *Wallonie* where they were certain to find prestige and action.

In a report of 10 December 1944, forwarded to the *SS-Hauptamt*, Degrelle in an attempt to analyze the situation of the French *Waffen-SS*, wrote that they were composed of 30% of Darnand's followers, 30% of Doriot's men and 40% of soldiers who did not support either party, and at the same time were opposed to all factions. According to Degrelle, it was high time Darnand's *Miliciens* were put under his control by transferring them to the *Wallonie*. Consequently, it was clear that only a foreign leader could unite and gather the divergent forces of the French collaboration. And this providential man could only be the commander of the Division *Wallonie*!

Von Ribbentrop's services also expressed the view that friction among Darnand's supporters and *doriotistes* was to be avoided, not by rallying to Degrelle's plans but by weakening Darnand's position! The latter had asked to join the *Charlemagne* not as a *SS-Sturmbannführer*[27] – too low a rank for an important command – but as *Secrétaire-Général au Maintien de l'Ordre*.[28] Moreover, since Darnand was also the head of the *Milice* – more or less 4,000 members and the most important group within the *Charlemagne* – he thought he had a good chance of taking over command. It would have given him authority and influence at which Doriot and the *SS-Hauptamt* would have taken offence. However, Darnand's fate was sealed since Hitler had opted in the meantime for the solution Doriot: ultra *SS* collaboration until the end.

Apparently, higher *SS* authorities in Berlin, remembering the setbacks that Degrelle had caused them, were very little inclined to associate the turbulent Belgian with the *Charlemagne*. The general impression was that Degrelle had already given them enough trouble.

As a good observer of the political scene, Degrelle had been surprised by the German attitude more than once. The latest development took place the day before his arrival at Sigmaringen. That day, he attended the swearing-in ceremony of the *Charlemagne* at Wildflecken barracks. Darnand, as well as General Bridoux, had been summoned not to appear other than in civilian clothes. As to Doriot, he was refused access to the parade ground. It was a broad hint to Degrelle on behalf of the Germans: no military or political role for foreign collaborators. The Belgian did not care at all and persisted in believing that the French collaboration represented real hopes for a future political role and the supplementary prestige that this would generate.

Darnand soon concluded that he had been put aside. However, there was one hope left: Degrelle. Darnand called on the Walloon and offered to join him – he

Fig. 20.4. Joseph Darnand between *Brigadeführer* Karl Oberg, *HSSPF* and as such representing Himmler in France (left), and *SS-Standartenführer* Helmut Knochen, chief of the *Sipo-Sd* (right) (*Collection J.-L. Roba*).

and his men – in the common struggle against Bolshevism within a *Corps West* under Degrelle.

Unfortunately for Degrelle, Gottlob Berger was to set his face against that design. The reason he officially set forth was politico-ethnic in nature: Wallonia was to be annexed to the *Reich* and not to France and consequently any form of French-Walloon Collaboration was out of the question. Although Berger, in a note to Himmler, had justified his refusal by stating that Doriot would be a better leader than Darnand, the *SS-Hauptamt* was secretly concerned just as much, if not more, by its desire to bar the way to the Walloons. Giving more weight to his analysis, Berger reminded Himmler that Degrelle's territorial claims had annoyed the French collaboration to such an extent that Degrelle had no chance of being accepted as a representative of them. Furthermore, Berger claimed that Doriot, as an ex-Communist, would protect the French workers in the *Reich* from the contagion of Bolshevism much better; that the tandem Darnand-Degrelle would create a situation which sooner or later would escape from German control.

Nevertheless, during a speech that excited local interest in the *Deutsches Haus* at Sigmaringen, in the presence of Abetz, de Brinon, Déat,[29] General Bridoux and the anti-Semitic writer Louis-Ferdinand Céline, the *Volksführer der Wallonen*, pleading his cause, gave full measure to his oratorical capacities. The topic of evening was: *The New Europe and the recovery of France:*

> *[...] 'The soldier is speaking to you. We shall return to our countries. We shall be the first in Brussels. Be the first in Paris! Long live France!' [...].*

Less than a month from the Ardennes offensive these words could seem premonitory of the state of mind and the excitement that the German attack would cause among the exiled collaborators.

Although the journey to Sigmaringen had ended in a complete fiasco, Degrelle had not lost hope of playing a dominant role in New European Order politics. A few weeks later, during a visit to the military academy at Kienschlag-Beneschau, near Prague, where Walloon and French candidate officers were undergoing their military instruction, he declared:

> ... "We cannot allow ourselves to simply let our German comrades free our countries from the capitalist and communist powers. We must be strong enough to be the spearhead of the troops, which will enter Brussels and Paris. I want to be on the first tank entering Brussels" ...

Then, facing the French platoon:

> ... "At Wildflecken barracks, I attended the swearing-in of your formation. I do repeat here what I said over there. What a happy choice you have made by christening your magnificent formation 'Charlemagne'. It delights me all the more, as Charlemagne was born near Herstal[30] and thus was an authentic Walloon!" ...[31]

After completing his tour, Degrelle forwarded a memorandum to the *SS-Hauptamt* summing up his arguments in favour of the establishment of a Corps West. There was no response.

The only consolation was a letter from Fernand de Brinon thanking the Walloon leader for his visit to Sigmaringen and in which he expressed the hope " ... that we consider the possibility of a complete mutual understanding, so as to get into collaboration" ...

The von Rundstedt offensive was imminent, pushing Degrelle forward to new horizons.

C. Obscure Walloon Formations

Jagdkommando Wallonien / Sonderkommando Wallonien

1. Preliminaries

In the course of the month of July 1942, Heinrich Himmler ordered the *Reichssicherheitshauptamt – RSHA* – be expanded with a special section that would be in charge of sabotage and subversive actions. This new section received the code name *Unternehmen Otto* or *Ottolagen*, and was part the *VI-F* (Technical and training centre of the *RSHA*). Dissatisfied with its results Himmler suppressed the *Ottolagen* and replaced it with a new desk, *Amt-S*, – the *S* standing for sabotage – headed by *SS-Obersturmbannführer* Otto Skorzeny.[32] When in May 1944, the *Gruppe II* (sabotage / under Col. Erwin von Lahousen[33]) of the army-tutored *Abwehr* was absorbed by the *Mil. Amt D* (*Militärisches Amt*) of the *RSHA*, Otto Skorzeny emerged as the undisputed chief of special operation forces.

Shortly before the Normandy landing, *Amt VI* planned to train stay-behind teams in case of an eventual evacuation of France and Belgium. These underground agents would then remain in radio contact with Berlin, and supply *Amt VI* with military information. This program was in the process of realization when the Allied armies landed in Normandy, obliging the Germans to modify their plans. The *RSHA* then decided to raise elite troops – *SS-Jäger Bataillone*, later *SS-Jagdverbände* – with a view to carrying out either large airborne operations behind Allied front-lines or smuggling smaller infiltration groups into enemy territory.

In the last months of the war, the leaders of the *RSHA* had to change plans once more. As the High Command intended to organize a last bastion of resistance in the south of Germany, Berlin planned to use foreign agents trained in special counter-espionage centres. These independent long-range agents were to be sent into their countries of origin in order to organize secret groups favouring confusion so as to maintain a spirit of panic and political uncertainty. Rapid Allied advances put a stop to the execution of these ultimate plans.

2. *Jagdkommando Wallonien*

In the weeks prior to the ultimate counter-offensive attempt of Field-Marshal Gerd von Rundstedt, Otto Skorzeny called in Walloons, more particularly former agents of the *Sipo-Sd*,[34] urging them to join the sabotage teams he was forming at Bad-Ems special training centre, near Koblenz.[35] It was not Skorzeny's first attempt. Already during the summer of 1944, through an intermediary,[36] he had requested Léon Degrelle part with the White Russians serving in the Assault Brigade as he intended to use them in his *Jagdverband-Ost* for special operations in the East. However, Degrelle gave Skorzeny a flat refusal. As usual, the Walloon leader was very reluctant as soon as the question of weakening his potential battle strength was put forward.[37] It was not before January 1945 that Skorzeny succeeded in interfering in Degrelle's affairs. On 30 January 1945, *Sonderführer* Nicolas Sakhnowski,[38] a White Russian, was detached from the Walloon Division with the mission to raise a special unit of individuals mastering the Russian language. After a prospecting tour which took him to Lüben, Altenburg, Bad-Wauben, Vienna, Prague and finally Berlin, where he arrived on 12 February 1945, Sakhnowski had recruited 20 individuals of whom only three or four succeeded in reaching the *Jagdkommando-Ost* as, in the meantime, the Friedenthal training centre had moved from Berlin to Bad-Reichenhall, near Salzburg.

As the idea of a *Jagdkommando Wallonien* had come to discussion on several occasions, Degrelle finally agreed. A restricted group of six people was selected and put under command of the Walloon *SS-Ustuf*. Albert Sapin.[39] On 25 February 1945, the latter received a special written order[40] from Léon Degrelle requiring that he form a sabotage team to be parachuted into the Belgian Ardennes. This order was a (very) late response to Himmler's departmental circular letter of 9 June 1944 requesting all foreign *SS* units draw up lists of volunteers for Skorzeny's special forces. These forces would be assigned sabotage missions in the rear of the Allied troops. Following Himmler's order, a list of volunteers was drawn up in every company of the Walloon Assault Brigade and forwarded to Degrelle for execution. However, in June 1944 (and the following months) Degrelle was sulky with Himmler and Berger's services on the grounds of a scheduled German take-over of the Walloon Assault Brigade,[41] the reason for which Degrelle first refused Skorzeny's request and later transgressed Himmler's plans.[42] In February 1945, the situation was different as Degrelle had become the undisputed (political and military) leader of the *28. SS-Freiw. -Gren. Div. Wallonien*.

SS-Ustuf. Sapin chose six men in the platoon he had commanded during the battle at Cherkassy and headed for Neustrelitz where he was to be briefed. The team received workers' clothes and were ordered to travel to Hamburg and wait for further orders: to blow up the railway bridge over the Meuse River at Liège.

By mid-April 1945, after a few weeks of complete inactivity, the six men disappeared leaving Sapin no other choice than to return to the Oder frontline.

The *Jagdkommando Wallonien* ceased to exist even before it had been put into action.

3. *Sonderkommando Wallonien*

On the eve of the evacuation of the Belgian territory in September 1944, *SS-Ustuf.* Otto Kraatz from the Brussels *Amt-VI* section,[43] left a stay-behind network (*I-Netz*) of fifteen Walloon and Flemish teams. Three of these fifteen teams were to be operational from September 1944 to March 1945, keeping radio contact with the main radio communication station based at Waldsee/Berlin, which in its turn transmitted the required information to the *Leitstelle Siegfried*.[44] Otto Kraatz had provided the stay-behind teams with substantial financial means.[45] At Düren/Aachen, where the Walloon *Sipo-Sd* personnel had gathered in September 1944, *SS-Obersturmbannführer* Eduard Strauch, *Kommandeur Sipo-Sd Wallonien*, carried a list of 120 Belgians who had received funds to finance their respective networks.

In September 1944, the *RSHA* centralized espionage activities in Western

Fig. 20.5. Left: Jef Van de Wiele, *Landleider of the DeVlag* and chief of the Flemish puppet government in Germany (*Collection J.-L. Roba*).

Europe in a special Department, the *Kommando-West*, of which the Marburg-based *Leitstelle Siegfried* was to cover the francophone part of Belgium. Preliminary administrative talks with Berlin took the whole month of September and half of October 1944. One of the Berlin discussion topics was an agreement (18.09.1944) between Léon Degrelle and Jef Van de Wiele, on the one hand, and Heinrich Himmler, on the other hand. Talks resulted in the programming of one Walloon and one Flemish radio communication station. The Walloon transmitter received the code name *Schreivogel* (*Brachvogel* being the Flemish counterpart) and was to be monitored from the *Leitstelle Siegfried* at Marburg. Its mission was to assist sabotage agents operating in Wallonia.

Degrelle and Van de Wiele had committed themselves to supplying the organization with men, the Berlin *VI.B.2* keeping complete control over both of the Marburg counter-espionage training centre and the missions to be decided upon.

As chief of the Walloon detachment Degrelle had no other choice than assign the disquieting *VI.B.2* candidate Charles Lambinon, former chief of the *D.S.I.* (*Département de Sécurité et d'Information* – Department of Security and Investigation), a Rexist internal police force, which, in the last month of the occupation had been heavily implicated in looting and murdering. Lambinon was put in charge of raising a *Sonderkommando Wallonien* consisting of more or less 75 men, all volunteers from the *28. SS-Freiw. -Gren. Div. Wallonien*. But as Degrelle feared interference from Berlin – Lambinon being *SD* trained – the *Chef* secretly ordered all volunteers be discouraged from joining Lambinon's unit and instead volunteer for an identical unit – controlled by Degrelle – under the reactivated former chief of the Signals platoon during the Caucasian campaign, *SS-Hscha*. Willy d'Hayer. The latter was presented a list of 60 radio-telegraph operators who had just completed a radio operator course at Vipiteno (Italy). He selected nine volunteers and left for the Lehnitz (Berlin) radio operator-training centre. As to Lambinon, checkmated by Degrelle's determination to keep entire control over all Walloon formations, he surrounded himself with the disreputable thugs of the former *D.S.I.*, all *Gestapo* auxiliaries in the *Reich*, over whom Degrelle had no authority.

When Lambinon transferred his *Sonderkommando Wallonien* from Breslau-Wohlau to Marburg (14.10.1944) he had recruited more or less 30 men. Commissioned *SD-Obersturmführer*, Lambinon was assisted by Marcel Vervloet, former chief of staff of the *D.S.I.*, and Paul Lespagnard, a long-time *Sipo-Sd V-Mann* (main agent) in Arlon/Province of Luxemburg.

During the von Rundstedt offensive, Lambinon, Vervloet and a few men showed up in the Ardennes and advanced as far as Houffalize. On their way, they visited town halls, police stations and law courts in search of documents and evidence implicating people involved in anti-Rexist activities (*i.e.* reporting non-evacuated Rexists to the police). As soon as Degrelle heard of the presence of Lambinon in the Ardennes, he personally ordered him and his men to return to Marburg without delay.

By March-April 1945, Lambinon had completed the training of three sabotage groups:

- *Groupe Téléphone* (two male agents and one female agent)
- *Groupe Ardennes* (3 male agents)
- *Groupe Meuse* (3 male agents)

None of the three groups was put into action.

Radio and spying instruction took place in three successive phases. The first consisted of a severe physical training. The candidates were also taught the practice of gathering information. During this training session, aspirants underwent a deep and thorough character and personality study. Training took place at Kolbe, Wetter-Niederwalgeren barracks and at Marburg.

The second phase focused on radio transmission. The most promising agents were sent to the *Leitstelle Siegfried* radio school housed in the *Gau Studenten Führung* at Marburg. Radio transmission training took 6 weeks. By the end of the training period, the future sabotage specialist had to be able to transmit 105 characters a minute and to receive 120. In a subsequent two week course, they were taught how to cipher and decode a message.

It was not before the third phase, when teams of three men each were formed, that Heinz Völlker[46] made them familiar with specific espionage techniques.

Seven groups (3 Flemish, 3 Walloon and 1 independent[47]) were planned to be dropped into Belgium by the Dora squadron stationed at Wiesbaden. However, during a mission in Egypt, this unit had lost most of its planes so that it was not able to fly in the Belgian agents.

4. Epilogue

Albert Sapin was made prisoner on 3 May 1945. Condemned to death by firing squad, his death penalty was commuted to hard labour. Like most of Degrelle's officers, Sapin was released from prison in the early 1950s.

By the end of April 1945, *SS-Hscha*. d'Hayer and his men from the Lehnitz radio-training centre evacuated towards Munich and surrendered there.

In the last days of April 1945, Lambinon, Vervloet, Lespagnard and others fled from Marburg, heading for Italy. Vervloet and most of his companions were arrested in the north of Italy, Lambinon slipping through the meshes of the net. He was never discovered.

Lespagnard was arrested near Munich on 23 January 1946. Sentenced to the death penalty, he was executed by firing squad on 3 June 1948.

D. The Von Rundstedt Offensive

A few days before the German attack through the Ardennes, Degrelle, together with other leaders of the European collaboration, attended the final sitting of the Congress of the European Press in Vienna where he gave a speech on the theme of National Socialism:[48]

> ... "Nowadays, speaking of Europe is no longer the point; the point is how to save Europe. To save Europe means to establish a new Europe on a National Socialist pattern. Only Germany can realize this. Fate gave her this great opportunity" ...

Apart from the Swedish and Spanish journalists, all the other delegations present had fled to the Reich: the French delegation was represented by Marcel Déat and Jean Luchaire, the Walloon one by Léon Degrelle and former journalist of the *Pays Réel SS-Ostuf.* Jean Vermeire.[49] On his way back to the division, Degrelle broke his journey at Berlin and took accommodations at the *Adlon* hotel where he was informed of the German offensive.

On 17 December 1944, one day after the start of the operation *Wacht am Rhein,* Victor Matthys, Degrelle's deputy chief of the Rexist Movement in Belgium who had fled in September 1944, organized a spectacular meeting in Hildesheim, the hometown of the Rexist evacuees. For the first time since they had arrived on German soil, a revival of Rexist political activities was openly discussed as a forthcoming German military success was being expected.

The next day the *Kommandeur* of the Walloon division attended two important meetings: first at the *Führungshauptamt* (Hans Jüttner), the second at Gottlob Berger's *SS-Hauptamt.* Jüttner's services informed Degrelle that the Walloon formation was put on stand by position with a view to assuring the maintenance of order in reoccupied Belgium. By way of consequence, Degrelle was ordered to move his troops westwards. At the *SS-Hauptamt* Matthys was informed that the evacuated Rexist politicians were given permission to return to Belgium and resume their political activities.

The announcement of the offensive was the sign for von Ribbentrop to restart diplomatic activity.[50] He assigned Roland Krug von Nida, civil servant with the rank of Minister, and State Counsellor Keyn, with the administration of Belgian (Walloon) affairs.

Following Berger's orders Matthys decided that the Rexist politicians would regroup at Gummersbach, near Cologne, and wait there for the events to develop.[51]

The aforesaid preliminary discussions resulted in two telegrams issued on 19 December 1944. The first came from Himmler's General Headquarters and mentioned that the *28. SS-Freiw. -Gren. Div. Wallonien* was to be attached to Army Group B (under Field-Marshal Walter Model), as a reserve force of the *6. SS-Pz. Armee* under *SS-Oberstgruppenführer* Sepp Dietrich. At the same time, via the Department of von Ribbentrop' s Foreign Office, Degrelle was given limited powers to act in the Walloon territories, which were expected to be reconquered by the Germans.[52]

When Degrelle finally arrived at Gronau he informed his *Ia* (officer of operations) – and second in command – *SS-Sturmbannführer* Frans Hellebaut – that ... "the cities of Liège, Namur and Huy had been captured, that Brussels was about to be occupied and that the Panzer spearhead troops were pushing towards Antwerp (...) that Belgium would not be occupied any longer but would be liberated" ... and, hardly controlling his excitement, Degrelle added that he ... "would be the first in the Ardennes".[53]

Fig. 20.6. Career officer of the Belgian Royal Army, Frans Hellebaut (18.01.1898) was the son of a General and grandson of a Minister of Defence. At the age of 16 he volunteered for WWI and eventually attended the Royal Military School and Staff College as well (*Ecole de Guerre*). By the outbreak of the WWII, he served as Chief of Staff of the 2nd Inf. Div. Prisoner of war until the end of May 1944 when he joined the *5. Freiw. -Sturmbrigade Wallonien*. Hellebaut was strongly opposed to a Walloon military intervention on the Western Front (*Doc. F. Hellebaut. Arch. E. De Bruyne*).

On 22 December 1944 Degrelle left for Cologne where he planned to meet *Gauleiter* Josef Grohe.[54] Former head of the civil administration of Belgium and northern France (*Reichskommissar für Belgien und Nordfrankreich*), in July 1944 he had replaced General *Freiherr* Alexander von Falkenhausen's military administration; Grohe had been put in office again on the very first day of the German attack.

In Wipperfürth/Cologne Degrelle also met Rexist Julien Carlier. Since September 1944, the latter had been running the Walloon radio broadcasting station *'Radio Wallonie'*. Degrelle put Carlier in charge of the Rexist propaganda in Wallonia.

Degrelle's next planned visit was with Sepp Dietrich, whom he met at Marmagen (Nettersheim) on Saturday afternoon, 23 December 1944.

In the meantime, the local military transport services (*Transportkommandantur*) had informed *SS-Sturmbannführer* Frans Hellebaut that ten trains would be ready at Gronau and Else railway stations on 24 and 25 December, the coaches bearing the inscription *Brüssel über Lüttich* (Brussels via Liège).

Degrelle's sudden departure for the Rhine had placed Hellebaut in a critical situation.[55] The motives which had pushed Hellebaut to join the Legion were fundamentally different from those that once had animated Degrelle. The Belgian career officer wondered what could be the military motives for such a sudden movement, which completely disorganized the articulation and the training of the division, which were still in progress. Actually, the Belgian career officer was less worried by the tremendous difficulties of raising a division than by the ethic and legal aspects of a Walloon presence on the Western Front. Hellebaut openly expressed the opinion that an intervention in the Ardennes was in flagrant opposition with the basic principles of the reason for the existence of the *Légion Wallonie*: the anti-Bolshevik struggle at the Eastern Front.

Considering that it was necessary to dissipate what Hellebaut thought to be a regretful misunderstanding, *SS-Oberführer* Nikolaus Heilmann, the German field officer supervising the military instruction of the Division, offered to back up Hellebaut's objections against the deployment of Walloon troops in the West. In the evening of 23 December 1944, both men left for Cologne and eventually succeeded in discovering – on Christmas day at 2:00 *a.m.* – Field-Marshal Walter Model's operational command post hidden in a forest near Münsterfelde. Their minds were set at ease immediately: the Field-Marshal's Chief of Staff was unaware of the arrival of Walloon forces! A telephone call to the Berlin *OKW* confirmed that a Walloon participation in the military operations had never been planned. As a matter of fact, the mission that the *Reichsführer-SS* had assigned to Degrelle was only a political one. The *Feldgendarmerie* received the order to block Degrelle's escort when it arrived at the Belgian border.

Degrelle's escort (under *SS-Hstuf.* Henri Derriks) arrived at Nettersheim, near the Belgian border on 24 December and stayed there until the *6. SS-Pz Armee* got rid of the Walloon forces on 6 January 1945, by detaching them to *XII SS-A.K.* of the *15. Armee*.[56]

In the end, if Degrelle could take about ten men into the Ardennes (elements of 3rd platoon of 1st Company under Stavelot-born *SS-Hauptscharführer* Maxime Havet) he owed it to Sepp

Fig. 20.7.

Dietrich from whom the cunning Degrelle had wrung 'local' facilities.

On 25 December, Dietrich's headquarters moved to Meyerode, near St-Vith. So did Degrelle. Together with his personal guard and a newly arrived Walloon Signals group (whose mission it was to establish communication liaison between Dietrich's HQ and the Walloon leader), he arrived at Steinbach, on Belgian territory.

Present at Steinbach were: Léon Degrelle; *SS-Ostuf.* Roger Wastiau (Signals officer); *SS-Ustuf.* Raymond Camby (orderly); *SS-Ustuf.* Tony Gombert (orderly); *SS-Ustuf.* Robert du Welz (Supply officer); *SS-Ostuf.* Paul Suys (once assisting chief *Rex-Vlaanderen*); *SS-Hscha.* René H ... (second in command of the Signals group); Degrelle's personal protection squad and *SS-Hstuf.* Karl Schaeffer, German orderly and Himmler's spy.

On 1 January 1945, a coach transporting Rexist politicians arrived at Limelé, with Victor Matthys heading the delegation.

On 2 January 1945, Degrelle moved to Limerlé, too. He was to stay there until 7 a.m., 10 January 1945

During his presence in the Belgian Ardennes, while waiting for the Germans troops to drive to the Meuse River, Degrelle spent his time visiting Sepp Dietrich's HQs and reading the *Mémoires de Honoré, valet de Chambre de Napoléon*, a book that he had discovered on one of Mr Dufourny's bookshelves.[57]

Between 2 January and 10 January 1945, Degrelle's entourage grew bigger by the arrival of:

- a group of Walloon war correspondents
- a second group of Rexist politicians (3 January)
- the rest of 3rd platoon of *1/I/69Rgt* under *SS-Ostuf.* Henri Thyssen
- Catholic Chaplain (Padre *Gérard*) who was to celebrate the mass on 7 January
- Paul Mezzetta, chief of the *Jeunesse Légionnaire*.

A *SD* squad led by Charles Lambinon showed up (3 January) but was sent back immediately.

But the main event occurred on 6 January 1945 when the widow of a local Rexist politician showed up at Degrelle's headquarters. She told Degrelle her husband had been arrested in La Roche and had committed suicide in prison after ill-treatment. As this had happened under

Fig. 20.8. Degrelle's car was left behind at Limerlé.

the authority of the local mayor, Degrelle decided to arrest Baron Jean Orban de Xivry, mayor of Laroche. Paul Mezzetta, Paul Suys and Robert du Welz were assigned the mission to capture the Baron. This operation took place on 7 January 1945. The Baron was locked up in the cellar of the Limerlé HQs as Degrelle intended to hand him over in return for his sisters, who had been imprisoned, too.[58]

During the next few days the Baron was questioned on a number of subjects: the political situation in Belgium after the Rexists had fled, the fate of one of Degrelle's uncles residing in La Roche, activities of the Resistance, etc.

Early in the morning of 10 January 1945, Degrelle left the Ardennes for other horizons.

E. Degrelle's Spanish Volunteers

During the autumn of 1944, Degrelle was restlessly in search of increasing his numerical strength. The idea of a new division to be established with the nucleus of the Flemish *6. SS-Sturmbrigade Langemarck* not only worried Degrelle, it also stimulated him as it was clear that Degrelle, for political reasons, could not lag behind his Flemish rivals. It was even more important that Degrelle could line up his division before the Flemish! Politically, it was a must as this was also an important matter of personal prestige.

In spite of Frans Hellebaut's scarcely disguised skepticism, quite aware as he was of the technical difficulties that such a project would generate, Degrelle stuck to his idea of commanding what he hoped to be a division.[59]

This was the very moment when the enlistment of Spaniards came up for discussion.

Two Belgian legionnaires serving in the *Wallonie*, Alphonse Van Horembeke and Paul Kehren, both veterans of the Francoist armies during the Spanish civil war, were entrusted with the recruiting campaign among the Spaniards residing in the Reich.[60]

After the *Division Azul* and the subsequent Spanish Legion had been disbanded, a number of Spaniards, for different reasons, did not to return to Spain.[61] Some of them worked for the Sauckel or Speer organizations, others tried to enrol into the *Wehrmacht*,[62] and some had been imprisoned on grounds of unauthorized and illegal stay in Germany.

By the end of March 1944, Alphonse Van Horembeke, at that moment a clerk in the Provincial Delegation of the Phalange Youth Front at Vizcaya/Spain, was asked to take care of the Spaniards scattered all over the Reich. The plan consisted in sending two confidential agents to Germany with the mission to contact as many Spaniards as possible with a view to enrolling them into the *Waffen-SS*, more particularly the Flemish *27. SS-Frw. Gr. Div. Langemarck*. The Flemish formation had been chosen above any other unit because the *Azul* and the *Langemarck* had been engaged side by side on the Leningrad front from 1941 to 1943. Together with his companion, Juan Beltrán de Guevera, Van Horembeke arrived at Versailles-Paris where his comrade left him to join a group of Germans and Rumanians, leaving Van Horembeke in the lurch.[63] Nevertheless the latter continued the mission on his own and reported at the *Langemarck* enlistment office in Lichterfelde West/Berlin. As he spoke neither German nor Flemish, he was advised to enrol in the *Wallonie*.[64]

On 7 July 1944, Van Horembeke entered *Heidelager* (Debica/Poland) barracks[65] and ran across Paul Kehren, his former comrade-of-arms from the 4th Bandera.

By the end of July 1944, Van

Horembeke was incorporated in the *Kampfgruppe Ruelle* called up to operate in Estonia. There, Van Horembeke had the opportunity to inform Degrelle of his initial mission, which consisted in providing social and welfare duties among the Spanish civilians working for Sauckel and Speer in order to convince them to join the *Waffen-SS*. Degrelle immediately understood the advantages he could derive from this situation. Since Spaniards needed welfare care, there could be no better place for them than ... the *Wallonie*!

A new mission awaited Van Horembeke: to recruit Spaniards for the *Wallonie*.

After the Estonian campaign Degrelle joined Breslau headquarters. There he informed an as much skeptical as astonished Frans Hellebaut about his plans: to raise a ... regiment of Spaniards! Accomplishing this important task fell to Van Horembeke and Kehren.

Meanwhile, the *Azul* and Spanish Legion veterans who had enrolled in the *Wehrmacht* had been sent to Stablack Süd barracks and were to meet new recruits arriving from France. A few months later they were transferred to the *Waffen-SS*.[66]

From April 1944 on, Spanish clandestine volunteers crossing the Pyrenees gathered at Lourdes, Perpignan or St-Jean-de-Luz.[67] A special unit, the *Sonderstab F*,[68] with HQ at Versailles/France, centralized the induction of Spanish volunteers into the *Werhmacht*. At the *La Reine* barracks, 5, Rue Carnot, in Versailles, the volunteers were welcomed by Louis Garcia Valdajos, an *Azul* and Spanish Legion veteran, detached from Stablack training centre to coordinate and escort the first contingent to Stablack barracks. Noteworthy is the fact that later contingents leaving Versailles were directed to Hall Tyrol/ Austria rather than to Stablack.

Valdajos took an administrative role in the military instruction of the recruits from 20 April to 6 June 1944, Miguel Ezquerra being in charge of the drill and tactics. Valdajos then went back to Paris again to attend an *SD* course after which he was sent to the Normandy front with an officer's rank. Before retreating with the German troops from France he also participated in anti-partisan operations against Spanish republican maquis along the Pyrenees. In September 1944, Valdajos joined Dr Faupel's[69] office to take care of Spanish affairs.

After the Estonian campaign, Van Horembeke and Kehren started their recruitment tour through the *Reich*, visiting plants, workers' camps, and other places where Spaniards could be met. Their tour took them to Linz/Austria where the two men came across an Austrian Francoist veteran who informed them about the presence of Spaniards at Stockerau/Vienna barracks.[70] These men had been incorporated into a Croatian unit against their will, among them Juan Beltrán de Guevars. Dissatisfied with their situation as second rank soldiers, having lost the ranks they had held in the *Azul* or the Spanish Legion, they found no difficulty in deserting the Croatian formation. Van Horembeke succeeded in recruiting a first group of 36 Spaniards and sent them to Alfeld, seat of the Walloon division since the end of October 1944. A few days later this group was sent to Hemmendorf/Oldendorf and joined other Spanish volunteers who had

Fig. 20.9. Two Walloon officers were in daily contact with the Spanish volunteers. One was SS-*Ustuf.* Rudi Bal (†Lübow 06.03.1945), the other being SS-*Ustuf.* Albert Steiver, who survived the war. Here he is (right) during a ski session after completing the *11. Kriegslehrgang* at Bad Tölz. The man on the left is *SS-Ustuf.* Jean Roman, L. Lippert's brother-in-law. He was to become Degrelle's liaison officer to the *SS-Hauptamt* in Berlin (*Doc. A. Steiver/Collection E. De Bruyne*).

enrolled spontaneously. A second Stockerau group was to be recruited a few days later by Beltrán. The first group comprised a number of NCOs like Pedro Zabala, Ocañas,[71] Cabrejas, Vadilio and others who immediately recovered their respective ranks.

During the following months Van Horembeke was to continue his recruiting tour, this time in company with Beltrán.

On 8 December 1944, patron saint's day of the Spanish infantry, the Spanish volunteers of the *Wallonie* honoured the Alfeld population with a *corrida*.

In the meantime, in the course of October 1944, Valdajos (like Ezquerra, a *SD*-officer, and not a regular *Waffen-SS* officer) had met Léon Degrelle at the *Adlon* Hotel, his usual *pied-à-terre* in Berlin. On this occasion Degrelle availed himself of the opportunity to entrust him with the administrative organization of a Spanish unit within the Walloon division:

> « Es encargado por el jefe de la división Valona Léon Degrelle de la organización dentre de la division de una unidad Espanola como jefe de la misma con la categoria que obstentaba. »

From October to 11 December 1944, Valdajos was busy with administrative matters relating to the instruction of the Spanish unit involving frequent trips to the general *SS* headquarters in Berlin. However, Valdajos accompanied the Walloon division when it was sent to the Rhine during the von Rundstedt offensive. From January 1945 on, he resided most of the time in Berlin leaving the command of the *3/I/70* to one of his subordinates.

After the Krüssow disaster (12.02.1945) where more or less 75% of the Spanish company was annihilated, Valdajos was sent to Postdam where he was to take command of an *Einsatz Gruppe*. In his service record Valdajos claims he participated in the battles for the defence of Spandau, Tempelhof-Potzdammerplatz area.

Valdajos survived the Berlin combats, hid in the Spanish embassy on 10 May 1945, and reached Spain in December 1945 after crossing Germany, Holland, Belgium and France.

The Spanish volunteers were grouped in the *3/I/70Rgt* under the command of (*Ostuf.*) Valdajos, the Walloon SS-*Ustuf.* Rudi Bal acting as liaison officer. In fact, Valdajos, as an administrative officer with duties in Berlin, was replaced by one of his platoon commanders, *Hauptscharführer* Bottet.[72] Two other *Hauptscharführer* (La Puente and Ocañas)[73] completed the cadre.[74]

Whereas some authors[75] mention the number of 350 to 400 Spaniards as having served in the *Wallonie*, a detailed account by *SS-Ustuf.* Albert Steiver, former deputy commander of the *I/70Rgt*, shows the following:[76]

> During the von Rundstedt offensive, 40 Spaniards (from Hemmendorf/ Oldendorf) under Valdajos accompanied the Walloon division to the Western Front
>
> A group of 40 Spaniards in disparate uniforms escorted by a German *Feldwebel*, arriving from Berlin and bearing individual route orders,[77] joined the *Wallonie* at Stettin on 3 February 1945. They were accompanied by a second group of 60 more or less well-equipped Spaniards bearing a collective route order signed by a Walloon officer operating in Berlin[78]
>
> The next day, another 120 Spaniards arrived at Stargard railway station coming from Vienna.

On the eve of the Pomeranian campaign, the *Wallonie* had available 240 (20 had been refused as temporarily unfit[79]) instead of a whole regiment, as announced by Degrelle in September 1944!

The Spanish recruits were immediately sent to the frontline on the Ihna River position (south-east of Stargard), participated in the first combats of the division (more particularly at Krüssow on 12 February 1945) and got involved in the bitter defence of Stargard. Only 60 Spaniards escaped the encirclement of Stargard

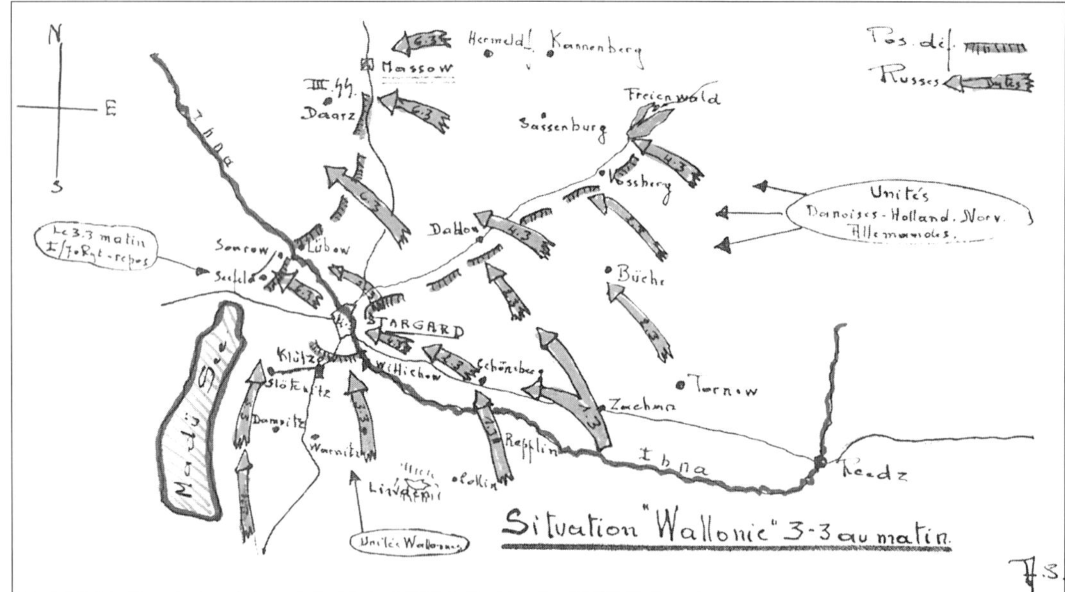

Fig. 20.10. A post-war hand-drawn chart by A. Steiver. Situation on 3 March 1945. As CO of the *1/I/70* and *Kdr a. i.* of the *I/70*, he defended the Seefeld area, north-west of Stargard (*Doc. A. Steiver/ Arch. E. De Bruyne*).

(4 March 1945). The survivors were regrouped at Scheune (south of Stettin).

By mid-March 1945, the Flemish *Langemarck* and the *Wallonie* were attached to the *XXXII Armee Korps*. At the same time, the Walloon command received the order to transfer the remainder of its Spanish forces to the III Germanic *Panzerkorps*.

1. Epilogue

One might wonder what happened to Degrelle's former Spanish volunteers.

The Spaniards, among them Van Horembeke, were ordered to Berlin where they were to form an *Einsatz Gruppe*. Initially Valdajos had been designated to command that unit but as he was more of a society gentleman than a frontline officer he suggested Ezquerra[80] be put in command of what was to be known as the *Einsatz Gruppe Ezquerra*. This unit was composed of the last volunteers who had refused the offer to be repatriated as foreign workers. Only a handful of older volunteers, a few sick and light casualties were evacuated by Beltrán who succeeded in escorting them as far as Rome where they found a hiding-place in a convent until their return to Spain.

Ocañas participated in the battle for Berlin and defended the neighbourhood of the Excelsior cinema-hall near Alexander Platz until 28 April 1945, the date of his capture by the Soviets. He was repatriated to Spain on the SS *Semiramis*.

The *Einsatz Gruppe Ezquerra* was engaged around the Chancellery bunker and buildings of the Air Ministry. On 1 May 1945, the remainder of the *Einsatz Gruppe* defended the Steglitz underground station and desperately tried to link up with the remainder of the *Gross Deutschland Wacht Rgt* holding the Alexander Platz underground station. They could not achieve this as Soviet infiltration blocked the Friedrich Straße underground station.

On 2 May 1945 the *Einsatz Gruppe* fell apart. All volunteers had been given a Spanish passport and false documents stating they were foreign workers.[81] Taking off their uniforms and getting rid of all military documents the Spanish tried to make their way through so as to avoid capture by the Soviets.

Van Horembeke was taken prisoner. Seeing what happened to the Spanish volunteers (one of his comrades was shot for having declared he was Spanish), he declared himself to be Belgian.

On transit from camp to camp he finally arrived at Kovno POW camp. After the visit of an Allied Commission Van Horembeke was sent back to Belgium. He was tried by the Military Court of Brussels and sentenced to 20 years imprisonment. In prison he taught his fellow prisoners Spanish. Liberated in the early fifties, Van Horembeke returned to Spain and obtained Spanish citizenship.

F. The Pomeranian Campaign

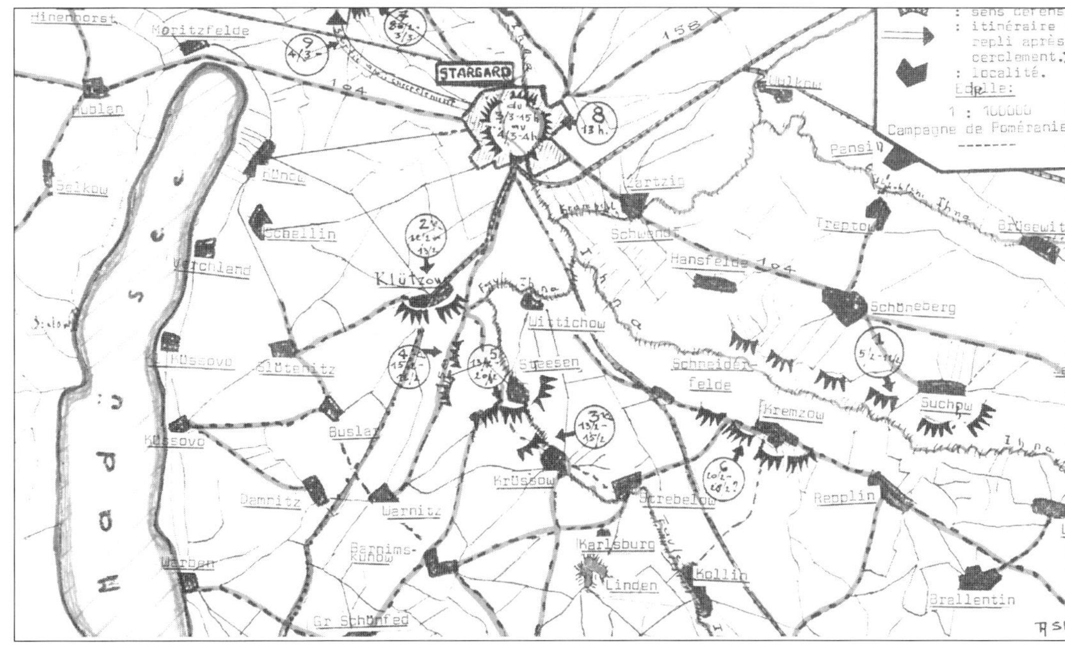

Fig. 20.11.
(Doc. A. Steiver/ Arch. E. De Bruyne)

1. Stargard

Since January 1945, a powerful Soviet offensive across the Vistula River had driven deeply into the German defence system in the Warsaw and Bromberg area. Soviet armoured corps had penetrated into the heart of the German *Warthegau* and had reached the Oder River in some places. Complete German armies were flowing back in disorder while a few of their best divisions had let themselves be overrun and were holding strategic points.

The Walloon division disembarked at Stettin on 2 February 1945, and was immediately sent to the town of Stargard threatened by the Soviet advance. The *Wallonie* was to engage the following forces along the Ihna River:[82]

- The Derriks Bn (*I/69*), with the mission of defending Kremzow
- The Lakaie Bn (*II/69*), with the mission of defending Kollin and Strebelow
- The Denie Bn (3 companies of the *I/70*), with the mission to defend Schöneberg
- The *PAK* and *FLAK* Companies
- A Signals Company

A total of 1,800 to 2,000[83] men in liaison with a *Pz. Gren. Rgt* of the *10. SS-Panzer Division Frundsberg* on the right and the *Langemarck* on the left.[84]

A few local and limited actions by the Walloons soon were countered by violent Soviet artillery fire and, on 12 February Soviet tanks succeeded in investing the vicinity of Krüssow. A counter-attack led by the *5/II/69* stabilized the situation for a short moment but its commander *SS-Ustuf.* Rudi Bal was killed during the action. In the meantime, the 1st and 3rd Companies (Spanish) of *II/70* had been called in as reinforcement to cover the only escape

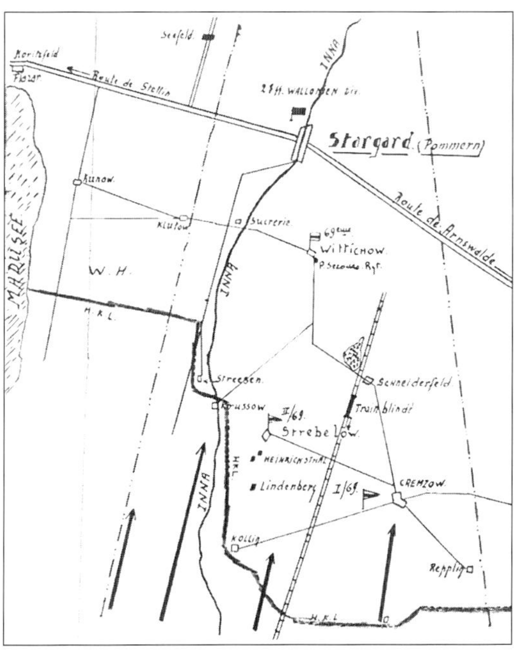

Fig. 20.12.
(Doc. F. Hellebaut/Arch. E. De Bruyne).

route via Wittichow. A counter-attack led by a battalion of the *Frundsberg* having failed, the remainder of the Walloon forces withdrew into the swamps around Streesen.

Although the situation in the sub-sector *Wallonie* had become rather critical, the protection mission, imposed on 5 February to the *Wallonie*, had been fulfilled successfully. The time gained had allowed the German High Command to undertake important indispensable strategic transport between Stettin and East Prussia.

In mid-February 1945 important reinforcements arrived on the frontline and General Steiner was ordered to resume the operational initiative in order to liberate the encircled town of Arnswalde.[85]

In this important operation the Walloons were given an offensive mission, which consisted of a diversionary attack on Lindenberg. On 16 February, the *7/II/69* under *SS-Ostuf.* Jacques Capelle achieved this operation successfully. Orders were to hold the position for 24 hours. The next day, overwhelming Soviet forces attacked the Walloon position. Capelle and his men were annihilated on the spot after having resisted for 27 hours. *SS-Ostuf.* Capelle and *SS-Ustuf* Jacques Poels were killed, the latter while attacking a tank with a *Panzerfaust*. The whole operation cost 2 officers and 52 men. This feat of arms was mentioned in the dispatches of the Armed Forces (*Wehrmachtbericht*).

Hard resistance by the Soviets forced Steiner to cancel his offensive. Moving backwards, the *Nordland* and the *Langemarck* Divisions were charged with holding a new defence line along the Ihna River while the *Wallonie*, in liaison with the *322. Div.*, occupied the frontline between Kremsov and Streesen.[86]

On 19 Februay 1945, the Walloon subsector was transferred to the authority of the *Nordland*.

Walloon positions were as follows:

- *I/69* at Kremzow
- *II/69* at Strebelow-Krüssow
- *I/70* in reserve of the *III/24* (Danish) at Kremzow
- Combat post at Schneiderfelde

By 1 March 1945, the Soviets had achieved a vast enveloping movement around the German lines near Stargard.

In position in front of Krüssow the Walloon forces found themselves in the same position as on the Olschanka River (Cherkassy): isolated on a salient with the delicate mission of rearguard combats, fighting delaying actions.

On 3 March, the majority of the *Wallonie* was concentrated on the Wittichow plateau.

In spite of all around pressure, there was nothing else to be done than to stick to a few square kilometres on the Wittichow plateau with the risk of being cut off. As a consequence of this development a new grouping was necessary on the Schneiderfelde-Streesen heights. The Lakaie Bn curled up towards the left of the 2nd echelon at Schneiderfelde, the Derriks Bn resumed the defence of the Streesen positions so as to assure a robust support, covering the last retreat road to Klützow and to keep contact with the *322. Div* while the remainder of the Denie Bn was sent to Seefeld, northwest of Stargard.

On 4 March 1945, the Derriks Bn was attacked by surprise. Only an immediate, determined and cool-headed intervention by *SS-Ustuf.* Bervaes[87] (*4/I/69*) saved the Bn from being annihilated.

First Company (*SS-Ustuf.* André Régibeau) was holding an advanced position between Streesen and Krüssow, 2nd and 4th Companies being entrenched in Streesen village. During the morning, the German defences on the outskirts of Stargard were overrun by Soviet infantry and tanks. At around midday, tanks managed to penetrate into the city and engaged in bitter fighting in the streets. 1st Company had to face a strong attack in front of Streesen, which caused the death of 12 men and 36 other casualties. *SS-Ustuf.* Régibeau, although wounded twice, refused evacuation during the combat. *SS-Oscha.* Mezzetta[88] and Fraikin were mortally wounded. Platoon CO *SS-Hscha.* Pierre Hancisse managed to hold his positions until 2:00 p.m. in spite of heavy losses. A bit farther, Soviet infantry tried to make a passage through the swamps north of Wittichow, threatening the positions of the *Wallonie*. *SS-Ostuf.* Henri Thyssen, together with a handful of volunteers, successfully held them off till the evening. Telephone communications with the HQ of the *Wallonie* headquarters were broken off. At 4:00 p.m., the city of Stargard was definitively lost. A new attack in front of Streesen obliged 1st Company to retreat to the village.

The mission allotted to the *Wallonie* was to hold at all costs the position Wittichow-Streesen until 10:00 p.m. so as to allow the retreat movement of the German units, the artillery and the train.

Another group of volunteers succeeded in containing Soviet pressure west of Stargard, on the road to Moritzfelde until midnight. Meanwhile Soviet troops tightened their grasp everywhere. Stargard was on fire in the north. Around 7:00 p.m., the train and the wounded left Wittichow via the last open road from Klützow to Künow, jammed by the train of the *322. Inf. Div.* The Derriks Bn evacuated Streesen and, echelon by echelon, retreated towards Klützow. Around 9:50 p.m., the Lakaie Bn and the *Wallonie* headquarters abandoned Wittichow.

SS-Ostuf. Dr. Med. Robert Buy and *Padre* Gérard, the Catholic divisional chaplain, thanks to repeated individual actions, managed to evacuate all the severely wounded. At 1:00 a.m. (5 March), the Derriks Bn, serving as an ultimate rearguard force, was still holding the Klützow crossroads, allowing the last German forces to escape Stargard from the south.

On 5 March 1945, the remainder of the *Wallonie* regrouped at Moritzfelde.

A new urgent mission awaited them: to return to Seefeld, 4 km north-west of Stargard, and take up position between Saarow and Lübow. Only 116 men of *I/69Rgt* and even less from the *II/69Rgt* reached Seefeld in time. Hellebaut and Mathieu (*69Rgt*) established their HQs at Brückhausen, next to *Oberstleutnant* Strelow (*322. Inf. Regt*) who was in charge of the area. In the meantime, Degrelle had joined the divisional (*322. Inf. Div*) HQ at Friedrichswalde.

On 6 March 1945, at dawn, the Lakaie Bn, positioned at Lübow (only one-third of the battle strength was left and 9 officers had been killed or injured), was attacked by surprise and completely annihilated. Only a handful of legionnaires under Thyssen and Gillis were able to resist as they were covered by shelling from the Derriks Bn on the other bank of the Ihna River. Soon Saarow was attacked too and Soviet forces drove into the Walloon positions, forcing the different companies to retreat urgently. Régibeau, who had stayed on in the positions until the very last moment, could only save his life by swimming across the ice-cold Ihna River, followed by Soviet infantry shooting at him.

Derriks and his officers regrouped a part of their men at Brückhausen in most difficult conditions. The Brückhausen position was in no way defendable. The terrain offered no protection, and *Nordland* and the *322. Inf. Div.* could not offer any support despite repeated desperate requests by Hellebaut. The orders were: to hold the positions at all costs! Mathieu's Command Post was shelled and as a result all telephone communications were cut. Moreover, in the meantime, Derriks had sustained a bullet wound in the knee and had been replaced by Marcel Bonniver. The remnants of the *I/69*, 250 men in all, tried to resist the Soviet pressure, in vain. At 6:00 p.m., Hellebaut ordered Bonniver to withdraw during the night and regroup at Friedrichswalde where they were to join the rear-guard of the *Nordland*.

2. Altdamm

In spite of successive setbacks, the *III.(germ.) Pz. Korps* had retained a certain cohesion. Thanks to skillful delaying actions it avoided a general collapse. The right flank (Lake Madü) was secured thanks to the resistance of the *281. Inf. Div.* (General Ottner) and two Walloon battalions, the left flank being covered by the *SS-Pz. Div. Frundsberg*, which had been dispatched on the spot coming from Greifenhagen, west of the Oder River.

Meanwhile Zhukov had ordered his

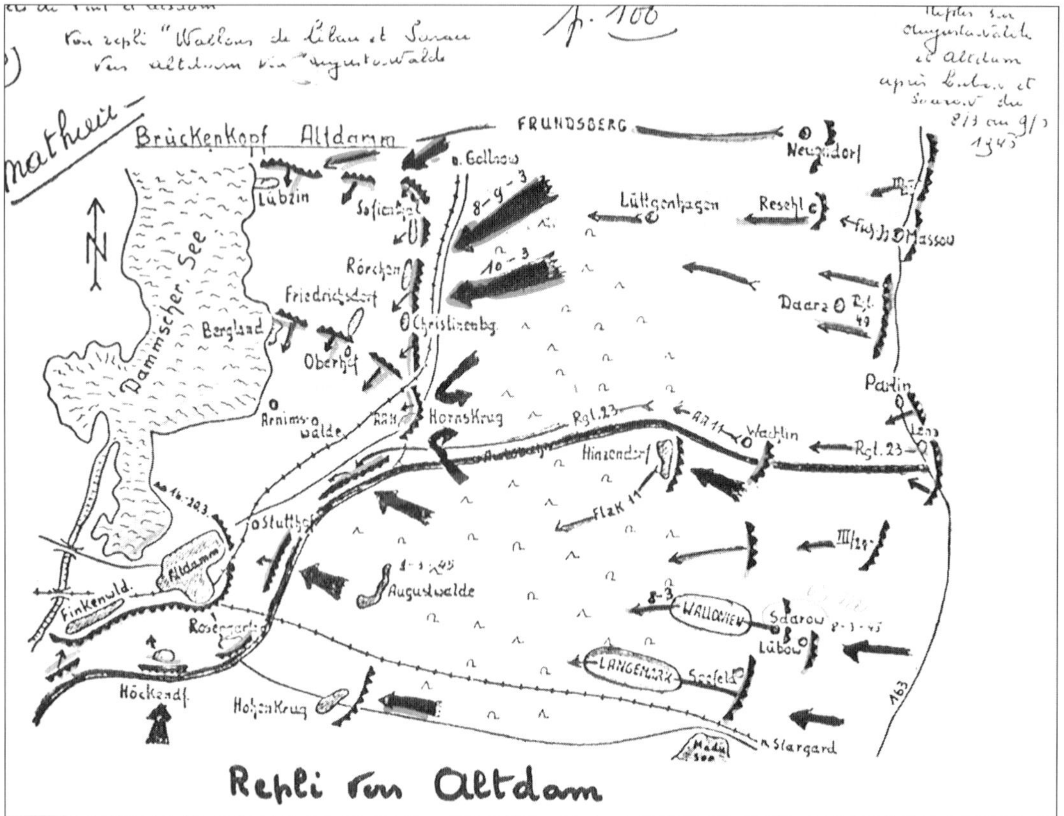

Fig. 20.13. Retrograde movement towards Altdamm (6–10 March 1945). Post-war hand-drawn chart by J Mathieu. (*Doc. J. Mathieu/ Collection E. De Bruyne*).

61st Army to overpower Altdamm by a double enveloping attack, and to cut the retreat of the *III.(germ.) SS-Pz. Korps*.

Since the start of the Pomeranian campaign the *Wallonie* had lost 125 men killed, with 7 of its officers and more than 200 men becoming severe casualties. Nine *s. Pak* and 12 *Flak* guns had been destroyed or abandoned. A greater part of the heavy weapons were lost, light infantry equipment had been abandoned during the successive combats, the train reduced to a few vehicles, and hundreds of Walloons were scattered all over the area, having lost contact during the difficult nightly retrograde movements.

A few days of rest was absolutely necessary. The Walloon division, now reduced to *Kampfgruppe* size, was sent to Scheune/Stettin (west of the Oder), where the auxiliary non-combat forces of the *Wallonie* had been grouped for recovery.

Despite a vigorous speech by Degrelle himself, most survivors had become demoralized and expressed the feeling they had done more than enough, that further engagement was useless ... Only a nucleus of hardcore legionnaires was found ready to continue.

On 12 March 1945, *SS-Hstuf.* Henri Derriks, nicknamed the *Boss* by his men, having recovered from his wound, gave a speech ending as follows:

> " ... those who have the guts, step forward!"

Twenty-three officers and 625 men lined up.[89]

The new unit, called *Kampfgruppe Derriks*, was raised at Bismarck. It was allotted 400 rifles, 150 *St. Gew. 44*, 60 *l. Mi. 42*, 4 *s. Mi 42* and 16 mortars (*m.Gr.W.* 8 cm) taken from the disbanded formations.

The *Kampfgruppe Derriks* was organised as shown in the shaded box on page 161:

The non-combatant forces of the *Wallonie*, under *SS-Hstuf.* Mathieu, were sent to Bergholz where they stayed until

Fig. 20.14. By the end of March and April 1945, Degrelle did not share frontline life with his men any longer. His visits to the frontline were sporadic. Here is a propaganda shot showing Degrelle among his men in the trenches. (*Arch. E. De Bruyne*).

3 Assault Companies:

1st Company	*SS-Ustuf.* André Régibeau
1st Pl	*SS-Ustuf.* Daniel Wouters
2nd Pl	*SS-Hscha.* Pierre Hancisse (wounded 17.03.45)
3rd Pl	*SS-Hscha.* Maxime Havet (wounded), Chavanne (wounded), *SS-Ustuf.* Jacques Leroy.
2nd Company	*SS-Ustuf.* Mathieu De Coster
1st Pl	*SS-Ustuf.* Jean Piron
2nd Pl	*SS-Ustuf.* Maurice Deravet
3rd Pl	*SS-Ustuf.* Abel Delannoy.
3rd Company	*SS-Ostuf.* Léon Gillis
1st Pl	*SS-Ustuf.* Eduard Serlet,
2nd Pl	*SS-Ustuf.* Jean Hallebardier
3rd Pl	*SS-Ustuf.* Gé. Pé. (wounded).
4th Company (heavy weapons)	*SS-Ostuf.* Henri Thyssen, comprising an assault platoon (former *Flak* Company), a platoon *s. Mi 42* and 2 platoons *m.Gr.W.8;*
1st Pl (*Stoßreserve*)	*SS-Ustuf.* Roger Gondry comprising 4 groups of 12 men (2 *le.M.G.* + *M.K*)
2nd Pl	*SS-Ustuf.* Georges Suain (4 *s.M.G.*)
3rd Pl	*SS-Ustuf.* Louis Bervaes (4/8cm mortars)
4th Pl	*SS-Ustuf.* René Serlet (†18.03.1945)

Totaling 60 *le.MG* 's, 4 *se.MG.42*, 150 *St.Gew.44* and 16 mortars (8cm)

the end of April 1945. As to Degrelle, he had his personal command post installed in the local castle of Brüssow belonging to the von Mackensen family, 30 km west of Stettin. From now on, apart form sporadic appearances among his men, he stayed in the rear area as matters relating to the end of the war absorbed him.

On 14 March, the armies of Zhukov resumed attacking the Altdamm bridgehead defended by Gen. Unrein.

In the afternoon of 15 March 1945, the *Kampfgruppen Wallonien* and *Langemarck* were placed on the alert and sent to Stettin.

On 16 March, Derriks and his men had reached the rallying point at the Stettin docks.

The situation was desperate. The remainder of the *SS-Pz. Gren. Rgt24 Danmark*, more or less 50 men (its commander *SS-Ostubaf.* Krügel had been killed at the Aldamm railway station combats) were relieved by 2 Flemish companies.[90] The *Pz. Rgt. 10* (*Frundsberg*), whose CO, *SS-Ostubaf.* Otto Paetsch, had also been killed,[91] only had a few tanks left.

On 16 March, in the evening, the Walloon battalion received the order to reinforce the *281. Inf. Div.* (General Ottner) entrenched between Altdamm and Höckendorf.[92] The Walloons were ordered to secure a 1,200 metre gap as far as the road to Stargard. Derriks dispatched 1st Company (Régibeau) to Rosengarten, 2nd Company (De Coster) was given the mission to link up with German forces on the left, 3rd Company (Gillis) being held in reserve behind the railway embankment, while 4th Company (Thyssen) took position on the left across the railway.

1st Company lined up at 1:00 a.m. and

Fig. 20.15. Stettin docks (*Futterfabrik*), 16 March 1945, only a few hours before going into action. *SS-Ustuf.* André Régibeau, CO/1st Company and his 3rd platoon CO, *SS-Ustuf.* Jacques Leroy, severely mutilated at Cherkassy. Note that *SS-Ustuf.* Leroy is wearing an NCO belt buckle, probably because this was the belt buckle he wore during his re-education and was easier to unbuckle for an one-armed man than an officer's one. The very young men right and left are Régibeau's despatch riders, Robert Thuillez (left, a Frenchman from St Omer) and Marcel Leplae (right), coming from the *Jeunesse Légionnaire*. (*Doc. A. Régibeau/Collection E. De Bruyne*).

deployed in the fields along the Rosengarten woods, its left flank towards the Aldamm sugar refinery. The position relieved by 1st Company was held by a *Wehrmacht* company, which was reduced to 20 men. 2nd Company followed in support. 3rd and 4th Companies took position in the sandy hills and on the railway embankment, between the Aldamm railway station and Finkenwalde, and constituted a second echelon of resistance and anti-tank obstacle.

By daybreak, the position of 1st Company appeared very critical: without cover or entrenchments, it underwent a frontal attack by Soviet forces emerging from the surrounding forest. Régibeau and his men had dug themselves in and resisted under a violent shelling, suffering substantial losses. A group of Walloons (*SS-Ustuf.* Leroy), overrun by Soviet tanks, not only withstood the Soviet infantry for 72 hours but succeeded in freeing itself by destroying several T34's. For this action *SS-Ustuf.* Leroy was to be recommended for the Knight's Cross.[93]

In the course of the afternoon, Régibeau succeeded in extricating himself and his men, having lost a quarter of them (30 men), and was put in reserve, 2nd Company taking over.

During the night the Soviets intensified their pressure forcing 2nd Company into heavy defensive combats during which several Soviets tanks were destroyed.

Intense artillery shelling marked the day of March 18th. 2nd Company retired to the railway embankment positions. Massive concentrations of fire were directed on all artillery and infantry positions. The *SS-Pz. Div. Frundsberg* defended inch by inch the hills east of Finkenwalde while the two small mortar platoons of 4th Company countered Soviet attack preparations. In the meantime *SS-Ustuf.* René Serlet of 4th Company had been killed. *SS-Hstuf.* Derriks established his new command post in a cellar east of Aldamm. In the evening, the essential positions had been

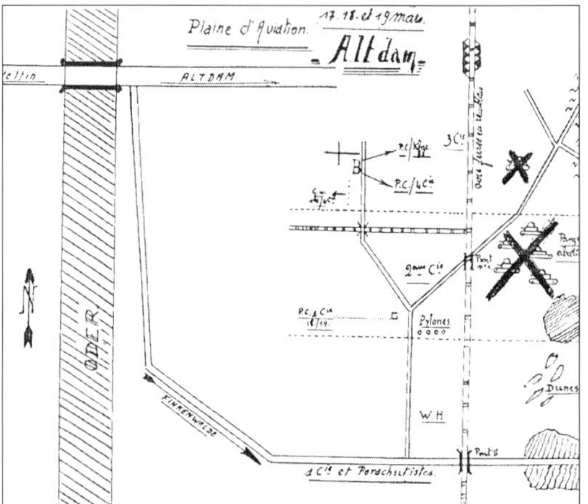

Fig. 20.16. Deployment of the four Walloon companies during the Altdamm fighting. (*Arch. E. De Bruyne, via R. Devresse*)

maintained, once more at the cost of heavy losses.

On 19 March, the Soviet forces carried all their efforts on the right flank at Finkenwalde and Podejuch, where decisive battles were about to be fought. These villages were crushed by terrible bombardments and could not be secured. Groups of isolated men were rounded up by the *Feldpolizei* and sent back to the frontlines. Whoever retired without permission exposed himself to a *Standgericht* (Field Court Martial), that is: immediate sentence by hanging from the nearest tree.

However, at 10:00 p.m., the Walloons received permission to withdraw from the Altdamm bridgehead via the main railway bridge, the very last to exist over the eastern Oder.

During the 72 hours of combat the *Kampfgruppe* had lost 110 men. SS-*Ustuf.* Hallebardier, Liènart, Gé. Pé. and *SS-Hscha.* Pierre Hancisse were wounded.

3. *Oder ist Hauptkampflinie – H.K.L.*

By 22 March 1945, the Walloon battalion was sent to *Gut Schmagerow*, 20 km west of the Oder for rest and refitting.

The day before, *Reichsführer-SS* Heinrich Himmler had been removed from his command of Army Group Vistula and replaced by *Generaloberst* Heinrici.

On the main line of resistance (*H.K.L.*), a thin curtain of mist ensured the positions remained free of enemy surveillance. The whole Pomeranian army (*Pz. Armee Oberkommando 3 / Pz. A.O.K. 3*) under *General der Panzertruppe* Hasso von Manteuffel had suffered severely but was refitting actively in the region west of Stettin. The civil population and hundreds of thousands of evacuees were fortifying the area as far as the line Pasewalk – Prenzlau.

Hellebaut's combat post was established at Gut Salzow, 2 km south-east of Löcknitz. More or less 1,000 legionnaires were gathered at Bergholz under Mathieu, waiting for new developments while Degrelle still had his personal CP (*Stab Degrelle*) set up at von Mackensen's castle at Brüssow and was feverishly preparing what many of his men, after the war, would consider as a 'French leave'.

In the meantime, the *Wallonie* and the *Langemarck* had been attached as a tactical reserve to the *XXXII.A.K.* (Schack) occupying the Politz sector, north of Stettin, and actively participated in the fortification of the Pozlow-Seehausen sector.

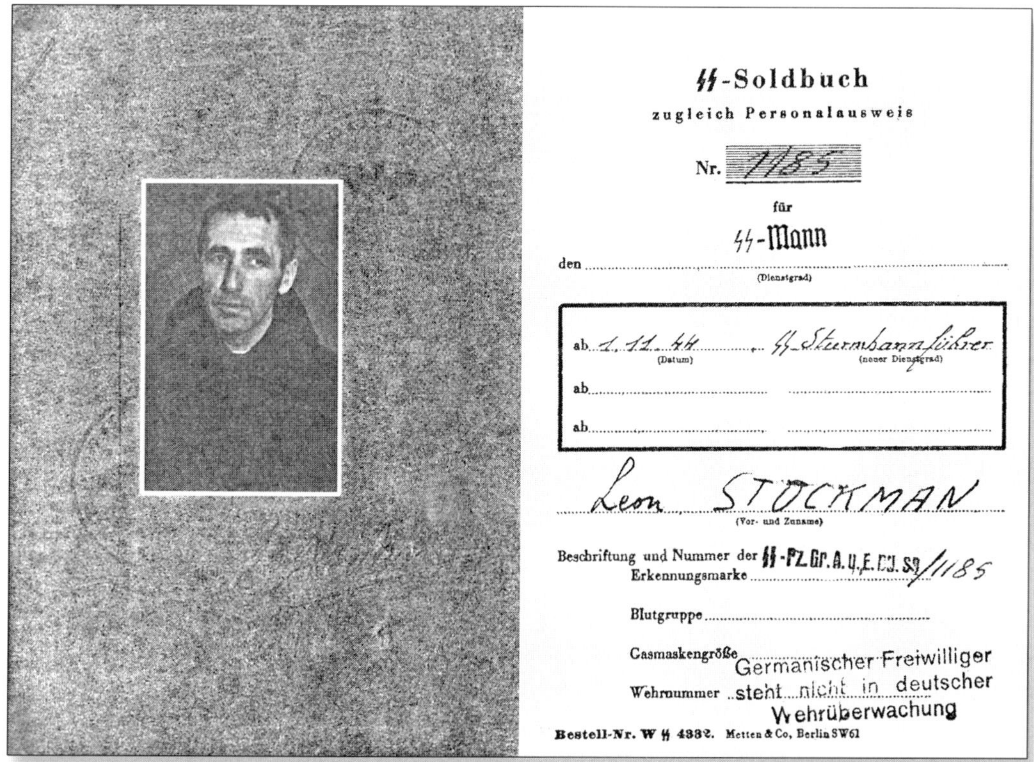

SS-Soldbuch
zugleich Personalausweis
Nr. [illegible]
für
SS-Mann
den .... (Dienstgrad)
ab 1.11.44 (Datum) SS-Sturmbannführer (neuer Dienstgrad)
ab ....
ab ....
Leon STOCKMAN
(Vor- und Zuname)
Beschriftung und Nummer der Erkennungsmarke SS-Pz.Gr.A.u.E.[illegible]/1185
Blutgruppe ....
Gasmaskengröße ....
Wehrnummer Germanischer Freiwilliger steht nicht in deutscher Wehrüberwachung
Bestell-Nr. W SS 4332. Metten & Co, Berlin SW61

Fig. 20.17. As Reverend Father *Gérard* (Léon Stockman) of the abbey of Chimay was suspected of Rexist sympathies and in order to protect him from being assaulted by the Resistance, the abbot sent him to Brussels in August 1944. In the Belgian capital city, Gérard Stockman was asked to take spiritual care of the Walloon legionnaires, an offer that he accepted. (*Private collection*).

On 1 April 1945, Padre Gérard, divisional Catholic Chaplain and *SS-Sturmbannführer*, celebrated the Easter mass.

The next day, several hundreds of Walloon workers, who had been forced to enlist into the Division during their stay in the *RWAD* (*Reichswallonischer Arbeitsdienst*, the Walloon section of the *Reichsarbeitsdienst*) camps arrived at Schmagerow. As to a man they refused to serve in the Division they were ordered to dig anti-tank ditches at Löcknitz under the surveillance of *SS-Hstuf.* Jean Vermeire, Degrelle's former liaison officer in Berlin. The artillery detachment in formation at Seltchan/Bohemia also arrived (without its guns), followed by the *Pi. Btl.* under *SS-Ostuf.* Mirgain, coming from Hradiscko/Bohemia. The personnel of the *Ers. Btl. 36*, which had been driven back by the advance of the Allied forces, were directed to Schneideberg (30 km south of Prenzlau) and also participated in the fortification preparations.

On 15 April, the partially trained *II/69 Rgt* at Löcknitz, under *SS-Hstuf.* Jean Vermeire, was sent into reserve at Randowsbrück. The other part of the *II/69 Rgt* regrouped the final volunteers for the last combats at Bismarck barracks under *SS-Hstuf.* Marcel Bonniver. In that way the *69 Rgt* was built up again, comprising more or less 900 men under *SS-Stubaf.* F. Hellebaut, the *I/69* under Derriks and the *II/69* under Bonniver.

On 15 April 1945, the remaining Walloon and Flemish combat units were placed under the general command of *SS-Standartenführer* Thomas Müller, commander of the *27. SS-Frw. Gren. Div. Langemarck*, with Conrad Schellong commanding the *Kampfgruppe* at the front.

On 17 April 1945, the *69 Rgt* was sent to Pomelen (Derriks) and Hohenholz (Bonniver), a few kilometers from the banks of the Oder, ready to intervene whenever the situation required it.

On 20 April 1945, the Soviets launched an attack between Kürow and Schillerdsdorf.

A new *Kampfgruppe* under *SS-Stubaf.* F. Hellebaut comprising three battalions,

Fig. 20.18. In October 44, Henri Derriks was in charge of the military instruction at the Wohlau-based *Ers. Btl. 36*. Here he is welcoming new recruits, among them very young members of the *Jeunesse Légionnaire*. The *Adjutant* on the left with sabre is *SS-Ostuf.* P. Dengis. The two Walloon officers are accompanied by *SS-Ostuf.* Dr Oetzmann (left), the German welfare officer of the Walloon division. The *Wehrmacht* officer next to Derriks is *Hptm* Pohl, drill officer of the Walloon *NSKK* and G.W. (*Collection J.-L. Roba*).

one Flemish (*SS-Hstuf.* Jan De Mulder) one Walloon (*SS-Stubaf.* Derriks) and the Pomeranian *Kolberg Btl* was constituted in the course of the morning of April 20th with the mission to reoccupy Hühnenberg (De Mulder), Derriks received the order to invest Neu-Rosow and throw back eventual Soviet infiltration coming from Schillersdorf, with the *Kolberg Btl* being invested with a similar mission at Schöningen.

SS-Stubaf. Derriks' Battalion, also known as *Kampfgruppe Derriks* (number two), was organised as shown in the shaded box on page 165.

In the afternoon of 20 April 1945, Derriks had reached Neu-Rosow and it immediately was reported that Soviet infantry was infiltrating the area. Together with Hellebaut, who had arrived on the spot for inspection, he decided to launch a counter-atttack. 3rd Company, under *SS-Ostuf* Léon Gillis, managed to occupy a favourable firing position without being spotted. While Gillis stopped the Soviet advance, 1st Company (*SS-Ustuf.* Régibeau) and 2nd Company (*SS-Ustuf.* De Coster) quickly reached the outpost of 3rd Company and resolutely launched a successful counter-attack, immediately followed by 3rd Company and 2 platoons of 4th Company, taking 50 to 60 prisoners. In the meantime, Soviet artillery had come into support and shelled the Walloons, obliging them to dig in. By 4:45 p.m., after a 2 km advance, 1st Company had reached the outskirts of Schillersdorf but had lost contact with 2nd Company. However, the Oder was in sight at about 500 metres distance.

The temptation was great to reach the river! Régibeau and his men bravely attacked again, but it proved to be a

Kommandeur	*SS-Stubaf.* Henri Derriks
1st Company	*SS-Ustuf.* André Regibeau (wounded 20.04.1945)
1 Pl	*SS-Ustuf.* Daniel Wouters (†20.04.1945)
2 Pl	*SS-Ustuf.* Jacques Leroy (wounded 20.04.1945)
3 Pl	*SS-Hscha.* Maxime Havet (†20.04.1945)
2nd Company	*SS-Ustuf.* Mathieu De Coster (wounded 22.04.1945)
1 Pl	*SS-Ustuf.* Jean Piron (wounded 20.04.1945) replaced by *SS-Oscha.* Raoul Roland
2Pl	*SS-Ustuf.* José Görtz (†21.04.1945)
3 Pl	*SS-Ustuf.* Roland Devresse
3rd Company	*SS-Ostuf u. Ritterkreuzträger* Léon Gillis
1. Pl	*SS-Ostuf. Gé. Pé.* (wounded on 21 and 23.04.1945)
2 Pl	*SS-Hscha.* Lucien Lambert
3 Pl	*SS-Hscha.* Fidèle Hendrickx
4th Company	*SS-Hstuf.* Henri Thyssen (†20.04.1945), replaced by *SS-Ustuf.* Monfils
1 Pl	*SS-Ustuf.* Roger Gondry
2 Pl	*SS-Ustuf.* Charles Monfils
3 Pl	*SS-Hscha.* Hector Landucci (†23.04.1945)

bloody action. This time the Soviets had pulled themselves together and riposted with machine-gun fire from the upper floors of the first houses of Schillersdorf, obliging the Walloons to dig themselves in once more. At the very moment that platoon CO *SS-Ustuf.* Daniel Wouters was attempting to bypass this nest of resistance, enemy fire nailed him to the ground. A Soviet counter-attack failed but the Walloon officers and leading NCOs, due to snipers, fell one after the other. SS-*Hscha.* Maxime Havet had been killed; *SS-Ustuf.* Jacques Leroy and *SS-Scharführer* Georges Piessevaux[94] were wounded. Régibeau, trying hard to replace them, skipped from bush to bush, encouraging his men or helping to put under cover the most badly injured ones. All of a sudden, Régibeau collapsed, seriously wounded in both thighs. It was his third injury in six weeks,[95] the eighth since he had arrived on the Eastern Front. *SS-Ustuf.* Wouters – 21 years old – took over command of 1st Company.

In the meantime, 3rd Company (*SS-Ostuf.* Gillis), reinforced with the platoon of *SS-Oscha.* Hector Landucci (4th Company) had moved forward so as to fill the gap between 1st and 2nd companies but could not achieve its goal. Thyssen, who was to be promoted *SS-Hstuf.* that very same day, offered to restore liaison with the remainder of 1st Company. A few moments later, he was shot dead by a sniper.

The situation was serious on the right flank. The weakened 2nd Company had been stopped along the road to Schöningen and 3rd platoon CO, *SS-Ustuf.* José Görtz, had been killed. It still had to cover 800 metres of open terrain before reaching the enemy positions. 2nd Company's commander had no news from his platoon CO, *SS-Ustuf.* Roland Devresse, whose mission it was to drive the Soviets out from the dunes along the Oder. Despite all efforts, he and his men had been blocked 1 km south of Schillersdorf.

By 5:00 p.m., the Assault Btl *Kolberg* had arrived, and its *Jagd-Pz Komp.*

(Glöckner) quickly progressed through the dunes towards Schillersdorf, freeing the Walloon companies from their difficult position. However, the Soviets were not long in returning fire. 3rd Company, which had taken advantage of the Kolberg unit's action to move on, was definitely halted.

General Hasso von Manteuffel was determined to continue the counter-attack efforts and by the end of the afternoon 3 battalions of the *27. SS-Frw-Gren. Div. Langemarck* had been sent in reinforcement in the Schöningen-Greifenberg sector.

In the meantime, the Walloons prepared themselves for passing the night in their positions. Farther north, nightly combats had driven the Soviet forces back to the Oder River banks with the result that the German command once more ordered Konrad Schellong of *Kampfgruppe Langemarck* to reoccupy Hühneberg.

Frans Hellebaut was to coordinate the action of the Walloon, Flemish and German forces. This third attack was due at 4:00 a.m. on 21 April. An artillery preparation scheduled to last two hours was limited to 10 minutes during which only a few *s. Flak 8.8*cm salvoes were fired.

The Walloon Bn deployed on a 500 metre wide frontline and headed for Schillersdorf. The three companies were: 3rd Company with about 30 survivors of 1st Company and the Landucci platoon to its left, 2nd Company with the Gondry platoon on the right and the support of five *Panzer* and two *m. Gr. W.*, plus elements of 4th Company. Gillis was quickly halted by intense shelling after

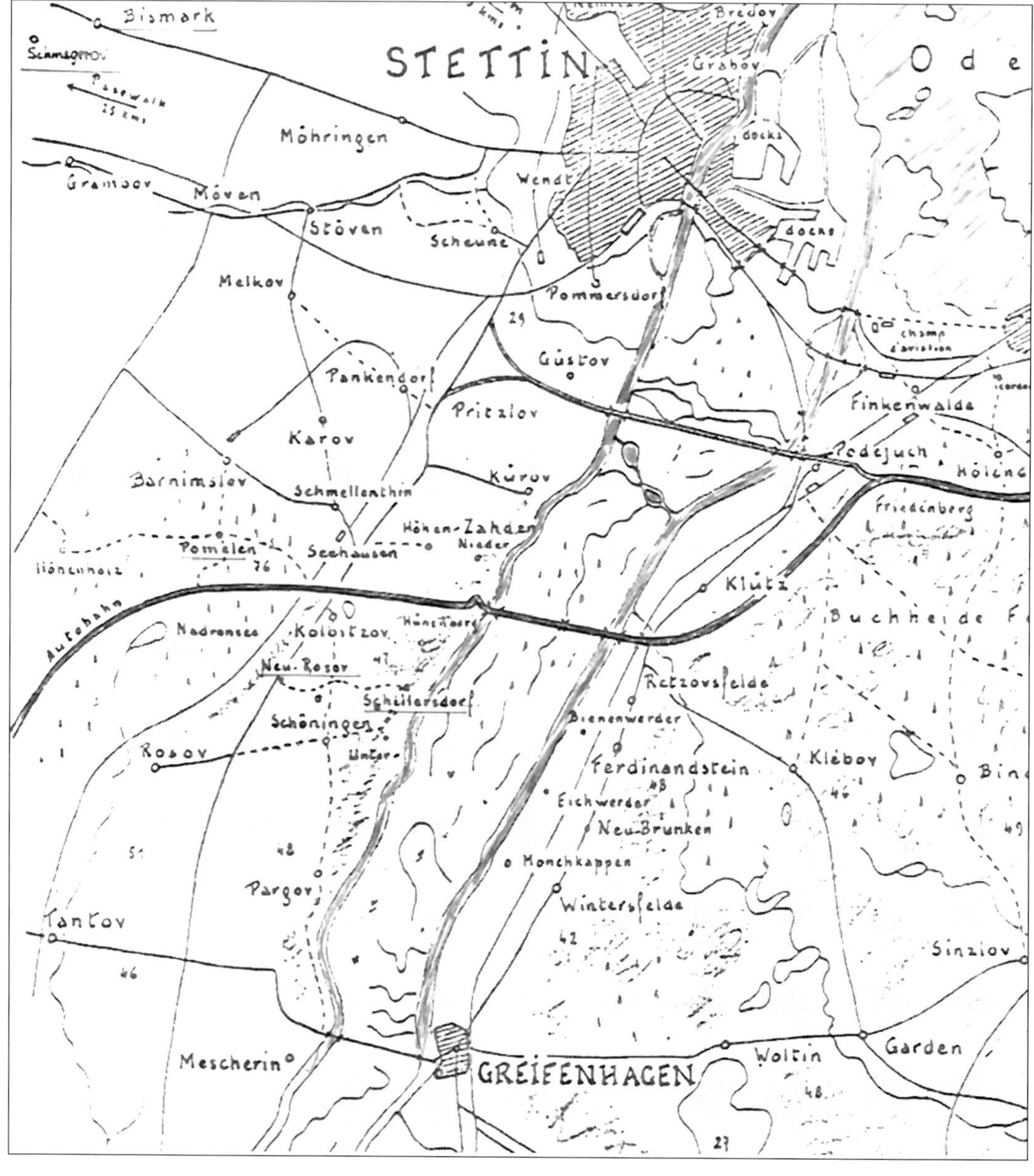

Fig. 20.19. Post-war hand drawn chart by F. Hellebaut. (*Arch. E. De Bruyne*).

Fig. 20.20. During the post-war trials, a *Soldbuch* was an incriminating document. Roland Devresse survived the war and managed to keep his *Soldbuch* out of the hands of the Belgian Justice. Promoted SS-*Ustuf.* on 20 April 1945 he had this promotion entered in his *Soldbuch* during his captivity on 5 May 1945. (*Doc. R. Devresse. Arch. E. De Bruyne*).

an advance of 100 metres. De Coster's Company managed to cross a rather long distance in spite of heavy flank firing. When he reached the Soviet lines there were only 15 men left. However, they had to return to their night-time positions, bringing back their wounded and dead.[96]

At dawn, it was clear that the attack was a complete fiasco as liaison with both the Flemish Bn on its left and the Kolberg on its right had been lost. In the afternoon, the main Soviet effort had moved northwards and threatened Kolbitzov and Neu-Rosow obliging Hellebaut to withdraw the Walloon Bn (reduced to 130 more or less fit men) to the initial Neu-Rosow positions of the day before.[97] During the night Derriks and his men crossed the highway Berlin-Danzig and reached the better protected Pomelen.

The next day, 22 April 1945, relentless fighting continued around the Oder River positions. Mixed units of the *Langemarck* and the *Wallonie* resisted desperately. At around midday, a fraction (2 incomplete companies) of the partially regrouped Derriks Bn resumed artillery support positions in the dunes of Neu-Rosow. The *7/II/69* under *SS-Ostuf.* Graff, dispatched in reinforcement at Rosow, became engaged and suffered heavy losses.

During the night, as enemy activity had calmed down in the sector, Schellong authorized that Derriks' exhausted men be sent back to Pomelen, on the condition a rearguard of 20 men stayed on the spot until the scheduled relief. These 20 men were all volunteers: *SS-Ostuf.* Gé Pé, *SS-Ustuf.* Albert Verpoorten, Jean Hallebardier, Roland Devresse[98] and Roger Gondry, SS-*Hscha.* Hector Landucci, SS-*Scharf.* Bayard and Van Malderen and 12 men.[99] In the morning of April 23, the Walloon rearguard was sent to Neu-Rosow, which had been abandoned by a group of *Jg. Pz*, and pushed back several Soviet infantry advances. Within a few hours, 10 men had been killed or wounded. Hector Landucci was killed at 3:00 p.m. A few moments later a grenade exploded in the ditch where Gé Pé, Verpoorten and two dispatch riders had been sheltering, killing the two couriers and mortally wounding Verpoorten. Although seriously wounded, Gé Pé was to survive! At 4:00 p.m., only four Walloons were left in the positions: Gondry, Devresse, Van Malderen and Quinaud! Shortly after, they received the order to join 7th Company.

The *Kampfgruppe* Schellong was disbanded due to lack of battle strength. The last Walloon units then joined the non-combatant Bn at Bergholz.

On 24 April 1945, all Walloons had been regrouped in the Brüssow-Wollshow area and sent in reserve behind the Ücker River, north of Prenzlau.

4. Rearguard battle at Schöningen-Prenzlau

While the train and the non-combatant units were marching west from April 26th onwards, the remainder of the two Walloon battalions of *69 Rgt* took position behind the Ücker River. Their task was to defend Bandelow (2nd and 3rd companies of *I/69*), Trebenow (HQ and *Pi. Btn.*) and Schönwerder-Ellinen (5th, 6th and 8th companies of *II/69*).

During the night of 26/27 April, Prenzlau was attacked by Soviet armoured troops who were resisting at the western outskirts of the city. The Bonniver Battalion (*II/69*) had been occupying Schönwerder for several hours together with a Bn of the *Wehrmacht*. At around midday, a group of Soviet tanks showed up coming from the Prenzlau-Neu-Brandeburg main road, but was stopped in front of the improvised anti-tank obstacles. At the beginning of the afternoon, Soviet infantry attacked Schönwerder village from the south and the east. Taking advantage of the weakness of a *Wehrmacht* company, the Soviets managed to surround the village.

Two Walloon platoons (*5/II/69 – SS-Ustuf.* Foulon and de Backer de Réville) counter-attacked at once and engaged in house-to-house combat. In hand-to-hand fighting *SS-Ustuf.* Count de Backer de Réville was mortally wounded as a handful of volunteers cleared the houses with hand grenades, while Soviet rocket launchers systematically shelled the place.

At 6:00 p.m, the Walloons were allowed to resume their retreat.[100]

On 28 April 1945, the Walloon formation, now as a general reserve of *III. (germ.) Pz-Korps*, began a 5 day retreat march towards Schwerin via Woddeck-Neu-Brandenburg-Zahren, Stavenhagen, Nachin, Krakow, Damerow, Klein Poserin and Krivitz.

On 1 May 1945, the American army of the Elbe reached Lübeck and Schwerin. At 1:00 p.m., as a result of a local armistice, the Anglo-Americans entered Hamburg.

On 3 May 1945, at 10:30 a.m., 400 veterans of the *Kampfgruppe Wallonien*, among them many wounded legionnaires, grouped in good order under Hellebaut and Derriks, appeared in front of Schwerin. A few moments later they were taken prisoner.

A few days earlier Degrelle had disappeared, leaving his men behind: … important matters awaited him.

Uscha. DEVRESSE, Roland.

NAHKAMPFTAGE

d.	Tag	Ort	Unterschrift
1	21. 6.42	Burkanowo	
2	24. 6.42	Ferma	
3	10. 7.42	Krasni-Liman	
4	17. 8.42	Apscheronskaja	
5	19. 8.42	Pruskaja	
6	21. 8.42	Tscherjakow	
7	22. 8.42	"	
8	23. 8.42	"	
9	24. 8.42	"	
10	4. 9.42	Ostmailowka	
11	9. 9.42	Kubano-Armiansk	
12	28.10.42	Psisch	

also 12 Nahkämpfe die als 5 Nahkampftage gerechnet werden. (gem. A.H.H. vom 7.12.42, 1030,8b)

d.	Tag	Ort	Unterschrift
6	22.12.43	Irdjin	
7	4. 1.44	Sakrewka	
8	14. 1.44	Teklino	
9	15. 1.44	"	
10	17. 1.44	"	
11	6. 2.44	Starosselja	
12	7. 2.44	"	
13	8. 2.44	Derenkowez	
14	9. 2.44	"	
15	10. 2.44	"	
16	11. 2.44	"	
17	13. 2.44	Nowo-Buda	
18	15. 2.44	"	
19	16. 2.44	"	
20	17. 2.44	Percée	
21	18. 2.44	"	

Fig. 20.21. R. Devresse counted 12 Close Combat days before the Close Combat Clasp was introduced by the end of 1942. New stipulations meant that those 12 days only counted for 5 days. The entries are signed by *SS-Ostuf.* Robert Denie CO/ 3rd Company. Note that the Close Combat days for the Schilldersdorf counter-attacks (April 20–23, 1945) are not entered. The total would then have been 24 Close Combat days. (*Document Roland Devresse. Arch. E. De Bruyne*).

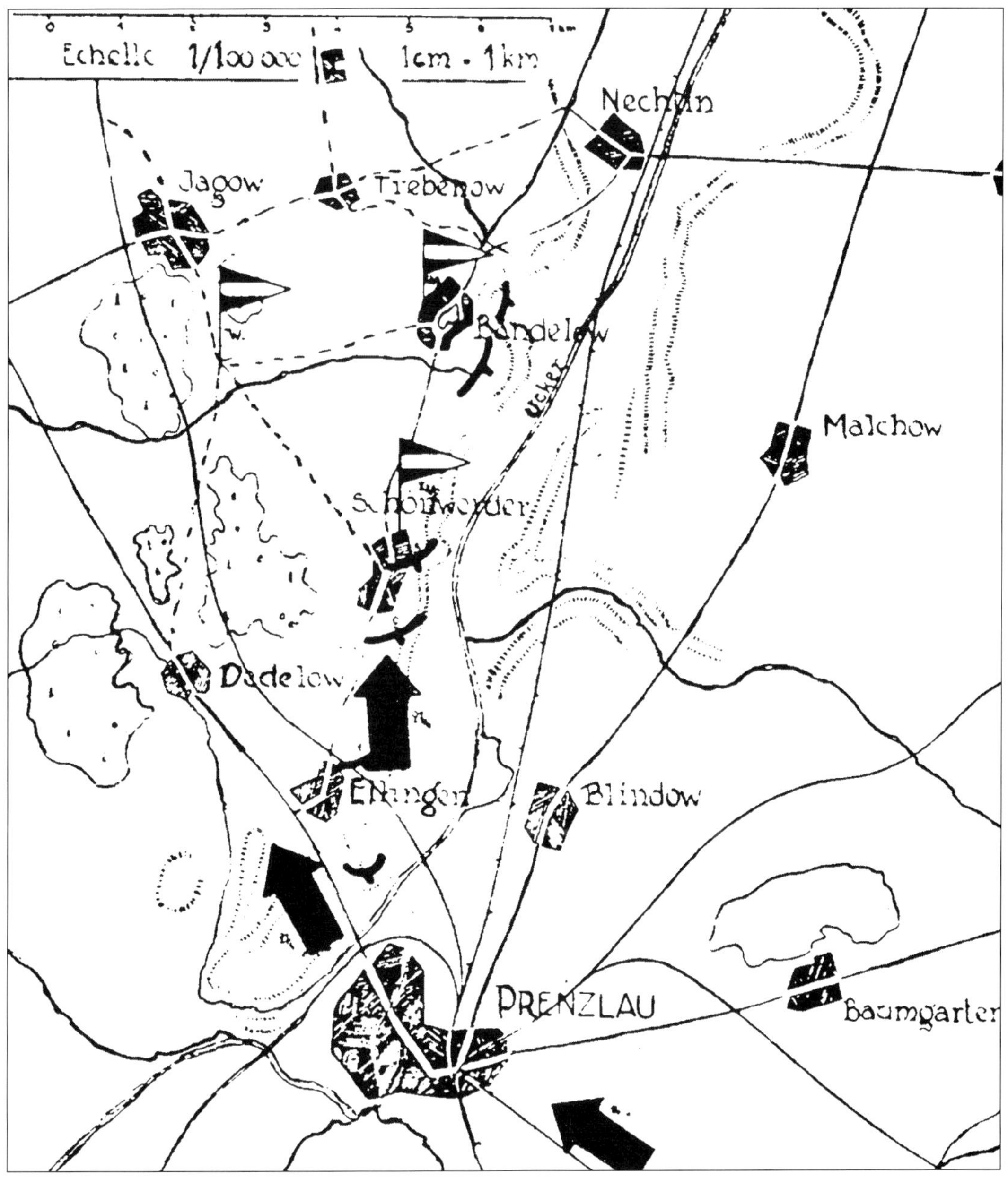

Fig. 20.22. Chart by F. Hellebaut. (*Arch. E. De Bruyne*).

CHAPTER XXI

The Lost Game

A. *Exit Léon Degrelle*

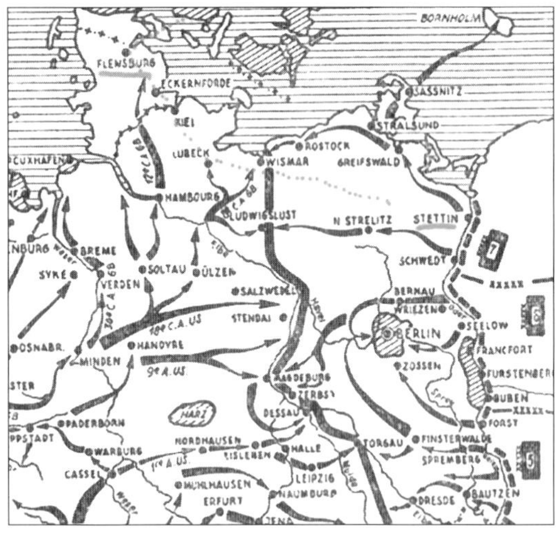

Fig. 21.1. Doc. J. Mathieu showing Degrelle's escape route (*Arch. E. De Bruyne*).

On 24 April 1945, Degrelle made his last appearance amongst his men.[1] That day, at Pomelen, he presided over a short award ceremony, many decorations being presented posthumously. Degrelle was to stay in the battle zone until 28 April 1945.

The day before he had ordered Dr Heinz Forsteneichner to personally take care of mysterious heavy suitcases. Then, without notifying Hellebaut, he left Zahren castle at dawn on 28 April 1945, together with SS-*Ostuf.* Charles Generet, *SS-Ostuf.* Robert du Welz, Degrelle's orderly, *SS-Ostubaf.* Hahn,[2] *SS-Ostuf.* Jules Sandron,[3] *SS-Ustuf.* Fl. E ... and *SS-Ustuf.* Willy Graide.[4] However, Graide and E ... already left the group the following day.

On 29 April 1945, on his way to Lübeck, at Nossinger-Hütte, Degrelle had a last conversation with *SS-Standartenführer* Müller, commander of the *SS-Divisionsgruppe Müller*, regrouping the remainder of the *Langemarck* and the *Wallonie* since the end of April 1945. The conversation focused on the fatal outcome of the fighting and on what had to be done to re-establish contact between the scattered units. Already, the archives of the Legion had fallen into the hands of the Soviets in spite of Degrelle's explicit orders to save them. *SS-Stubaf.* Georges Jacobs, the first Commander of the *Légion Wallonie*, whose task it was to secure them, had to abandon them. He was however able to save Degrelle's political will, which Léon had confided to him at Stettin on 14 March 1945.

The non-combatants, that is the majority of the division, were scattered on the roads towards Schwerin-Lübeck. Desertions did not count any more. A great number of legionnaires put on plain clothes and got rid of their military documents and uniforms. The most cunning ones had been able to get false papers stating they were foreign labourers. Only a small group under Hellebaut-Derriks-Bonniver had kept a certain cohesion. They surrendered to the Americans at Schwerin on 3 May 1945.

Two days earlier, on 1 May 1945, Derriks and Hellebaut had received from *SS-Ustuf.* Albert Steiver a sealed envelope containing the following message from Degrelle, dated of 30 April 1945:[5]

> Majors Hellebaut and Derrickx (sic),
>
> Captain Bonivert (sic),
>
> I am leaving for armistice talks with the RFSS, who is in Lübeck. I fear that an abrupt armistice will immobilize all our people on the spot. Therefore, it is urgent that all our men be sent to the west sector of Lübeck. The official orders are to keep our troops moving, in groups, by all means, on lorries heading for Lübeck and regroup over there. It would even be better to have them hitchhiked – it would give our men more freedom – rather than multiply march columns and risk

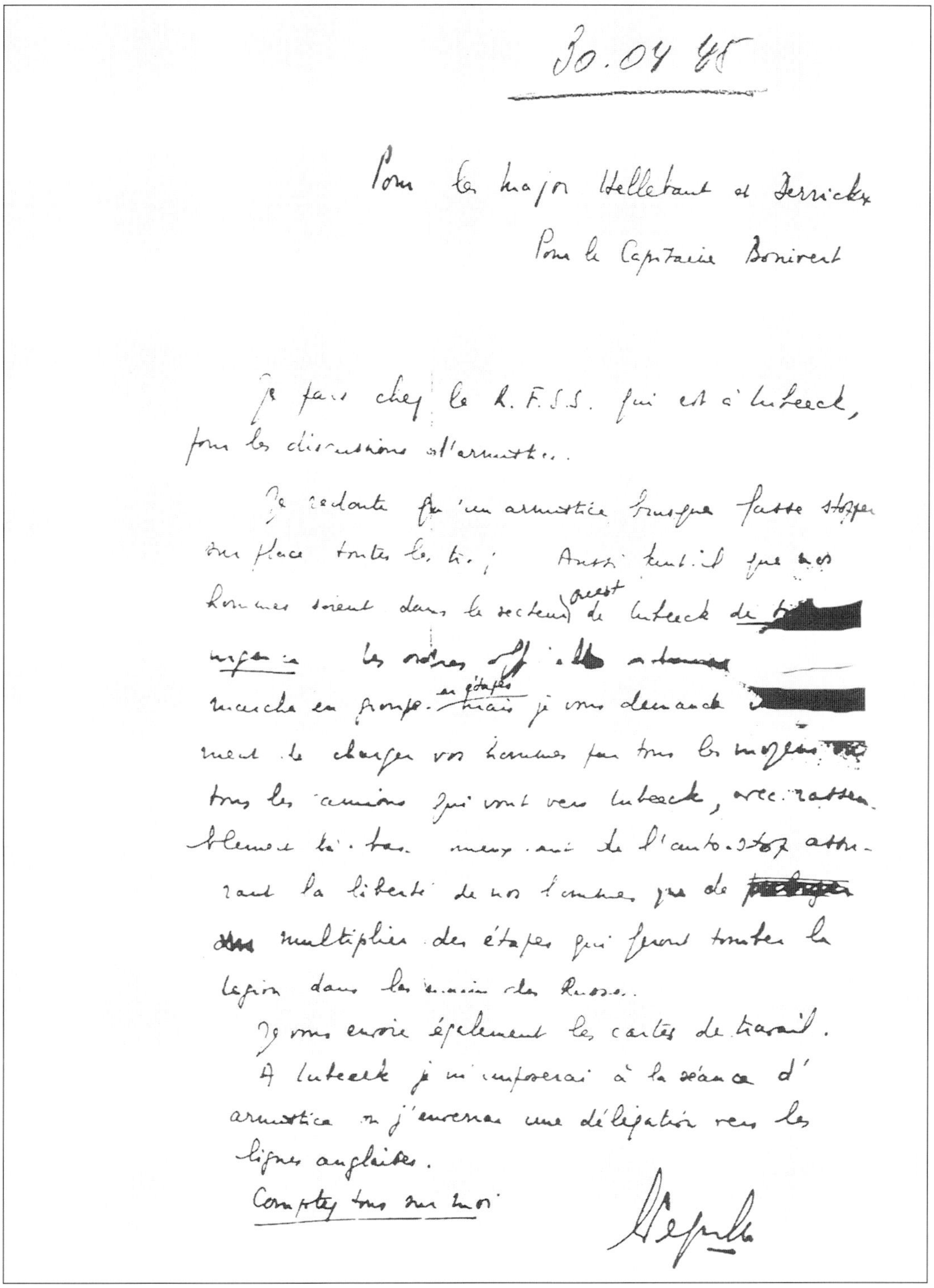

Fig. 21.2. Note Degrelle's spelling of Derrickx (Derriks) and Bonivert (Bonniver). Even in his post-war books, Degrelle never spelled the names of his most important officers properly (*Arch. E. De Bruyne*).

30.04.45

Pour le major Hellebaut et Derrickx
Pour le Capitaine Bonivert

Je pars chez le R.F.S.S. qui est à Lubeck, pour les discussions d'armistice.

Je redoute qu'un armistice brusque fasse stopper sur place toutes les tr.; Aussi faut-il que nos hommes soient dans le secteur ouest de Lubeck de [illegible] urgence. Les ordres [illegible] marche en groupe en étapes mais je vous demande [illegible] ment de charger vos hommes par tous les moyens [illegible] tous les camions qui vont vers Lubeck, [illegible] mieux avec de l'auto-stop assurant la liberté de nos hommes que de [illegible] multiplier des étapes qui feront tomber la legion dans les mains des Russes.

Je vous envoie également les cartes de travail.

A Lubeck je m'imposerai à la séance d'armistice ou j'enverrai une délégation vers les lignes anglaises.

Comptez tous sur moi.

Degrelle

being captured by the Russians.

I am also sending the work permits. In Lübeck, I shall impose myself at the armistice session, or I shall send a delegation to the English lines.

Rely on me.
(Signed) Degrelle.

As *SS-Ustuf.* Albert Steiver did not succeed in locating Hellebaut, it was Derriks who received the note. As to the second message Steiver was bearing, it said to meet-up at Bad-Seeberg, then Lübeck and to pass to Denmark with weapons and luggage to join the northern front . . .

Hellebaut (and many a Walloon legionnaire) never forgave Degrelle's using the pretext of political talks to abandon his men.[6]

On 1 May 1945, Degrelle and the men in his train spent the night at Kalkhorst. Himmler passed by in the course of the morning of 2 May without Degrelle having the time to meet him. The irony of the fate was that du Welz was busy sewing the insignia of a *SS-Standartenführer* on Degrelle's uniform when Generet informed Degrelle that a hardly recognizable Himmler had just left the place.

As Degrelle was not in a position to meet Himmler he called on Dr Brandt, Himmler's secretary, and handed him a memorandum. This document contained all the points, which had been discussed in detail previously in Berlin during the month of March and early April 1945:

1. So as to avoid that Walloon and Flemish legionnaires fall into the hands of the Soviets, it is important to remove the divisions north of the line Hamburg-Lübeck in order to be refitted;
2. To allow the legionnaires to live in Germany after the war without the risk of being handed over to the Soviets;
3. To allot every legionnaire a sum of money of 1,000 to 2,000 *Reichsmarks;*
4. To give to Degrelle the possibility to reach Sweden or Portugal with funds by aircraft or submarine;
5. Degrelle be given as surname that of Cherkassy so that he could safely live abroad under the cover of that name;
6. To help Degrelle's family who were living in Hanover without any resources.

Still worried to represent as many people as possible, Degrelle informed Brandt that during the meeting he had had with *SS-Standartenführer* Müller a few days earlier, the latter had given him command over both the Walloon and Flemish divisions. Despite this new situation, Degrelle was given to understand that the divisions *Langemarck* and *Wallonie* had to reach the Bad-Segeberg region under the command of their respective military chiefs. This last clause resulted in energetic protests by Degrelle because it was Degrelle's firm intention to take direction over both of the Belgian units. Hahn hardly could make Degrelle admit that if, politically, the action could be justified, militarily speaking it was not. Following Generet, Degrelle also met a refusal as far as the assumed name Cherkassy (if possible with the title *von*) was concerned. Degrelle was so obsessed by this demand that the subject was put on the table several times again in Copenhagen, during conversations with Pancke, the leader of the police forces for Denmark.

At Bad-Segeberg, Degrelle was informed of Hitler's death.

The general impression was that Degrelle and his companions embarrassed the Germans.

A first meeting with Himmler, at Malente on 2 May 1945, failed. It was then decided to return to Bad-Seegeberg, to spend the night there and then to head again in the direction of Lübeck the following day. All this resulted in a return trip to Malente. This time, Degrelle was luckier. He met Himmler's motorized column by chance. The latter was apparently pleased to meet Degrelle. Being unaware of the disgrace, which in the

Fig. 21.3. The wreck of Degrelle's escape plane in the Concha Bay/San Sebastian (*Le Soir Illustré*, May 1946).

Fig. 21.4. Walloon *SS* taken prisoner near Kiel and gathered on the tennis court of a hotel at Timmerdorfer Strand (*Collection Terlinden, via J.-L Roba*).

meantime had struck Himmler, Degrelle immediately assured Himmler of his complete allegiance and that of his men. Himmler promised that he would do all that he could to send Degrelle and his 'division' to neutral Sweden. He then questioned Degrelle on how many men he was accompanied by? ... three people, Degrelle replied.

During the night of 2 to 3 May 1945, Degrelle followed the column of the *RFSS* on the road from Malente to Flensburg. Arriving at Kiel, the column had to stop as a result of the last local bombardment by the *R.A.F.* In the darkness, Degrelle's car, a small Volkswagen, lost contact with the powerful limousines of Himmler's suite. Moreover, Degrelle's car had an engine failure. Generet and Degrelle put themselves in search of some authority to obtain assistance while du Welz and the driver stayed on the spot to keep a close eye on the suitcases piled up in the Volkswagen.

In Flensburg, Degrelle obtained a new car and a German driver as well.

In the afternoon of 3 May 1945, the papers were ready at last. Crossing the border offered some supplementary difficulties. Degrelle got impatient and flared up at his companions. The transfer towards Copenhagen was facilitated by Degrelle's joining the German colonel responsible for military transport in Denmark. The latter was to remain with Degrelle as far as Nyborg.

There the group had to take the ferryboat. Two opportunities presented themselves: one was a cargo boat transporting Danish political prisoners escorted by members of the Swedish Red Cross, the other one being a vessel carrying troops of the *Wehrmacht*, and for which Degrelle finally opted. Degrelle arrived at Copenhagen on 4 May 1945, at 2:00 a.m. After spending the rest of the night in the embassy, he had a meeting with Dr Best at 1.00 p.m the next day. (Dr Werner Best – German Plenipotentiary in Denmark – was expected to work out the details of Degrelle's evacuation). Once again, and for the very last time, Degrelle tried to make someone accept the plan he had elaborated for so long. The discussions between Best and Degrelle ended in a very satisfactory way for Degrelle. Indeed, he would be transferred to Norway and could even be accompanied by a team of Walloon war correspondents.[7]

After Best, it was Pancke's turn to face Degrelle. The latter plied him with questions about his relatives left behind in Hanover, and what would become of them in his absence. During the brief stay in Copenhagen, Degrelle took every

Fig. 21.5. Severe condemnations awaited the people having collaborated in some way or another with the Germans. Nr 71 is Léon Closset, here at the Courcelles trial in 1948.

opportunity to approach any Party dignitary or serviceman of some rank, requesting them to consider his demands. Only, Degrelle was living on a cloud and seemed not to notice that, in the great drama which was unfolding, he no longer represented the image he had imposed on the Germans.

In the evening, Generet was sent on a mission in the Danish capital from which he did not return.

And thus Degrelle, accompanied by his last companion, *SS-Hstuf*. Robert du Welz – since Degrelle himself had promoted the devoted luggage bearer to the rank of captain – succeeded in reaching Oslo from where they departed by plane during the night of 7/8 May 1945.[8]

Meanwhile, Derriks, as a captive of the Allies, sounded out the Americans on the possibility of him and his men joining the American forces in their fight against Japan, the only immediate means to avoid being arrested by the Belgian authorities, and sent back to Belgium for court-martial.[9]

CHAPTER XXII

Epilogue

One might wonder what fate was kept in store for Degrelle's closest followers.

The *Ers.Btl.36* was threatened by U.S. troops and evacuated Alfeld on 6 April 1945. It settled down very temporarily in Biesenbrow, west of the Oder. It was driven back a second time during the Soviet offensive in the direction of Stettin. *SS-Ostubaf.* Bruno Schulz, replacing G. Tchekhoff,[1] surrendered the unit to the Americans in the region of Lübeck.

As to Georges Tchekhoff, he had left Alfeld on 6 April together with the sick and wounded. His intention was to reach Berlin where, according to the latest instructions, all White Russians of the division *Wallonie* were to report at the headquarters of Skorzeny's *Jagdverband Ost*. In the meantime, however, the latter had evacuated from Oranienburg and

Fig. 22.1. The Walloon colony in Argentina celebrated the 10th anniversary of the establishment of the *Légion Wallonie* by means of a souvenir sheet (*Widow G. Tchekhof/ Collection E. De Bruyne*).

withdrawn to Bavaria. While heading for the south in search of Skorzeny's unit, Tchekhoff was stopped by the *Feldgendarmerie* in Sangbittel (he had even been very close to being hanged for desertion!). He finally arrived at Zell-am-See. Under the identity of Scheer (his mother's maiden name), he turned into a Belgian worker employed by the *A.E.G.* works. Then began a three year stay in German camps for displaced persons. Passing in transit from one camp to another, avoiding investigation of the different repatriation committees – the Soviet one being the most dangerous – Tchekhoff managed to get in touch with his family and to obtain a passport for himself and his family to Argentina on 12 May 1948.

A last difficulty: the *North-Express* Hanover-Paris stopped at Herbestal and Liège/Belgium, last place of residence of the former Commander of the *Légion Wallonie*, where his identification, even in 1948, could still be feared. Without meeting any major obstacle, Tchekhoff arrived safely in Buenos Aires. He eventually ran across other Walloon companions in misfortune. Sentenced to the death penalty *in absentia*, he died in exile on 25 November 1961.

The commander of *69 Rgt, SS-Stubaf.* Jules Mathieu, had stayed with his men at Bismarck. At the end of the month of April 1945, he sent all remaining legionnaires north-westwards. Together with Georges Ruelle, Jules Sandron and Joseph Pévenasse he regrouped the different columns scattered on the roads.

On 1 May 1945, 11 km away from Lübeck, the trio stopped along the road to shelter from strafing by an American aircraft, during which their car was riddled with bullets. At the Schmerdorf village crossroads, a few kilometers from Lübeck, a British tank blocked the three Walloon officers across the road. Sandron and Pévenasse asked to be released from their military duties and Mathieu demobilized them. They immediately took off their uniforms and left the place heading to Hanover where they hoped to meet their respective families. Joseph Pévenasse vanished. No doubt he managed to achieve what he had advised to many a legionnaire: to reach the Soviet zone and, under a false identity, escape arrest by the Belgian authorities.

The following day Mathieu gave himself up to the British in Lübeck. However, changing his mind the very next day he decided otherwise, and escaped very easily. An overall discovered in a garden shed soon replaced his uniform. The first person whom he met was Degrelle's former liaison officer in Berlin, Jean Vermeire. The latter, bearing false papers, was trying to hide in the stream of refugees. Uniting their fates, Mathieu, Vermeire, together with two other false civilians, succeeded in being accommodated in a Hamburg barracks. At the local swimming pool Mathieu was recognized by a Belgian, living in the same city as he, who reported him to the authorities. Taken to Hamburg Altena prison first, he finally was placed in the Gnadeland prison camp, near Neumünster/Schleswig-Holstein. The camp was guarded by the 6th Artillery Regiment. There he was surprised to meet the former commander of the Brussels *Kommandostab Z*, Major Baumann. Mathieu stayed there one year, just long enough to draw up a detailed account on Soviet night-time tank tactics for the American Army Intelligence Service. Only after supplying all this information was Mathieu repatriated to Belgium. Condemned to death *in absentia* on 20 October 1944, this first sentence was ratified on appeal on 14 May 1948. It was later commuted to hard labour. Released from prison in 1952, he devoted his leisure time to writing his memoirs. He died on 16 April 1990.

Frans Hellebaut's fate also deserves a few lines. On 2 May 1945, Léon Degrelle's Chief of Staff arrived in the Schwerin area with hundreds of Walloon legionnaires, and waited there for the Americans to arrive. The latter showed up in the form of airborne troops, and indicated the shortest route to a *Sammellager*. Hellebaut, then went in the direction of Schwerin aboard a vehicle and spent the night on the square in front of the city hall. The following day, tormented by hunger, the Walloon officer approached a castle along the road in the direction of Hamburg. The landlord, Baron von Schwerin, who was to be a part of the future Dönitz government, received him.

He had hardly settled down when an American patrol proceeded to search the castle. Hellebaut was taken prisoner and transferred to the nearby *Sammellager*.

A few days later, he was taken to a transit camp and finally arrived at a British POW camp on a peninsula in the Baltic Sea. Living conditions being particularly painful, Hellebaut reported to the highest ranked German officer in the camp and via this officer requested repatriation.

On the following day, Hellebaut was informed of the presence, in Kiel, of Georges Danloy, a Belgian officer commanding a battalion of the well-known airborne *Piron Brigade*. Hellebaut immediately requested he be handed over to this officer. Danloy's bewilderment was great when he was put in the presence of Hellebaut.[2] The latter was accommodated in a local hotel, a Walloon orderly being put at his service. Later in the evening, in the mess, and in the presence of British officers (who couldn't believe their eyes when noticing the WWI ribbon of the Military Cross on Hellebaut's uniform), Danloy announced that he had received orders to escort the Belgian officer to Belgium and hand him over to the Magistrate of the Brussels Military Court.

Hellebaut was condemned to death by firing squad. However, the issue of the royal family saved his life. Victor Larock, chief editor of the socialist newspaper *Le Peuple* was conducting a virulent anti-Leopoldist campaign and openly criticized the attitude of King Léopold III during the war. He presented Hellebaut's execution as a radical means to make him keep silent as Hellebaut was an important witness.

On 23 August 1953, Hellebaut refused to sign a 'spontaneous' statement imposed by the corps of career officers. Signing this statement was the *conditio sine qua non* to obtain from the influential resistance groups their agreement to Hellebaut's release on parole, that the Minister of Justice Joseph Pholien was inclined to grant by virtue of the Lejeune Law.[3] Having declined the offer on grounds that the contents of the statement were outrageous to his honour, Hellebaut served seven more years before being released from the St Gilles prison in 1960. Hellebaut died on 18 June 1984.

After the dissolution of the Rex Movement Victor Matthys did not return to Berlin, where he had been running the *Toison d'Or*, a Rexist newspaper, but stayed at Badeke, in the *Hannover-Gau*. It seems that Matthys intended to stay and wait there for the Americans in spite of the fact that, according to his own postwar statements, he was given the opportunity to reach Spain by air from Switzerland. Unlike Degrelle, Matthys refused the offer for an individual rescue. Other sources, on the contrary, report that the deputy chief of the Rex Movement had planned and prepared an escape route to the south since March 1945. Matthys left Badeke the day before the American forces showed up, heading for the Swiss border.

As soon as he had arrived at Nanders, near the Swiss border, Matthys took steps to obtain political asylum in Switzerland. American troops arrived before he could get an answer. Matthys and his wife then left Nanders for Landeck. However, it was not possible to continue farther southwards. Victor Matthys returned to the Hanover area and was arrested. He was condemned to death and executed by firing squad on 10 November 1947.[4]

Due to increasingly violent bombing, Charles Lambinon and his *Siegfried* team had left Marburg in the middle of March 1945, heading for Weimar. The next day Lambinon left the group and returned to Hildesheim by motorcycle. His intention was to make a clean sweep of the funds amassed by the Rex Movement. Lambinon vanished and never could be arrested. According to some rumors, he

Fig. 22.2. A group of Belgians enrolled in the German armies are being led away for repatriation to Belgium. This group is only guarded by one single man wearing a British uniform (second row left) (*Collection Terlinden, via J.-L. Roba*).

resided for some time in an abbey in the region of Marseille. Lambinon was condemned to death *in absentia*.

During the last weeks of April 1945, another more enigmatic individual was roaming in the forbidden zone along the Swiss border aboard a car of the local *Gestapo*: Fernand Rouleau, Degrelle's ex-lieutenant. After his dismissal from the Legion in September 1941, he offered his talents as an organizer to the French *Waffen-SS*. In June 1944, as an *SS-Ostuf.*, he was transferred to the *Stabsschwadron Reiter Regiment 17* of the *8. SS-Kavalerie Divsion Florian Geyer* engaged in Hungary. Rouleau managed to cross the Swiss border and reached Spain under the cover of a false identity. He died in Madrid without being troubled by Belgian justice on 31 July 1984.

During the first days after the surrender of the German armies, the Allies left the great mass of the POWs in semi-liberty. The most cunning ones, and more particularly all those who had good reasons not to fall into the hands of the justice, took advantage of this situation to vanish. Assumed identity cards allowed them to cross Germany and France and, through Spain and Portugal, to reach South America. For others, the French Foreign Legion was a secure means to escape arrest. Others fell into the hands of the Soviets and were sent to labour camps along the Volga, more particularly camp nr 188 (Tambow). Most of them were released in 1948–49 and handed over to the Belgian justice. Few were lucky enough to hide in Germany, under a false identity. A handful of fortunate ones had married German wives and could hide easily. Others worked in out-of-the-way farms, etc. However, this semi-underground situation did not last. By the end of the month of May 1945, the Americans had received lists of names: the most wanted individuals were not the Rexists or the legionnaires but the people who had belonged to the *Sipo-Sd* and Skorzeny's special formations.

By mid-June 1945, the Walloon legionnaires who had been taken prisoner were sent to Hamburg-Neuengamme concentration camp, where the officers and rank-and-file were separated. A few weeks later, the first repatriation convoys were organized.

Finally, as a rough guide, of all Walloon officers who served in the *Legion Wallonie* from 1941 to 1945, 26 were killed in action; 5 died in 1948, either from illness or suicide; 48 incurred a death sentence; there were 19 death sentences *in absentia* and 26 cases of life imprisonment. Twenty-three officers were condemned to 20 years behind bars; 9 were sentenced to 10–20 years of ordinary detention. There was one condemnation to 5 years of imprisonment and one nonsuit (Catholic Chaplain L. Fierens), not to mention 8 non-listed officers, probably foreigners or stateless individuals to whom the Belgian penal code was not applicable.

Fig. 22.3. Ypres, May 1948: a priest, a medical doctor and two public prosecutors before the local Court Martial attend the execution of a Flemish collaborator. 239 Belgian citizens (and 3 Germans) were executed by firing squad. No Walloon Eastern Front veteran was executed for simply enrolling in the German armies. However, a few legionnaires who had participated in reprisal actions against the population in Belgium were shot. Note that traitors to the country were shot in the back (*Doc. E. De Bruyne*).

On 6 November 1948, 35 of the condemned officers were pardoned. One was shot on 21 June 1948 (Pierre Pauly, 2nd Commander of the *Légion Wallonie*, on grounds of his involvement in the Courcelles reprisals).

PART III

Historical and Critical Analysis of Degrelle's War-time Years 1940–45

CHAPTER XXIII

The Case of Lucien Lippert, Belgian Kommandeur of the Légion Wallonie and the 5.SS-Freiw.Sturmbrigade Wallonien

Fig. 23.1. *SS-Sturmbannführer* Lucien Lippert, whether he liked it or not?

Lucien Lippert's fate, a Belgian career officer abiding by strict military tradition, i.e. Exaltation of the Nation, Respect of the Constitution and Loyalty to the Dynasty, duly sealed with an oath of allegiance, killed in action at Novo-Buda on 13 February 1944, within the ranks of the *5.SS-Freiw.Sturmbrigade Wallonien* as CO of the unit, wearing the *feldgrau* of a *SS-Sturmbannführer*, is hardly known, as he continuously stood in the shadow of Léon Degrelle.

Nothing predestined this station master's son of the Belgian railways to commit a breach of honour by putting on the uniform of those who, twice in a quarter of a century, had invaded his country. The only person who could have released him from his oath was the highest moral authority in Belgium, King Leopold III.

Consequently, at the establishment of the *Legion Wallonie* in July 1941, Rexist circles – and this was no surprise – immediately propagated the rumour that the King showed sympathy for an anti-Bolshevist legion.[1] Later, as they had to face the disturbing silence of the Sovereign, these circles claimed that the King's silence was in fact a tacit approval, since on this illusion depended the recruitment of the officers of the active and the reserve corps who were necessary to cadre the formation.

A few rare requests for permission to serve at the Eastern Front were directed to the King but remained unanswered, the *Office of the Works of the Demobilized Army – OTAD*[2] kept silent on the subject (but professional soldiers applying for permission were granted an unpaid leave!). Only the *Kommandostab Z* (Z standing for *Zeppelin*) – a section within the *Militärverwaltung* in Brussels charged with tutoring the auxiliary collaborating paramilitary formations – answered favourably, backed up by Degrelle's loud and biased propaganda campaign.[3]

Lucien Lippert belonged to an officer corps that traditionally stood aside from politics as its members, at the risk of disciplinary sanctions, were not authorized to join a political party, or to attend a political meeting in uniform. The war did not change these rules. And when General Van Den Bergen, Chief of Staff of the Belgian Army and Senior Officer of *Oflag II A* (Prenzlau), on request of the German camp *Kommandantur*, authorized the posting of an agenda, 18 July

1941, in which officers who wished to fight at the Eastern Front could apply at his office the next day, 51 officers showed up despite the reserve that this could only be done under the cover of the King's approval (a clause that the General had carefully inserted into the text of the communiqué himself). But on learning that enlistment could only take place through the Rex Movement, all 51 officers withdrew their candidatures.[4] In other POW camps, inquiring as to the possibilities to fight at the Eastern Front was considered anti-patriotic and punished without delay. On 21 July 1941, Captain-Commander of the Reserve Corps, Jean Malherbe, POW at *Oflag VIII C* (Juliusburg) expressed the wish to take service with the *Garde Wallonne*, a ladder to climb up to a command within the *Légion Wallonie*. The Belgian Senior officer of the *Oflag* immediately imposed a 14 days close arrest. This penalty was made public and entailed an immediate quarantining by Malherbe's fellow prisoners.

As a matter of fact, even if the officer corps could only be apolitical, there can be no doubt that it was, all the same, tinged with conservatism and thus more tilted to reactionary behaviour than revolutionary attitudes. Even, if generally speaking, the officer corps had a natural bent towards order and discipline, one cannot deny that some francophone officers, a minority, were in favour of an authoritarian regime (under the leadership of the King) while the number of career officers with close links to the Rex Movement was close to nil.

However, after the armistice, the officers' *esprit de corps* was cracked. Many an officer, especially among the younger ones, had been shocked by the marriage of the King, 'prisoner at Laeken Palace'. Others were scandalized, feeling they were victims of discipline by accepting to be taken into captivity while some of their chiefs had chosen a 'French leave' to France, the case of one of General Van Overstraeten's protégés being flagrant. Others had been shaken in their convictions by the speech of Prime Minister Pierlot, 28 May 1940:

"By breaking the link uniting him to his people, the King placed himself under the power of the invader. As a consequence, he is no longer in a position to govern, as obviously the function of Chief of the State cannot be carried out under foreign control. Officers and civil servants are released from their duty of obedience as imposed on by their oath of allegiance."

And as if this statement were not sufficient, General Denis, Minister of Defence, added 8 June 1941:

"The Oath taken by the members of the Army can only be valid in presence of a free King, fulfilling his duties as set by the Constitution, while for the time being the Sovereign is in the impossibility of doing so, the specific case being laid down by art. 82 of the Constitution."

The disintegration of the Officer Corps and the resulting general *état d'esprit* were so disturbing, and had become such a concern, that a committee – named after the officer in charge *Committee ' t Serclaes* – was established in the course of 1942. This Committee was charged with providing the POWs with moral help and material assistance. Its main goal, however was twofold: to target officers flaunting anti-Royalist opinions and to assess the importance of their republican feelings, on the one

Cap. Fig. 23.2. *Your Majesty, we were waiting for you . . .* (Caricature taken from Victor Larock, *Pour combattre Léopold III – Arguments et Documents no. 4.50 Griefs, faits, arguments,* 1951).

hand; to spot the royalist circles striving for a strong (or even authoritarian) regime, especially among the French-speaking officers, on the other hand.[5]

Such was the general atmosphere when, at the request of the *OTAD*, Lucien Lippert was released from *Oflag III B* (Tibor) in September 1940, and transferred to the *Service Volontaire du Travail pour la Wallonie – SVTW* (Service of Volunteer Labour in Wallonia), a new organization initiated by circles close to General Van Overstraeten, the King's Military Adviser, and individuals belonging to the Officer Corps of the Reserve. The *SVTW* advocated and promoted moral education through volunteer labour for the benefit of the nation.

At the time the Soviet Union was invaded, great fuss was made over anti-Bolshevist idealism to make possible the establishment of the different legions, which were to fight alongside the Germans at the Eastern Front. In the specific case of the *Légion Wallonie*, anti-Bolshevism certainly was, at least in the eyes of the public and the volunteers themselves, a determining and even decisive element. However, according to Frans Hellebaut, other interests, less avowed than that of anti-Communism, were at stake.

Fernand Rouleau, a newcomer to the Rex Movement, who in no time made his way up to Commander of the *Formations de Combat de Rex* (Rexist militia) and *Lieutenant du Chef*, is one of the keys to the mystery.

Rouleau, an adventurer and close to all pre-war European right wing movements, proved to be the go-between on behalf of influential circles of the capital city, mainly francophone Royalists and Belgicists (i.e. favouring a united Belgium as opposed to a Wallonia-Flanders split up of the country). This coterie (in fact the real instigators of the Walloon anti-Bolshevik legion, much more than Degrelle) charged Rouleau with the public announcement of a *Corps Franc Wallonie* (*Freikorps* Wallonia) in order to counterbalance the Flemish separatists, who had raised their own *Legioen Vlaanderen*.

Was there any relation between Lippert's enlistment into the *Légion Wallonie* and the interests of aforementioned circles?

Lucien Lippert enrolled in the *Légion Wallonie* during July 1941, and left for Meseritz barracks in August 1941. Incorporated into the *Wehrmacht*, he participated in the different winter campaigns. He rose up to *Kommandeur* on 6 April 1942, and he continued to hold command when the *Legion Wallonie* was transferred, under the appellation *SS-Freiw. Sturmbrigade Wallonien*, to the *Wafffen-SS* on 1 June 1943.

In mid-December 1942, the Walloon legionnaires were granted a first leave. Meanwhile, things had developed in an unexpected manner. The first talks for a transfer to the *Waffen-SS* had started confidentially in September-October 1942, and were publicly announced on 25 October 1942. Lippert was deeply upset by the negative comments this new orientation had generated in Belgium.

After an absence of seventeen months, Lippert had to bow to the facts: the *Légion Wallonie* was not popular among the population. Robert Poulet, chief editor of the censored *Nouveau Journal* was to draw the same conclusions after the 21 December 1942 editorial. But there was something still worse going on! The confidential circles of the capital city, the very ones that had very discreetly demonstrated their sympathy in July 1941, carefully avoided him now that the fortune of arms seemed to change sides. And when Lippert wanted to sound out these personalities on the attitude that he was to adopt in the face of these new developments, all doors closed. This upsetting statement of facts probably had to do with Lippert's intention of retaking service with the Walloon Voluntary Labour Service, in which he had been a cadre before the *Barbarossa* operation.

During the first months of 1943, this service was about to be absorbed by the Rex Movement and it first leader, Henri Bauchau, had resigned from his post as he stubbornly refused to cooperate with Rexists.

In the meantime, the German occupying forces were looking for a new *SVTW*-leader. Knowing that Lippert had already had a preliminary conversation with *Reichsarbeitsführer* Konstantin Hierl, Victor Matthys, *a. i.* leader of the Rex Movement in Belgium, came to the conclusion that the Commander of the *Légion Wallonie* was the suitable person guaranteeing all required qualities. However, his choice proved to be a critical decision as Lippert's departure for the *SVTW* could be interpreted as a moral desertion. In fact, Lippert's plans were not an elegant way to abandon the *Légion Wallonie* (but they could have been looked on as such by the legionnaires). They were much more a defensive falling back towards those who had maintained a stubborn silence during his December 1942 furlough, a kind of tactical withdrawal on the positions where the *OTAD* had placed him in 1940 even though the new Rexist-tutored *SVTD* was far from showing the same values as the ones advocated by the former Bachau team. At the same time, Lippert was determined to protect the new *SVTW* from too much Rexist influence and ordered legionnaire officer Léon Closset (the very one who was to replace Lippert at the head of the *SVTW* once it had become clear that Lippert would not be transferred to the *SVTW*) to keep a close eye on this matter. Meanwhile, Lippert's permanent presence in Belgium was likely to facilitate the possibilities of renewing contacts with the circles that were leaving him in the lurch for the moment.

And yet, premonitory signs announcing a change in the mentalities and the attitudes had not failed to appear, some of them had even come to daylight during Lippert's furlough, as it seemed clear that by the turn of 1941–42 the *Légion Wallonie* no longer reflected the image that Lippert had in mind since August 1941. Being a few months away from the transfer of the *Légion Wallonie* to the *Waffen-SS*, (informal discussions had started in September-October 1942), Lippert was quite aware that this new orientation would blur the image of the Walloon unit and definitively annihilate the Belgian unitarian spirit the Legion was supposed to radiate. By joining the *Waffen-SS* Lippert knew that the Legion would inevitably become an instrument of the anti-national Flanders-Wallonia split up policy in the hands of the Germans. This orientation was a mental torture to Lippert, as it was bound to end in a firm reprobation by the francophone and unitarian royalist circles who until then had given him their blessings and who, paradoxically enough, 17 months later, while retracting themselves, in restricted circles, behind closed doors, continued to call Lippert a " ... brilliant officer and a man of the elite!"[6]

Lippert, unlike Degrelle, was not in favour of a Legion being mainly a means of political propaganda. According to the young *Kommandeur*, the Walloon formation had to limit its image to the military aspect without (too many) political implications and above all without upsetting public opinion in Belgium. This had also been the opinion of the circles that had favourably welcomed the establishment of the *Légion Wallonie* in 1941.

Degrelle's speech of 17 January 1943, at the Palais des Sports, in the centre of Brussels, announcing that the Walloon people had all of a sudden Germanic roots, emphasized by a loud *Heil Hitler*, not only shocked public opinion but also resulted in a massive defection of Rexist militants, to start with José Streel, the main Rex ideologue. But at the same time, Degrelle's policy was brought to light: the *Légion Wallonie* was to serve exclusively his steadily growing own personal interests and ambition, the military aspect being limited to those exploits likely to glorify Degrelle. By accepting the organization of a Nazi-dominated Europe where the integrity of Belgium was not secured, Degrelle really set very little value on the pre-war National Program of the Rex Movement.

In one word, Degrelle had made the *Légion Wallonie* his. The *Reich* was suffering its first important reverses and Lucien Lippert had manoeuvered himself into a dilemma.

The only way out remaining was Lippert's replacement by a fellow career officer. This is what happened in June 1944 with the arrival of Major B.E.M. Frans Hellebaut, four months after Lippert's death.

In the end, Hellebaut's hesitations (preliminary talks to join the *Legion* had started while Lippert was still alive), on the one hand, and Degrelle's reluctance to part with Lippert (far more inclined to yield than Hellebaut), on the other hand, ensured that Lippert, in the absence of an adequate relief by a professional officer (the only possibility for the Walloon formation to keep its military character), continued to assume command until 13 February 1944, without failing in his honour. He finally purchased with his life the choice he had made in 1941, but was comforted by a piece of advice Hellebaut had given him during a dramatic meeting at Fischeck-Hamburg *Oflag XD*, 12 February 1943: "to continue requires more courage than to abandon".[7]

CHAPTER XXIV

Degrelle's War-Time Years in a Nutshell

In 1940, at the age of 34, Léon Degrelle was the youngest West European fascist leader with parliamentary experience.[1]

During 1941–45, unlike most of the other West European non-axis fascist personalities having chosen for military collaboration,[2] Degrelle was to spend the war-time years at the Eastern Front, among his men, from the beginning until nearly the end. And yet, in the summer of 1941, Degrelle was close to missing the unique opportunity, which in the end, and with the help of military collaboration, would allow him to re-start a political career.

Entirely absorbed by activities he essentially focused on political actions in Belgium, ignored by a German military administration favouring Flemish separatism[3] to the detriment of Belgian unitarian integrity (that the Walloon fascist had been loudly advocating ever since before the war), Degrelle underestimated by far the establishment of the *Légion Wallonie* as an instrument likely to serve his personal ambition.

To him, the action and the existence of the *Légion Wallonie* (known to be an offshoot of the Rexist Movement, more or less bound to be limited in time and space as German armies were expected to overrun the Soviet Union before the end of summer 1941) were nothing else but elements, among many others, allowing him to elbow himself up to the top.

After maintaining a wait-and-see attitude, only unexpected developments induced Degrelle's enrolment into the *Légion Wallonie*.

From the start the establishment of the *Légion Wallonie* had been presented as a gesture of mere willingness, a kind of moral guarantee toward the German occupying authorities before whom the Rexist Movement and its leader had been grovelling in vain ever since May 1940.[4]

Due to Degrelle's interfering, the establishment of the *Légion Wallonie* became a fact, a political reality of which the implications in occupied Belgium would be considerable. There is no doubt that Degrelle's personality hastened such an outcome since he is the perfect example of the sort of man guided by momentary impressions and impulses. This explains why most of the time he could not honour the promises he had rashly uttered in moments of unconsidered bursts of enthusiasm and passion. The ones pertaining to the terms of enlistment into the *Légion Wallonie* are noteworthy.[5] They even gave birth to a lyrically-remodelled marching song, soon forbidden by the Walloon staff at *Regenwurmlager*: "Léon, keep telling me your lies, you are so good at lying".[6]

Instant brilliant and dazzling success, noisy publicity, a Barnumesque decorum and above all the challenge of enrapturing an audience were the sensations Degrelle was really after. Much more than the dull and boring job of a politician, these were things Degrelle was attracted to in the first place. This explains why, later on, at the Eastern Front, Degrelle proved to be a better *Menschenführer* than *Volksführer*.

Not only a truly gifted public speaker, Degrelle had also developed the intuition of always being present on the very spots where matters of prestige and personal interest were involved. These were two notable advantages the leaders of the Flemish collaboration cruelly missed.[7]

Pure luck, in the full sense of the word, was an even more important element in Degrelle's meteoric rise from

Fig. 24.1. Degrelle avoided being drafted in the Belgian army ... but served in the German army. Here he is as a private in *Feldgrau* (*J. Mathieu/Collection E. De Bruyne*).

Schütze to *SS-Obersturmbannführer* and commander of the *28. SS-Freiw.-Gren. Div. Wallonien.*[8] In the end, it appeared to be a decisive element of success.

During his presence at the Eastern Front, Degrelle was wounded several times. None of the injuries he sustained were severe enough to necessitate evacuation or immediate admission to a hospital.[9] All were used for purposes of personal propaganda, and were widely commented on in the Belgian (censored) press.

Not only was Degrelle served by physical luck, a succession of fortuitous events also came to his rescue in a most opportune way:[10]

> Firstly, there was the pure accidental meeting with Robert Poulet[11] in July 1941, which, on top of the Rouleau affair, accelerated Degrelle's final decision to depart for the Eastern Front;[12]
>
> Secondly, John Hagemans' death in action, in August 1942. It freed him from another ambitious character suffering a lack of space, and who, once back in Belgium, would not have hesitated in trying to outrun Degrelle. Both dreamed of the same *grandeur* in a world where there was only room for a single leader;
>
> Thirdly, the tragic death of Lucien Lippert. If it is true that it deprived Degrelle from an outstanding technician, Lippert's death nevertheless opened the way and permitted Degrelle to grasp at the supreme command of the later *Wallonie* division.

What would have been Degrelle's position if Lucien Lippert had survived the Cherkassy outbreak? No doubt, the Walloon professional soldier would have been promoted to a higher rank and would have continued to hold command of the Walloon unit.[13] Eliminating Lippert would have been a risky operation, so great was his popularity among his men. Degrelle, unfit for any military command, would then have been nothing more than a kind of parading *visiteur aux armées*, an Axis-friendly foreign politician in *feldgrau* among so many, who, like Doriot, Darnand and others, were only tolerated for the number of enlistments they represented.

Fate decided otherwise ...

By the end of 1944, Degrelle was highly decorated and had been appointed commander of a division, moving a step ahead on his Flemish rivals. At the same time, he had taken a serious option on a future political and military role that he wanted to be supra-national.[14]

What Degrelle had not been able to achieve via mere political action, he was to obtain thanks to the military merits of the *Légion Wallonie*. By way of consequence, there was no other choice left for Degrelle than at all costs be recognized as the undisputed military commander of the Walloon formation that he wanted to be as prestigious as possible, not a reinforced brigade as his more realistic officer of operations Frans Hellebaut had recommended, but a division, even lilliputian-sized.

Furthermore, a surviving Lippert would have disapproved of the Cherkassy parades that Degrelle organized in Brussels and Charleroi.[15] In the same way, there can be no doubt that Lippert would have agreed with Hellebaut in his objections against Degrelle's plans to form a division simply because it was nonsense, militarily speaking. Both officers united in the same effort would then have curbed Degrelle's impetuous aspirations.[16]

None of this was to happen ... On the contrary!

As to his place within the Walloon formation, Degrelle had no other choice than to firmly settle down in a position of force and undisputed authority, protecting him from any interference threatening his interests, be it Walloon or German. Not to take this measure of self-protection would unavoidably have led to failure. That is why Degrelle dismissed from the Legion all individuals who did not agree with his views or all those who, for any reason, were likely to become a threat to his personal rise. As for the rest, everybody – without any exception – was welcome. This is why Henri Derriks was tolerated within the Walloon formation until the end of the hostilities. After all, his presence in the ranks of the Legion served Léon Degrelle more than it could possibly harm him.[17]

All through the war, Degrelle had one main concern: to rally sufficient people who would be representative enough of his ambition. The recruitment of foreigners such as Frenchmen, Spaniards, White Russians and even Flemings had no other purpose than to put the screw on Gottlob Berger so as to emerge as the champion of West European military collaboration, the very springboard to Degrelle's reason for being: political power.

Next to the military command Degrelle had already held since his return from Estonia, on 23 November 1944 he was granted civil authority in his capacity of *Volksführer der Wallonen*. This new appointment meant that from that moment on Degrelle was to act with full power over all French-speaking Belgians residing within the borders of the Reich.

As a Commander (and *Gerichtsherr*/judge) of a division Degrelle exercised full military and judicial authority over his legionnaires. The haste with which he ordered enlistment into the newly formed division of all uniformed para-military types having fled Belgium could only comfort and strengthen his position.

As *Volksführer der Wallonen*, he had supreme control over the civil administration of the francophone Belgians scattered all over the *Reich*. His first task as leader of the Walloon people was to spot all Belgian male civilians aged 17–55 and to convince them to join the *Waffen-SS*. Lack of success in voluntary enlistment resulted in radical coercive methods of enrolment. If in July 1941 idle promises had sufficed to convince Rexist militants to go to war, in autumn 1944 moral pressure proved to be necessary to make people join the division. In 1945, personal restraint and actual coercion (*vis absoluta*) were required.[18]

If successful, the von Rundstedt offensive, mid-December 1944, could have restored the prestige of the Rexist Movement led by Victor Matthys, Degrelle's deputy chief.

Abandoned by Degrelle at the end of 1942 to the exclusive benefit of a political speculation of which Degrelle had anticipated the advantages, Victor Matthys and the Rexist Movement in Belgium experienced a totally different reality than the one sensed by the legionnaires at the front, as the Rexist Movement had to face the anger of the population and the raids of the Resistance. From an instrument originally meant to be at the service of a moderate collaborating policy advocated by the Rexist Movement, the Legion, throughout the war-years, had finally outshone the action of the Movement, relegating its leaders to accomplishing loathsome *Sipo-Sd* round-up duties.

The Rexist Movement was dissolved on 30 March 1945, in the dark back room of a *Stube* in Bockenrode (Hanover) in the total indifference of the very one who once had been its founder.

The Legion, contrary to the Rexist Movement, was not disbanded. It simply ceased to exist on 3 May 1945, ... also in the absence of its commander.[19]

After the Pomeranian campaign, the Legion had undergone serious changes, the main one being Frans Hellebaut's initiative of creating a *Kampfgruppe*, grouping volunteers for the last heavy rearguard combats in April 1945.[20] This modification rang the death knell of the Rexist influence. For the first time in its history, the Legion was led into action by the non-Rexists Frans Hellebaut and Henri Derriks. This development was symptomatic and already premonitory of Degrelle's attitude in the last days of the war.

His dear Legion already belonged to the past ...

After the war, many a Walloon legionnaire felt Degrelle had left his comrades-in-arms in the lurch, that speculative talks with Himmler on the road to Lübeck had only been an ... elegant manner to bow out, by no means worthy of a commanding chief ... and *Waffen-SS* officer.[21]

Epilogue

Years ago, but long after the war, we interviewed one of Degrelle's most daring frontline officers, a legionnaire from the first 1941 contingent who had worked his way up to *SS-Ustuf.* and company commander in 1944, wounded 8 times, the last injury being sustained on 20 April 1945, while leading a counter-attack on the banks of the Oder. On the crucial question as to how he finally judged and considered Léon Degrelle, this former officer, after a long hesitation, answered; "Degrelle had the quality of his faults and the weakness of his qualities" and after an even longer silence, he then added " ... mais il était des nôtres ..." ("but he was one of our party" – meaning by this that Degrelle had shared the sufferings and dangers of frontline life like any other legionnaire, that this in itself was sufficient to forgive his shortcomings, even the worst ones).

CHAPTER XXV

Military Collaboration in WWII, a Matter of Idealism?

The case of the Walloon Eastern Front volunteers and their leader Léon Degrelle.

The establishment of the *Légion Wallonie* in July/August 1941, mainly resulted from the ambition of Fernand Rouleau, Léon Degrelle's deputy. Temporarily set aside by the intrigues of his lieutenant while away in Paris for talks with ambassador Otto Abetz, Degrelle, after returning, managed to preserve appearances thanks to an active, personal and above all spectacular participation in the recruitment campaign.[1] By doing so, he soon overshadowed his rival and even succeeded in passing himself off as the real generator of the anti-Bolshevik formation.

Determining the motivations, beliefs and reasons which pushed thousands of Walloons to follow Léon Degrelle is quite a challenge.[2]

Astonishingly enough, apart from the first two contingents composed of politically committed men, volunteering for the Legion was in many ways more coincidental than it was a well-judged decision. During the war-time years a great number of legionnaires enlisted for entirely different reasons than those which had animated the first nucleus around Degrelle in July 1941: Rexist militants hoping their presence next to their leader would result in rewards, on the one hand; on the other hand, those who had followed Degrelle with no other ambition than serve what they sincerely thought to be a just cause, whatever this just cause was supposed to represent – anti-Bolshevism, preservation of Christianity, a better place for Belgium in a Germanized Europe, or plain Rexist militant discipline obeying orders.[3]

Generally speaking, few legionnaires bore the Germans in their hearts. During the *Wehrmacht* period the supporters of the integration of Belgium into the *Reich*, the unconditional supporters of Hitler and Germanism preferred joining the *Waffen-SS* and avoided the Legion.[4] Those who nevertheless had ventured into the ranks of the Walloon formation were given a bad reception and Degrelle

Fig. 25.1. Already before the war, anti-Communist propaganda was the favourite topic of right wing groupings, actively backed up by an influential Catholic Church during and after the Civil War in Spain (*Collection E. De Bruyne*).

personally saw to it that they were expelled without more ado.[5]

The initial recruitment had drawn its first elements among the members of the Rexist Movement, more particularly from the *Formations de Combat*, the militia of the Rexist Movement. As at that time German troops were victorious on all fronts, the married men could easily be convinced they would soon be back with their families without suffering significant dangers and could resume their professional activities haloed with the prestige of having participated in the struggle against Communism. As to the students, they would hardly miss the start of school in September ... so, they were told.

The ambitious ones and careerists, for whom the war against Bolshevism was not based on genuine idealism, forsook the Legion after coming face to face with the sufferings of frontline life and the danger of the first combats in 1941–42. Once back in Belgium, a number of these so-called super idealists soon got involved in *Sipo-Sd* round-up duties.

Without generalizing, the mature legionnaires of the first contingent did not consider Bolshevism to be a mortal danger worth combating but rather considered it as a regime likely to jeopardize personal plans of access to public services and the advantages to be derived from them. The rest of the first contingent – apart from a few isolated individuals, adventurers as well as a handful of Nazi supporters and pro-German enthusiasts – comprised sincere Rexists, convinced of the sincerity of those who had recruited them, animated by a true ideal. They had left their families with the belief that they were acting in the best interests of the Fatherland and were, in the first moments of enthusiasm, ready to give their lives for what they assumed to be a noble cause.

After the disaster of the first combat in February 1942, Degrelle immediately realized the isolated performance of his men would not, on its own, be enough to bring him into the spotlight, that he and his Legion, the chosen instrument of his rise to power, were likely to remain anonymous ... unless something spectacular intervened ...

Taking advantage of the second contingent supplied by Rexist Youth leader John Hagemans in March 1942, a group composed of teenagers willing to expose themselves generously like any youth, easy to manipulate, saturated with slogans glorifying heroism, Degrelle was to show neither hesitation nor scruples when enrolling these new forces, giving the Legion a second wind it badly needed to survive.

The youngsters he was about to throw into the battle were stimulated by a sincere enthusiasm, by an unlimited allegiance to their leader John Hagemans, whose utopian visions had transported his *Knights* into a surrealist universe of unrealistic dimensions. Truly convinced of the rightness of their action, they offered their young lives with the courage and the self-sacrifice with which they had been crammed.

By the end of 1942, the Caucasus campaign had decimated the ranks of the Legion. In order to face this situation Degrelle intensified propaganda and multiplied steps with German authorities with a view to recruiting more men.

In June 1943, the Legion was transferred to the *Waffen-SS*. The nucleus of the *Sturmbrigade* consisted of the remainder the first contingents and recruits

Fig. 25.2. The presence of the *Edelweiß* on the cap shows that this propaganda poster was issued after the Caucasus campaign (and before being transferred to the *Waffen-SS*), during a period when the Walloon unit was badly in need of new blood.

enlisted in Germany. In the meantime, National Socialist propaganda had intensified. Serious efforts were made to persuade the Walloons they were of Germanic lineage. Cherkassy came to the rescue of Degrelle, too. The heavy breakthrough battles south-west of Korsun in February 1944, created a great stir in Germany, the press echoing and magnifying the event all over occupied Europe. At last, Léon Degrelle had achieved his goal: to emerge from the anonymity in which he had been confined for more than two years.

The Cherkassy affair substantially contributed to attracting new volunteers, inspired as they were by a momentary irresistible impulse of the moment, result of a well-organized propaganda campaign. However, it did not take long before they realized the fatal consequences of a hasty and inconsiderate step. With the arrival of these legionnaires, the Legion had to face a phenomenon that it had not known until then: repeated desertions. And in spite of the rigours to which the deserters exposed themselves, their number increased in a direct proportion to Hitler's chances of losing the war.[6]

In the meantime, Degrelle had increased his influence in a decisive way and consequently intended to enlarge the battle strength of the *Sturmbrigade*. At the same time, he set his mind on the Walloon POWs and workers in Germany for whom the struggle against Communism was certainly not a main concern. Many a POW or labourer enlisted as a consequence of the opportunity it offered to escape monotonous captivity in *Stalags* or the constraints of life in an *Arbeitslager*. In many cases, the promise of a two-week leave in Belgium when enlisting tipped the scale. No need to tell that the promise was never kept …

In 1944, the fate of the war had changed sides. The reservoir of idealists in Belgium had dried up with no hope of renewal. To increase recruitment, Walloon collaboration propaganda then highlighted the material advantages that enlistment would procure. A special effort was made to recruit the Walloons residing in Germany. All classes and circles were called up: POWs, workers, students; anybody likely to sign up was welcome, provided he could bear arms. Even convicts were given the opportunity to join the Legion offering them the choice between prison or military service.[7] As ranks grew bigger, the Legion took on a mercenary character it had never shown before and slowly lost its initial identity.

The liberation of Belgium in September 1944, forced the paramilitary collaborators[8] to flee to Germany where they were immediately transferred to the newly-formed *28. SS-Freiw. -Gren. Div. Wallonien*. The same fate affected the numerous Rex civilians who had followed the German armies in their retreat: they too were forced to enrol as a result of a decree ordering general mobilization issued by *SS-Sturmbannführer* Léon Degrelle, recently appointed *Führer der Wallonen* (Leader of the Walloon People). Among these latecomers, there was a strange mixture of unyielding idealists (there were a few left!), adventurers and scoundrels, not to mention the very few soldiers of the lost causes that an intellectual and psychic process had irresistibly attracted to the final *baroud d'honneur*.

And last but not least, in November-December 1944, about 500 Walloon workers in Germany were called up for service in the *Reichswallonischer Arbeitsdienst*, the Walloon branch of the *R.A.D.*, a decision taken by Degrelle as *Führer der Wallonen*, on the pretext that a three month stay in the Walloon *R.A.D.* camps would allow them to recover from hard work in the German factories. As a matter of fact, the *RWAD* was nothing other than the antechamber of the *Waffen-SS*. The conscripts protested in vain when they realized Degrelle had trapped them. Under the threat of arms, they were forced to enrol and sent to the Oder front in March 1945.[9]

In short, the motivations of the Walloon Russian front combatant can be identified as follows:

1) those legionnaires who had Belgium (and its future) in mind and on

whom totalitarian propaganda did not have as much grip as faith in their country protected them from Nazi German influence;

2) the Rexists who had tried to take advantage of the German presence to impose a New Order regime;

3) volunteers blinded by National Socialist social achievements and who had ended up by showing sympathy or even admiration for Nazi Germany and its regime, and who, maybe for other reasons too, ardently wanted a German victory;

4) practising Catholics yielding to their religious ideal who had gone to war to fight Communism with the same spirit that once had animated the Crusaders, as they truly considered Bolshevism to be the greatest danger of Christianity;

5) individuals attracted by material advantages for themselves and their families; individuals eager to avoid a criminal conviction or forget either sorrow, grief or a domestic disagreement; individuals willing to put on the *feldgrau* uniform even knowing this gesture was reprehensible on moral or legal grounds;

6) the ones who on behalf of the oath of allegiance to Degrelle, out of naïve admiration, out of boundless friendship,[10] out of inner conviction or party discipline, joined Degrelle without being aware the latter was (mis)using them merely for purposes of prestige and personal ambition.

In the end, one thing seemed clear: without preliminary military collaboration there would be no political activity at all ... and, by way of consequence, no Degrelle ...

Appendices

APPENDIX I

List of Walloon Officers Who Served in the Legion Wallonie, the 5.Sturmbrigade and the 28.SS-Freiw.Gren.Div.Wallonien[1]

The Walloon legionnaires were enlisted with the rank they held in the Belgian Army, whether within the Reserve Corps or the regular Army. The only exception were the Russian ex-officers of the White armies (anti-Communists during the Russian Civil War), who were enrolled with the hybrid rank/function of *Sonderführer*. When joining the *Waffen-SS* they were allotted a rank one degree below the rank they held in their national army.[2]

Walloon NCOs could become officers:

a. by graduating from one of the Military Academies [Bad-Tölz – mainly *11. Kriegslehrgang*[3]) – Kienschlag (*1. & 2. Kriegs-Waffen-Junkerslehrgang*) – Sophienwalde Academy (29 October 1944–20 December 1944)];
b. by recognition of frontline experience, the so-called F*rontbewährungsoffiziere* (*Wehrmacht* period only);
c. by achievement of personal exploits – *Tapferkeitsoffiziere* (literally "brave officer");
d. from September 1944, a number of officers of the *NSKK* and the *Garde Wallonne* were enrolled with a lower rank (one degree) than the one they held in their respective formations. The officers who refused to join the Division were sent to the *Ers. Btl. 36.*, 2nd Company;
e. by merit and seniority;
f. by pretending they were already officers of the Reserve Corps when enrolling (*i.e.* Fernand Rouleau).

*All officers having graduated from the *11.Kriegslehrgang* were permitted to wear their *SS-Ustuf* insignias from 1 April 1944 on.

SS-Obersturmbannführer

1. Lucien LIPPERT
25.08.1913–13.02.1944/August 1941-February 1944/Rank obtained posthumously/Belgian career officer/4th Kdr of the *LW* (and Assault Brigade) June 1942 – February 1944/*Hptm* 08.06.1942/*SS-Stubaf.* 28.6.1943/Winter Campaign Medal/ Gen.Inf. Assault Badge/Wound Badge in Black/Iron Cross II/Iron Cross I (24.08.1942)/German Cross in Gold (posthumously 20.02.1944) /.*SS-Ostubaf.* (posthumously).

2. Léon DEGRELLE
15.06.1906–31.03.1994/8 August 1941- 8 May 1945 /.
Schütze: August 1941
Gefreiter: 10.02.1942
Feldwebel: 22.03.1942
Leutnant: 01.05.1942
SS-Ostuf.: 01.06.1943
SS-Hstuf.: 01.01.1944 (*Führer* – but not *Kdr* – of the 5th Assault Brigade from 13.02.1944 to September 1944).

SS-Stubaf.: 20.04.1944

SS-Ostubaf. d. Res. u. Kdr 28. Freiw. -Gren. Div. Wallonien: 01.01.1945, which is, – according to the *Führer-Stellenbesetzung* of 1 March 1945 – his last official rank obtained.

Awards

03.03.42: Iron Cross II (*EK II*) awarded by Gen. Werner Sanne/*100.I.D.*

23.03.42: Wound Badge in Black (*Verwundenten-Abzeichen*).

21.05.42: Iron Cross I (*EK I*) awarded by the *101.I.D.*

03.06.42: *97. Jäg. Div.* Badge (*Edelweiß*).

15.08.42: Winter Campaign Medal (*Winterschlacht-Abzeichen*) awarded by Gen. Ernst Rupp/*97. Jäg. Div.*

25.08.42: Gen.Inf. Assault Badge (*Allg. Sturm-Abzeichen*) awarded by Gen. Ernst Rupp/*97. Jäg. Div.*

30.11.43: Close Combat Clasp in Bronze (*Nahkampfspange*).

23.12.43: Wound Badge in Silver awarded by *SS-Brigadeführer* Herbert Otto Gille/*5. Pz Div. Wiking*).

20.02.44: Kinght's Coss (*Ritterkreuz*). Recommendation No. 2474 by the Chief of the Section Personnel of the Army dated 8 May 1944 as a result of Gille's recommendation dated 15 February 1944.

19.03.44: Close Combat Clasp in Silver.

19.03.44: Wound Badge in Gold.

27.08.44: Oakleaves.[4] (*Eichenlaub*). Three direct recommendations by *Generaloberst u. Befehlshaber H.Gr.Nord* Schoerner, a first one to *SS-Gruppenführer* Fegelein of the *Führer Hauptquartier* dated 25 August 08:30 *p.m.*, and co-signed by Gen. Grasser, in charge of *the Armee-Abt. Narwa*; a second one to *OKH/PAP 5A /1. Staffel* on 25 August 09:00 *p.m.*, and a third one to the *Reichsführer-SS* Himmler – *Feldkommandostelle*, dated 25 August but dispatched on 26 August at 06:34 *p.m.* Subsequent recommendations by *SS-Brigadeführer* Jürgen Wagner (*4. SS-Frw. -Pz. Gren. Brig. Nederland*/Dorpat sector) on 29 August 1944, and by General Hasse, chief *II.Armeekorps* on 6 September).

14.09.44: Close Combat Clasp in Gold.

09.10.44: German Cross in Gold (*Deutsches Kreuz in Gold*). Recommendation by Herbert Otto Gille dated 21.01.1944, processed 26 September 1944, and awarded on 9 October 1944).

SS-Sturmbannführer

3. Frans HELLEBAUT
29.08.1898–18.06.1984/June 1944-May 1945/Career officer holding the rank of Major – B.E.M. (War Staff College Certificate)/*SS-Stubaf.* 01.06.1944/ Chief-of-Staff of the *28. SS-Freiw. -Gren. Div. Wallonien*, second in command/ Hellebaut was to attend the *Kdt Inf. Schule/Döberitz* from 04.12.1944 – 05.02.1945, but refused.[5]

Appendix I: Fig. 1.1
Frans Hellebaut

4. Georges TCHEKHOFF
14.12.1892 (Suchum/Russia)-Buenos Aires 25.11.1961/Ex-officer (Russian

Imperial Marine, and later Wrangel Army) *Hauptmann*/Second *Kdr* of the *Légion Wallonie* (April- June 1942)/*SS-Hstuf.* 01.06.1943/*SS-Stubaf.* 20.04.1944/ Attended *Schieß Schule Pz. Tr. Putloss Kdt* from 31.07.1944 to 09.09.1944/*Kdt 20. Rgt Führer Lehrgang/Döberitz* from 04.12.1944 to 07.02.1945/*Kdr 70Rgt*/ Winter Campaign Medal/Iron Cross II/Iron Cross I.

Appendix I: Fig. 1.12
Georges Tchekhoff

5. Georges JACOBS
07.12.1893-Madrid 1964/August 1941-January 1942/retired career officer/ Captain-Cdt of the regular Army but addressed to as Major, rank he held in the Reserve Corps/1st *Kdr* of the *Légion Wallonie*/Reactivated mid-October 1944 as head of the *Adjutantur*/*SS-Stubaf.* on 01.09.1944/Winter Medal/Iron Cross II (28.02.1945).

6. Jules MATHIEU
23.09.1909–16.04.1990/August 1941 as a NCO-May 1945/*Leutnant* in June 1942/*SS-Ustuf.* 01.06.1943/*SS-Ostuf.* 01.12.1943/*SS-Hstuf.* 20 April 1944/SS-*Stubaf.* 20.04.1945/Mathieu attended the *Kdt Schießschule* at Putlos (11.07 – 09.09.1944)/*Kdr 69Rgt* in October 1944/Winter Campaign Medal/Iron Cross I/Iron Cross II/Close Combat Clasp in Silver/Gen.Inf. Assault Badge/(German Cross in Gold 1945, according to document signed by Degrelle in 1985).

Appendix I: Fig. 1.3
Jules Mathieu

7. Henri DERRIKS
31.07.1904–06.11.1972/Belgian officer of the Reserve Corps/November 1942-May 1945/*Oberleutnant*/*SS-Ostuf.* on 01.06.1943/SS-*Hstuf.* 21.06.1944/*SS-Stubaf.* 20.04.1945/Commander of *I/69Rgt*/Commander of the *Kampfgruppe Derriks* in April 1945/Derriks claims he was awarded the German Cross in Gold on 4 March 1945 (Streesen retreat)/Iron Cross II/Iron Cross I/Gen.Inf. Assault Badge/Wound Badge in Black/Close Combat Clasp in Bronze/Rumanian Cross of Merit/Derriks also claims that General Ottner (*281. Inf. Div*) recommended him for the *Ritterkreuz* after the Altdamm bridgehead fighting.

8. Léon STOCKMAN
13.01.1899./ Divisional Catholic chaplain/15 October 1944-May 1945/Iron Cross II (16.03.1945)/Gen.Inf. Assault Badge (01.04.1945)/Rex Movement Medal in Gold (02.11.1944).

SS-Hauptsturmbannführer/Hauptmann

9. Gommaire ANTHONISSEN
06.02.1896–10.02.1944/Captain of the Reserve Corps/August 1941/*SS-Hstuf.* 07.08.1943.

10. Marcel BONNIVER
20.01.1905–26.12.1983/August 1941 as a private-May 1945/*SS-Ustuf.* 01.06.1943/*SS-Ostuf.* 20.04.1944/*SS-Hstuf.* 09.11.1944 after the Estonian campaign/Together with Degrelle and Gillis one of the 3 Walloons having participated in all the military campaigns of the Legion/Winter Campaign Medal/Iron Cross II/Iron Cross I/Inf. Assault Badge in Silver/Close Combat Clasp in Silver/Wound Badge in Silver. Last assignment: CO *II/69Rgt* in April 1945.

11. Victor BOULLIENNE
7.11.1881/Captain of the Reserve Corps/*Hptm.*/ August 1941 – demobilized in May 1943.

12. Pierre DENGIS
08.12.1916–13.2.1984/August 1941 as *Oberfeldwebel*-May 1945/*Leutnant* (01.03.43)/*SS-Ostuf.* on 01.12.1943/*SS-Hstuf.* on 09.11.1944/Winter Campaign Medal/Wound Badge in Gold/Iron Cross II/Iron Cross I/Gen.Inf. Assault Badge/Close Combat Clasp in Bronze/War Merit Cross II with Swords/Commander of the Convalescent Co (*Genesenden Kp*) of the *Ers. Btl. 36* in 1945.

13. René DUPRES
02.02.1909–02.12.1941/August 1941–02.12.1941/Career officer/*Hauptmann*/.

14. Willy HEYVAERT
Captain of the Reserve Corps/*Hauptmann*/August 1941 – Demobilized in December 1941.

15. Nicolas KAMSKY
14.12.1898 (Moscow)/Ex-officer of the Wrangel armies/August 1941 as *Sonderführer*-May 1945/*Leutnant* 01.05.1943/*SS-Ostuf.* 20.07.1944/*SS-Hstuf.* 01.09.1944/ Emigrated to Canada after the war/War Merit Cross II/Winter Campaign Medal/Iron Cross II (30.08.1942)/Wound Badge in Black (17.03.1944)/Gen.Inf. Assault Badge (27.04.1944)/Close Combat Clasp in Bronze (22.06.1944).

16. Léon LAKAIE
26.04.1901/Career officer/POW in *Oflag IIA* (Prenzlau) until June 1944/*SS-Hstuf.* 28.07.1944.

17. Pierre PAULY
25.04.1908–21.06.1948/January 1942-March 1942 as *Hptm u. Kdr*/Career officer – Captain – B.E.M. (War Staff College Certificate)/3rd *Kdr* of the *Légion Wallonie*/Iron Cross II/Iron Cross I/Fled to Germany in September 1944, but was not taken up in the cadre/Executed by firing squad in 1948.

18. Adolphe RENIER
18.07.1915-Paris, 1999/Career officer of the Belgian Air Force/10 October 1941-May 1945/Transferred to the *Luftwaffe* as a pilot in June 1944/*Leutnant*/*SS-Ostuf.* 01.06.1943/*SS-Hstuf.* 20.04.1944/Winter Campaign Medal/Iron Cross II/Iron Cross I/Wound Badge in Black/Entered a monastic order in 1952.

19. Georges RUELLE
23.4.1910–1981/August 1941-May 1945/Professional NCO/*Feldwebel* in August 1941/*Oberfeldwebel* on 20 January 1941/Mentioned in the 23 February 1942 dispatches of the Battalion for outstanding gallantry/*Leutnant* in June 1942 (*Frontbewährungssoffizier*)/SS-*Ustuf.* 01.06.1943/*SS-Ostuf.* 01.12.1943/*Kdr* of the *Kampfgruppe Ruelle* in August 1944 (Estonia)/*SS-Hstuf.* 09.11.1944/Attended the *26. Btl u. Abt. Führer Lehrgang/Heereschule* Güstrow from 17.02.1945 to 17.03.1945/Winter Campaign Medal/Iron Cross II/Iron Cross I/Gen.Inf. Assault Badge/Wound Badge in Silver/Close Combat Clasp in Black/Sick leave from September 1942 to 15 January 1943/He was then put at the disposal of the *Kommandostab* Z who assigned him as Chief *a. i.* of the *Formations de Combat* within the General Staff and Adjutant to the *Garde Wallonne* from 15.02.43 to October 43.

20. Henri THYSSEN
15.7.1920–20.04.1945/March 1942–20.04.1945/Lieutenant of the *Garde Wallonne*/*Leutnant*/SS-*Ustuf.* 01.06.1943/*SS-Ostuf.* 20.04.1944/*SS-Hstuf.* 20.04.1945/ Gen.Inf. Assault Badge/Iron Cross II/Iron Cross I/Close Combat Clasp in Black.

21. Jean VERMEIRE
28.09.1918/August 1941 as a *Leutnant* although NCO of the Reserve Corps-May 1945/*SS-Ostuf.* 01.06.1944/*SS-Hstuf.* 30.01.1945/Liaison officer to the *RSHA* in Berlin from June 1943 to August 1944, with offices at the *Wallonische Verbindungsstelle*, Hedemannstraße, 24, Berlin SW16/Attended the *Lehrgang Inf. Schieß Schule Döberitz/Heer. Sch. Güstrow* from 17.12.1944 – 28.01.1945/Winter Campaign Medal/Iron Cross II/Iron Cross I/Gen.Inf. Assault Badge.

22. Albert VANDAMME
06.04.1893/August 1941-Demobilized on 12 January 1942/Captain of the Reserve Corps/*Hptm.*/.

- Dr Albert JACQUEMIN (see 132)
- Jean MALHERBE (see 139)

SS-Obersturmführer/Oberleutnant

23. Camille BOSQUION
13.08.1905-died in a car accident in Belgium, June 1944/August 1941 as NCO/*Oberfeldwebel* on 10 February 1942 for gallantry during the Gromowaja-Balka fighting/*Leutnant* in June 1942/Demobilized after the Caucasus campaign/*SS-Ustuf.*/ Commander of the Recruiting Centre and *Ers. Btl* in Namur (Belgium)/Winter Campaign Medal/Iron Cross II/Iron Cross I.

24. Arthur BUYDTS
27.05.1899–28.02.1942/August 1941/Lieutenant of the Reserve Corps/*Oberleutnant*.

25. Jacques CAPELLE
24.05.1914-(?) 17.02.1945)/August 1941/Graduated from the *11. Kriegslehrgang* at Bad-Tölz/*SS-Ustuf.* 21.06.1944*/*SS-Ostuf.* 09.11.1944/Winter Campaign Medal/Gen.Inf. Assault Badge/Iron Cross II/Iron Cross I.

26. François CHOME
15.11.1913/March 1942-May 1945/Graduated from the *11. Kriegslehrgang* at Bad-Tölz/*SS-Ustuf.* 21.06.1944*/*SS-Standarte Kurt Eggers* as head of the Walloon war correspondents on 31.08.1944/*SS-Ostuf.* 20.04.1945/Made prisoner in Copenhagen on 7 June 1945.

27. Léon CLOSSET
29.5.1911/Former *Sabena* airline pilot/August 1941 as an NCO-May 1944/*Leutnant* as *Frontbewährungsoffizier* in June 1942/*Kommandeur a. i.* during Lippert's 1st furlough in December 42/Became the head of the Rexist Labour Service (May 1944 – April 1945) with the rank of *Oberarbeitsführer* on 01.05.1944/Winter Campaign Medal/Iron Cross II.

28. Mathieu DE COSTER
30.01.1924/Joined the *L.W.* on 23.06.1942-May 1945/Graduated from the *11. Kriegslehrgang* at Bad-Tölz/*SS-Ustuf.* 21.06.1944*/*SS-Ostuf.* per 20.04.1945/Gen.Inf. Assault Badge/Iron Cross II/Iron Cross I.

29. Roger DE GOY
22.10.1919–27.06.1979/March 1942 as an NCO-May 1945/Rexist Youth cadre and John Hagemans' adjutant/Graduated from the *11. Kriegslehrgang* at Bad-Tölz/*SS-Ustuf.* 21.06.1944*/*Junkerschaftsführer* (*16. Junkerschaft*) at Kienschlag Academy/*SS-Ostuf.* 20.04.1945/Gen.Inf. Assault Badge/Iron Cross II/Iron Cross I.

30. Robert DENIE
24.08.1908/Officer in the merchant marine/March 1942-May 1945/*Leutnant*/*SS-Ustuf.* 01.06.1943/*SS-Ostuf.* 20.04.1944/Attended the *Kdt Inf. Schule* of Döberitz (12.12.44 – 20.04.1945)/Gen.Inf. Assault Badge/Iron Cross II/Iron Cross I (presented on the battlefield at Teklino-Cherkassy, 17.01.44)/Close Combat Clasp in Bronze/Wound Badge in Black./ (Probably *SS-Hstuf.* 20.04.1945).

31. Joseph DUMONT
23.03.1914/Lieutenant of the Reserve Corps/Joined the *Garde Wallonne* on 02.02.1942/*L.W.* as a *Leutnant* on 12.04.1942/*SS-Ustuf.* 01.06.1943/*SS-Ostuf.* 01.12.1943./Wound Badge/Iron Cross II/Iron Cross I/. (Probably *SS-Hstuf.* 20.04.1945).

32. Charles GENERET
24.10.1907 – †Indo-China 1948 in the ranks of the French Foreign Legion/August 1941-May 1945/Graduated from the *11. Kriegslehrgang* Bad-Tölz/Immediate promotion to *SS-Ustuf.* 20.04.1944* as highest ranked/Instructor (*Heerwesen*) at Kienschlag-Beneschau Military Academy /Winter Campaign Medal/War Merit Cross II with Swords/*SS-Ostuf.* 20.04.1945.

Appendix I: Fig. 1.4
Léon Gillis

33. Gé. Pé ... 14.01.1925/August 1941 – as youngest legionnaire of the contingent -May 1945/Graduated from the *11. Kriegslehrgang* at Bad-Tölz/*SS-Ustuf.* 21.06.1944*/*SS-Ostuf.* 20.04.1945/Winter Campaign Medal/ Iron Cross II/Iron Cross I/Wound Badge in Silver.

34. Léon GILLIS
11.02.1913–28.03.1977./ August 1941 as a *Gefreiter* (corporal)-May 1945/ Together with Degrelle and Bonniver,

one of the three legionnaires having participated in all the *Wallonie* campaigns/Severely wounded at Tcherjakow (Caucasus)/Spent one year in different hospitals for recovery/*SS-Standartenoberjunker* (*Tapferkeitsoffizier*) on 01.03.1944 on grounds of exceptional gallantry during Cherkassy breakout/*SS-Ustuf.* on 20.04.1944/*SS-Ostuf.* 09.11.1944/Knight's Cross (30.09.1944) for outstanding action in *Kamfpgruppe Ruelle* in August 1944/Winter Campaign Medal/Inf. Assault Badge in Silver/Iron Cross II (February 1942)/Iron Cross I (26.08.1942)/Close Combat Clasp in Silver/Wound Badge in Silver/Knight's Cross.

35. Adrien GODSDEEL
02.03.1898/August 1941-March 1942/ Seriously wounded at Gromowaja-Balka and demobilized/Successively *Feldwebel*, *Oberfeldwebel* (20.02.1942) and *Leutnant*/Reactivated as *SS-Ustuf.* (21.06.1944)/*SS-Ostuf.* on 21.07.1944/ Commanding officer of the Dilligsen-Alfeld instruction centre in 1944/45/ Winter Campaign Medal/Iron Cross II/Wound Badge in Silver.

36. Josy GRAFF
02.12.1917/Career NCO/August 1941-May 1945/*Oberfeldwebel* 01.03.1943/ *Leutnant* in May 1942/*SS-Ustuf.* 01.06.1943/*SS-Ostuf* 20.04.1944./ Escaped to Argentina where he died in a motor-cycle accident. (Probably *SS-Hstuf.* on 20 April 1945).

37. Marcel LAMPROYE
31.05.1914/August 1941 as NCO-May 1945/*SS-Ustuf.* on 01.06.1943/*SS-Ostuf.* 20.04.1944/Winter Campaign Medal/Iron Cross II/Iron Cross I/Close Combat Clasp in Silver/(Probably *SS-Hstuf.* on 20 April 1945).

38. Albert LASSOIS
12.7.1911/Former *Sabena* airline pilot/August 1941 as a NCO-May 1945/*Leutnant* in June 1942/CO of 1Co from 5 August 1942 to 9 September 1942./ Head of the social service of the *Légion Wallonie* (*L'Honneur Legionnaire*) from January 1943 to June 1943/*SS-Ustuf.* on 01.06.1943/*SS-Ostuf* on 31.01.1944./ In May 1944, Lassois took command of the social service (*Fürsorgeoffizier*/Welfare Officer) within the *Erstazskommando Wallonien* in Brussels/Transferred to Namur as Commander of the Training and Replacement Centre (*SS Walllonie*) after Bosquion's death in June 1944/Commanding officer of the Grünenplan (near Alfeld) instruction centre in 1944/45/Winter Campaign Medal/Iron Cross II/(Probably *SS-Hstuf.* on 20 April 1945).

39. Alfred LISEIN
28.7.1902/August 1941-March 1942/Demobilized to fulfill political duties in Belgium/A friend of Degrelle and as such his Co/CO/Iron Cross II.

40. Oscar MAHIEU
04.04.1906/Sept. 1944-May 1945/SS-*Ostuf.*

41. Joseph MIRGAIN
08.03.1911/Career NCO/August 1941-May 1945/*SS-Ustuf.* 01.06.1943/*SS-Ostuf.* 20.04.1944/Iron Cross II/Winter Campaign Medal/(Probably *SS-Hstuf.* on 20 April 1945).

42. Albert NORTIER
11.11.1918/August 1941-May 1945/Graduated from the *11. Kriegslehrgang* at Bad-Tölz/*SS-Ustuf.* 21.06.1944*/*SS-Ostuf.* 20.04.1945.

43. Jules SANDRON
16.10.1915/August 1941-May 1945/Graduated from the *11. Kriegslehrgang* at Bad-Tölz/*SS-Ustuf.* 21.06.1944*/*SS-Ostuf.* 20.04.1945.

44. Albert STEIVER
26.09.1917/August 1941-May 1945/Graduated from the *11. Kriegslehrgang* Bad-Tölz/*SS-Ustuf.* 21.06.1944*/CO *1/I/70Rgt* and *Kdr a. i. I/70Rgt*/*SS-Ostuf.* 20.04.1945.

45. Georg von SCHAFROFF
17.10.1903 (Inkoo – China)/*Sipo-Sd* Brussels from January to October 1943/Joined the *L.W.* in October 1943 as a *Sturmmann,* then *Sonderführer*/*Waffen SS-Ustuf.* 01.06.1944/*Waffen SS-Ostuf.* 09.11.1944 as result of the Estonian Campaign/Iron Cross II/Iron Cross I/Gen.Inf. Assault Badge.

46. Marcel THOMAS
13.12.1915/August 1941-May 1945/Graduated from the *11. Kriegslehrgang* at Bad-Tölz/*SS-Ustuf.* 21.06.1944*/*SS-Ostuf.* 09.11.1944 as result of the Estonian Campaign/Iron Cross II/Iron Cross I/Gen.Inf. Assault Badge/Wound Badge in Silver.

47. Roger WASTIAU.
31.10.1911–1985/August 1941-May 1945/Graduated from the *11. Kriegslehrgang* Bad-Tölz as an administrative officer (*Verwaltungsoffizier*)/*SS-Ustuf.* 21.06.1944*/ *SS-Ostuf.* 01.09.1944/Head of the *Adjutantur* untill mid-October 1944/CO of the Signals Co from mid-October 1944 on/Replaced Jean Roman as liaison officer to the *RSSH* in April 1945/Winter Campaign Medal/War Merit Cross I/Gen.Inf. Assault Badge/Iron Cross II/Wound Badge in Black/(He claims he received the rank of *SS-Hstuf.* on 20 April 1945).

48. Jacques WAUTELET
05.01.1922/Graduated from the *11. Kriegslehrgang* at Bad-Tölz/*SS-Ustuf.* 21.06.1944*/*SS-Ostuf.* 09.11.1945 as result of the Estonian Campaign.

- Dr Sylvère MIESSE (see 133)
- Baron Robert SLOET d'OLDRUYTENBORGH (see 146)
- Paul DAULIE (see 142)
- Armand DOR (see 143)
- René VERDEUR (see 148)

SS-Untersturmbannführer/Leutnant

49. Robert AMBROES
24.8.1920/Former officer of the *G.W.*/ Graduated from Sophienwalde Academy (29.10.44 – 20.12.1944)/*SS-Ustuf.* February 1945/Last appointment: *Adjutant I/69Rgt.*

50. Rodolphe BAL
30.04.1911–06.03.1945/August 1941/Graduated from the *11. Kriegslehrgang* at Bad-Tölz/*SS-Ustuf.* 21.06.1944*.

51. Guy BARTHELEMY

52. Raymond BERNARD
06.02.1920/Graduated from Kienschlag (1st session)/*SS-Ustuf.* 09.11.1944/Last appointment: Assistant *Adjutant 28.SS-Freiw.-Gren.Div.Wallonien.*

53. Louis BERVAES
08.03.1918/October 1944-May 1945/Career NCO/Officer of the *G.W.*/ Graduated from Sophienwalde Academy (29.10.44–20.12.1944)/*SS-Ustuf.* February 1945/Iron Cross II (04.03.1945)/Gen.Inf. Assault Badge/Wound Badge in Black.

54. Marcel CAPOEN
11.04.1921–19.08.1944/August 1941/Graduated from the *11. Kriegslehrgang* at Bad-Tölz/*SS-Ustuf.* 21.06.1944*.

55. Paul CHENUT
30.06.1918/August 1941-May 45/*SS-Ustuf.* 30.01.1945.

56. Léon COLLARD
29.07.1920/Graduated from Kienschlag (1st session)/*SS-Ustuf.* 09.11.1944.

57. Léon CREMERS
20.04.1920/10 March 1942-May 45/Career NCO of the Belgian Army/Graduted from the *Nachrichtenschule Nürenmberg*/*SS-Ustuf.* 21.12.1944.

58. Joseph CREUVEN
05.10.1920/October 1944 as *Leutnant* of the *G.W.*/ Graduated from Sophienwalde Academy (29.10.44–20.12.1944)/*SS-Ustuf.* February 1945.

59. François DARAS
25.02.1919–17.02.1944/August 1941/*Leutnant*/*SS-Ustuf.* 01.06.1944/Winter Campaign Medal/Gen.Inf. Assault Badge/Iron Cross II/Iron Cross I .

60. Joseph DAULNE
/ *Leutnant*/August 1941–12.08.1942/(Dismissed on grounds of personal conflict with Degrelle).

61. Pierre de BACKER de REVILLE, Count.
†Schönwerder 27.04.1945/Officer of the Reserve Corps/*SS-Ustuf.*

62. Georges DE BONGNIE
14.12.1916/Member of Staff of the *Formations de Combat* in Germany among the volunteering Walloon labourers/Joined the *L.W.* in March 1942/Successively *Schütze, Gefreiter, SS-Unterscharführer* (01.08.43), *SS-Oberscharführer* (01.02.44)/Graduated from Kienschlag Academy (1st session)/*SS-Ustuf.* 09.11.1944/Last appointments: *Adj-Maj I/70Rgt* (27.01.45–15.03.45); *Adjutant 69Rgt* (01.04.45–03.05.45)/Iron Cross II/Inf. Gen.Inf. Assault Badge/Close Combat Clasp in Bronze/Shared F. Hellebaut's cell (cell *33. A* /prison St-Gilles, Brussels) for 16 months (October 46-March 48).

63. Jacques DE HEUG
22.04.1922–08.02.1982/August 1941-May 1945/Graduated from Kienschlag (1st session)/SS-*Ustuf.* 09.11.1944.

64. Abel DELANNOY
17.12.1925–06.12.1989/March 1942-May 1945/Graduated from Kienschlag Academy (1st session)/*SS-Ustuf.* 09.11.1944/Wound Badge in Black/Iron Cross II/Iron Cross I.

65 Philippe della FAILLE d'HUYSE
21.08.1923/Joined the *L.W.* on 8 April 1943-May 1945/Graduated from Kienschlag Academy (1st session)/*SS-Ustuf.* 09.11.1944/Wound Badge in Black/Iron Cross II.

66. Maurice DERAVET
03.06.1902/August 1941-May 1945/Graduated from Kienschlag Academy (1st session)/*SS-Ustuf.* 09.11.1944/Iron Cross II/Winter Campaign Medal/Gen.Inf. Assault Badge/Close Combat Clasp in Bronze/Wound Badge in Black.

67. Léon DESTATTE
04.04.1912/Graduated from Kienschlag Academy (1st session)/*SS-Ustuf.* 09.11.1944.

68. Alfred DEVAUX
13.11.1922/Theology Student/Joined the *L.W.* on 15 April 1942-May 1945/Graduated from the *11. Kriegslehrgang* at Bad-Tölz/*SS-Ustuf.* 21.06.1944*/*Junkerschaftsführer (14. Junkerschaft*) at Kienschlag Academy from May 1944-November 1944/Then Artillery instruction at Beneschau until March 1945/(Probably *SS-Ostuf.* 20.04.1945).

69. Stéphane DEVREESE
04.04.1912/August 1941-May 1945/Career NCO/*SS-Ustuf.* 21.06.1944 */ War Merit Cross II with Swords/*K.T.L.d.SS-Wien* from 15.8.44–16.9.44/*K.T.L.d.SS–Wien* from 16.10.44–15.11.44.

70. Roland DEVRESSE
30.8.1924–23.10.2001/March 1942-May 1945/Graduated from Kienschlag (2nd session) as highest graded of his promotion/Due to collective punishment immediate promotion to *SS-Ustuf.* was delayed for 1 month/*SS-Ustuf.* on 20.04 1945/Gen.Inf. Assault Badge/Iron Cross II/Iron Cross I (Nowo-Buda)/Close Combat Clasp in Bronze.

71. Georges DUPIRE
29.03.1907/*SS-Ustuf.* 30.01.1945.

72. Albert DUPONT
07.06.1911/Graduated from Kienschlag (1st session)/*SS-Ustuf.* 09.11.1944.

73. Florent EMSIX
04.11.1920/August 1941-May 1945/First joined the *Légion Wallonie,* then Headquarters of the *Jeunesse Legionnaire* in 1943/Graduated from Kienschlag Academy (1st session)/*SS-Ustuf.* 09.11.1944/*Junkerschaftsführer* at Kienschlag Academy.

74. Henri FELDBUSCH
15.03.1913/August 1941-May 1945/Graduated from Kienschlag Academy (1st session)/*SS-Ustuf.* 09.11.1944.

75. Raphaël FOULON
29.06.1919/August 1941-May 1945/Graduated from Kienschlag Academy (1st session)/*SS-Ustuf.* 09.11.1944.

76. Fernand FOULON
18.03.1916/*SS-Ustuf.*

77. Henri GILLEMON
19.12.1916/Former *G.W.* officer/*SS-Ustuf.* February 1945/Last appointment: *Ib /69Rgt.*

78. Tony GOMBERT
30.03.1924/September 1944/Flemish Rexist/Degrelle's aide, coming from the *Langemarck.*

79. Roger GONDRY
16.06.1923–28.02.1983/March 1942-May 1945/Graduated from Kienschlag (1st session)/*SS-Ustuf.* 09.11.1944/Gen.Inf. Assault Badge/Iron Cross II (Altdamm)/Iron Cross I (25.04.1945).

80. José GÖRTZ
15.09.1921–21.04.1945/August 1941-demobilized/Re-*L.W.* in September 1942–15 March 1943/Demobilized/Re-re–enrolment on 28 April 1944/Graduated from Kienschlag (1st session)/*SS- Ustuf.* 09.11.1944.

81. Mathieu-Charles GRISAY
10.01.1920/*SS-Ustuf.* 30.01.1945.

82. Jan GIJZELS

83. Willy GRAIDE
11.04.1914-(suicide in prison 18/19.10.1945)/POW May 1940–11.11.1942/Graduated from the *11. Kriegslehrgang* at Bad-Tölz/*SS-Ustuf.* 21.06.1944*/(Probably *SS-Ostuf.* 20.04.1945).

84. John HAGEMANS
28.08.1914–26.08.1942/10 March 1942 as an NCO and Chief of the Rexist Youth/*Leutnant* posthumoulsy.

85. Jean HALLEBARDIER
01.05.1922/October 1944 as former officer of the *G.W.* -May 1945/Graduated from Sophienwalde Academy (29.10.44–20.12.1944)/*SS-Ustuf.* February 1945/War Merit Cross II with Swords (01.09.1944)/Iron Cross II (19.03.1945)/Wound Badge in Black (22.03.1945)/Gen.Inf. Assault Badge (06.04.1945)/Iron Cross I on 24.04.1945.

86. Robert JOURDAIN
02.07.1925/Former officer of the *G.W.*/ October 1944-May 1945/Graduated from Sophienwalde Academy (29.10.44–20.12.1944)/*SS-Ustuf.* February 1945/Iron Cross II/Wound Badge in Black.

87. Jean-Marie LANTIEZ
25.08.1920/August 1941-May 1945/*SS-Hscha.* promoted to *SS-St.O.Ju.* (01.03.1944) on grounds of exceptional gallantry during Cherkassy campaign/SS-*Ustuf.* (*Tapferkeitsoffizier*) on 20.04.1944/Winter Campaign Medal/Gen.Inf. Assault Badge/Iron Cross II/Iron Cross I. (Probably *SS-Ostuf.* on 20 April 1945).

88. Désiré LECOCQ
10.03.1922–06.03.1945/August 1941/Graduated from Kienschlag (1st session)/*SS-Ustuf.* 09.11.1944/Winter Campaign Medal/Iron Cross II/Iron Cross I/Gen.Inf. Assault Badge/Close Combat Clasp in Bronze.

89. David LELIEVRE
14.12.1900/10 March 1942-May 1942/*Leutnant*. Dismissed on grounds of notorious incapacity.

90. Raymond LEMAIRE
13.10.1922–2002/August 1941-May 1945/Graduated from Kienschlag (1st session)/*SS-Ustuf*. 09.11.1944/Winter Campaign Medal/Gen.Inf. Assault Badge/Wound Badge in Black/Iron Cross II/Iron Cross I.

91. Jacques LEROY
10.09.1924–05.08.1996/March 1942-May 1945/Graduated from Sophienwalde Academy (29.10.44 – 20.12.44), section for severely wounded personnel/SS-*Ustuf*. February 1945/Recommended for the Knight's Cross in March 1945 for his action as platoon commander *1/I/69* during the Altdamm bridgehead battle/(Knight's Cross according to post-war document signed by L. Degrelle)/Iron Cross I/Iron Cross II/Gen.Inf. Assault Badge/Wound Badge in Silver/Obtained German citizenship in 1961.

92. Jean LIENART
12.10.1920/Graduated from Kienschlag (1st session) *Ustuf*. 09.11.1944.

93. Henri-Marie LOVINFOSSE
23.02.1914–1985/POW/12.11.1942-May 1945/NCO of the Reserve Corps/Graduated from Kienschlag (1st session)/*SS-Ustuf*. 09.11.1944/CO/1Co of the instruction centre at Grünenplan/Alfeld training centre from November 1944 on/Platoon CO/ *8/II/69Rgt*./ Severely wounded at Lindenberg/War Merit Cross II/Iron Cross II.

94. Jules MAHIEU
16.07.1911/7 November 1942-May 1945/NCO of the Reserve Corps/POW (*Stalag XI B*)/Graduated from Kienschlag (1st session)/*SS-Ustuf*. 09.11.1944/Iron Cross II for action at Nowo-Buda (Cherkassy).

95. Robert MEAN
17.08.1923/Joined the *Wallonie* on 28.04.1944-May 1945/Graduated from Kienschlag (1st session)/*SS-Ustuf*. 09.11.1944.

96. Pierre MIGNON
30.03.1923/Joined the *Légion Wallonie* on 23.07.1942-May 1945/Member of the *G.W*. on 29.12.1941/Graduated from Kienschlag (1st session)/*SS-Ustuf*. 09.11.1944/Wound Badge in Black/Gen.Inf. Assault Badge.

97. Charles MONFILS
04.05.1920/August 1941-May 1945/Graduated from the *11. Kriegslehrgang* at Bad-Tölz/*SS-Ustuf*. 20.4.1944*/(Probably *SS-Ostuf*. 20.05.1945).

98. Jean MOREAU
26.11.1922/Joined the *L.W*. in March 1942-May 1945/Member of the Rexist Youth Movement/Graduated from Kienschlag (1st session)/*SS-Ustuf*. 09.11.1944/*Junkerschaftsführer* at Kienslchag Academy (2nd session) in replacement of A. Régibeau/Iron Cross II/Iron Cross I/Gen.Inf. Assault Badge.

99. Henri NIZET
14.6.1910/Graduated from Kienschlag (1st session)/*SS-Ustuf*. 09.11.1944.

100. Jean PIRON
20.05.1921/15.01.1944-May 1945/Graduated from Kienschlag (1st session)/ *SS-Ustuf.* 09.11.1944.

101. Jacques POELS
13.12.1922–17.02.1945/March 1942/Graduated from Kienschlag (1st session)/ *SS-Ustuf.* 09.11.1944.

102. André REGIBEAU
04.09.1917–15.02.1987/August 1941- May 1945/Highest graded of the 1st Kienschlag course/*SS-Ustuf.* 01.09.1944/Withheld at Kienschlag as *Junkerschaftsführer* (until November 1944) notwithstanding repeated requests to be transferred to front service/Commander of the *1/I/69*/Commander of the 1Co of the *Kampfgruppe Derriks*/Wounded 8 times during the period 1941–45/Winter Campaign Medal (30.08.1942)/Iron Cross II (21.01.1944)/Iron Cross I (16.03.1945)/Gen.Inf. Assault Badge (21.01.1944)/Close Combat Clasp in Bronze (22 recorded days)/Wound Badge in Gold (20.03.1945).

103. Raphaël ROORYCK
25.08.1920/August 1941 – May 1945/Graduated from Kienschlag (1st session)/ SS-*Ustuf.* 09.11.1944/Winter Campaign Medal/Wound Badge in Black.

104. Henri RUE
03.06.1920–12.02.1945/POW/Joined the *L.W.* on 16.12.1942 as *Schütze*/Graduated from the *11. Kriegslehrgang* at Bad-Tölz/*SS-Ustuf.* 20.04.1944*.

105. Albert SAPIN
24.11.1916/August 1941-May 1945/*SS-Ustuf.* as result of gallantry at Cherkassy as 3rd Platoon CO of 2 Company (*Tapferkeitsoffizier*)/Winter Campaign Medal/Gen.Inf. Assault Badge/Iron Cross II/Iron Cross I/Close Combat Clasp in Bronze.

106. Paul SCHREIBER
19.09.1921/August 1941- May 1945/Graduated from the *11. Kriegslehrgang* at Bad-Tölz/*SS-Ustuf.* 21.06.1944*/*Junkerschaftsführer* (*14. Junkerschaft*) at Kienschlag Academy/(Probably SS-*Ostuf.* 20.05.1945).

107. Charles SCHUMACHER
20.06.1911/August 1941-May 1945/Graduated from the *11. Kriegslehrgang* at Bad-Tölz/*SS-Ustuf.* 21.06.1944*/(Probably *SS-Ostuf.* 20.04.1945).

108. Edouard SERLET
04.03.1915/Career NCO/Former *NSKK* officer/March 1942-May 45 1945/ Graduated from the *11. Kriegslehrgang* at Bad-Tölz/*SS-Ustuf.* 21.06.1944*.

109. René SERLET
11.06.1923–18.03.1945/Graduated from Kienschlag (1st session)/*SS-Ustuf.* 09.11.1944.

110. Victor SMETS
19.01.1908/August 1941 as an NCO – May 1945/Graduated from Kienschlag Academy (1st session)/*SS-Ustuf.* 09.11.1944/Winter Campaign Medal/Wound Badge in Black.

111. Jean STIEBERT
29.06.1925/Graduated from Kienschlag (1st session)/*SS-Ustuf.* 09.11.1944.

112. Georges SUAIN
04.04.1920/Graduated from Kienschlag Academy (1st session)/*SS-Ustuf.* 09.11.1944.

113. Jean THEATRE
29.11.1916/POW/15.10.1942-May 1945/Graduated from the *11. Kriegslehrgang* at Bad-Tölz/*SS-Ustuf.* 21.06.1944*/(Probably *SS-Ostuf.* 20.04.1945).

114. Léopold THYS
05.01.1917–28.02.1942/*Leutnant*/Career officer.

115. Noël VACHAUDEZ
12.10.1915/October 1944 as *Leutnant* of the *G.W.* -May 1945/Graduated from Sophienwalde Academy/*SS-Ustuf.* February 1945.

116. Virgile VANDERWALLE
11.12.1913/POW/16.02.1943 as an NOC-May 1945/Graduated from Kienschlag Academy (1st session)/SS-*Ustuf.* 09.11.1944/Iron Cross II/Gen.Inf. Assault Badge/Close Combat Clasp in Bronze.

117. Hubert VAN EYSER
†13.12.1944/August 41/NCO commissioned *Leutnant*/Winter Campaign Medal/Gen.Inf. Assault Badge/Iron Cross II/Iron Cross I /

118. Georges VAN EESBEECK
26.11.1919/*L.W.* on 23.07.1942-May 1945/Graduated from the *11. Kriegslehrgang* at Bad-Tölz/SS-*Ustuf.* 21.06.1944*/(Probably *SS-Ostuf.* 20.04.1945) /

119. Paul VAN GYSEGHEM
06.07.1923/Graduated from Kienschlag Academy (1st session)/*SS-Ustuf.* 09.11.1944.

120. Jacques VERENNE
03.07.1924–14.08.1944/*L.W.* on 1.11.1941/Graduated from the *11. Kriegslehrgang* at Bad-Tölz/*SS-Ustuf.* 21.06.1944*/(Probably *SS-Ostuf.* posthumously).

121. Albert VERPOORTEN
20.10.1916–23.04.1945/Member of the Staff of the *Jeunesse Légionnaire*/Joined the division in September 1944/Graduated from Sophienwalde Academy (29.10.44 –20.12.1944)/*SS-Ustuf.* February 1945 /

122. Charles VERPOORTEN
/01.01.1942-May 1945/Graduated from Kienschlag Academy (1st session) 09.11.1944/SS-*Ustuf.* 09.11.1944.

123. André VINCKENBOSCH
03.08.1914/Labour Service (volunteer) in Germany/Joined the *L.W.* on 30.08.1942/Suspected of having deserted to the Russians in March 1945, as *Ic* officer of the *28.SS-Freiw.-Gren.Div.Wallonien*/Graduated from Kienschlag Academy (1st session)/*SS-Ustuf.* 09.11.1944/Wound Badge in Black/Pi. Assault Badge in Black.

124. Guy WARNIER.
26.11.1920/March 1942-May 1945/Graduated from the *11. Kriegslehrgang* at Bad-Tölz/*SS-Ustuf.* 21.06.1944*/(Probably *SS-Ostuf.* 20.05.1945).

125. Albert WEHINGER

21.07.1914/August 1941-May 1945/Winter Campaign Medal/Gen.Inf. Assault Badge/Iron Cross II/CO of 2nd Co of Grünenplan-Alfeld training centre.

126. Marc WILLEM
21.06.1919–16.08.1944/Graduated from the *11. Kriegslehrgang* at Bad-Tölz/*SS-Ustuf.* 21.06.1944*/(Probably *SS-Ostuf.* posthumously).

127. André WINANDY
13.04.1922/August 1941-May 1945/Graduated from *Nachrichtenschule* Nüremberg 21.12.1944/Winter Campaign Medal/Iron Cross II/Gen.Inf. Assault Badge/Close Combat Clasp in Bronze.

128. Daniel WOUTERS
02.12.1923–20.04.1945/Member of the Rexist youth Movement/*L.W.* in March 1942/Graduated from Kienschlag Academy (1st session) 09.11.1944/*SS-Ustuf.* 09.11.1944/Iron Cross II (Sakrewka 06.01.44)/Iron Cross I (Novo- Buda)/Gen.Inf. Assault Badge/Close Combat Clasp in Bronze.

129. Rotislav ZAVADSKY
22.12.1908/*Sonderführer*/Reported missing during Cherkassy breakout.

Addenda
130. Louis Garcia VALDAJOS
/5 October 1944-March 1945/ Spaniard/Platoon Co *3/I/70Rgt*/*Ostuf.*

131. Fernand-Marie COLLARD
05.07.1912/Journalist/Chief of the *DeWag*/SS-*Pz-Gren. Ers. Btl. 11* (*Nordland*) on 27.05.1943/*SS-Ustuf.* on 01.01.1944.

Medical Corps

SS-Hauptsturmbannführer/ Hauptmann

132. Dr Albert JACQUEMIN
30.8.1896/August 1941-demobilized 1942/Transferred to the *1. SS Pz. Div. L.A.H.* on 15.10.1944/*SS-Ostuf.* on 13.09.1943/*SS-Hstuf.* 21.06.1944/Winter Campaign Medal/Iron Cross II.

- Dr Raymond BUY

25.02.1902 (Rochefort-sur-Mer/France)/Frenchman/Regimental medical doctor (*69Rgt*).

- Dr Robert STAHL (from the Alsace)

Appendix I: Fig. 1.5
Dr Albert Jacquemin

SS-Obersturmführer/Oberleutnant

133. Dr Sylvère MIESSE
09.01.1909/August 1941- March 1942 as *Sonderführer/AGRA* member dismissed by Degrelle/Then medic in a *SS*-hospital from 17.02.43 to 01.08.43/Appointed Chief medic within the Assault Brigade Wallonien but not accepted by Degrelle/Joined the *Waffen-SS* as SS-*Ustuf.* (*16. SS-Pz. Gr. Div. RF-SS*)/*SS-Ostuf.* on 30.01.1944/Made prisoner in Italy/Winter Campaign Medal/Gen.Inf. Assault Badge/Iron Cross II/Iron Cross I.

- Dr Ignace BAANANTE. (Spaniard)

/ In charge of the *3/I/70Rgt.* composed of Spaniards.

SS-Unsturmführer/Leutnant

Candidates medical doctors

134. Emile LAMBRICHTS
15.05.1926.

135. Paul ROEKEN
20.02.1919/*St.O.Ju.*

Dentists

136. Roger LEJEUNE
08.07.1911/*Leutnant*/Graduated from Bad-Tolz on 21.06.1944*. Transferred to *SS-FHA Amtsgr. D.* on 01.02.1945 /

Chemists

(11). Victor BOULLIENNE
17.11.1881/*Hauptmann Stabsapoteker*/ Demobilized in May 1943 /

137. Camille PETRE.
26.06.1915–1984/*Oberfeldwebel*/*Leutnant*/*SS-Ustuf.* 01.06.1943 /

Non-Combatant Personnel

SS-Sturmbannführer/Major

138. Charles PETERS
18.01.1898/*Staffelführer* (Major) & liaison officer Rexist *NSKK*/Transferred to the *Ers. Btl. 36* in September 1944.

SS-Hauptsturmführer/Hauptmann

(14). Willy HEYVAERT
/August 1941-December 41/Demobilized.

139. Jean MALHERBE
06.01.1886/POW (*Oflag* Hammerstein and *Oflag VIII* C-Breslau) from 01.09.1940–01.01.1942/Major within the *G.W.*/Joined the *Ers. Btl. 36* on 01.11.1943/ *SS-Hstuf.* on 03.10.1944/*SS-Ausblg* Sennheim in October 1944/In charge of the instruction of the *Art. Rgt. 28* on 20.11.1944.

SS-Obersturmführer/Oberleutnant

140. Victor BOURDOUXHE
27.10.1912/Former *G.W.* officer/*SS-Ostuf.*

141. Joseph DANGUY
19.11.1890/Former officer of the National Gendarmerie (Police Force)/Joined the *G.W.* as a Lieutenant on 12.04.1943/Gradutated from Sophienwalde Academy (29.10.44–20.12.44)/*SS-Ostuf.* February 1945.

142. Pierre DAULIE
Dismissed by Degrelle on grounds of personal conflict.

143. Armand DOR
08.08.1891/August 1941-Demobilized in December 1941.

144. Robert du WELZ
12.10.1897/August 1941-May 1945/Aide-de-camp and Degrelle's handy man/Accompanied Degrelle on his flight to Spain on 08.05.1945/*SS-Ostuf*/(Claims he obtained the rank of *SS-Hstuf.* on 20.04.1945).

145. Fernand ROULEAU
09.12.1904-Madrid 31.07.1984/August 1941-September 1941/Degrelle' lieutenant and recruiting officer/Dismissed from the *Légion* on grounds of personal conflict with Degrelle and was later even expelled from the Rex Movement/Joined the *Erstazkommando Frankreich der Waffen-SS* (Recruitment *Charlemagne*) on 01.08.1943/*SS-Ostuf.* on 21.06.1944 (*SS Kav.A.u.E.Abt.*).

146. Robert SLOET d'OLDRUYTENBORGH
23.10.1897/August 1941-demobilized 01.10.1942/*Oberleutnant/Hauptmann* of the *G.W.* on 01.10.1942/Liaison officer for the Rexist *NSKK* with the rank of *Staffelführer* (Major/September 1943).

147. Paul SUYS
23.07.1908/Member of *Rex-Vlaanderen. Freiwillige Leg. Niederland* on 06.08.1941/*Freiw. Leg. Flandern* on 01.11.1941/*6. Sturmbrigade Langemarck* on 01.05.1944/*28. SS-Freiw. -Gren. Div. Wallonie* on 01.10.1944/*SS-Ustuf. d.R.a.K.* on 06.08.1943/*SS-Ostuf. d.R.a.K.* (:*der Reserve außer Kader*) 30.01.1944.

148. René VERDEUR
02.05.1893/August 1941-May 1942/Former colonial officer of the Congolese *Force Publique*/Commanding officer of the *Ers. Btl. 36* from August 1941 to November 41/*SS-Ostuf.*

SS-Untersturmführer/Leutnant

149. Raymond CAMBY
07.01.1922/1942-May 1945/Graduated from the *11. Kriegslehrgang* at Bad-Tölz/*SS-Ustuf.* 21.06.1944*/Degrelle's orderly during the Ardennes offensive/(Probably *SS-Ostuf.* 20.04.1945).

150. René CARNOY
19.01.1908/October 1944 as *Leutnant* of the G.W. -May 1945/Graduated from Sophienwalde Academy (29.10.44–20.12.44)/*SS-Ustuf.* February 1945.

151. Françis CAUDRON
30.08.1923/Officer of the *Garde Wallonne*/Graduated from Sophienwalde Academy (29.10.44–20.12.44)/*SS-Ustuf.* February 1945.

152. Jacques DUCATE
SS-*Ustuf.*

153. Henri DUMONT
SS-*Ustuf.*

154. Jean GALERE
11.03.1912/September 1944-May 1945/Former *Oberleutnant* of the *G.W.*/Graduated from Sophienwalde Academy (29.10.44–20.12.1944)/*SS-Ustuf.* February 1945.

155. Fritz GRUBBE
15.10.1913/Former officer of the G.W./Octobr 1944–1944 May 1945/Graduated from Sophienwalde Academy (29.10.44–20.12.1944)/*SS-Ustuf.* February 1945.

156. Louis JACOBS
01.12.1901/Head of the Walloon detachment (under SS-*Hstuf.* Moskopf) within the *Dienststelle Jungclaus* in Brussels/SS-*Ustuf.* in September 1944.

157. Jules JANSSENS
25.05.1893/*Feldwebel* of the *Feldgendarmerie*/Lt of the *Garde Wallonne*/SS-*Ustuf.* in February 1944.

158. Roger KAISERGRUBER
05.01.1919/*G.W.*/SS-*Ustuf.* February 1945.

159. Jean ROMAN
13.01.1915/9 September 1941-March 1945/Graduated from the *11. Kriegslehrgang* at Bad-Tölz/SS-*Ustuf.* 21.06.1944*/Liaison officer to the *RSHA* on 01.08.1944/Deserted in April 1945/Married Lippert's sister in 1944.

160. Gérard SOENEN
10.08.1915/Graduated from the *11. Kriegslehrgang* at Bad-Tölz/SS-*Ustuf.* 21.06.1944*/(Probably SS-*Ostuf.* 20.04.1945).

161. Valère ROEMAET
20.10.1897/Graduated from the *11. Kriegslehrgang* at Bad-Tölz/*SS-Ustuf.* 21.06.1944*/Head of the saving and pension funds of the Walloon Legion/(Probably SS-*Ostuf.* 20.04.1945).

Detatched for special service

162. Felix FRANCK
Degrelle's former private secretary/August 1941-demobilized January 1942/Reactivated in September 1944 as a *SS-Ustuf.*

163. Jean GEORGES
30.09.1899/August 1941 as an NCO-demobilized in December 1941/Reactivated in September 1944 as an *SS-Ustuf.*

164. Joseph PEVENASSE
10.10.1900/March 1942-March 1943/In September 1944, Degrelle promoted him to

Leutnant of the *G.W.* so that he could obtain the rank of a *SS-Ustuf.* within the *Waffen-SS*/As a lawyer he was then directed to the divisional judicial service (Military Court).

Addenda
165. Edmond COLLARD
21.03.1911/Second session at Kienschlag Academy/*SS-Ustuf.* on 01.02.1945.

166. Gérard SALES
Catholic Chaplain/September 1941-March 1942.

167. Louis FIERENS
Catholic Chaplain/15 December 1942-March 1944.

Struck off the list

168. Louis CALONNE
31.12.1904/SS-*Ustuf.*

169. Henri HANNICQ
Leutnant.

Of a total of 115 Walloon frontline officers, 26 were killed in action, 5 had died by the end of 1945.

The Belgian judicial system pronounced 48 death penalties, 19 in *absentia.*

- 1 was executed by firing squad (Pierre Pauly, for his participation in the Courcelles massacre on 17–18 August 1944, and not in his capacity as a legionnaire officer).
- 26 were condemned to life imprisonment.

By 1952, all legionnaires (except the ones involved in blood crimes in Belgium during the occupation and Frans Hellebaut) had been released from captivity.

The following nationalities were represented in the *Légion Wallonie* 1941–45:

Belgium (both Walloons and Flemings), France, Monaco (one individual), White Russians (a few dozen), Finland (one), Poland, Rumania, Switzerland (three individuals), Italy, U.S.A. (one individual), Spain, Hungary, Czechoslovakia, Sweden (one) and one Jew (10 March 1942 contingent – discovered when transferring to the *Waffen-SS* and sent back to Belgium).

Note that most of these individuals lived in Belgium.

After the war (at least) 6 Frenchmen, 47 Italians, 20 White Russians, 35 Poles, 3 Yugoslavs, 2 Hungarians, 1 Finn, 1 Spaniard, 2 Czechs, 2 Luxemburgers, 2 Rumanians, 1 Lithuanian, 2 Swiss, 2 Dutchmen, 2 Armenians, 1 Canadian, 1 Turk, 1 Greek, 1 Iranian were wanted by the Belgian Judicial Services, charged with the crime of Collaboration with the Enemy of the State.

Out of a total of 1,700 legionnaires listed at Meseritz (*Wehrmacht* period) 57 were foreigners (*Cfr* List Philibert Canva, former *Gefechtsschreiber* (Combat secretary) of the *Kampfgruppe Ruelle;* arch. E. De Bruyne).

BUETER, William-Thomas, né à Tarenton (U.S.A.), 25-9-1920, noyauteur, dom. à Courcelles, rue Paul Pastur, 73, Américain, Légion Wallonne, A. M. Charleroi, I. F.

Appendix I: Fig. 1.6. Among the many nationalities represented in the ranks of the Légion Wallonie there was at least one American citizen (*Collection E. De Bruyne*).

APPENDIX II

Lineage

July-August 1941:

- *Corps Franc Wallonie*
- *Légion Wallonie*
- *Légion 'Belge' Wallonie*

August 1941:

- *Légion Wallonie/Wallonische Inf. Btl. 373.*

Temporarily attached to:

- *101. le. Div.* [10.12.1941 – (16.05.1942)])
- *Kampfgruppe* Markulj /*100. le. Div.* (January 1941–16.02.1942)
- *Kampfgruppe Tröger/100. le. Div.* (17.02.1942)
- *100. Jäg. Div.* and back to *101. le. Jäg. Div.* (17.02.1942 – 16.05.1942)
- *68. I.D.* (General Meissner – 17.05.1942 – 20.05.1942)
- *97. Jäg. Div.* (General Ernst Rupp – 21.05.1942 – 18.11.1942)

By 08.08.1942, the Walloons had been awarded 6 Iron Cross I, 55 Iron Cross II and 11 War Merit Cross II. Three officers, 16 NCOs and 62 privates had been killed; 1 officer and 15 privates were missing; 1 officer, 22 NCOs and 87 privates had been wounded while 9 officers, 15 NCOs and 47 privates had been dismissed for physical unfitness.

1 June 1943:

- *SS-Freiwilligen-Brigade Wallonien* (01.06.1943 – 03.07.1943)
- *SS-Sturmbrigade Wallonien* (03.07.1943 – 03.1944)
- *5. SS-Freiw. -Sturmbrigade Wallonien* (03.1944 – 18.09.1944)

Temporarily attached to:

- *5. SS-Pz. Div. Wiking* (November 1943 – February 1944)
- *Gruppe Wagner/III.(germ.) SS-Panzerkorps* (August 1944)

September 1944:

- *SS-Freiw. -Gren. Div. Wallonien* created 19.10.1944 following order of 18.09.1944
- *28.SS-Freiw.-Gren.Div.Wallonien* (19.10.1944)
- (*28. SS-Freiw. -Pz. Gren. Div. Wallonien* – never to be)[1]

Temporarily attached to:

- *III.(germ.) SS-Panzerkorps* (Steiner/February 1944 – March 1945)
- *SS-Divisionsgruppe Müller* (15 April 1945)

APPENDIX III

Feldpostnummer[1]

The most common *Feldpostnummer* allotted to the *Légion Wallonie/Wallonische Inf. Btl. 373* was 38918.

38918A (Staff + Staff Co + train)
38918B (1 Co)
38918C (2 Co)
38918D (3 Co)
28918 E (4 Co)
38918 was allotted to
from 08.1941: – *Inf. Btl. 373;* Staff and companies 1 to 4.
from 01.06.1943: – *Sturmbrigade Wallonien*

- SS-Frw. Sturmbrigade Wallonien
- from 22.12.1943: – 5. SS. Sturmbrigade Wallonien.
- from 08.09.1944: – SS-Brigade Wallonien.
- from 20.12.1944: – 28. SS-Freiw. -Gr. Div. Wallonien.
- *Feldpostnummer* of separate Walloon units:

16821:	*Stab II u. 5–8 Kp/5. SS-Sturmbrigade Wallonien* (July 1944). *Stab II u. 5 – 8 Kp/5. SS-Brigade Wallonien* (September 1944).
18909:	*Feldersatz-Kp/5. SS-Sturmbrigade Wallonien.* *Feldersatz-Kp/SS-Rgt. Wallonien.*
25151:	*1. Flak-Kp. 5. SS-Wallonien* (August 1944). *1. Flak-Kp. SS-Brigade Wallonien* (September 1944).
28193:	*I. Btl/5. Frw. Sturmbrgiade Wallonien* (July 1944).
31954:	*SS-Kriegsberichter-Zug/5. SS-Wallonien* (July 1944). *SS-Kriegsberichter-Zug/SS-Brig. Wallonien* (August 1944, cancelled in December 1944).
36637:	*Inf. – Geschütz Kp./ 5. SS-Wallonien* (July 1944).
37572:	*1. Sturmgeschütz-Bttr/5. Frw. Sturmbrig. Wallonien* (November 1943). *Sturmgeschütz-Bttr/SS-Wallonien* (March-cancelled in September).
38714:	*Große Kraftw. Kolonne/5. SS-Wallonien* (July 1944). *Große Kraftw. Kolonne/SS-Brigade Wallonien* (September 1944).
41163:	*2. Sturmgeschütz-Bttr/5. Frw. Sturmbrigade Wallonien* (November 1943). *3. Sturmgeschütz-Btrr/5. SS-Wallonien* (March 1944, cancelled in September 1944).
41461:	*2. Flak-Kp/5. SS-Wallonien* (July 1944). *2. Flak-Kp/SS-Brig. Wallonien* (September 1944).
42059:	*Feldersatz-Kp/5. Frw. Sturmbrigade Wallonien* (December 1943). *SS-Feldersatz-Kp. 5 SS-Wallonien* (April 1944, cancelled February 1945).
43857:	*Panzerjäger-Kp./ 5. SS-Wallonien* (August 1944). *Panzerjäger-Kp./ SS-Brigade Wallonien* (September 1944).
64074:	*Sonderbetreuungs-Trupp des Kampfsenders Flandern u. Wallonien/ SS-Standarte Kurt Eggers* (March 1945).

Feldpostnummer allotted to Legion Wallonie Officers and Bureaus in Belgium

04092: *Sammelfeldpostnummer* at Charleroi.
04092 G: *Wallonische – Legionärs-Genesenden-Kp* (July 1942).
07515: *Sammelfeldpostnummer* at Brussels.
07515 CB:[2] *Ersatz-Kommando der Waffen-SS Wallonien.*
07515 CN: *Fürsorge-Offizier der Waffen-SS in Flandern und Wallonien* (October 1943).

Offices in Northern France

01402: *Sammelfeldpostnummer Lille*
01402 BN: *Fürsorge-Offizier der Waffen-SS Flandern u. Wallonien* (October 1943)
Fürsorge-SS Führer in Flandern u. Wallonien (February 1944)

Addendum:
Following *Feldpostnummer* were used during the Estonian Campaign:
28.07.1944: 57475 W
03.08.1944: 58103 A
11.08.1944: 588028 A

APPENDIX IV

German Liaison Officers

1. *Leutnant* Leppin (August 1941-January 1942).
2. *Hptm* Dr Erich von Lehe (March 1942-November 1942).
3. *Hptm* Dietzl *ad interim* in absence of No. 3 till arrival of No. 4.
4. *Rittmeister* von Rabenau[1] (March 1942 with second contingent).
5. *SS-Obersturmbannführer* Alfred Wegener[2] (June 1943-February 1944).
6. *SS-Haupsturmführer* Hans Drexler (17.01.1944–13.02.1944).
7. *SS-Obersturmbannführer* Bruno Schulz[3] [Liaison and discipline officer for the German personnel of the *SS-Pz. Gren. Aus. u. Ers. Btl. 36* at *Tr. Ü. Pl.* Wildflecken (*Verbindungsoffizier u. Disziplinarvorgesetzter f. d. reichsdeutschen Führer, Unterführer u. Männer*) from 13.02.1944 to 05.09.1944, assigned *Kommandeur* from 26.04.44 onwards)].
8. *SS-Oberführer* Johan Nikolaus Heilmann (12.12.1944–15.01.1945 as head of the Divisional Formation Staff – *Führer d. Aufstellungsstabes*).
9. *SS-Ustuf.* Deckers (during *von Rundstedt* offensive)[4]
10. *SS-Hstuf.* Schaeffer (Estonian campaign).
11. *SS-Ostbaf.* Hahn (March 1945).

Miscellaneous

- Major Bode, commander of the *Regenwurmlager* training centre (*Ers. Btl. 477*)
- Dr Heinz Forsteneichner, liaison officer to the Foreign Office.
- *Hauptmann* Pohl, instructor of the *G.W.* and *NSKK* contingents at Delligsen/Alfeld training centre.
- *Hauptmann* Heiser, commanding officer of *Regenwurmlager* barracks.

APPENDIX V

Catholic Chaplains

1. Joseph SALES, priest, Luxemburger. Joined the unit in September 1941 – dismissed in March 1942.

2. Louis FIERENS, priest, joined in December 1942 – resigned after Cherkassy. He was the first Catholic chaplain within the *Waffen-SS* (but he wore the *Wehrmacht* uniform).

3. Léon STOCKMAN, – *Padre Gérard*, – joined the unit in October 1944, with the rank of an *SS-Mann*. In November 1944, he was promoted to divisional chaplain with the rank of an *SS-Sturmbannführer*.

APPENDIX VI

Special Operations

Charles LAMBINON
07.12.1911./ Head of the *D.S.I./ SD-Ostuf.* in October 1944, Chief of the Walloon section of the *Siegfried* spying school at Marburg./ He was assisted by:

Marcel VERVLOET
09.05.1919./ *SD-Ustuf.*

APPENDIX VII

Walloon Senior Officers of Military and Paramilitary Formations

A. Légion Wallonie

SS-Obersturmbannführer	Lucien Lippert (posthumous) Léon Degrelle
SS-Sturmbannführer	Georges Tchekhoff Georges Jacobs Frans Hellebaut Léon Stockman Henri Derriks Jules Mathieu

B. Garde Wallonne

Major	Jean Malherbe

C. Rexist Labour Service

Oberarbeitsführer (Lt-Col)	Léon Closset

D. NSKK

Staffelführer (Major)	Jacques Reylandt (Rex) Baron Robert Sloet d'Olduytenborg (Rex) Charles Peters (Rex) Joseph Augustin (*AGRA*)

APPENDIX VIII

Total Recruitment 1941–45[1]

1941	1,200
1942	1,843
1943	1,929
1944	2,500
1945	260 (Spaniards)
Total	**7,732**

APPENDICIES IX

White Russians

A. Officers

SS-Stubaf. Georges TCHEKHOFF

Former naval officer of the Czar. Member of General Denekin's General Staff in Bulgaria and as such he was assigned as aide-de-camp to the Chief of the Naval Forces in 1920.

SS-Hstuf. Nicolas KAMSKY

Former Captain of the Denekin Army

SS-Ostuf. Georg von SCHAFROFF

Former private of the Ataman Bulak-Balachowitch detachment (1919); Lieutenant (1935) within the *R.O.V.S.* (Association of Russian Veterans)

B. Sonderführer/Waffenführer

Rotislaw ZAVADSKY

St-Petersburg, 22.12.1908/Interpreter /*Sonderführer*/reported missing during Cherkassy breakout

Alexis SAKHNOWSKY

Petrograd, 16.11.1905

Leonide STOUPINE

Blagadornari /Caucasus, 04.03.1898. Stayed in the Caucasus with his family.

Appendix IX: Fig. 1.7. Pre-war meeting of exiled White Russians in Brussels. Seated from left to right: Georges Tchekhoff, Colonel Klimchevitch, General Arkhangelsky, Admiral Pakrovsky and General Miller. Standing between Gen Arkhangelsky and Gen. Miller: Ratislaw Zavadsky (*Widow Tchekhoff/Collection E. De Bruyne*).

APPENDIX X

Losses[1]

	Battle Strength	Killed	Missing	Wounded or Unfit	%	Sick or Evacuated
08.08.41 Departure Brussels	860					
10.08–16.10.41				68		
Meseritz Ers. Btl . 36 03.11.41–31.01.42						
Donetz 03.11.41–26.01.42	792	8				200
17.02–28.02.42 Gromowaja-Balka	411	71		155	55	
17.05.42 Jablenskaja	450	12		17	6	
10.06. –21.06.42 Spakovska	150	2		10	8	
10.07–14.08.42 *Vormarsch* (800km)	850					350
19.08.42 Pruskaja (Caucasus)	100	10		15	25	
23.08. –28.08.42 Tcherjakov	460	15		74	20	
14.10. –15.11.42 Pschich	370	5		20	7	
Cherkassy						
20.10.43–02.02.44 Olschanka positions	2000 [2]	15	28	40	4	250
12/13.44–19.01.44 Teklino	700	80	20	90	27	30
03.02. –18.2.44 Outbreak	1,460	150	650	20	56	
Narwa front						
14.08.44 Liiva (4 Co)	35		35	15	100	
19.08.44 Patschka (2 Co)	120	15	30	10	46	
21.08.44 Ema (Dorpat)	335	10		25	10	
22.08. –28.08.44. Keerdu-Peerna	300	20		30	17	
Oder front						
05.02. –07.03.45 Stargard	1,800	55	65	200	18	

(continued overleaf)

17.02–20.03.45 Altdamm	650	22		84	16
20.04. –23.04.45 Schillersdorf	550[3]	90	10	150	36
27.04.45 Schönwerder (Prenzlau	350	10		50	17
Total:	**6,000**[4]				
killed during air-raids in Germany or victim of assault by the resistance:					
		75	25	75	
Total		**657**	**863**	**1,035**	
Grand Total	**6,000/(657+863+1,035) = 42.58% casualties**				

APPENDIX XI

Close Combat Days

The following combat days were allotted to the *Légion Wallonie*.

Close Combat days prior to the establishment of the Close Combat Clasp on 01.12.1942 are taken into account as follows:

CLOSE COMBAT DAYS as settled per 1 February 1944:

- 15 months of uninterrupted stay in Russia corresponds to 15 close combat days;
- 12 months of uninterrupted stay in Russia corresponds to 10 close combat days;
- 8 months of uninterrupted stay in Russia correspond to 5 days close combat days.

However this advantage was not granted to the Train personnel. An interruption due to a furlough, a mission, a transfer, a disease or a wound was not taken into account provided it did not exceed a quarter of the duration of the total time of presence.

Dates	Place	Units involved
04.11.41	Samara	Elements of a Platoon of 4Co and 1Co
11.11.41	Karabinowka	1 platoon 1Co
17.02.42	Nowo-Andreiewka-Gromo	1,2,3,4 Companies.
28.02.42	Gromowaja-Balka	Battle force
01.03.42	Hill/Gromowaja-Balka	HQ
17.05.42	Jablenskaja	Battle force
18.05.42	Prelesnoje-Barwenkowo	Battle force
08.06.42	Spachowka	3Co and Pioneer
09.06.42	Spachowka	3Co and Pioneer
10.06.42	Spachowka	3Co and Pioneer
21.06.42	Burkanowo	1Co and 1 Platoon HQ
24.06.42	Ferma	1Co and 1 Platoon HQ
10.07.42	Krasni-Liman	Battle force
14.08.42	Hill 233/Maïkop	Platoon Mezzetta (3Co) + 2Platoons/4Co
17.08.42	Apscherowskaja	1Co
19.08.42	Pruskaja	1Co
21.08.42	Tcherjakow Foulon, PAK, IG, and group Kehren.	3Co, Platoon Mirgain, Platoon
22.08.42	Tcherjakow	idem + 1Co
23.08.42	Tcherjakow	Platoon Dumont
24.08.42	Tcherjakow	Platoon Dumont
08.09.42	Ismaïlowka	1Co
09.09.42	Kubano-Armyanski	Battle force + supply
28.10.42	Psisch	Battle force
22.12.43	Irdynn	2Co + 3Co
01.01.44	Sakrewka	1platoon 3Co
14.01.44	Teklino	1,2,3,4Co+platoon motorcycles
15.01.44	Teklino	idem+ Signals
17.02.44	Teklino	idem

(continued overleaf)

31.01.44	Steblew	Feld Ersatz Btl
01.02.44	Steblew	idem
02.02.44	Steblew	idem
03.02.44	Losowok	2Co, 1 Platoon IG.
04.02.44	Moschny	2Pl/8Co
06.02.44	Starosselje	Pi, 1pl/3Co, Signals, 4Co, PAK, IG.
07.02.44	Starosselje	Idem
07.02.44	Derenkowez	2Pl/1Co, Pl/3Co
08.02.44	Skity	Pl. Motorcycles, Flak 2, Pl. Landucci. Group Degrelle, group Daras
08.02.44	Derenkowez	1Pl/1Co+ 2Co,3Co,PAK.
09.02.44	Derenkowez	Brigade
09.02.44	Starosselje	Pi,1Pl/3Co,Signals,4Co, PAK,IG+2Pl/6Co,1Pl/8Co.
10.02.44	Derenkowez	Brigade
11.02.44	Derenkowez	Brigade
12.02.44	Nowo-Buda	2Pl/1Co, PAK, Flak 2, 4Co.
13.02.44	Nowo-Buda	Brigade
15.02.44	Nowo-Buda	Brigade
16.02.44	Nowo-Buda	Brigade
16.02.44	Schanderowka	Wounded and Tross (Degrelle)
17.02.44	Breakout	Brigade
18.02.44	Breakout	Brigade
18.02.44	id.	Brigade
19.08.44	Patska	
20.08.44	id.	
21.08.44	Kambja	
22.08.44	id.	
23.08.44	Noô/Lemmatsi	
24.08.44	id.	
25.08.44	Kärkna-Noëlla	
26.08.44	Pärna	
27.08.44	Lombi	
28.08.44	id.	
29.08.44	Keerdu	
30.08.44	id.	
31.08.44	id.	
01.09.44	Bhf Karkna	
03.03.45	Schneiderfeld-Klützow	
04.03.45	Streesen-Wittichow	
06.03.45	Lübow-Saarow	
17.03.45	Altdamm	
18.03.45	id.	
19.03.45	id.	
20.04.45	Schillersdorf	
21.04.45	id.	
22.04.45	Rosow	
23.04.45	Neu-Rosow	
27.04.45	Schönwerder	

75 close combat days, in all 5.50 % of the time spent at the Eastern Front 41–45 (1,363 days).

APPENDIX XII

Commanding Officers of the Légion Wallonie/Assault Brig./Div.

1. *Hptm* ('Major') Major Georges Jacobs (08.08.1941–30.12.1941).
2. *Hptm* (B.E.M.) Pierre Pauly (30.12.1941–01.04.1942).
3. *Hptm* Georges Tchekhoff (01.04.1942–06.06.1942).
4. *SS-Stubaf.* Lucien Lippert (06.06.1942–13.02.1944).
5. *Lt* Léon Closset, *Kommandeur a. i.* from mid-December 42 to mid-March 43, replacing L. Lippert during his first leave in Belgium while a Walloon combat group was still in the Caucasus.
6. *SS-Ostuf.* Jules Mathieu, *ad interim*, commanding the breakout forces in the absence of Léon Degrelle (13.02.1944–18.02.1944).
7. *SS-Stubaf.* Georges Tchekhoff *ad interim* (01 April 1944–20 June 1944)
8. *SS-Oberführer* Karl Burk (21.06.1944–09.1944).
9. *SS-Ostubaf.* Léon Degrelle (17 September 1944–03 May 1945), second in command being *SS-Stubaf.* Frans Hellebaut.

APPENDIX XIII

The Ers. Btl. 36

Wehrmacht Period

Regenwurmlager/Meseritz: *Lt* René Verdeur (August 1941-November 1941).

Regenwurmlager/Meseritz: *SS-Hstuf.* Georges Tchekhoff (June 1942-April 1944).

Pieske transit camp. (Mai 1943).

Waffen-SS Period

- Wildflecken (June 1943–13.04.1944).
- note that on 15 December 1943, a new appellation appeared: *SS-Panzergrenadier-Aus. und Ersatz Btl 36*, the previous one being *SS-Grenadier Aus. u. Ers. Btl. 36*.
- *Heidelager* (Debica b. Krakau 14.04.44–14.08.44): *SS-Stubaf.* Bruno Schulz (*Hstuf.* Biens-assisted by *Hptm* Pohl-being second in command), heading the German staff, *SS-Stubaf.* G. Tchekhoff being in charge of the Walloon staff.
- Breslau (15.08.44–30.10.1944): *SS-Ostuf.* A. Lassois. From 15 October 1944, military instruction by personnel of *7/II/Rgt* under *SS-Ostuf.* Jean Vermeire.
- Wohlau/Breslau (01.09.44–14.11.44): *SS-Stubaf.* Georges Tchekhoff (Bruno Schulz remaining in office for administrative matters); second in command being *SS-Ostuf.* Pierre Dengis.
- Military and Field instruction: *SS-Hstuf.* H. Derriks.
- Alfeld (15.11.44-April 1945).
- Alfeld: sick *SS-Stubaf.* Georges Tchekhoff replaced by *SS-Hstuf.* Pierre Dengis, Bruno Schulz remaining in office for administrative matters.

The Alfeld-stationed *Ers. Btl. 36* had two training centres:

1. Delligsen: Commanding officer *SS-Ostuf.* Godsdeel and CO/1Co, while 2Co was under *SS-Hstuf.* Biens (the former officers of the *G.W.* who had refused to join the *Waffen-SS* formed a platoon within this Co, and some of them participated in the military training of the forced enlisted 'volunteers' coming from the Walloon Labour Front in February-March-April 1945).

2. Grünenplan: Commanding officer *SS-Ostuf.* A. Lassois,

   - 1Co: *SS-Ustuf.* H. M. Lovinfosse.
   - 2Co: *SS-Ustuf.* A. Wehinger.

Note that prior to their departure for Germany Walloon volunteers enrolled in Belgium were grouped:

- at Charleroi, as far as the *Wehrmacht* period is concerned;
- at the *SS-Vorschule* at Namur, first under the command of *SS-Ostuf.* Camille Bosquion, then SS-*Ostuf.* A. Lassois, assisted by *SS-Hscha.* R. Verhiest.

The medical service of the *Ers. Btl. 36* was headed by the Rumanian doctor Marcus (January-April 1945).

APPENDIX XIV

Battle Force
Wall. Inf. Btl. 373 – 1 November 1942

A. Battle Force

Wounded, sick and soldiers on leave	850
Inf Ers. Btl. 477	252
Total:	**1,102**

B. Departures since Establishment of the Légion Wallonie (8 August 1941)

1. Deaths	
Killed in action	109
Illness	3
Accident	3
Total:	**115**
2. Missing	
Made prisoners, mortally wounded, probably dead	16
3. Demobilized as a result of casualties, illness, or unfitness (among these 85 men of the classes prior to 1908)	160
4. Demobilized for physical unfitness during the Regenwurmlager/Meseritz training (among the latter 58 men of classes prior to 1908)	140
5. Dismissed on moral grounds and punishment	36
6. Other reasons	5
Total:	**357**
Total of departures	**1,574**

APPENDIX XV

Members of the Belgian Nobility within the Legion Wallonie 1941–45

- Count René de BACKER de REVILLE. *SS-Ustuf*. †27.04.1945
- Philippe della FAILLE d'HUYSE. *SS-Ustuf*
- Knight Robert du WELZ. *SS-Ostuf*
- Baron Jacques van ZUYLEN. †1944
- Knight François de MEESTER de HEYNDONCK. †28.02.1942
- Baron Christian VANDER-STRAETEN WAILLET. †February 1942
- Baron SLOET d'OLDRUYTENBORGH. *NSKK Staffelführer*
- Idésbald del FOSSE et d'ESPIERRES. (10 March 1942 contingent, made prisoner at Sakrewka/Cherkassy on 04.02.1944)
- Jean PETIT de THOZEE. *Oberfeldwebel*
- Jacques de *** de ***. Career officer of the Belgian army. Dismissed from the Legion for having refused to take the oath of allegiance to Hitler in August 1941

The following French noblemen served in the *Légion Wallonie*

- Pierre de la HAMAIDE (February 1945 – CO/3rd Pl */1/I/70Rgt*)
- Aimé ROYAN de KERLINE

APPENDIX XVI

Exceptional Promotions

Wehrmacht period

Camille BOSQUION
Promoted to *Oberfeldwebel* on 10.03.1942 for gallantry during the Gromowaja-Balka action (28.02.42)

Hubert VAN EYZER
Promoted to *Oberfeldwebel* on 10.03.1942 for gallantry during the Gromowaja-Balka action (28.02.42)

Frontbewährungsoffiziere

The following *Oberfeldwebel* were commissioned *Leutnant* on grounds of their frontline experience (also known as *ohne Patent angelegte Offiziere i.e.* commissioned officer without having attended a military academy). All of them were commissioned *Leutnant* before the transfer to the *Waffen-SS*.

- Jules Mathieu
- Georges Ruelle
- Camille Bosquion
- Léon Closset
- Albert Lassois
- Pierre Dengis
- Marcel Bonniver
- Robert du Welz (no frontline experience, but Degrelle's handy man)
- Adrien Godsdeel
- Joseph Mirgain
- Robert Denie
- Hubert Van Eyzer
- Marcel Lamproye
- Josy Graff
- Albert Wehinger

Waffen-SS period

A. *Tapferkeitsoffizier*
Albert SAPIN Promoted to *SS-Standartenoberjunker* for exceptional courageous behaviour as platoon CO/(2Co) at Teklino for restoring a difficult liaison with 3Co.

Léon GILLIS Promoted to *SS-Standartenoberjunker* (01.03.1944) for exceptional courageous behaviour during the Cherkassy retreat as CO of the 2nd platoon/5Co (*PAK*).

Jean-Marie LANTIEZ Promoted to *SS-Standartenoberjunker* for exceptional gallantry during the Cherkassy campaign as CO of the Signals platoon within the HQ/Co.

B. Exceptional Promotions
Léon DEGRELLE was anticipatively promoted to *SS-Hauptsturmführer* on 01.01.1944 ahead of the normal date of 30.01.1944.

As a 'Cherkassy present' all Walloon graduates from the *11. Kriesglehrgang* (Bad-Tölz) were promoted to *SS-Ustuf.* anticipatively (01.04.1944) ahead of the 21.06.1944 date for their classmates.

All officers (except Degrelle) having participated in the Estonian Campaign obtained a higher rank by one degree.

APPENDIX XVII

Military Academies

Walloon officers graduated from:

A. Bad-Tölz(*11. Kriegslehrgang/ VI Inspektion – 15. Junkerschaft*, from 06.09.1943 to 15.03.1944)

Highest graded: Charles GENERET, SS-*Ustuf.* on 20.4.1944.
The rest received their commission on 21.06.1944 with operative effect from 20.04.1944. However, mention must be made that all graduates of *11. Kriegslehrgang* were given permission to wear their *SS-Ustuf.* insignias from 1 April 1944, a favour obtained by Degrelle as a direct result of the Cherkassy breakout. They were called back from Bad-Tölz to participate in the Cherkassy parade at Charleroi and Brussels.

A few isolated Walloons attended various other courses. As an illustration, let us mention the *18. Kriegslehrgang* (5 Walloons–4 *Standartenoberjunker d.Res.d.W.-SS* and 1 *Standartenjunker d. Res. d. W-SS*).

B. Kienschlag/*SS Panzer Grenadier Schule* (Neweklau über Beneschau)

Three sessions were organized:

1. *(Wall-Franz.) Kriegs-Waffen-Junkerlehrgang* from 15.05.1944 to 01.09.1944 (*Lehrgruppe IV* (D)/*10. (Wall- Franz) Inspektion* composed of three Walloon *Junkerschaften* (14/15/16) and one French (13).

   Instructors:

   - *Heerwesen*: *SS-Ustuf.* Charles Generet
   - Tactics: *SS-Hstuf.* Jauss
   - *SS* philosophy (*Weltanschauung*): *SS-Ostuf.* Bender
   - *Junkerschaftsführer*: *SS-Ustuf.* Paul Schreiber (*14. Junkerschaft*); Alfred Devaux (*15. Junkerschaft*); Roger DeGoy (*16. Junkerschaft*);
   - Highest graded: André REG IBEAU, *SS-Ustuf.* on 01.09.1944, the other participants were promoted to *SS-Ustuf.* on 9 November 1944.

   - Twenty-nine Walloons graduated *Waffen-Standartenoberjunker* and ten graduated *Waffen-Standartenjunker*.

2. *(Wall-Franz.) Kriegs-Waffen-Junkerlehrgang* from 9 September 1944 to 31 March 1945 (for disciplinary reasons promotion was postponed for 1 month as result of a collective punishment)

   Instructors:

   - *Heerwesen*: *SS-Ustuf.* Charles Generet
   - Tactics: *SS-Ostuf.* Helmut Klaindienst (coming form the *L.A.H.*) assisted by Walloon SS-*Ustuf.* Paul Schreiber
   - *SS* Philosophy: *SS-Ostuf.* Bender
   - *Junkerschaftsführer*: *SS-Ustuf.* André Régibeau (replaced by Jean Moreau in November 1944) and Florent Emsix
   - Highest graded: Roland DEVRESSE (*SS-Ustuf.* on 20.04.1945)

3. *(Wall. -Franz.) Kriegs Waffen-Junkerlehgang* from 1 April 1945 but interrupted on 20 April 1945 (probably the *18/19. Oberjunkerlehrgang* scheduled from 16.04.1945 to 30.06.1945).

C. Sophienwalde Academy (29 October 1944 – 20 December 1944)

Attended by the officers of the *Garde Wallonne* who had agreed to join the *Waffen-SS*.

APPENDIX XVIII

Battle Force, Pomeranian Campaign (05.02.1945 – 27.04.1945)[1]

More or less 2,000 men were lined up for the combats around Stargard. By 7 March 1945, 407 men had been killed, wounded or were missing (2,000–407:1,593).

10 March 1945: a first *Kampfgruppe* was raised under *SS-Hstuf* Derriks comprising 625 men + 23 officers (:648). The rest of the forces (945 men) were sent to Bergholz under *SS-Hstuf*. Mathieu.

The battle force (648) engaged at Altdamm (15.03–20.03.1945) suffered 110 casualties (:538).

Total strength (*Kampfgruppe* + Reserve at Bergholz):1,483.

A second Bn (*II/69Rgt* – 04.04.1945) under *SS-Hstuf*. Vermeire was split up. Remained at Plöwen/Löcknitz: the men participating in fortifications works behind the Randowsbrücke under Vermeire, while a combat reserve was put under command of *SS-Hstuf*. Bonniver and grouped at Bismarck (Mathieu).

On 15 April 1945 the situation was as follows:

- *Kdr 69Rgt*: *SS-Ostubaf*. Frans Hellbaut (900 men);
- *I/69Rg:* (Derriks) 600 men;
- *II/69Rgt:* (Bonniver) 300 men.

Oder River fighting (17.04. – 23.04.1945):

- *I/69* (Derriks) at Pomelen;
- *II/69* (Bonniver) at Höhenholz as a reserve.

On April 1945, losses amounted 258 (900–258:642).

Total strength of the remainder of the *28.SS-Freiw.-Gren.Div.Wallonien* is 642 + 583:1,225 men.

The Schönwerder counter-attack (27.04.1945) cost 60 men (642–60:582 men).

On 3 May 1945, 430 out of the 582 surrendered to the Americans.

APPENDIX XIX

Contingents of the Legion Wallonie /Assault Brigade Departing from Belgium[1]

08.08.1941:	Departure from Brussels (more or less 860 men)
19.08.1941:	50 men, among whom were the Catholic Chaplain and Kommandeur Jacobs
01.09.1941:	
10.03.1942:	Contingent comprising J Hagemans's Rexist Youth and members of the G.W.
10.04.1942:	60 volunteers leave Brussels
22.07.1942:	150 volunteers
25.08.1942:	40 volunteers
15.09.1942:	
26.10.1942:	Departure of Henri Derriks.
20.03.1943:	
13.04.1943:	
26.06.1943:	Departure from Schoten (Antwerp) of Flemish volunteers for the Walloon Assault Brigade.
29.07.1943:	Departure from Namur. Ceremony is presided over by Degrelle in the presence of SS-Ostuf. François of the Langemarck.
29.11.1943:	Departure from Binche (accompanied by a detachment of Walloon DRK nurses).
24.05.1944:	
01.08.1944:	

APPENDIX XX

German Liaison Staff Officers

Left-hand column:
Appendix XX: Fig. 1.8. SS-Ostuf. Reinfahrt

Right-hand column:
Appendix XX: Fig. 1.9. SS-Hstuf. Jehn

Left-hand column:
Appendix XX: Fig. 1.10. SS-Ostuf. Flechsig

Right-hand column:
Appendix XX: Fig. 1.11. Winterscheidt

APPENDIX XXI

Regalia

Pre-War Rex Movement Insignia

Appendix XXI: Fig.2.1. The Rexist cross and crown emblem was often placed with the Belgian colours (on the hood of the car) as a sign of loyalty to the Kingdom. (*Collection E. De Bruyne*).

Wartime Rex Movement Insignia

Left-hand column:
Appendix XXI: Fig.2.2. Contrary to what some authors claim, the Rex Movement Insignia is not the blood order. (The latter was instituted by Matthys as late as February 1944). The inscription says: Bravoure-Honneur-Fidélité. (*Collection E. De Bruyne*).

Right-hand column:
Appendix XXI: Fig.2.3. Walloon NCO wearing the Winter Campaign ribbon, the Wound Badge and the Rex Movement insignia. (*Collection E. De Bruyne*).

Jeunesse Legionnaire

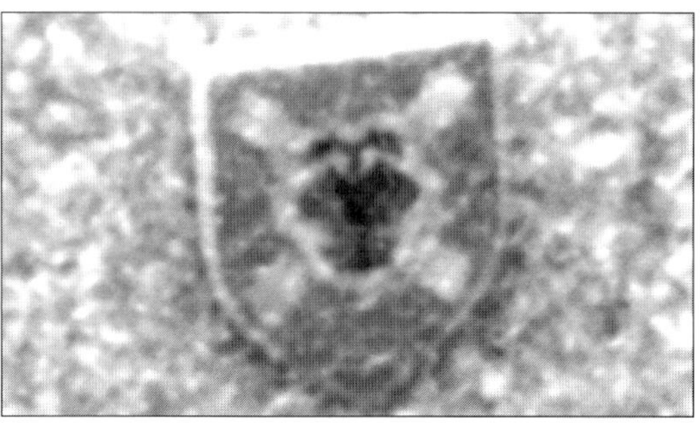

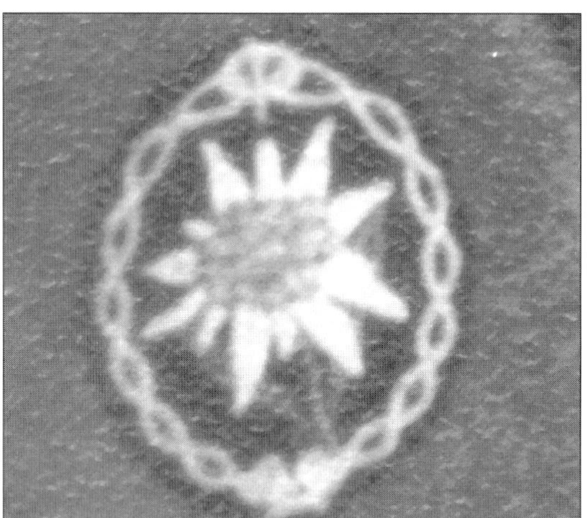

Left-hand column:
Appendix XXI: Fig.2.4.
Walloon SS-Sturmmann wearing J.L. insignia on left breast pocket.
(Private Collection)

Right-hand column top:
Appendix XXI: Fig.2.5.
Magnified JL insignia.

Right-hand column bottom:
Appendix XXI: Fig.2.6.

Legionn Wallonie

Left-hand column:
Appendix XXI: Fig.2.7.
Führer-Anwärter. Edelweiß badge worn by the Caucasus campaign veterans.
(*Collection E. De Bruyne*).

Right-hand column:
Appendix XXI: Fig.2.8.
Member of the Langemarck but wearing on his left breast pocket what seems to be the Rexist insignia showing he is a member of Rex-Vlaanderen, a Flemish offshoot of the Walloon Rexist Movement.
(*Collection E. De Bruyne*).

Tactical Signs

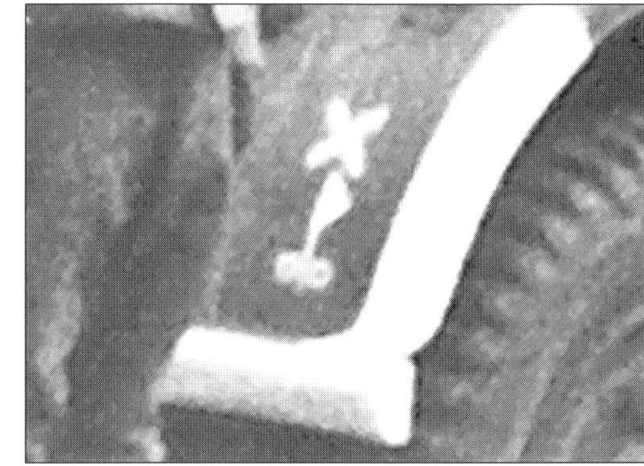

Left-hand column:
Appendix XXI: Fig.2.9. Mercedez-Benz 170V used by the Walloon Assault Brigade. (*J. Mathieu/ Collection E De Bruyne*).

Right-hand column:
Appendix XXI: Fig.2.10. Under the Brigade symbol (Burgundy Cross) is the tactical sign showing that this vehicle belongs to the (motorized) Staff of the Brigade.

APPENDIX XXII

Forced Enrolment into the 28.SS-Freiw.-Gren.Div.Wallonien and use of the Burgundy Collar-patch

During September 1944, Degrelle ordered compulsory enlistment into the *28.SS-Freiw.-Gren.Div.Wallonien* of all Rexist refugees aged 16–55 who had fled to Germany in September 1944. Alleged full battle strength of the Walloon unit reached 3,500 to 4,000 men. The reality, however, was different. Only a small number of these 'volunteers' were fit for battle duties.

geboren am 13.1.93 in .... (Ort, Kreis, Verwaltungsbezirk)

Religion kath. Stand, Beruf telephonist.

Personalbeschreibung

Größe 1.68 Gestalt mittel

Gesicht — Haar d. braun

Bart — Augen braun

Besondere Kennzeichen (z. B. Brillenträger)

fehlt ein Knochen a. l. Unterarm.

Schuhzeuglänge .... Schuhzeugweite ....

(Vor- und Zuname, eigenhändige Unterschrift des Inhabers)

Die Richtigkeit der nicht umrandeten Angaben auf Seite 1 und 2 und der eigenhändigen Unterschrift des Inhabers bescheinigt:

Waffen-SS
(Dienststempel)
SS-Pz.-Gren.-Ausb.- u. Ers.-Btl. 36

den 8.10.44 194

SS-Pz. Gren. Ausb. u. Ers. Btl. 36

(Ausfertigender Truppenteil, Dienststelle)

SSf (Z.) u. Adjutant

(Eigenhändige Unterschrift, Dienstgrad u. Dienststellung d. Vorges.)

2

Appendix XXII: Fig.2.11 (*below*) and **2.12** (*left*). This 52 years old Rex refugee was enrolled on 8 October 1944. Note the Burgundy Cross collar patch. Issued officially it was soon forbidden and disappeared as quickly as it had appeared. (*Private Collection*).

At the same time the Burgundy Cross collar patch was to replace the usual *SS* runes.

Appendix XXII: Fig.2.13. Another younger Rexist refugee (October 1944) wearing the Burgundy collar patch. (*Private Collection*).

APPENDIX XXIII

Full Strength Order of Battle of the 28.SS-Freiw.-Gren.Div.Wallonien/ February 1945

28. SS. Freiw. Gren. Division
"Wallonien"
IIa.

O.U., den 10-1-45.

Führerstellenbesetzung

Dienststellung.	Dienstgrad.	Name.	Bemerkungen.
Div. Kommandeur	SS-Stubaf.	Degrelle	
Stellvertr.u.Ia	SS-Stubaf.	Hellebaut	
0 1	SS-Ostuf.	Nortier	
Gasschutzoffz.	SS-Hscha	von Saenowsky	
Ic	SS-Ostuf.	Forstenoichner	beim Stubaf. Degrelle.
03	SS-Oscha.	Wenzel	Nachkdo. Gronau
04	SS-Ostuf.	Schaffer	beim SS Stubaf Degrelle
Ib	SS-Ostuf.	Hermann	
07	SS-Ostuf.	Greif [illegible]	
Führer Wa.u.G.	SS-Ostuf.	Thiemann	Stutzpunkt Mohlem.
Div.Feldgn.Kp.			
Kp. Führer	SS-Ustuf.	Ringelhan	Nachkdo Elze.
Zugführer	SS-Oscha	Licht[illegible]	
IVa.			
Div. Intendant	SS-Ustuf	Jehn	
1. Mitarbeiter	SS-Ustuf	Plaumann	
IVb			
Div. Arzt	SS-Ostuf	Stahl	
Div. Apotheker	SS-Ustuf	Petre	
Leiter Zahnstat.	SS-Ustuf	Friederich	
IVc			
Div. Veterinär	SS-Hstuf.	Bodorke	
V.			
Div. [illegible]	SS-Ustuf	[illegible]vreese	Lazarett Breslau
T.F.K.	SS-Hscha	Stoetz	

Feldgendarmerie			
Führer d.t.	SS-Stscha	Klugo	
Kraftf. Kp.			
Kp. Führer	SS-Ustuf	Jacobs	Bodendorf
Vet. Kp.			
Komp. Führer	SS-Hstuf	[illegible]ast	
Sani.Kp.			
Kp. Führer	SS-Ostuf.	Stahl	
Hilfsarzt	SS-Hscha.	Buhr	
Apotheker	SS-Ustuf	Quoidbach	
Kr.Kw.Führer	SS-Hscha	Görner	
I.-Zug-Führer	SS-Oscha.	König	
Adjudantur			
Div. Adjudant	SS-Stubaf	Jacobs	
Re	SS-St.O.Ju.	Bernard	
Div.Richter	SS-Hstuf	Flechsig	
Urkundsbeamte	SS-Ustuf	Zinser	
Div. Pfarrer	SS-Stubaf	Stockmann	
Stabsquartier-Kdt.	SS-Ostuf	Vermeire	
VI.			
Leiter	SS-Ostuf	Schlück	
Fürsorgeoffz	SS-Ostuf	Suys	beim Stubaf. Degrelle

Führerstellenbesetzung.

69. Régiment

Regt. Kommandeur	SS-Hstuf.	Mathieu	
Adjudant	SS-Ustuf.	Sandron	
1.C [illegible].	SS-Oscha.	Pevenasse	
2.C O.	SS-Oscha	Gilmon	
Off. z.b.V.	SS-Oscha.	Grube	
Stabskom. Führer	SS-Oscha.	Galere	
Verw.Führer	SS-Ustuf	Schetella	
Arzt			
I Batl.			
Btl. Kommandeur	SS-Hstuf	Derriks	
Adjudant	SS-Ustuf	Degoy	
O.O.	SS-Oscha	Deroy	
Arzt	SS-Ustuf	Buy	
Verw. Führer	SS-Ustuf	Zapetal	
1.Kie-Führer	SS-Ustuf	Regibeau	
Zugführer	SS-Ustuf	Serlet René	
2.Kp.Führer	SS-Ustuf	Deravet	
Zugführer	-		
3.Kp. Führer	SS-Ustuf	Serlet Edouard	
Zugführer	SS-Oscha	Nizet	
4.Kp.Führer	SS-Hstuf	Bonniver	
1.Zugführer	SS-Ustuf	DeCoster	
2. "	SS-Oscha	Bervaes	
	SS-Oscha	Ambroes	ohne Verwendung
	SS-Oscha	Vachaudez	ohne Verwendung
	SS-St.O.Ju	DeHeug	"
	SS-St.O.Ju	Cremers	"
Nachr. Ausbilder	SS-Ustuf.	Nikolaus	Kommandiert
II. Btl.			
Btl. Kommandeur	SS-Hstuf.	Lakaie	
Adjudant	SS-Ustuf.	Theatre	
O.O.	SS-Ustuf.	Liénart	
Arzt	SS-St.O.Ju	Roekens	
Verw. Führer	SS-Ustuf.	Wanka	
(5).Kp. Führer	SS-Ustuf.	Monfils	
1 Zugführer	SS-Oscha	Bacha	
2 Zugführer	SS-Oscha	Jourdain	

(5).Kp.Führer	SS-Ustuf.	Rue	
1. Zugführer	SS-Ustuf	Delafeille	
2. Zugführer	SS-Ustuf	Lovinfosse	
(6). Kp. Führer	SS-Ostuf	Gillis	
1. Zugführer	SS-Ustuf	Rooryck	
2. Zugführer	SS-Ustuf	Hean	
3. Zugführer	SS-Oscha.	Dargent	
7. Kp. Führer	SS-Ostuf	Cappelle	
1. Zugführer	SS-Ustuf	Poels	
2. Zugführer	SS-Ustuf	Wouters	
Flak Kp. Führer	SS-Ustuf	Foulon Fernand.	
1. Zugführer	SS-Ustuf	Collard	
2. Zugführer	SS-St.O.Ju	Gondry	
Nachr. Ausbilder	SS-Ustuf	K[illegible]singer	
	SS-Ustuf	Görtz	
	SS-Ustuf	[illegible]ots	
	SS-Oscha	Dal	
	SS-Oscha	Janssens	
	SS-Oscha	Govaerts	

Führerstellenbesetzung

70.Regiment

Rgt Kommandeur	SS-Stubaf	Tcheokhoff	
Btl. Kommandeur	SS-Hstuf	Ruelle	
Komp. Führer	SS-Hstuf.	Dumont	
Verw. Führer	SS-Ostuf	Motzger	
Zugführer	SS-Ostuf	Bourdouxhe	
Arzt	SS-Ustuf	G[illegible]esemann	
Adjudant	SS-Ustuf	Debougnies	
Zugführer	SS-Ostuf	Valdajos	
Nachr. Zugführer E.	SS-Ustuf	Cremers	
Zugführer	SS-Ustuf	VanEsbeeck	
Zugführer	SS-Ustuf	Suain	
Komp. Führer	SS-Ustuf	Steiver	
Zugführer	SS-Ustuf	Foulon Raph.	
Zugführer	SS-Ustuf	Lecocq	
Zugführer	SS-Ustuf	VanGyseghem	
Kom. Führer	SS-Ustuf	Bal	
Kom. Führer	SS-Ustuf	Schumacher	
Zugführer	SS-Ustuf	[illegible]iannoy	
Auf Lehrgang			
	SS-Ostuf	Debhal[illegible]off	
	SS-Ostuf	D[illegible]ie	
	SS-Ustuf	Beldbusch	
	SS-Ustuf	Piron	
	SS-Ustuf	VandenWaele	
Sans affectation			
	SS-Ostuf.	Lassois	
	SS-Ostuf.	Calonne	
Kandidaten-Offizier			
Adjudant Pel.SUR	SS-Oscha.	Sarveis	
Adjudant Pel.	SS-[illegible]	Cau[illegible]ron	
Adjudant Pel.	SS-Oscha	Carn[illegible]	
Adjudant Pel.	SS-Oscha	Pague	

Adjudant Pel.	SS-Oscha	Bandron	
Adjudant Pel.	SS-Oscha	Kaiser	
Zugführer	SS-Oscha	Bottet	
Sans affectation	SS-Oscha	Leenen van Mechelen.	
		Cuvelier	
		Daulie	
		Danguy	
		delaHamaide (François)	

Führerstellenbesetzung.

Pionier Abtlg.	(auf Lehrgang)		
Kommandeur	SS-Ostuf.	Mirgain	
Kom. Führer	SS-Ustuf.	S[illegible]pin	
Zugführer	SS-Ustuf.	Mignon	
Gem. Nachr. Kp.			
Komp. Führer	SS-Ostuf.	Wastiau	beim Stubaf. Degrelle
Adjudant u.Vertreter	SS-Ustuf	Lantiez	
L.d.N.	SS-Ustuf	Winandy	
F.S.N.	SS-St.O.Ju.	Czapp	
Zugführer	SS-St.O.Ju.	D'Hondt	
Art. Abt.	(auf Lehrgang)		
Kommandeur	SS-Hstuf.	Malherbe	
Battr. Führer	SS-Ostuf.	Graff	
V.B.	SS-Ustuf	Devaux	
Adjudant-Major	SS-Ustuf	Winterscheidt	
Battr. Führer	SS-Ostuf.	Dumont	
V.B.	SS-St.O.Ju.	Grisay	
Battr. Führer	SS-Ustuf	Soeneen	
V.B.	SS-Ustuf	Destat	

Left column top:
Appendix XXIII: Fig. 2.14.

Left column bottom:
Appendix XXIII: Fig. 2.15.

right column top:
Appendix XXIII: Fig. 2.16.

right column middle:
Appendix XXIII: Fig. 2.17.

right column bottom:
Appendix XXIII: Fig. 2.18.

Appendix XXIII:
Fig. 2.19.

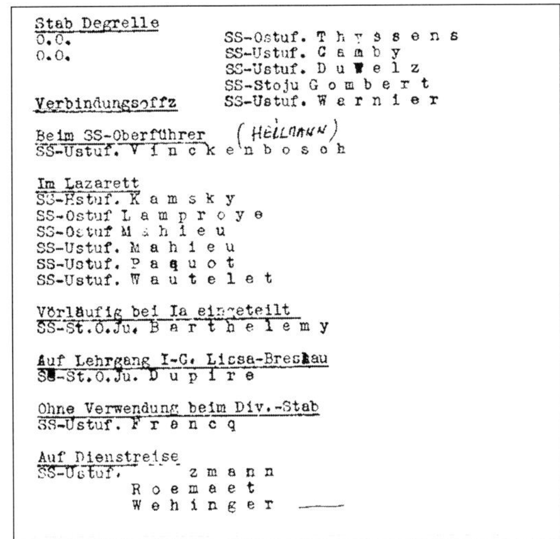

Stab Degrelle
O.O. SS-Ostuf. Thyssens
O.O. SS-Ustuf. Camby
SS-Ustuf. Du[illegible]elz
SS-Stoju Gombert
Verbindungsoffz SS-Ustuf. Wernier

Beim SS-Oberführer (HELLMANN)
SS-Ustuf. Vinckenbosch

Im Lazarett
SS-Hstuf. Kamsky
SS-Ostuf Lamproye
SS-Ostuf Mahieu
SS-Ustuf. Mahieu
SS-Ustuf. Paquot
SS-Ustuf. Wautelet

Vörläufig bei Ia eingeteilt
SS-St.O.Ju. Barthelemy

Auf Lehrgang I-G. Licsa-Breslau
SS-St.O.Ju. Dupire

Ohne Verwendung beim Div.-Stab
SS-Ustuf. Frencq

Auf Dienstreise
SS-Ustuf. [illegible]zmann
Roemaet
Wehinger

APPENDIX XXIV

Document Degrelle in the Matter J. Mathieu

Document signed by Léon Degrelle after the war stating Jules Mathieu was awarded the *Deutsches Kreuz in Gold*. (Arch. E. De Bruyne).

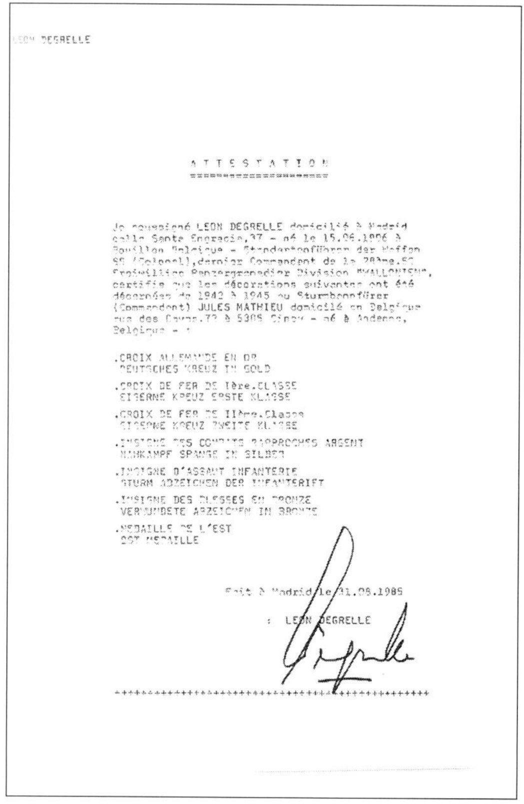

LEON DEGRELLE

A T T E S T A T I O N

Je soussigné LEON DEGRELLE domicilié à Madrid calle Santa Engracia,37 - né le 15.06.1906 à Bouillon Belgique - Standartenführer der Waffen SS (Colonel),dernier Commandant de la 28ème.SS Freiwilligen Panzergrenadier Division "WALLONIEN", certifie que les décorations suivantes ont été décernées de 1942 à 1945 au Sturmbannführer (Commandant) JULES MATHIEU domicilié en Belgique rue des Cayns.72 à 5305 Ciney - né à Andenne, Belgique - :

.CROIX ALLEMANDE EN OR
DEUTSCHES KREUZ IN GOLD

.CROIX DE FER DE Ière.CLASSE
EISERNE KREUZ ERSTE KLASSE

.CROIX DE FER DE IIème.Classe
EISERNE KREUZ ZWEITE KLASSE

.INSIGNE DES COMBATS RAPPROCHES ARGENT
NAHKAMPF SPANGE IN SILBER

.INSIGNE D'ASSAUT INFANTERIE
STURM ABZEICHEN DER INFANTERIE

.INSIGNE DES BLESSES EN BRONZE
VERWUNDETE ABZEICHEN IN BRONZE

.MEDAILLE DE L'EST
OST MEDAILLE

Fait à Madrid le 31.08.1985

: LEON DEGRELLE

Appendix XXIV: Fig. 2.20. Document signed by Léon Degrelle after the war certifying Jules Mathieu was awarded the Deutsches Kreuz in Gold. (*Doc. J. Mathieu/Arch. E. De Bruyne*).

APPENDIX XXV

Documents in the Matter J. Leroy

Left column:
Appendix XXV: Fig. 2.21. Document signed by Roger Wastiau certifying that Jacques Leroy was awarded the Knight's Cross. French handwritten text by Leroy says: *'haven't seen Wastiau since 1946'*. (*Arch. E. De Bruyne*).

Right column:
Appendix XXV: Fig. 2.22. Post-war document signed by Degrelle certifying Jacques Leroy was awarded the Knight's Cross. (*Arch. E. De Bruyne*).

n'ai plus revu Wastiau depuis 1946

Bruxelles, le 20 mai I95[illegible]

A T T E S T A T I O N

Je soussigné WASTIAU , Roger , né à Grammont le 30 octobre I92I , et domicilié à Bruxelles II, rue de l'Industrie, déclare certifié que le nommé :
LEROY, Jacques ,né à Binche le IO septembre I924
a obtenu la Ritterkreuz sur le Front de Stettin, à Altdam le 20 avril I945 .

SS. Hauptsturmführer
d. Div. Adjudant

LEON DEGRELLE

Madrid, le 8 décembre 1973.

Attestation

Je soussigné Léon Degrelle, né à Bouillon le 15 juin 19[illegible] certifié que le nommé : [illegible] Jacques né à Binche le 10 septembre 1924 a obtenu la Ritterkreuz sur le Front de Stettin à [illegible], le 20 [illegible]

APPENDIX XXVI

Degrelle's Last Will (March 1945)

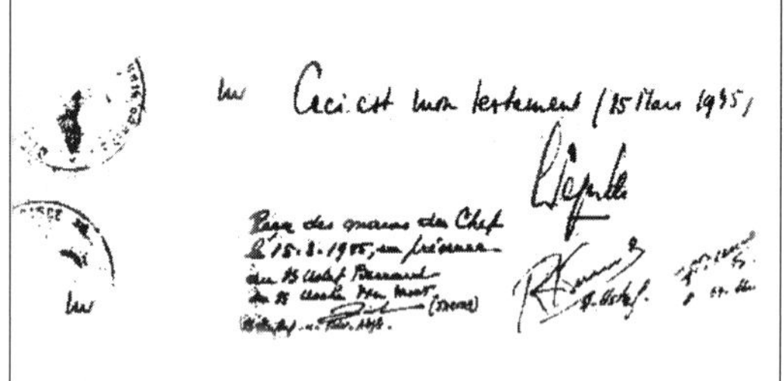

Ceci est mon testament (15 Mars 1945)

Reçu des mains du Chef le 15.3.1945, en présence du SS Ustuf Bernard et du SS Uscha Van M...

Ceci est mon testament

Pour témoigner à mon épouse très-aimée Marie-Paule Degrelle, née Lemay, ma confiance et ma reconnaissance infinies je lui lègue, avec le droit le plus absolu la totalité de mes biens. Elle aura aussi le droit de choisir ses conseillers.

Ce testament annule toutes les dispositions que j'aurais prises précédemment.

Fait au front de l'Oder, le 15 Mars 1945

Degrelle

Appendix XXVI: Fig. 2.23. + 2.24. Text says: received from the Chef (Degrelle) on 15 March 1945 in presence of *SS-Ustuf*. Bernard and *SS-Uscha* Van M...(signed *SS-Stubaf. u. Div.Adj*. G. Jacobs). (*Arch. E. De Bruyne*).

APPENDIX XXVII

Propaganda

1. Pre-War Period

Appendix XXVII: Fig. 2.25.
(*Collection E. De Bruyne*).

Rex ou Moscou

MEETING DE REX

LE JEUDI 30 JUILLET, à 20 heures

Léon Degrelle

parlera au

PEUPLE de BRUXELLES

au "PALAIS DES SPORTS" Avenue Louis Bertrand, Schaerbeek

Ouverture 18 h.
Entrées N°s 4 et 6

Soutien au fond de combat
5 FRS

Appendix XXVII: Fig. 2.26.
(*Collection E. De Bruyne*).

Appendix XXVII: Fig. 2.27. Rexist contribution fee stamps. (*Collection E. De Bruyne*).

Appendix XXVII: Fig. 2.28.
(*Collection E. De Bruyne*).

2. *Wehrmacht* Period

Appendix XXVII: Fig. 2.29.
(*Collection E. De Bruyne*).

WALLONIE

Des chasseurs sont formés sous la direction du commandant de la Légion.

Appendix XXVII: Fig. 2.30.
(*Collection E. De Bruyne*).

WALLONIE

Le printemps sur le front de l'Est.
Mais le combat contre l'ennemi de l'Europe continue.

En avant avec la
KRIEGSMARINE!

Left-hand column:
Appendix XXVII: Fig.2.31.
(*Collection E. De Bruyne*).

Right-hand column:
Appendix XXVII: Fig. 2.33.
More or less 150 Walloons served in the *Kriegsmarine*.

CARIBOU

(nom scout de Gaston Chavanne).

Le 24 août de cette année, Caribou était tué sur le front russe au cours d'une reconnaissance dans les lignes ennemies.

Entré assez tardivement à la troupe scoute, il s'y révéla un gai compagnon, ardent au jeu, profondément désireux de suivre sa loi.

Il avait le tempérament d'un entraîneur.

C'est ce qui le fit désigner pour la charge de chef de patrouille des Sangliers, puis pour celle de Ier C. P.

Fidèle à sa promesse, il accomplit ses tâches de son mieux, dans des circonstances parfois difficiles.

Il passe au clan au printemps 1941. Avec lui disparut la patrouille des Sangliers.

Au sortir de la rhétorique, il quitte le Collège et l'Unité pour aller là où l'appelait son destin!

Il a laissé parmi nous le souvenir d'une âme droite et loyale et c'est avec une émotion gonflée d'espérance que nous songeons à lui.

Rév. P. L......, aumônier scout,
le 18 octobre 1942.

Vous qui l'avez connu, priez pour lui.

WALLONIE

A LA MÉMOIRE DE

Gaston A. CHAVANNE

sous-officier
à la Légion belge « Wallonie »
tombé à Tscheryakow (Caucase)
le 24 août 1942, à l'âge de 20 ans.

Croix de fer de 2e classe.
Médaille de l'Est (campagne d'hiver 1942).

Symbole de fierté et d'héroïsme, il a lutté courageusement aux côtés de son Chef, contre le communisme et pour sauvegarder les droits de sa Patrie.

Seuls comptent, dans la vie des peuples, ceux qui, poussés par l'amour lucide de leur Pays, frayent les routes !

Les autres, tôt ou tard, suivront! Ce sont les cœurs forts qui changent les nations. C'est l'exemple, le don et l'audace qui entraînent. D'abord savoir ce qu'on veut, où on va, puis foncer tout droit, quels que soient les obstacles. Léon Degrelle.

Appendix XXVII: Fig. 2.32.
Obituary of legionnaire G.Chavanne, KIA in the Caucasus on 24 August 1942. (*Collection J.-L. Roba*).

Left-hand column:
Appendix XXVII: Fig. 2.34.
(*Collection E. De Bruyne*).

Right-hand column:
Appendix XXVII: Fig. 2.35.
(*Collection E. De Bruyne*).

3. Waffen-SS Period

Left-hand column:
Appendix XXVII: Fig. 2.36.
(*Collection E. De Bruyne*).

Right-hand column:
Appendix XXVII: Fig. 2.37.
(*Collection E. De Bruyne*).

Engage-toi à la

SS Brigade d'Assaut Wallonie

Chevalerie des Temps Modernes

Elle comprend les ARMES suivantes

Chars d'Assaut

Section Anti-Chars -- Formations Motocyclistes

Sections Anti-Aériennes - Génie

Formations Sanitaires - Troupes de Transmission

ARTILLERIE

Herstellung und Alleinvertrieb: Kunstverlag E. A. Schwerdtfeger & Co. AG., Berlin

La

SS Brigade d'Assaut Wallonie

est entièrement motorisée

Tous renseignements

SS Brigade de Wallonie

Bureau de Recrutement

Place du Martyr, 2

VERVIERS - Tél. 125.57

Engagez-vous à la Waffen-SS!

Foto: SS-Kriegsberichter Roth

Nous avons l'honneur
de vous inviter à assister
à la

Commémoration du Départ
de la
" Légion Wallonie "
8 août 1941 — 8 août 1944
au Palais des Beaux-Arts de Bruxelles,
le dimanche 13 août 1944, à 15 heures

La place correspondant à la présente invitation sera réservée jusqu'à 14 h. 45

FAUTEUIL n° 227

Left: **Appendix XXVII: Fig. 2.38.** (*Collection E. De Bruyne*).

Below: **Appendix XXVII: Fig. 2.39.** (*Collection E. De Bruyne*).

Above: **Appendix XXVII: Fig. 2.40.** (*Collection E. De Bruyne*).

Right: **Appendix XXVII: Fig. 2.41.** (*Collection E. De Bruyne*).

Camarade!

Toi aussi La Waffen-SS t'appelle

Pourquoi te tiens-tu encore à l'écart?

L'élite de la jeunesse marche avec nous et envoie encore aujourd'hui son inscription au bureau de Recrutement de la "**SS-Brigade Wallonie**" à **Dinant** (Province de Namur).

(détacher ici)

Je sollicite mon engagement à la

"**SS-BRIGADE WALLONIE**"

Nom .... Prénom ....

Né le ....

Domicilié à .... rue ....

....

(Signature)

Above: **Appendix XXVII: Fig. 2.42.** (*Collection E. De Bruyne*).

Top right: **Appendix XXVII: Fig. 2.43.** (*Collection E. De Bruyne*).

Right: **Appendix XXVII: Fig. 2.44.** This picture of Léon Degrelle bears the seal of the *Honneur Légionnaire*, the Rexist Welfare care for the Walloon Eastern Front combatants. (*Collection E. De Bruyne*).

Below: **Appendix XXVII: Fig. 2.45.** The Walloon Assault Brigade weekly. (*Collection E. De Bruyne*).

Le Combattant

ORGANE HEBDOMADAIRE DE LA BRIGADE D'ASSAUT SS WALLONIE

Bulletin d'abonnement

Left: **Appendix XXVII: Fig. 2.46.** (*Collection E. De Bruyne*).
Right: **Appendix XXVII: Fig. 2.48.** (*Collection E. De Bruyne*).

Appendix XXVII: Fig. 2.47. Not all Walloon legionnaires wore the Wallonie armbadge. The officer on the right is is Jules Mathieu. (*J. Mathieu/Collection E. De Bruyne*).

4. Post-War Period

Appendix XXVII: Fig. 2.49. Probably (unusual) post-war imitation of the *Légion Wallonie* arm-badge. (*Collection E. De Bruyne*).

Criminel de guerre, traitre notoire, chef d'une bande d'assassins qui ont combattu contre les Alliés, Léon Degrelle s'est dérobé à la justice de son pays et il a trouvé, en Espagne, un refuge contre le châtiment qu'il mérite.

Avec cynisme, il porte ostensiblement la Croix de Fer que lui décerna Hitler, en récompense

Notre Photographe "LUI" a rendu visite

DEGRELLE SE PORTE BIEN

Bien qu'il soit interné, en ce moment, à l'hôpital militaire Mola à Saint-Sébastien, le chef de « Rex » a tout l'air d'être en parfaite santé et de s'émouvoir assez peu du bruit fait autour de sa peu intéressante personne et des demandes d'extradition dont il est l'objet de la part des Autorités belges. Notre ambassadeur à Washington vient d'en écrire au secrétaire général de l'O.N.U., en précisant les accusations formelles qui pèsent sur Degrelle, criminel de guerre, assassin de ses compatriotes, officier de l'armée allemande, condamné à mort par contumace par les tribunaux belges.

Appendix XXVII: Fig. 2.50. The Belgian post-war press liked to remind its readers of Degrelle's exile in Spain. (*Le Soir Illustré* - May 1946).

APPENDIX XXVIII

The Legionnaires

Appendix XXVIII: Fig. 2.51 and **2.52** Oath-taking ceremony at Meseritz barracks presided over by L. Degrelle. (1943). (*Collection E. De Bruyne*).

Appendix XXVIII: Fig. 2.53.
1 April 1944. The Cherkassy parade at Charleroi. Once again, *SS-Ustuf.* H. Thyssen is the colour-bearer. R. Devresse is the 3rd from the right. (*Collection R. Devresse*).

Appendix XXVIII: Fig. 2.54.
Meseritz 1943: from left to right: Rex Movement Cadres Serge Döring and Victor Matthys, Major Bode (*Ers.Aus.Btl 477*) and *Adjutant*, Lucien Lippert, Georges Tchekhoff and Léon Degrelle. (*J.-L. Roba*).

Appendix XXVIII: Fig. 2.55. 1942: PAK 37 instruction. (*PAK 37:* 440 Kg; length: 3m; range 550m; 8 to 10 rounds per minute). (*J. Mathieu/Collection E. De Bruyne*).

Appendix XXVIII: Fig. 2.56. Léon Degrelle was keen on addressing his men. (*Collection E. De Bruyne*).

Appendix XXVIII: Fig. 2.57. January 1942: a Walloon patrol crosses the frozen Samara River. *Unteroffizier* Jean Pirmolin (4th Company), in charge of the patrol, is being sledge-pulled by *Gefreiter* Albert Dosquet. Pirmolin was eventually executed by firing squad (1948) for his participation in the murder of Belgian patriots. (*Collection Bunt, via J.-L. Roba*).

Above: **Appendix XXVIII: Fig. 2.58.** During the Cherkassy breakout: scattered elements are heading for Chanderowka. (*J. Lekeux/ via J.L. Roba*).

Top left: **Appendix XXVIII: Fig. 2.59.** MG40 instruction under the supervision of a veteran of the Caucasus campaign. (*Collection E. De Bruyne*).

Middle left: **Appendix XXVIII: Fig. 2.60.** Lucien Lippert (foreground) among his men. The officer on the right is J. Mathieu. (*J. Mathieu/Collection E. De Bruyne*).

Bottom left: **Appendix XXVIII: Fig. 2.61.** Walloon *SS-Ustuf.* Albert Wehinger (here during Cherkassy parade) served under Henri Derriks as a platoon Co (2nd Company). (*Collection J.-L. Roba*).

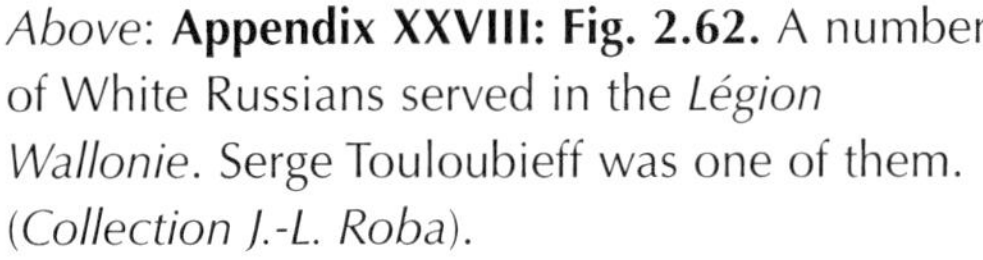

Above: **Appendix XXVIII: Fig. 2.62.** A number of White Russians served in the *Légion Wallonie*. Serge Touloubieff was one of them. (*Collection J.-L. Roba*).

Top right: **Appendix XXVIII: Fig. 2.63.** Four young members of the 10 March 1942 contingent while attending a catholic mass. From left to right: Prosper Hebbelinckx (KIA), Jacques Leroy, Jean Moreau and Georges Thonon. (*G. Thonon via J.-L. Roba*).

Middle right: **Appendix XXVIII: Fig. 2.64.** Anti-Bolshevik meeting held at Brussels on 29 June 1943. Léon Closset is marching ahead. Two Walloon legionnaires are bearing the Rexist colours. The man on the right with armband is George Woyciekowski, Director of the pro-German Office for Russian Refugees in Belgium. (*J. Mathieu/Collection E. De Bruyne*).

Bottom right: **Appendix XXVIII: Fig. 2.65.** Leon Gillis demonstrating the use of the *Sturmgewehr* 44 to the men of the anti-tank element of *KG-Wallonien*. He has not yet added the collar patches of an SS-Ostuf., the rank he reached on 9 November 1944, though it was not uncommon for men to wear their old insignia for weeks or months after a promotion. This photo may have been taken during a training exercise in the autumn of 1944, but related photos have been captioned as being taken in Pomerania in February 1945. Gillis replaced the wounded Marcel Lamproye as the commander of the *PAK* Company during that campaign. Note the wear to his sheepskin jacket. (*Collection J.-L. Roba*).

APPENDIX XXIX

Documents

IM NAMEN DES FÜHRERS

VERLEIHE ICH

DEM

SS-Sturmmann

F Georges

I./5.SS-Freiw. Sturmbrigade "Wallonien"

DAS

EISERNE KREUZ

2. KLASSE

K.Gef.St. den 6.9. 1944

Der Kommandierende General

SS Obergruppenführer und
General der Waffen SS

(DIENSTGRAD UND DIENSTSTELLUNG)

Appendix XXIX: Fig. 2.66. The diploma is signed by Gen. Steiner, commanding officer of the III. (germ.) *SS-Panzer-Korps*. (*Private Collection*).

San. Schule der Waffen-SS
Prag
Az.: 40 k 12

(11b) Prag, den 21. VIII. 1944

Zeugnis

Der SS- Sturmmann
geb. am 1923 Einheit: SS-Freiwillg.Div."Wallonien"
hat an einem zweimonatigen Lehrgang an der San. Schule der Waffen-SS Prag teilgenommen und nach theoretischem und praktischem Unterricht die Prüfung als Sanitätsdienstgrad der Waffen-SS, mit der Note

5 (genügend) bestanden.

Das Tragen von Unterführer-Anwärter - A[illegible] gemäss V. Bl. d. W.-SS, Ziffer 78/1941 ist genehmigt.

Der Leiter
der San. Schule der Waffen-SS - Prag
SS-Hauptsturmführer.

Above: **Appendix: Fig. 2.67.** Note the appellation *SS-Freiwillg. Div. Wallonien* in August 1944! (*Private Collection*).

Einheit: SS.Art.Abt.Wallonien Stabsbatterie
Offene Bezeichnung, keine Feldpostnummer, nur allgemeinverständliche Abkürzungen

Wehrnummer:

Erkennungsmarke: SS.Gr.A.u.E.Btt.36
Beschrift. (Truppenteil, Dienststelle)
Lfd. Nr.: 54

Kriegsstammrollennummer: Stabs/A/a/14

1 Familienname

2 Jacques
Vorname (Rufname unterstreichen)

2a Rue Belgique
Ständiger Aufenthaltsort zur Zeit der Einberufung
Ort, Kreis, Straße, Hausnummer

3 Tag | Monat | Jahr d. Geburt

4 Geburtsort: Belgique
Kreis, Bezirk, Amt usw. — Reg. Bezirk

6 catholique — Religiöses Bekenntnis
7 Célibat. — Familienstand — Tag | Monat | Jahr

8 a) électricien — erlernter Beruf
b) idem — ausgeübter Beruf

18 Datum des erstmaligen Diensteintritts in die Wehrmacht: 21.02.1944

13 Anschrift der Frau oder der Eltern oder der zu benachrichtigenden Person (maßgebend für Verlustanzeige)

SS.Sturmann — Dienstgrad
15 — Stellengruppe

19 **Zugang:** Eingetroffen am: 11.11.1945
Überwiesen von:
Bisheriger Feldtruppenteil oder Ersatztruppenteil oder Wehrersatzdienststelle
Dortige Stammrollennummer:
Kriegs- oder Truppenstammrolle der bisherigen Einheit
Wehrpaß eingetroffen oder abgenommen am:

42 SS.Gr.Aus.u.E.Btt.36
Zuständiger Ersatztruppenteil
Alfeld /Leine
Standort

43 steht nicht in deutscher Wehrüberwachung
Zuletzt zuständige Wehrersatzdienststelle. (Siehe Wehrpaß S. 1 bzw. 4)

41 **Abgang:** Überwiesen am: 13.3.1945
an: 3e.Batterie
Truppenteil, Ersatztruppenteil, Lazarett, Wehrersatzdienststelle
Gefallen Gestorben am:
Nichtzutreffendes streichen.
Beerdigt in:
Vermißt seit:
bei:
Truppenteil, Kriegsschauplatz, Ort, Überfahrt

4a Wehrpaß abgesandt oder ausgehändigt am: an:

41b — nur bei Geb.-Jahrgang 1914 und jünger —
Aktive Dienstpflicht erfüllt*) von bis
„ „ ***)
„ „ ***)
Zur Erfüllung der akt. Dienstpflicht abgeleist. Wehrdienst**) von bis
„ „ ***)
„ „ ***)
*) Eintragung nur, wenn die 2jährige Dienstpflicht bei Abgang erfüllt ist.
**) Eintragung nur, wenn die 2jähr. Dienstpfl. bei Abg. noch nicht erfüllt ist.
***) Nur auszufüllen bei Unterbrechung der Dienstzeit.

Der stark umrahmte Teil ist sofort nach Zugang des Soldaten auszufüllen.

22 **Besondere Ausbildung, Lehrgänge, Kommandierungen**
Welche Waffe(n), Gerät usw.; erreichter Ausbildungsstand
Lehrgäng de radio — groupe sanguin : A

a) in erster Linie zu verwenden als:
b) in zweiter Linie zu verwenden als:
vom Einheitsführer **persönlich** einzutragen

23a **Beförderungen, Ernennungen, Stellengruppe**

Durch Befehl usw. vom	ernannt oder befördert zum	Stellengruppe	mit Wirkung vom	Bestätigung des Komp.- usw. Führers
SS.Art.Abt.Wallonien	SS.Sturmann	15	1.2.45	SS.Ustuf.u.Bie Führer

Right: **Appendix : Fig. 2.68.** (*Private Collection*)

APPENDIX XXX

Walloon Veterans

Appendix XXX: Fig. 2.69. Buenos Aires, 4 March 1952. Walloon veterans pose during a reunion. From left to right: N. Sakhnowksi (White Russian), J. Baujot, J. Liénart and his wife, Lucien Gaillard and his wife (holding shield), G. Tchekhoff and his wife. Next in line is Y. Chenot. (*G. Gilsoul/Collection E. De Bruyne*).

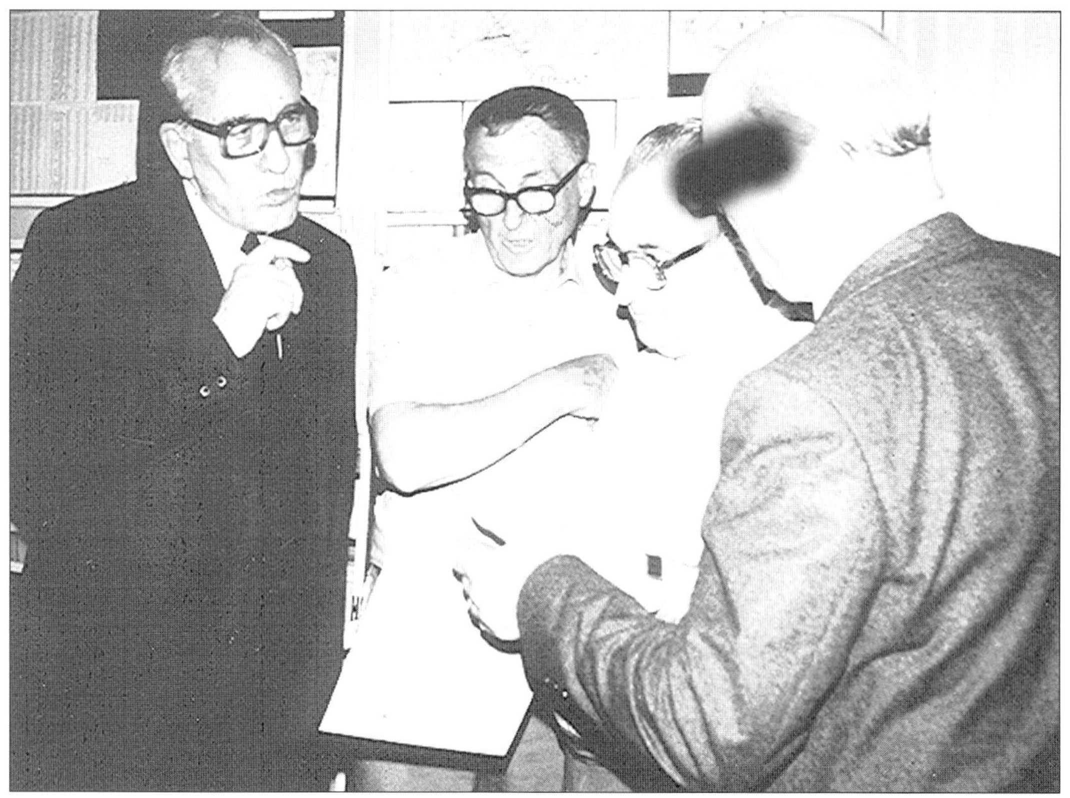

Appendix XXX: Fig. 2.70. Long after the war: from left to right, former *SS-Ostuf.* Mathieu De Coster (March 42 contingent-CO/2Co/*Kampfgruppe Derriks*); former *SS-Stubaf.* Jules Mathieu (August 41 contingent-*Kdr/69Rgt*); former *SS-Ustuf.* Roland Devresse (March 42 contingent-Platoon CO/ 3Co/*Kampfgruppe Derriks*) and former *SS-Ostuf.* Gé.Pé. (August 41 contingent-Platoon CO /3Co/ *Kampfgruppe Derriks*). (*Collection E. De Bruyne*).

Notes

Notes

Notes to CHAPTER I

1. He was crossed off as a member in 1941. He joined the Rexist youth movement *Jeunesse Légionnaire* in 1943. During May 1944, being a medical doctor, he became the head of the medical service of the Walloon (Rexist) Labour Service, fled with the Service to Germany in September 1944 and was arrested by the Belgian authorities in May 1945.
2. Martin Conway, *Collaboration in Belgium – Léon Degrelle and the Rexist Movement*, Yale University Press New Haven & London, 1993, pp. 9–20; Jean-Michel Etienne, *Le Mouvement Rexiste jusqu'en 1940*, Presses de la Fondation Nationale des Sciences Politiques, Paris, 1968, pp. 30–34.
3. As the treasurer of the *Avant-Garde* until 17 May 1928.
4. L. Degrelle, *Mes Aventures au Mexique*, Paris-Louvain-Milan, Ed. Rex, 94p.
5. Ernest Delvaux (31.10.1883), lawyer, was appointed head of the Walloon Cabinet within the Ministry of the Interior (under Gérard Romsée, Flemish *VNV* member). In 1936, E. Delvaux had been elected Rexist Senator for the Province of Luxemburg. François Boulanger, political advisor to the *Pays Réel*, assisted him in his task; M. Conway, *op. cit.* p. 82.
6. By virtue of art. 57 of the Law of 1928 he had been exempted from military service. As eldest son of a large family, he was given the possibility to refuse being subjected to the draft like any other young Belgian. (Note that Degrelle could have refused this benefice of the Law).
7. *Grimm report* (Officer within the German *Verbindungsstab* (liaison staff) in August 1941). Document transmitted by Prof. Francis Balace, Professor of Contemporary History at the University of Liège.
8. By 01 August 1943, all of the 4 Walloon provincial governors in office on 10 May 1940 had been replaced by New Order sympathisers. Former governor Van Mol of the Province Hainaut was accused of having abandoned his post as governor of the province too soon after the invasion and was replaced by the Rexist Antoine Leroy. Former governor Mathieu (Province of Liège) went to France in May 1940 to look after refugees from his province. He was not allowed to resume his functions and was replaced by Petit, a militant Rexist. Governor Van Den Corput, governor of the Province of Luxemburg, was forced to resign under the age-limit ordinance. He was replaced by a former officer of authoritarian principles, Baron Greindl, who, in his turn, was replaced by Rexist Jacques Dewez. François Bovesse, former liberal minister, an opponent of the policy of neutrality and governor of the Province of Namur, was first replaced by a barrister, Devos, but the latter was attacked by the collaborationist press for continuing the policy of his predecessor. He was dismissed and the post was given to a prominent member of the Walloon section of the *Verdinaso*, Prince Emmanuel de Croij. François Bovesse was assassinated on 1 February 1944 by members of the *DSI*, the Rexist Security Corps. In the bi-lingual province of Brabant, Baron Houtart, in an effort to escape the duty of dismissing the elected Mayor and Aldermen of the Communes of Greater Brussels, went on sick-leave in autumn 1942 and did not reappear. He was replaced *a.i.* by Dr Wildiers. Rexist Adrien Gillès de Pélichy replaced the latter; M. Conway, *op. cit.* pp. 141–42.
9. Personal account by Pierre Pauly (*Kdr* of the *Légion Wallonie*) of the Gromowaja-Balka battle, transmitted to Frans Hellebaut on the eve of his execution; arch. E. De Bruyne, facts confirmed by J. Mathieu.
10. Statement by José Streel. The exact word used by Streel is *'Peaux-Rouges'* (literally Redskin Indians), which had – and still has – no offending connotations in Europe.

11. M. Conway, *op. cit.* pp. 170–75.
12. From the German point of view the breakout of the encircled forces had been presented as a victory by the German propaganda, whereas, in reality, it was more a defeat, the Germans having lost an important battle.
13. M. Conway, *op. cit.* p. 247.

Notes to Chapter II

1. Martin Conway, *Collaboration in Belgium – Léon Degrelle and the Rexist Movement*, Yale University Press New Haven & London, 1993, pp. 151–53.

Notes to Chapter IV

1. Heading the *Waffen-SS-Dienststelle Fürsorgeoffizier Flandern und Wallonien*, Paul SUYS joined the *SS-Freiw. -Leg. Nederland* (06.08.1941) and later on the *Freiw. -Leg. Flandern* (01.11.1941) and eventually the *28. SS-Freiw. -Gren. Div Wallonien* in September 1944 with the rank of an *SS-Ostuf. d.R.a.K.* (*der Reserve auf Kriegsdauer*); that is, of the Reserve Corps for the duration of the war).
   The main task of the *Fürsorge und Versorgungsamt der Waffen-SS Ausland* (which came under the *Hauptfürsorge und Versorgungsamt* of *the Rasse-und Siedlungshauptamt*) was to give a variety of financial and material assistance to Flemish and Walloon *Waffen-SS* volunteers and their families.
2. Born in Essen 01.01.1911. *Hptm d. Res.* coming from the *Pz. Jäger Abt. Großdeutschland.* Joined the *Kommandostab beim Militärbefehlshaber in Belgien u. Nordfrankreich* on 11 November 1942. Transferred to the *Waffen-SS* with the rank of *SS-Hstuf.* on 8 August 1943.

Notes to Chapter V

1. The *Gildes Estudiantines* was a project for a National Socialist Students' Association. John Hagemans, leader of the Rexist Youth, planned to make it operational in October 1941.

Notes to Chapter VI

1. The *DeWag* was meant to advocate the Germanic ideology in the occupied countries (Northern and Western Europe) developed by the trio Himmler-Berger-Riedweg. *SS-Ostubaf.* Dr Franz Riedweg, a Swiss doctor and Gen. von Blomberg's son-in-law, headed (April 1941-November 1943) the *Germanische Leitstelle* (Germanic Coordination Office) or *Amt VI* of the *SS-HA*, before joining the *III.(germ.)SS-Pz. Korps.*
2. The task of the Berlin based *DWAK* (headed by Prof. Weber, and also vice-president of the *DeWag*), was to supervise the propaganda organization among the Walloon workers in the Reich.

Notes to Chapter IX

1. Martin Conway, *Collaboration in Belgium – Léon Degrelle and the Rexist Movement*, Yale University Press New Haven & London, 1993, p. 25.

Notes to Chapter XII

1. Stefan Gierets died on 25 June 1941. He was replaced by Karl Herwanger, a gymnastics teacher.

Notes to Chapter XIV

1. Blumenthal 29.10.1878 – †Nassau 31.07.1966. Von Falkenhausen became Lieutenant in 1897. Served in the international expeditionary corps during the Chinese Boxer Rebellion. After completing his military education at the *Kriegsschule*/War Academy (1904–08), he was sent to Tokyo and was appointed attaché. He participated in the WWI campaigns in Flanders, France, Russia and Turkey and became head of the German military mission in that country. After the German defeat, he joined the Weimar-tutored *Reichswehr*. From 1934 to 1939, he served as military advisor to Chiang Kaï-Chek. He ended his career as director of the Dresden Infantry School. Arrested by the *Gestapo* after the July 1944 plot and sent to Dachau concentration camp. Sentenced in Belgium to 12 years imprisonment on the charge of executing hostages and deporting Jews. Amnestied and released 27 March 1951.
2. Von Harbou was transferred to Belgium as he was at loggerheads with the *Auslands-Organisation* of the *NSDAP* of the Hague (Netherlands) where he served in the Rauter administration during May 1940. He openly criticized the *NSDAP* and its leaders. Dismissed from his command in December 1943, he committed suicide in the Moabit prison in Berlin on 12 December 1943. His successor was Heider.
3. Lawyer. *Regierungspräsident* of Aachen (1934), Cologne (1936) and Düsseldorf (1939). In November 1939, von Brauchitsch, fearing *NSDAP* interference in military matters, assigned Reeder with the secret elaboration of a Military Administration of the Netherlands, Belgium and the Grand-Duchy of Luxemburg. In April 1945, Reeder was arrested and tried by a Military Court in Brussels to 8 years imprisonment, but he too was soon released.
4. *OFK 672* (Brussels/Gen. von Hammerstein); *OFK 589* (Liège/Gen. von Claer, then Keim); *OFK* 520 (Mons/Col. von Walther), the *OFK 570* (Ghent) covering Flanders (with a special status for the Antwerp harbour).
5. Killed in a car accident in November 1940. His successor was *SS-Standartenführer* Constantin Canaris (Duisburg, 03.11.1906), replaced by *SS-Sturmbannführer* Ehlers in February 1942. Canaris resumed office in Brussels in February 1943. Constantin Canaris was no relation to Admiral Wilhelm Canaris.

   Canaris, Dr. jur. Konstantin [SS-*Standartenführer und Oberst der Polizei*] – commander of the German Security Police and Security Service (*Sicherheitspolizei und Sicherheitsdienst – Sipo/SD*) in Belgium and northern France; Inspector of German Security Police and Security Service (*Insp. d. Sipo u. SD*) in Military District I (*Wehrkreis I*) at Koenigsberg (Königsberg) 1944; {put on trial 1951 by a Belgian court on charges of responsibility for the murders of inmates at Breendonk concentration camp, torture, execution of hostages and deportations of Belgian Jews to the death camps of Poland; convicted and sentenced to 20 years imprisonment at hard labour 04 Aug. 1951 (LT 6 Aug 1951:3f); released from Belgian custody 12 Apr. 1952 (NYT 13 Apr 1952:25:6); impending trial by a West German court at Kiel on charges of participating in the deportation and death of 26,000 Jews from Belgium and northern France between Aug. 1942 and June 1944 announced 13 Feb 1980 (NYT 14 Feb 1980:3:1); subsequent disposition unknown (ABR-SS; Holo. Ency. 243).}; with credit to David Thompson.
6. Essen 17.08.1906–1955. Judge at the Civil Court of Essen in 1933. Counsellor to the Dortmund government and, in 1942, Counsellor of the Reich at Königsberg. Polish campaign as a Lieutenant in the *Wehrmacht*. Member of the *Allgemeine SS* since December 1931. *NSDAP* member since 1935. Convinced National Socialist. Transfer from the *Wehrmacht* to the *SD* in November 1941. *SS-Obersturmbannführer* and head of *Einsatzkommando 2*, Latvia, on 4 November 1941. During February 1942, he became head of the *Sipo-Sd* in Minsk. Transferred to the Headquarters of General von Dembach in July 1943 with the assignment of combating communist guerillas. Sent to Belgium in 1944 in order to reorganize the struggle against the Resistance, on the one hand, and commissioned with a surveillance mission against Jungclaus and Canaris, on the other hand.

   Belgium; German Security Police and Security Service *Wallonia* {arrested and put on trial by an American military tribunal at Nuremberg (the '*Einsatzgruppe case*') on charges of ordering and participating in mass shootings of Jewish civilians in the Soviet Union; convicted and sentenced to death by hanging 10 Apr. 1948 (NYT 11 Apr 1948:9:1); execution postponed due to defendant's insanity; extradited to Belgium; put on trial by a Belgian military court at Liege; convicted of war crimes and sentenced to death 30 Oct 1948 (NYT 31 Oct 1948:26:6); died in a Belgian prison 9 Sept. 1955 (Rueckerl 129; Holo Ency 1792–3; *Encyclopedia of the Third Reich* pps. 920; Field Men p. 117); with credit to David Thompson.

7. Successive Chiefs of the *Abwehr* in Belgium were:
   Lt-Col. Dischler (1940–1941);
   Col. Servaes (1942-April 1943);
   Col. Scholz (April 1943-March 1944);
   Lt-Col. Gieskes, chief of the *FAK 307* (from March 1944).
8. *Abwehr* chiefs in Belgium carried names of musicians as a cover.

Notes to Chapter XV

1. During January 1943, Degrelle decided upon the creation of a Red Cross battalion composed of Walloon (Rexist) nurses. As a result of a first agreement, a contingent would be recruited directly by the *M.F.R.* (feminine section of the Rexist Movement). After a severe selection, twenty candidates were sent to Wiesbaden for instruction under the leadership of Mad. Jeanne Biltrays, who had been appointed *Cheftaine de Bataillon* (Battalion Mistress).
2. Appointed in Belgium as Himmler's representative on 1 April 1942. Previously he had served in *HSSPF* Rauter' s staff (Netherlands). On 14 August 1944, he was appointed *HSSPF* in Belgium and *Generalkommissar für das Sicherheitswesen* (General Commissar for Security matters) within *Gauleiter* Grohe's Civil Administration. In the last weeks of the occupation, with the help of Rex auxiliary police forces, he organized the reprisal actions against the Resistance. After *Wehrmachtsbefehlshaber* General Grase, who commanded the *Wehrmacht* forces in occupied Belgium, had been dismissed, Jungclaus combined the functions of *Wehrmachtsbefehshaber* and *HSSPF* from 14 August 1944 on. Accused of defeatism for having released 600 political prisoners and ordered the evacuation of the collaborators without orders from Berlin, he was released of all his functions (*) on 16 September 1944 by Himmler himself after a dramatic meeting at Valkenburg (Netherlands). Jungclaus however kept his rank of *SS-Ostuf. der Reserve* (**) and was sent to the front in Yugoslavia (*SS-Gebirgsjäger Rgt 13*), where he was killed near Savidovice on 14 April 1945 (***). (The *SS-Gebirgsjäger Rgt 13* was part of the *7. Frw. -Gebirgs Division Prinz Eugen* which was fighting in Croatia at the time he was killed).

   (*) Jungclaus was relieved of his office as *HSSPF* and lost his rank of *Gruppenführer* of the *Algemeine SS* that he had been granted in November 1942. He also lost his title of *Generalleutnant der Polizei*.

   (**) After the war, during an inquiry by the Belgian Justice, Eggert Neumann, last *Kommandeur* of the *SS-Gebirgsjäger Regt 13*, stated (25 May 1947) *(...) As the Regiment was unexpectedly sent the to front-line, Jungclaus reported to me without having been assigned by the division. As he had no battle experience and having no need for him, I made him a surplus officer on the regimental staff (Hauptmann im Stabe) with no specified duties. (...).*

   (***) Death certified under oath by Alfred Hempel, Jungclaus' chauffeur, and Eggert Neumann (Darmstadt, 13 January 1947).

Notes to Chapter XVI

1. In March 1942, the Brussels *Reichsjugendführung* created the Central Office for Technical Collaboration with Youth Movements in Wallonia, and appointed the Walloon Robert Radelet to head it. In an attempt to unify all Walloon New Order Youth Movements into one single (*Hitler-Jugend*) tutored youth movement, Radelet was to act as a delegate of all existing Youth Movements.
2. When Hemesath left for the Eastern Front in March 1942, and prior to Bennewitz' appointment, *Bannführer* Jansen replaced Hemesath for a short time. Note that on 30 January 1944, *Hauptbannführer* Bennwitz became *Gebietsführer. Hauptmädelführerin* Helma Westphal (*Bund Deutscher Mädel*) represented the girls' section in Belgium.

Notes to Chapter XVII

1. Including 3 Germans tried in Belgium [among the latter *SS-Stubaf.* Philip Johann Adolf Schmitt, (Bad-Kissingen, 20.11.1902), head of the Breendonk *SS-Auffanglager* concentration camp, convicted of 83 murders].

Notes to Chapter XVIII

1. Officers of the Belgian regular army were not allowed membership of a political party, nor were they allowed to flaunt a political opinion in public or attend political meetings dressed in uniform. On 18 July 1941, after the raising of foreign anti-Bolshevik legions had been allowed, fifty-one POW officers of the regular Army and the Reserve Corps from Prenzlau *II.A Oflag* offered to serve on the Eastern Front. All cancelled their offer as soon as they were informed that departure for the Eastern Front implied Rexist membership and an oath of allegiance to Degrelle.
2. Although Jacobs normally held the rank of Cpt-Cdt he was addressed as Major. This is due to the fact that career officers, when retiring, automatically joined the Reserve Corps with a rank one degree higher.
3. Adapted from Cpt. Ph Heinderyckx, *L'Organisation et l'équipement de la Légion Wallonie 1941–1945*, privately published 1992, p. 2.
4. Degrelle served as a private in the 1st group (Laruelle) of the 1st platoon (Mathieu). 2nd platoon of 1st company was commanded by Albert Lassois, 3rd platoon by Léon Closset and 4th platoon by Jean Vermeire.
5. All the German Command was ready to offer was a commission as *Sonderführer*, which Degrelle actually refused; Erich Grimm, *Als Adjutant beim Aufstellungsstab der Légion Wallonie*; Ach. E. De Bruyne.
6. *Corpo Spedizionario italiano in Russia*, also mentioned as *Corpo italiano de Spedizione.*
7. *Armee Gruppe Süd* (autumn 1941): under Von Rundstedt until 01.12.1941, then von Reichenau, and composed of:

   1. Pz Armee (von Kleist) comprising 6 *Panzer* divisions (100 *Panzer* each instead of 260 as in 1939 and 150 in June 1941);

   6. Armee (von Reichenau – later Paulus) composed of 14 Inf. Divs. (took Kursk on 2 November 1941) in liaison towards Orel with *Armee Gruppe Mitte* (*2. Armee* von Weichs);

   17. Armee composed of 14 Inf. Divs. and reinforced with the *Torino* and *Pasubio* divisions of the *C.S.I.R.*;

   11. Armee (von Schöbert, later von Manstein);

   The Rumanian divisions of Antonescu: 19 Inf. Divs. and 1 Cavalry Div.

   Luftflotte (Loehr) and Rumanian, Italian and Hungarian forces.
8. B.E.M. (*Breveté d'Etat-Major*), officer holding a Staff College Certificate.
9. This reinforcement under *Hauptmann* Tahir Alagic also comprised two 3.7cm *PAK* guns.
10. Markulj, Ivan. Born in Mostar, Herzegovina on 11.02 1889 – executed in Belgrade, Yugoslavia in September 1945. Officer in the Austro-Hungarian, later in the Royal Yugoslav Army. Carried the rank of Colonel at the time of the Yugoslavian capitulation in April 1941. With the declaration of Croatian independence on 10 April 1941, Markulj joined the Croatian *NDH Domobranstvo.*

    In June 1941, he commanded the 369th Reinforced (Croat) Infantry Regiment, a legionnaire unit of Croatian volunteers within the *Wehrmacht*. He commanded the unit through its training, and then in their first battles on the Eastern Front as part of the *100. Jäger Div.* February 1942. *Oberstleutnant* Babic commanded the Croat unit as Markulj had returned to Croatia for recruitment problems. During July 1942, Markulj was withdrawn from the 369th, and Colonel Viktor *Vitez* Pavicic took over the unit. Note that *Vitez* was a Hungarian order of Knighthood.
11. Besides the remainder of the *Légion Wallonie*, the *Kampfgruppe Tröger* comprised one Bn of the *SS-Rgt/Germania*, one Croat *Inf. Btl*, a recce company, 12 tanks, an *Art. Gr.* (10.5cm), one *I.G.* 7.5cm battery, and a wing of *Stukas*.

12. Mesic, Marko. Born in Bjelovar, Croatia, on 30 September 1901 – executed (?) in Yugoslavia in 1948 (?). As a Lt-Colonel, Mesic was appointed as commander of the artillery detachment of the 369th (Croat) Reinforced Infantry Regiment from its founding. He replaced Colonel Viktor Pavicic as commander of the Regiment on 21 January 1943. Pavicic fought to the very last moment with the Croatian survivors in Stalingrad, and was captured with his few remaining men on 2 February 1943. Apparently, he was awarded the *EK I* in the last days of the Stalingrad pocket. In absentia, promoted to full Colonel and received the Hungarian title of *Vitez* for his heroism. Walked with his men from Stalingrad to Moscow, where he was placed in a POW camp. With credit to M. Allen Milcic.

13. So was Sergeï Smolensky, White Russian and former officer of the Czarist Army. Two noblemen out of three were killed on 28 February 1942: Baron Christian Vanderstraeten Waillet and Knight Frans de Meester de Heyndonck.

14. Hubert Van Eyzer was killed as a *SS-Ustuf.* in the Cherkassy sector (Kumuna-Kommintern) on 13 December 1943.

15. Degrelle's participation in this 10 hours battle has been questioned after the war. Degrelle, due to physical and nervous failing, had to be evacuated to the rear during the first part of battle by his commanding officer Alfred Lisein himself. After the departure of Lisein, Jules Mathieu took over command of 1st Company; cfr Pauly report, written statement by J Mathieu; arch. E. De Bruyne.

16. In August 1944, Georges Ruelle was in command of the *Kampfgruppe Ruelle* in Estonia, during which Léon Degrelle won the Oakleaves to his KC. After the Caucasus campaign, Camille Bosquion was transferred to Belgium where he took command over the *Erstaz* of the *L.W.* at Namur. Bosquion was killed in a car accident in 1944, probably set up by the Resistance.

17. Among other things, a letter by P. Pauly forwarded to the *Kommandostab Z* in Brussels with the request Léon Degrelle be called back to Belgium *[. . .] where his presence would be more appreciated than on the front-line. [. . .]; Nachlaß Baumann*, CEGES, Brussels.

18. The *Légion Wallonie* was withdrawn from the *97. Jäg. Div.* on 18 November 1942.

19. Divisions are labelled as mentioned on wartime documents. Note that the 97th, 99th, 100th and 101st Divisions were remodelled with regard to the Balkan campaign. The initial appellation of *le. Inf. Div.* was changed into *Jäger Division* in April 1942.

20. Jean Vermeire, a journalist of the *Pays Réel*, joined the *L.W.* on 8 August 1941. In January 1942, Léon Degrelle sent him on a recruitment tour in Belgium.

21. Former officer of the *Garde Wallonne*. Although Thyssen was not an officer of the Belgian army, he was commissioned to the rank of *Leutnant*.

22. Part of the Rumanian *VI.A.C.* (*Dragalina*).

23. In August 1942, the *97. Jäg. Div.* was composed of *Jäg. Rgt. 204* (+ 400 *Hiwis**); *Jäg. Rgt 207* (+ 350 *Hiwis*); *Rad. Abt. 97* (+ 40 *Hiwis*); *Pz. Jg. Abt. 97* (+ 25 *Hiwis*); *A.R.81* (reinforced with an *Aufklärungsabteilung* composed of 220 Cossack *Hiwis* + another 120 local people); *Pi. 97* (reinforced with an Ukranian *Bau-Kompanie* of 182 *Hiwis*); *Wall. Btl* (+ 100 *Hiwis*); *N.A.97* and *Feldgendarmerie Trupp 97* (reinforced with 14 Ukranian *Hiwis*). General Ernst Rupp was killed on 30 May 1943, at Miljutinscky (Caucasus) by the shrapnel of a Russian bomb. Date mentioned in Rupp daughter's diary (with credit to J.-L. Roba).
    * *Hiwi:Hilfswilliger* (auxiliary helper), or foreigners, especially Russians, who joined the Germans Army, and retreated with the Germans. This auxiliary personnel performed non-combatant duties.

24. Like Degrelle, Hagemans sought to gain a personal objective: to be the undisputed leader of all francophone New Order Youth Movements. While undertaking this, he acted on his own and completely ignored both the Rex Movement and Degrelle. By the end of 1941, he had renamed the *Jeunesse Rexiste* (Rexist Youth) into *Organisation de la Jeunesse Nationale-Socialiste – O.J.N.S* . (Organization of the National-Socialist Youth) and drew nearer to the Hitler Youth, whose aid he badly needed to achieve his goal. Like Degrelle, Hagemans' personal aims could not be reached without military collaboration. But Degrelle, because of his own ambitions, thwarted Hagemans' plans (Degrelle was to take over control of the later *Jeunesse Légionnaire*). While Hagemans was naïve enough to believe having his youngsters on the Eastern Front would accelerate his own projects, he soon had to come down a peg or two and had to bow to the

facts: Degrelle had taken over control of Hagemans' troops by disbanding (not only for military reasons) the Youth Company (former 6th Company), leaving Hagemans desperately isolated.

25. That is 5 officers, 33 NCOs and 170 privates from the first August 1941 contingent.
26. Note that even non-Caucasus campaign veterans also wore the *Edelweiß*. The most striking example was Henri Derriks, who did not participate in the 1942 summer campaign.

Notes to Chapter XIX

1. E. De Bruyne, *Le Recrutement dans les Stalags et Oflags en faveur de la Légion Wallonie*, Housse, 1998.
2. *Nachlass Baumann*, CEGES, Brussels.
3. By 13 July 1944, the number of desertions numbered 179; – OSOBY (Moscow), Archives/ No. 1372/3/1094, CEGES.
4. Derriks enlisted in the *Légion Wallonie* on 14 October 1942.
5. *Niederschrift über die Übernahme der Wallonischen Legion*; Berlin Document Center. Note that section 11 of the aforementioned minute stipulates that the collar patch of the *SS-Freiwilligen-Brigade Wallonien* had to sport the Burgundy Cross instead of the traditional *SS* runes. Curiously enough, this stipulation was never carried out. Point 14 of the same minutes stipulates that the Brigade was to keep its Catholic chaplain. Point 16 mentions that by mid-July 1943, the Brigade was to be attached in reinforcement to the *SS Kavallerie-Division* (anti-partisan actions).
6. Löwenberg/Mark, 3.3.1900/†17.02.1944.
   21.06.1918: *Landsturm* recruit.
   21.06.1918–27.11.1918: *I.R.Feldrkt. Dep/. I.Div.*
   24.01.1919–31.03.1922: *Etappenkommandantur* Döberitz, *Rw I.R.und.Rw.I.R.9*. Joined the Police Force on 28.11.1923.
   12.12.1931: *Polizei-Leutnant*.
   20.04.1934: *Oberleutnant d. Schutzpolizei.*
   30.01.1937: *Hauptmann d. Schutzpolizei.*
   01.05.1937: joined the NSDAP/No. 5.377.990.
   20.08.1938: *SS-Mann.SS-Nr* 309 367.
   25.10.1942: *Oberstleutnant der Schutzpolizei.*
   01.07.1938: commissioned *SS-Hstuf.* (this shows that his rank of *SS-Hstuf.*, while granted 20.08.1938, was backdated to 01.07.1938).
   06.01.1939: *Rittmeister* (Cavalry and artillery equivalent of *Hauptmann* & *SS-Hstuf.*) within the *SS Polizei Division*. Wegener had *Hauptmann/Hstuf.* as his military rank, while his police rank was two higher, *Oberstleutnant*, and his military rank was gradually brought up to the equivalent *SS-Ostubaf.*
   01.08.1940: *SS-Stubaf.*
   05.01.1942: *SS-Ostubaf.*
   23.01.1943: Attached to the *SS-Ausbildungs-Rgt* at Prague/Czechoslowakia. (Leadership of the *SS*-Training Reg. Prague).
   17.05.1944: posthumously promoted to *SS-Standartenführer* (effective from 30.01.1944). *EK II, EK I, Deutsches Kreuz* in Gold on 24.12.1941 as *Kdr* of the *Aufklärungs Abteilung* of the *SS Polizei Division*; Personal File Albert Wegener. Berlin Document Center.
7. The Walloon 9th Company was allotted 9 *Stu. Ges.* (3 sections of 3 *Stu. Ges.* each). Instruction took place at Debica/Heidelager. On arriving at Stieblev (Replacement Bn of the *Wiking* division) via Korsun, *Wiking* was in such a desperate need of assault guns that the Walloon *Stu. Ges.* were transferred to *Wiking*. Pierre Dengis was then assigned command of the Walloon section (strength: 17 men) of the *Wiking Feld. Ers. Btl* at Stieblev, while his men were transferred to the different companies. Instead a battery of *Stu. Ges.* from the *SS-Polizei Div.* was attached to the *Sturmbrigade* along the Dnepr. *Memorandum* Henri Philippet; interview Pierre Dengis (Amay, March 1980).
8. The normal battle strength of an Assault Brigade was 2,250 men plus the Replacement Battalion. As the Walloons only numbered 2,000 (including the *Ers. Btl. 36*), the Brigade only had one motorized battalion instead of two.
9. Dettenhausen, 22.11.1919. 1933–1938: *Hitler-Jugend*.

01.11.1939: *SS-Verfügungstruppe.*
09.11.1940: *SS-Ustuf.* (*Junkerschule* Bad-Tölz 01.11.39–24.02.1940).
07.07.1941: *EK II*
20.11.1941: *EK I*
30.01.1942: *SS-Ostuf.*
03.08.1943: *Deutsches Kreuz in Gold* (as chief of *10./Germania*).
28.09.1943: seriously wounded.
14.10.1943: *RK* (recommendation No. 2224) as *SS-Ostuf.* and emergency leader of *II./Westland.*
30.01.1944: *SS-Hstuf.*
01.09.1942: 2 *Abzeichen für die Niederkampfung von Pz. Kpfr. d. Einzel Kämpfer* (action of 10.7.1942 as *Zugführer* of *14. Kompanie*); Personal File Hans Drexler, Berlin Document Center.

10. In fact, Degrelle's behaviour was more a political concern than a military one as *Kdr* Lucien Lippert was strongly opposed to risking the main body of his unit in such a risky operation. Degrelle needed attention from the higher *SS* circles in Berlin, on the one hand (and only a military exploit could achieve this), and, on the other hand, Degrelle had to face serious internal problems resulting from the German intention of taking over command of the Brigade (Lippert had been temporarily set aside and replaced by Wegener who, together with Derriks as liaison officer, started the Teklino counter-attack It was not before 17 January 1944 that Lippert could resume command as a result of Degrelle's repeated protest).

11. See table of losses.

12. While retreating from Stieblev, Degrelle was wounded on arriving at Novo Buda when the roof of the *isba* (where he had been sheltering during a Soviet attack) fell in. According to Degrelle's memoir and post war comments, his injuries were such that he had to be evacuated toward Schanderowka. *SS-Ustuf.* Marcel Lamproye, CO of the *PAK* Company is less affirmative. After having witnessed the events described by Degrelle, Lamproye wrote in a post-war comment *[...] Degrelle is wounded (some plaster on his shoulders) and is running down the village [...]*; – Roland Devresse, *Un Mouvement de Jeunesse dans la Tourmente 1940–1945; Vol. 2, – Les volontaires de la Jeunesse à la Légion Wallonie, Chapter XII, La Campagne de Cherkassy – Derniers Combats et la percée,* p. 16.

13. Mention must be made that Degrelle had left Schanderowka with the sick and wounded long before Mathieu ordered the final retreat. Mathieu caught up with Degrelle late in the afternoon of 17 February 1944.

14. Note that Degrelle's Knight Cross was not merely for his own (perceived) actions, but that it also represented the real defensive success of the Walloons at Nova Buda. Even if Gille was misinformed that Degrelle commanded the *Sturmbrigade,* he certainly realized how important his role was in his capacity of inspirational and political leader.

15. Note that prior to the outbreak wounded and sick Walloons were evacuated, first by medical evacuation train, later by plane (from Korsun), the last medical evacuation plane leaving Korsun on 13 February 1944.

16. German propaganda attempted to portray the *Cherkassy Kessel* breakout as a defensive victory.

17. After the Cherkassy parades, the Walloons were encamped near Mons and received a three-week leave, another favour refused to the Flemings. Note that the three-week leave in Belgium was a disaster for the Brigade as hundreds of legionnaires availed themselves of the opportunity of being in Belgium to desert; records in the matter R. Wastiau, written testimony by Roger Wastiau, Military Court, Brussels.

18. Apart from *SS-Stubaf.* G. Tchekhoff, who was not interested in taking over command of the Walloon formation.

19. Karl Joannes Burk, Buchenau, 14.03.1898-Fritzlar, 23.09.1963. *SS Nr* 68 910 Party Nr: 1 848 222
SS-Ustuf.: 20.04.1935
SS-Ostuf.: 09.11.1935
SS-Hstuf.:13.09.1936
SS-*Stubaf.*: 12.09.1937 (*Kdr. II/12. SS-Totenkopf. Rgt*)
SS-Ostubaf.: 09.11.1938 (successively *Führer im SS-Art.Ers.Btl; Führer b.Rgt.z.b.V.SS-Art. Rgt/SS-Div.Wiking; SS-FlakAbt. Ost*).

SS-Staf.: 09.11.1940 (successively *2.SS-Inf.Brig., SS-Flak Ers.Abt*)
Transferred from the Reserve to the active cadre: 15.07.1943.
SS-Oberf.: 09.11.1943.

Successively: *SS-Flak Aus. u. Ers.Abt.; Höh. SS-und Pölizei Führer Ost;* 5.SS-Freiw.Sturmbrigade *Wallonien*, first as *Inf. Führer* then as *Kommandeur* (21.06.1944); *SS-Führer Hauptamt* (20.09.1944); liaison officer to G. Wlassow [(*mil.Verb.Fhr z. G. Wlassow; Kdr 15. Waff.Gren.Div.d. SS Lett.1* (12.02.1945)]. *Deutsches Kreuz in Gold* (05.11.1942); – Personal File Karl Burk, Berlin Document Center.

20. In June 1944, Himmler refused to sign Degrelle's appointment to *Kommandeur* of the *5.SS-Freiw.Sturmbrigade*, as requested by Degrelle himself. The original German text addressed to *SS-Obergrupenführer* von Herff (Chief of the *SS-Personalhauptamt*) is as follows:

    Ich gebe anliegend die Urkunde, mit der SS-Sturmbannführer Degrelle zum Chef der 5.SS-Freiw.Sturmbrigade "Wallonien" ernannt werden sollte, ohne Unterschrift des Reichsführers-SS zurück.

    Der Reichsführer-SS meinte dazu, daß Degrelle je als Chef der Wallonen bezeichnet werden soll. Er möchte aber diese Bezeichnung nicht mit seiner Urkunde festzulegen, sondern sie müsste sich vielmehr von selbst einführen; Persönlicher Stab der Reichsführer *von Herff, 12.07.1944; Personal File Léon Degrelle, Berlin Document Center.*

    (I hearby return the diploma with which Degrelle should have been appointed Chief of the 5.SS-Freiw.Sturmbrigade 'Wallonien' without the signature of the Reichsführer-SS. The Reichsführer-SS is further of the opinion that Degrelle is expected to be addressed as Chief of the Walloons. But he does not want to sanction this appellation with a diploma, but on the contrary, it should appear all by itself.).

21. *SS-Stubaf.* Georges Tchekhoff was acting then as *Kommandeur ad interim* of the Brigade.
22. *SS-Ustuf.* Marc Willem (†), Marcel Capoen (†), René Verenne (†), Marcel Thomas and Jacques Wautelet.
23. *Memorandum* Ph. Canva, former *Gefechtsschreiber* (Combat Secretary) of the *Kampfgruppe Ruelle*; arch. E. De Bruyne.
24. Born in Courdinne on 11.12.1913, Léon Gillis was a member of the Rex Movement and volunteered for the *Légion Wallonie* in July 1941. Enlisted as a private, he soon became a NCO, received the *EK II* and the *EK I* (26 August 1942). On 1 March 1944, he was promoted to *SS-Standartenoberjunker* on grounds of exceptional gallantry at Cherkassy (*Tapferkeitsoffizier*). On 20 April 1944, he obtained the rank of *SS-Untersturmführer*. By that time, he was already holder of the Wound Badge and the Close Combat Clasp in Silver. After the Estonia campaign, he was promoted to the rank of *SS-Ostuf.* on 9 November 1944. As he also participated in the whole Oder campaign, one may assume that, like Degrelle, he was also entitled to the Close Combat Clasp in Gold.

Notes to Chapter XX

1. Note that the official document was issued on 19 October 1944 (*Führungshauptamt – Umgliederung der SS-Freiw. Sturmbrigade Wallonien – Tgb nr 3712/44 g. Kdos*). As already mentioned, the appellation of *Kommandeur* appeared spontaneously in the official records and documents as Degrelle had already been identified as such in the press.
2. By virtue of the Convention of Augsburg (26 June 1548), the Circle of Burgundy was attached to the Holy Germanic Empire. By way of consequence, all Walloon provinces became part of the Germanic Empire from 1548 to 9 February 1801 (Treaty of Lunéville). Walloon noblemen, such as Tilly 't Serclaes, de Latour, Clerfayt, Baillet-Latour, etc. then served with distinction in the Imperial armies.
3. Charles de Longueval, Count de Bucquoy (1571–1621) Served in the Spanish armies as commanding officer of the Walloon mercenaries. In 1618, he was appointed Commander-in-Chief of the (Austrian Habsburg) Imperial Armies.
4. Of whom 62 underage (less than 16 years) were returned to their parents. Note that a number of *JL* members, having no relatives in the Hanover area, which had been allotted to the Walloon refugees, falsified their identity papers in order to accompany their comrades to the front. The youngest known was 14 years; *De Nieuwe Orde*, TV-series by Maurice Dewilde, BRT, Brussels, Belgium.
5. According to a post-war interview with Frans Hellebaut (Aarschot, 23 August 1982), 3,500 men would be a more accurate number. In December 1944/January 1945, about

240 Spaniards were enrolled as well as several dozens of Frenchmen, who had deserted the *Charlemagne* to join the more prestigious Degrelle.

6. Hellebaut had volunteered for the Russian front in May 1944, and for that purpose was liberated from *Prenzlau II A Oflag*.
7. The lack of Belgian officers caused most of the Services to be in the hands of German officers, a situation that led to friction.
8. The monthly allotment in fuel for the 50 or 60 motorized vehicles of the division was 800 litres of fuel and 400 litres fuel oil; interview F. Hellebaut (Aarschot, 1982).
9. As *Führer des Aufstellungsstabes* (Senior Staff Officer in charge of supervising the forming of the divisional staff – Note that Heilmann left this task entirely to F. Hellebaut).
   Born on 20.04.1903, in Gundhelm (Prussia). Joined the *Wafffen-SS* (Nr 327.324) in May 1939 coming from the Police force, where he held the rank of *Hauptmann der Polizei*.
   Last assignment before joining the *28.SS-Freiw.-Gren.Div.Wallonien*: *15. Div. Führer-Lehrgang* (Schulenberg-Hirschberg Schloß from 08.10–15.11.1944); Personal Record, Berlin Document Center.
   Note that Heilmann won the Knight's Cross on 23 August 1944, for his distinguished leadership of the Latvian *15. Waffen-Grenadier Division* during the retreat from the Velikkaya River in early July of that year. Heilmann was an experienced staff officer and regimental leader, who won the German Cross in Gold as *Ia* of the *SS-Polizei Division*. He was sent to a division commander's course to solidify his education. Heilmann went missing in Pomerania in late January 1945; he was presumably going to take command of some unit there.
10. *SS-Obersturmbannführer* per 01.01.1945.
11. Schaeffer was also charged with reporting to the *SD* about Degrelle's (political and social) activities.
12. But suspected of deserting to the Soviets; interview J. Mathieu.
13. *SS-Stubaf.* per 20.04.1945.
14. *SS-Stubaf.* per 20.04.1945.
15. Platoon commander *1/I/69* in March 1945.
16. Coming from the *Garde Wallonne*.
17. Coming from the *Garde Wallonne*.
18. Former cultural attaché in the embassy of the Reich to Brussels and since 9 November 1942, (von) Ribbentrop's Foreign Ministry interpreter and liaison officer; *Memorandum* Dr H. Forsteneichner; arch. E. De Bruyne.
19. General delegation to represent French interest in Germany. Later Commission replaced the word Delegation.
20. On 1 October 1944, they were given extraterritorial rights.
21. Headed by Otto Abetz until his dismissal in December 1944.
22. An Office for evacuated francophone Belgians had been established in Hildesheim and comprised a *Stab Degrelle* taking care of the political matters.
23. On 6 January 1945.
24. G.-T. Schillemans, *Philippe Pétain. Le prisonnier à Sigmaringen*, *m p* éditions, Paris, 1965, p. 113; M. Déat, *Mémoires Politiques*, Denoël, Paris, 1989, p 920; M. Garçon, *Les procès de la Collaboration*, Albin Michel, Paris, 1948, p. 137; A. Brissaud, *Pétain à Sigmaringen (1944 – 1945)*, Librairie Académique Perrin, Paris,1960.
25. V. Barthélmy, *Du Communisme au Fascisme, L'histoire d'un engagement politique, Albin Michel*, Paris, 1978, p. 390.
26. Of all non-Axis units, the *28. SS-Freiw. -Gr. Div. Wallonie* was the only exception. During the preliminary talks with a view to forming a Germanic Corps in the course of spring 1943, Himmler planned to split up the *Légion Wallonie*. Some 200 to 300 legionnaires among the ethnic best (*rassisch besten Männer*) would then have been transferred to the *Germania Standarte/Pz-Jäg. Abt* or *Pi. Btl*, the rest could only be used as a *Korps-Kradschützen Btl*. Degrelle resisted and finally had his way: no split up and command in Belgian hands; *Aufstellung des Germanischen Korps*, Himmler to Berger, 03.03.1943. Berlin Document Center.
27. Rank he was granted when he joined the *Waffen-SS* in August 1943.

28. Secretary-General for the Maintenance of Order (January 1944). On 14 June 1944, Darnand was appointed Secretary of State for the Interior.
29. Leading French socialist (neo-plannist) who turned to fascism and collaboration. Leader of the *Rassemblement National Populaire – RNP*.
30. Town situated on the Meuse River, about 10 km from Liège (Belgium).
31. Communication André Régibeau, (Herstal, March 1985), witness to Degrelle's address.
32. By the turn of 1944/45, the operational services of the *VI-S* were based at Schleiden (Eifel).
33. Born in Vienna, 1897. Professional soldier, served as a junior infantry officer in the First World War. Entered Austrian War School for General Staff training. After graduating served as an intelligence officer with the Second Austrian Division. In 1936 promoted to Lieutenant-Colonel of the Austrian General Staff, where he served in the Intelligence Division. After the *Anschluß* served in the *Abwehr*, the intelligence organization of the High Command of the German Armed Forces (*OKW*), Division I.
34. Mainly former *Sipo-Sd* auxiliaries of the main office of Brussels and the outposts of Liège, Arlon, Charleroi and Mons, who had evacuated to Germany in September 1944. Exempted from military service in the *Division Wallonie*, most of them had been temporarily assigned to the Hamburg *Gestapo*.

    Note that the Flemish auxiliary *Sipo-Sd* members, unlike their less numerous Walloon colleagues, were all transferred to a special unit, the *SS-Polizei-Bataillon Flandern*. There was no such Walloon counterpart.
35. Bad-Ems was the training centre of the *Jagdverband Süd-West*. (Although operations in Belgium fell to the *Nord-West*, the Walloon agents were sent to the *Süd-West*. The reason for this is that the *Süd-West* trained the francophone agents for operations in France and Wallonia).
36. The emissary was Karl Hammer, an Alsatian, who had made acquaintance with Degrelle in the *'Tcherkassy Kessel'*. At the time of his mission Hammer belonged to the Berlin General Headquarters of Hadj Amin El Hussein, Great Mufti of Jerusalem; E. De Bruyne, *Les Wallons meurent à l'Est*,. D. Hatier. Brussels, 1992, pp. 124–125.
37. Noteworthy is the fact that more or less 100 Flemish legionnaires were transferred – by order of Jef Van de Wiele, head of the Flemish puppet government in Germany – without further ado to the *Jagdkommando 502* whereas the Walloons, for the purpose of special operations, only supplied volunteers.
38. Memoir Georges Tchekhoff; interview Alexeï Sakhnowski (Nicolas' brother), Brussels, April 1985; interview Alex Stroïtnowski, Madrid, February 1983.
39. Russian (Krinitchanaya) born Albert Sapin from Walloon parents had the reputation of being a *Draufgänger* (daredevil). After the Cherkassy breakout, he was promoted to *SS-Ustuf.* (*Tapferkeitsoffizier*) for exceptional personal gallantry during the Teklino forest attack (mid-January 1944).
40. Order received at Hradischko (Bohemia) where Sapin was supervising the instruction of the elite *Sturmpionniere* (Assault pioneers).
41. E. De Bruyne has extensively developed this hardly known episode in *Les Wallons meurent à l'Est*.
42. When transferring the *Légion Wallonie* to the *Waffen-SS*, June 1943, it had been agreed upon that Degrelle would have complete control over all legionnaires and that the Germans could not dispose of Degrelle's men without his consent.
43. The Brussels services of the *Amt-VI* was housed at Rue Emile Claus. The first chief of the Brussels *VI* (Walloon section) was *SS-Hstuf.* Marcel Zschunke (till 1943). His successor was *SS-Hstuf.* Kurt Lawrenz (alias Max Heller). Note that Zschunke was going to be in charge of the Walloon desk at Waldsee/Berlin in 1944/45. In March 1945, Zschunke's Walloon desk was transferred from Waldsee to Pritzerbe, south-west of Berlin, near the main *RSHA* radio station of Wannsee (*Havel Institute*). Lawrenz headed the *Leitstelle Siegfried* at Marburg from the beginning (14.10.1944) until 18.11.1944 date on which he was replaced by *SS-Hstuf.* Reinhardt Wolf (coming from *VI.D*).
44. The *Siegfried Leitstelle* covered sabotage activities in Wallonia and operated from Marburg. As such it was part of the Berlin stationed *VI.B.2* (sabotage actions in Belgium-France-Holland under *SS-Ostubaf.* Bernhardt). Liaison officer between the Berlin *VI.B.2* and the *Leitstelle Siegfried*/Marburg was *SS-Hstuf.* Ludwig Wiedemann.

Note that *Leitstelle Walter*, established in Constance, was the Sigmaringen-French counterpart of the *Leitstelle Siegfried*.

45. Thanks to *SS-Hstuf.* Heinrich Massbender, last chief of the section *III.D* (Wirschaft/Economy) at Brussels.

46. Actually, Heinz Völlker von Collande, specialist of German espionage since WWI. He was in charge of espionage activities in the non-occupied part of France with an office at Lyon. At Heydrich's request, he helped to organize the *Amt-VI*.

47. Composed of two experienced agents-informers of the Verviers *Geheime Feldpolizei*.

48. *The Völkischer Beobachter* (15.12.1944, page 1). *Um die Rettung Europas – Eichenlaubträger Degrelle sprach auf der Journalistentagung*.

49. There were delegations representing Flanders, the Netherlands, Denmark, Croatia, Bulgaria, Italy, France, Hungary and Rumania.

50. After the evacuation of the Belgian territory in September1944, the *SS* took over Flemish and Walloon affairs.

51. Gummersbach had been chosen because the former Brussels *Ersatzkommando Wallonien* (under *SS-Hstuf.* K.-T. Moskopf) had elected domicile at the local Körster hotel. The presence of Moskopf 's services would facilitate the arrival of the Rexist officials.

52. Degrelle always pretended he was given full power similar to the one he had been granted as *Volksführer der Wallonen* (Leader of the Walloon People) whereas, in reality, he was only given a propaganda mission and by no means was he entrusted with military authority; *Memorandum* Dr Heinz Forsteneichner. Arch. E. De Bruyne. (Dr Heinz Forsteneichner was the liaison officer of the German Foreign Office (*Auswärtiges Amt*), representing (von) Ribbentrop since the latter pretended to recover his prerogatives now that Belgium was again invaded; Dr Albert De Jonghe in his intervention in a debate organized by Flemish television (30.11.1990): *Na september 1944 – De Droom is uit*.

53. Interview F. Hellebaut; Aarschot, 23 August 1982.

54. Degrelle's escort was composed of elements from 1st and 5th Companies of the *I/69Rgt*.

55. Degrelle left with 15 lorries and about 10 cars after he had commandeered almost the whole fuel allotment of the division; interview F. Hellebaut, Aarschot 23 August 1982.

56. Until then, the Walloon division was billeted at Auenheim (Staff), Niederhausen (*69Rgt*) and Huchenhoven (*I/Rgt 70*), and resumed military training.

57. At Steinbach Degrelle stayed in a castle owned by Mr. Schmidt. The house in Limerlé was owned by Mr. Dufourny.

58. The trade did not take place. Baron Jean Orban de Xivry was taken to Germany as a civil prisoner and later (end January 1945) handed over to V. Matthys' political Staff in Hannover. After the war, the Baron stated in Court that Henri Derriks, disobeying Degrelle's orders, had saved his life by preventing him from being shot – letter by Baron Jean Orban de Xivry to the Public Prosecutor before the Court Martial of Liège, *dd* 7 March 1947; Personal Record Henri Derriks. Court Martial of Liège.

59. Frans Hellebaut, Degrelle's operations officer, had calculated that the cadre of a total strength (*soll Stärke*) division would require some 1,800 officers and NCOs, a figure far beyond the possibilities of the Walloon unit as its total strength never exceeded 4,500 men. Moreover, some 1,000 legionnaires had been detached to different instruction centres scattered all over the *Reich*.

60. Van Horembeke first served in the 4th *Bandera* and afterwards in the 67th Company of the 17th *Bandera* and took part in the Bielsa pocket fighting. Before the war Kehren had been a member of the right wing group *Légion Nationale*. He joined the Francoist armies during the Spanish civil war and served within the *Travelera de la Reina*. He tried to volunteer for the anti-Communist legion in Finland but in vain. At the end of May 1940, he took a job in the German *Reichsbahn* (railway). He came back to Belgium to enlist in the *Légion Wallonie* in August 1941. As a result of friction with his superiors in general, and Degrelle in particular, he was demobilized after the Caucasus campaign. He then took service in the *Sipo-Sd* of Liège and Ghent. He rejoined the *Sturmbrigade* at the beginning of the 1944. He then served as an *SS-Oscha.* in the *3/I/69Rgt* and eventually in the *Kampfgruppe* Derriks. Condemned to death, Kehren was finally released from prison in October 1957.

61. The *Azul* division was disbanded in October/November 1943 as a result of the political pressure from the British and Americans, who threatened to occupy the Canary Islands. Franco then started negotiations for the withdrawal of the *Azul* division but at the same time authorized the establishment of a Legion (*Legion Espagñola of Voluntarios*) commanded by Col. Navarro. The Spanish Legion was finally to be disbanded in March 1944.

62. "The first Spaniards to be accepted within the *Wehrmacht* were sent to the Volunteer Unit Stablack in June 44. The Spaniards who were recruited via the *Sonderstab F* in France during the summer of 44 formed two battalions billeted near Vienna. The Spanish *Ers. Btl.* at Hollabrunn apparently fed the Spanish Volunteer Training Battalion activated on 25 October 44 at Stockerau as part of the 1st Croatian Brigade." (Cfr K. W. Estes, *A European Anabasis : Western European Volunteers in the German Army and SS*, 1940–1945, Thesis, University of Maryland, 1984, p. 167.); R. Van Leeuw, Degrelle's private secretary, mentions (letter of 09.06.1985) that the Spaniards served with the 357th, 302nd Div. and the 3rd *Gebirgsjäger* on different fronts in Rumania, Czechoslovakia and Yugoslavia.

63. In Versailles was situated the *Quartier de la Reine* barracks, the French general recruitment centre for the *Waffen-SS*.

64. *Ami mandaron a Berlin, donde me presente, en Lichterfelde West en al Cuartel General de la Waffen-SS, en la Representacion de la Division Flamenca donde les expuse el caso. Estos, al ver que yo ne parlabre de Flamenco me mandaron à la Division Walona, manda par Léon Degrelle; Memoir* Van Horembeke; arch. E. De Bruyne via R. Van Leeuw.

65. Seat of the *Ers. Btl. 36* of the Walloon Assault Brigade.

66. Scheduled for mid-December 1944 onwards in what was to become the *SS-Freiwilligen-Kompanie 101* and, in March 1945, the *SS-Freiwilligen-Kompanie 102.*

67. A semi-clandestine recruiting office was operating in the German embassy in Madrid.

68. For a short time Miguel Ezquerra Sanchez, head of the later *Einsatz Gruppe Ezquerra* during the final combats in Berlin, was active within the *Sonderstab F*.

69. Former German ambassador to Franco during the Spanish civil war. During WWI, as a member of the General Staff, he headed the Spain-South America desk. In 1919, he was sent to Bolivia where he was active in the organization of the Bolivian army. In 1926, he headed a military mission in Peru. During the Chaco war opposing Paraguay and Bolivia, Faupel returned to Bolivia.

70. Housing the Spanish Volunteer Training Battalion.

71. In fact Lorenzo Ocañas Serrano.

72. According to Raymond Van Leeuw, Pedro Zabala, rather than Louis Valdajos (an administrative officer) took command of the Spanish *3/I/70*. Note that Zabala was to be one of Ezquerra's warrant officers during the Berlin combats; Letter R. Van Leeuw, dated 22 July 1985.

73. According to Ocañas' memoir, all platoon commanders held an officer's rank. According to A. Steiver they all were NCOs.

74. According to A. Steiver, a fourth platoon existed whose commander was an Abel Ardoos.

75. Carlos Caballero, *El Batallón Fantasma*, p. 24.

76. Letter dated August 1985.

77. Which seems to indicate that they came from different places.

78. Recruitment probably arranged by Valdajos, the collective route order (probably) being signed by *SS-Ustuf.* Jean Roman.

79. These 20 volunteers never had had any military instruction. They belonged to the first Stettin group of 40 all azimuth volunteers (probably recruited by Ezquerra).

80. Miguel Ezquerra Sanchez: a lieutenant first with the *Azul* and than with the Spanish Legion. After returning to Spain in the course of spring 1944, he went to Germany some time later. He also attended a *SD* course at Versailles and was to take command of the *SS-Freiwilligen-Kompanie 101* at Stablack; letter by R. Van Leeuw, dated 7 February 1984.

81. Those documents had been furnished even before the battle of Berlin.

82. Note that the regimental *I.G.* and *Panzerschreck* platoons were not available, nor were the *Stu. Ges.* and the *Pi. Btl.*

83. The remainder of the initial battle force was still undergoing training at schools or with the *Er. Btl. 36.*

84. On 7 February 1945, the *Langemarck* was transferred to the III. Germanic *Panzerkorps.*

85. As a part of Operation *Sonnenwende* under Gen. Wenck. This was actually intended to be the north wing of a massive two-pronged offensive to destroy the head of the Soviet forces advancing on Berlin. The south wing from around Küstrin, never got started. And the north wing, which was to advance deeply, only managed a few kilometres. Arnswalde was only a preliminary objective, not the ultimate one.
The *11. Pz Armee* under Steiner (replaced by Raus on 24 Febr. 1945) comprised the following forces:
the new *II.A.K. Oder* (Hoerlein) between the Oder and Lake Madü, comprising:
Bahn *K.Gr.* (Schmeling);
Pyritz *K.Gr.* (Weiss);
9. Fallsch. Jäger Div (Brauer);
the *XXXIX Pz Korps* (Decker) between Madü See and the Ihna river, comprising:
Pz. Div. Holstein (Hess);
10. SS-Pz. Div. Frundsberg (Harmel);
K.Gr Wallonien (Hellebaut);
4. SS-Polizei Pz. Gren. Div. (Harzer);
the *III.(germ.)SS-Pz Korps* (Unrein, then Steiner) between Stargard and Neuedell, comprising:
11. SS-Freiw. -Pz. -Gren. Div. Nordland (Ziegler);
K.Gr. Langemarck (Schellong);
K.Gr. Arnswalde (Voigt);
the *23. SS-Freiw. -Pz. -Gren. Div. Nederland* (Wagner, former commandant of the Dorpat Front);
the *281. Inf. Div.* (Ottner);
the *1. Pz-Korps-Gruppe Munzel* in protection behind the Drage lakes, comprising:
Fhr Begl. Div. (Remer);
Fhr Gren. Div. (Mäder);
the *X.SS-Korps* (Krappe) in protection west of Kallies, comprising:
K.Gr Pz. Jäger SS-Nordland (Schulz-Streeck);
5 Jäger Div. (Sixt);
parts of the *402.* and *163. Inf. Div.*

86. Defended by the *III/24* (motorized *Pz. -Gren. Btl* Sörensen/Danish) of the *Nordland.*

87. Former *G.W.* officer Louis Bervaes commanded the mortar platoon.

88. Chief of the *Jeunesse Légionnaire*, Mezzetta's corpse was evacuated beyond the Oder River for burial. He was the only Walloon legionnaire to be treated that way. All other killed legionnaires were left on the spot.

89. Mention must be made that moral pressure was made upon the Walloon legionnaires to volunteer for this *Kampfgruppe*, as each man had to appear in front of his Company/CO and explain to him the reasons for refusing to join the *Kampfgruppe.*

90. *SS-Ustuf.* Jacobs and Ghyssens.

91. Paetsch was posthumously awarded the Oakleaves and promoted to *SS-Standartenführer.*

92. Höckendorf was defended by the Flemish *Kampfgruppe*, the remainder of the *Nordland, Nederland* and the *25Rgt* of the *9. Fallschirm-Jäger Div.*

93. Jacques Leroy. Born at Binche on 10 September 1924. His father was the Rexist war-mayor of Binche. Member of the *Jeunesse Rexiste.* Enrolled in the *Légion Wallonie* on 10 March 1942, he participated in all eventual battles (except Estonia).
According to Leroy himself, as stated in a post-war interview, he left hospital in July 1944, after having suffered severe injuries (loss of right eye and right arm) at Teklino/Cherkassy, action for which he received the *EK I* and the rank of *SS-Oberscharführer.* After recovery, he expressed the wish to return to frontline duties and Degrelle sent him to Sophienwalde academy (mid-October- mid-December 1944. His appointment as Degrelle's orderly did not satisfy him and he sought more action. He then joined the first *Kampfgruppe* Derriks (the second being the one used for the counter-attacks on Schillersdorf 20–23 April 1945) to participate in the Altdamm battle

(mid-March as commander of the 3rd Platoon/1st Company) where, according to his statements, Degrelle awarded him the *RK* for heroic resistance at Rosengarten-Finkenwalde. Leroy was injured once more on 20 April 1945 (within the ranks of the 2nd *Kampfgruppe Derriks*, composed of volunteers only). After the collapse, Leroy (like all Walloon combat officers) was imprisoned at Neuengamme concentration camp before transport to Belgium for the post-war trials. On 16 November 1946, the Military Court condemned him to 20 years imprisonment.

94. High-ranking cadre of the *Jeunesse Légionnaire*. After Mezzetta's death at Streesen, and as most members of the *J.L.* had been regrouped in *1/I/69*, Piessevaux chose to serve in that Company.

95. André Régibeau survived the war. He died in a car accident on his way to a Walloon veterans reunion in 1986.

96. At the end of April 21st, of the 450 men initially engaged the day before, only 96 had no substantial injuries.

97. The *Kdr* of the *Polizei Rgt*, held responsible for allowing the Soviets to get through the first echelon, was court-martialed on the spot and shot.

98. Graded highest of the 2nd Kienschlag course, he should have been promoted *SS-Ustuf.* on leaving the session if he (and his comrades) had not been imposed a collective punishment, postponing graduation for 1 month, the other successful candidates holding the rank of *SS-Standartenoberjunker*. Roland Devresse was officially informed of his promotion to *SS-Ustuf.* by *SS-Ostuf.* Sandron (Adjutant *69Rgt*) on 5 May 1945. He had it recorded in his *Soldbuch* the same day in a POW camp; – cfr Roland Devresse, *Les Volontaires de la Jeunessse dans la Tourmente 1940–1945, tome 2 – les Volontaires de la Jeunesse à la Légion Wallonie – Chapitre XV: 1945, La fin à l'Oder*, p. 55. Unpublished. Note that his case is not an isolated one. A number of 20 April 1945 promotions seem to have been *'officialized'* after the 3 May 1945 surrender as shown below. The entry of the rank of *SS-Obersturmführer* bears the date of 20 May 1945! The indications *'10 März 1944 SS-Standartenoberjunker'* and *'1.4.44 SS-Unstersturmführer'* allows us to certify that the recipient belonged to the *11. Kriegslehrgang* at Bad-Tölz.

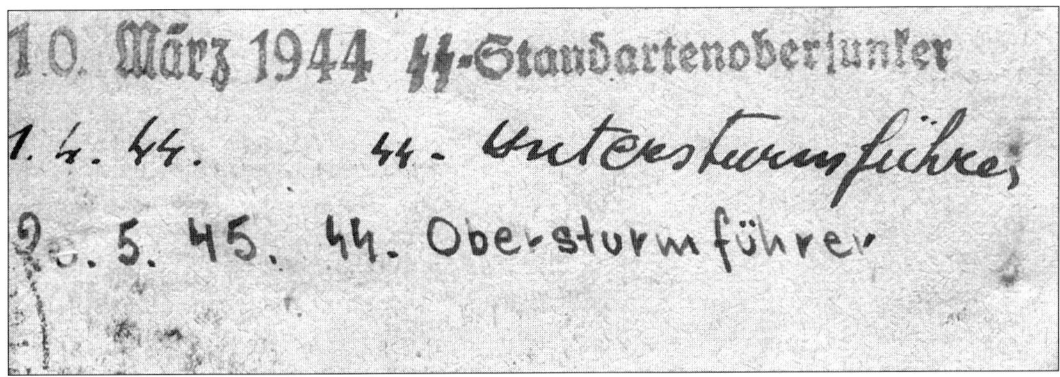

10. März 1944 SS-Standartenoberjunker
1.4.44. SS-Untersturmführer
20.5.45. SS. Obersturmführer

99. In fact this rear guard comprised 22 men; cfr *Gé. Pé, A l'Est coule l'Oder*, p. 57.

100. By echelon and supervised by the Staff of the *XXXII.A.K* (Gen. Schacht); communication Frans Hellebaut.

Notes to Chapter XXI

1. When he showed up at the Neu-Rosow medical aid station, headed by Dr Robert Buy and Walloon *DRK* nurse Mad. Neuteleers, whose third son (of three all to die fighting with the Germans) was to fall on the battlefield the same day.

2. Last German liaison officer to the *28.SS-Freiw.-Gren.Div.Wallonien*. In fact, the Germans intended to designate Hahn as the *Ia* of the Division, replacing Hellebaut. No need to mention that this never was achieved as Hellebaut continued to command the *Kampfgruppe* until the end of the war.

3. Adjutant *I/69Rgt*. Mathieu, *Kdr* of *69Rgt*, declined Degrelle's offer to accompany him to Lübeck on grounds that officers had to stay with their men.

4. Involved in bloody looting while accompanying Rexist refugees to Germany in September 1944. He committed suicide in prison.

5. Note that Degrelle had been on his way for two days already when it came to his mind that at least he should inform his Chief of Staff that he had left for talks.
6. Generet's opinion of Degrelle is severe. He certified that he had the impression that Degrelle was merely trying to save his own bacon.
7. A few Walloon war correspondents under *SS-Ustuf.* François Chomé of the *Standarte Kurt Eggers* reached Denmark.
8. The German crew was composed of the pilot Albert Duhinger, the mechanic Gerhard Stide and two other members: Georg Kubel and Benno Epner. The authors are indebted to Jean-Louis Roba for this info.
9. The legionnaires knew they had been condemned *in absentia* to the death penalty.

Notes to Chapter XXII

1. Bruno Schulz was the (administrative) German commander of the *Ers. Btl. 36* and as such is to be considered as a kind of liaison officer. After the Burk affair in June-July 1944, Tchekhoff took over command of the *Ers. Btl. 36*. In April 1945, like all White Russians (although he had obtained Belgian citizenship in 1938) of the Walloon Division, Tchekhoff was called up by Skorzeny's services to join the Friedenthal HQ of the *Jagdverband Ost*, leaving command to Schulz. As to Pierre Dengis, commanding the sick and wounded company, he too left the place to join the Oder front.
2. Hellebaut was widely known in military circles, as his father had been a general and his grandfather Minister of Defence.
3. Named after the man who inspired it, the Lejeune Law allowed liberation from prison after one-third of the penalty had been served.
4. Involved in the Courcelles massacre (August 17/18 1944), a Rexist reprisal for the murder of the Rexist Mayor of Charleroi-city.

Notes to Chapter XXIII

1. During the recruitment campaign for the L.W., F. Rouleau, speaking to career officers and officers of the Reserve Corps (bound by oath of allegiance to the King), asserted that he possessed a letter by Count Robert Capelle, the King's private secretary, ascertaining that military presence on the Eastern Front was not incompatible with the oath taken to the King. However, mention must be made that nobody has ever seen that letter. One month later, in the course of August 1941, Degrelle, with a view to lulling consciences, told his men the King had congratulated him by cabling a telegram to *Regenwurmlager*/Meseritz barracks. This telegram proved to be faked, too.
2. After the armistice, on the initiative of circles close to certain individuals of the King's entourage, and with the agreement of the German occupying forces, a new service called *Service de Travaux de l'Armée Démobilisée – O.T.A.D.* was created, which was charged with executing duties of the suppressed Ministry of Defence. Established by decree of 31 August 1940, its staff was chosen among the servicemen who belonged to the regular army. General Keyaerts, released from Tibor *Oflag* for that purpose and Colonel Goethals, (former military attaché in Berlin, arriving spontaneously from Switzerland), were put at the head of the *O.T.A.D.* In October 1940, the *O.T.A.D.* was allowed to repatriate several dozens of officers (Active and Reserve). On the list of the repatriated officers appeared a majority of officers of the Cavalry, a preference that led to hard feelings among the other branches for whom this kind of favouritism was a scandal.
3. Firstly, by asserting that King Leopold III had cabled a telegram of congratulations to the legionnaires and that he approved the forming and the action of the *Legion Wallonie*. Secondly, by a circular letter widely diffused in the *Stalags* stating that *(...) the German authority asked higher circles in Brussels whether the oath of allegiance to the King was compatible with the service in the Legion and the oath taken to the Führer, leader of the European armies (this oath only binds militarily speaking, and for the only duration of the campaign in Russia), the answer was affirmative (...);* arch. E. De Bruyne.
4. Eddy De Bruyne, *Le Recutement dans les Stalags et Oflags en faveur de la Légion Wallonie*, Housse, p. 11.

5. Written statement by Lieutenant André Catalaÿ, member of the Committee.

6. It seems a proven fact that Louis Fierens, Catholic Chaplain of *5. Freiw. Sturmbrigade Wallonien*, was received by Count Capelle on 22 July 1943 and that on that occasion the Count praised Lippert in the aforementioned words; L. Fierens, *C'est un journal, ce n'est que cela . . .*, CEGES, Brussels. In the same order of ideas, it is not uninteresting to make oneself acquainted with F. Hellebaut's analysis. Speaking of military collaboration, the latter noted: " . . . many francophones felt reluctant to appear as if they had espoused the ideas of the Flemish extremists; or, in their turn, to send their sons fight in the East hand in hand with the army that had invaded the national territory twice. In fact, the Belgians were abandoned in a completely unforeseen situation, without obtaining the slightest directive from their natural guide. No ruling personality wanted to compromise himself in front of the divided opinion, either in one sense or in the other – hesitating to openly encourage the young people who came to consult them discreetly, but often feeling a sincere admiration for these foolhardy persons who thought to contribute to the future of Europe, Belgium and her King. Exception made for Léon Degrelle, well-spoken warmonger, who, tempted by such an extraordinary adventure and while accepting all the risks, felt it was a unique chance to show off . . ."; Frans Hellebaut, *Historique de la Légion 'Belge' Wallonie – Les circonstances de sa création* ; arch. E. De Bruyne.

   Meanwhile, we do know the exact circumstances in which Degrelle departed for the Eastern Front; E. De Bruyne, *La difficile naissance d'une légion perdue (The difficult birth of a lost Legion)*, Jours de Guerre, Crédit Communal, 1992, vol. 8.

7. *(. . .) General Van Overstraeten had agreed with Lippert's enlistment and had given him 'carte blanche'. In 1943, he no longer wanted to receive him. Lippert came to consult me on this matter. I answered him that as an officer his duty was to stay with his men, for Van Overstraeten, through an intermediary, had given him (Lippert) the advice to desert by taking off to England (. . .)*; Interview Frans Hellebaut, Aarschot 07.08.1981; Jean-Louis Roba, *L'Honneur et la Fidélité – Essai de biographie de Lucien Lippert*, De Krijger, 1997, p. 103. In the same order of ideas, during the revision of Hellebaut's trial, which had condemned him to death on 10 May 1946, his lawyers pointed out that *(. . .) it is a proven fact, indeed, that Major Hellebaut, at the time he was in captivity in Germany, did not ignore the relations which existed in Belgium between some advisers of the King, among whom Count Capelle, and New Order movements, these facts were corroborated with all the possible guarantees by Captain of the Artillery Lippert, – who had become Commander of the Légion Wallonie, during a visit he paid Hellebaut on 12 February 1943 (. . .)*; arch. E. De Bruyne.

   It should be noted that F. Hellebaut was known to be one of General Van Overstraeten's protégés, too.

Notes to Chapter XXIV

1. The 2 April 1939, elections allowed Degrelle to become a Member of Parliament as a deputy representing the constituency of Brussels.

2. In July/August 1941, following West-European New Order grouping Leaders left for the Eastern Front with the first contingent to be raised in their respective countries: France, *PPF* Leader Jacques Doriot, Marc Augier co-founder of *Les Jeunes de L'Europe Nouvelle* grouping; Belgium, *VNV* militia (Black Brigade) Leader Reimond Tollenaere (†22.01.1942), *Verdinaso* Leader Jef François (no frontline duties), *Rex-Vlaanderen* Leader Paul Suys (no frontline duties), Rex Movement Leader Léon Degrelle, *F.C.* Commander Fernand Rouleau (no frontline duties); the Netherlands, *Weer Afdeeling* Leader A. J. Zondervan (no frontline duties), *Nederlandsche-SS* Leader Henk Feldmeijer; Denmark, *DNSAP* (Danish Nazi Party) Youth Leader Christian Fredrik von Schalburg; Norway, Chief of Police Jonas Lie and *Nasjonal Samling* founding members Björn Oestring, Charles Westberg and Ragnar Berg.

3. By doing so the Germans only continued the *Flamenpolitik* policy they had developed during WWI; cfr Friedrich Wilhelm Freiherr von Bissing, *Belgien unter deutscher Verwaltung*, München, 1915, pp. 17–18.

4. On 5 January 1941, at Liège, Degrelle openly professed a pro-Nazi course by ending his speech with a vibrating *Heil Hitler!* In a subsequent report (*Lagebericht*) sent to Berlin, General Eggert Reeder, head of the *Militärverwaltung* (military administration) in Brussels judged the situation misleading (*groß angelegte Reklame*) and called Degrelle

[. . .] ein unzuverlässiger Charlatan [. . .], a hardly reliable charlatan.

5. The Walloon legionnaires were promised a Belgian uniform, no frontline combat duties and a limited presence of a few weeks on the Eastern Front, all vain promises.
6. *Léon, redis-moi tes mensonges, tu mens si bien . . .;* interview Emile Muller, légionnaire of the 1nd contingent. Herstal (Belgium), November 1979.
7. An example among others: during the von Rundstedt offensive, while Flemish collaboration leaders were waiting for the offensive to be successful far away from the frontline, Degrelle had moved forwards into the Ardennes with the intention of entering Brussels-capital (considered Flemish territory!) and to seize power before the arrival of the Flemish collaboration.
8. Degrelle acceded to the rank of *SS-Obersturmbannführer* on 01.01.1945. After the war, Léon Degrelle claimed he held the rank of an *SS-Standartenführer* (20 April 1945) and *SS-Oberführer* (signed Himmler 2 May 1945). (Note that by 2 May 1945, Himmler had been removed from Office).
9. By the end of the war, Degrelle was granted the Wound Badge in Gold as a result of repeated injuries. Mention must be made that not all of them were caused by enemy fire . . . The first to be taken into account (February 1942) for the *Verw. -Abz.* was a sprained ankle (a sleigh having crushed Degrelle's foot).
10. When speaking of Degrelle's luck people would say *Chance Degrelle, chance éternelle*, which means something similar to *Lucky Degrelle, lucky forever*.
11. Officer and WWI hero, highly decorated as an *officier patrouilleur* (i.e. specialized in cleaning up enemy trenches). Editor of the *Nouveau Journal*, a moderate censored newspaper during WWII.
12. In the 6 December 1985 edition of French right-wing newspaper *Rivarol*, Robert Poulet wrote *[. . .] he (Degrelle) left for the Eastern Front as result of an admiring but impetuous impulse. I have already mentioned the short dialogue I had with him when he wondered why I did not support the recruitment campaign for the Légion Wallonie. I answered him that I was not the kind of person to send people to war without going myself.*
    Are you saying this for me? he (Degrelle) replied.
    Yes, indeed.
    So, you think I should enlist?
    From the moment you are recruiting . . . yes.
    And to the great astonishment of all the people present, he then replied:
    Well, if that is so, I am enlisting.
13. This appears clearly from the numerous interviews with Walloon Eastern Front veterans. Some even ventured themselves to stating that Lippert, rather than Degrelle, deserved the *Ritterkreuz*, the heroic action of the Walloons having been identified and merged with the name of Léon Degrelle, whom the German Command of the breakout forces – as late as 9 February 1944 (*) – erroneously believed to be the commander of the Brigade. Since Degrelle used to act in front of German officers as if he were the (military) commander of the Walloon unit, whereas in reality he was only the political leader, the confusion on behalf of the Germans is plausible; (*) *Department of the Army Pamphlet no. 20–234*, January 1952, Historical Study – Operations of Encircled Forces – German Experiences in Russia, Chapter IV – the Pocket west of Cherkassy – the inside view, p. 22.
14. In the winter of 1944, Degrelle explored the possibilities of being appointed commander of a *Corps Occidental* (Corps West), which would have comprised the *28. Wallonien*, the *27. Langemarck* and the *33. Charlemagne*, the political aim of the operation being: Degrelle, sole interlocutor of the German authorities for Belgium and France.
15. Although personal relations between Lippert and Degrelle were good, a number of diverging views divided the two men, the most important one being Lippert's disagreement about Degrelle's using the *Légion Wallonie* for purposes of personal prestige. Lippert also wanted to limit the role of the *Légion Wallonie* to a military intervention without political implications in Belgium and above all without shocking public opinion. The Cherkassy parades did shock public opinion.
16. Interview Frans Hellebaut, operations officer and second-in-command of the *Division Wallonie*, Aarschot (Belgium), August 1983; interview Jules Mathieu, former *Kdr 69Rgt*, Pessoux (Belgium), 1986.
17. Officer of the Reserve Corps of the Belgian Army, Henri Derriks joined the Legion in

October 1942, and proved to be an exceptional frontline officer. Soon at loggerheads with Degrelle, the latter never got rid of him for the good reason that Derriks was too good an officer, likely to enhance the prestige of the Walloon unit.

18. Among others, the case of 500 Walloon workers forced *manu military* to join the ranks of the *28.SS-Freiw.-Gren.Div.Wallonien* in January-February-March 1945; Eddy De Bruyne, *Dans l'Etau de Degrelle – Le Service du Travail obligatoire ou de l'usine à la Waffen-SS*, Foxmaster, Verviers,1994.
19. On April 28 1945, Degrelle and 6 companions left Zahren castle at dawn without notice, leaving Hellebaut and Derriks a handwritten note he was heading north for talks ...
20. *Kampfgruppe Derriks*, more or less 450 men were involved in counter-attacks at Schillersdorf from 20 to 23 April 1945.
21. Degrelle did meet Himmler by mere chance on the road to Malente on 2 May 1945. *Memoir* Charles Generet, one of Degrelle's companions on his road to Lübeck; arch. E. De Bruyne via J.-L. Roba; Eddy De Bruyne, *Les Wallons meurent à l'Est – Degrelle et les légionnaires wallons au front russe*, Didier Hatier, Brussels, 1991, pp. 170–174.

Notes to Chapter XXV

1. Degrelle and Abetz had become close friends thanks to the fact that their respective wives once attended to same boarding school. While Degrelle was looking for political support, Rouleau, manipulated by the true promoters of the *Légion Wallonie* – i.e. obscure royalist and Belgicist higher circles opposed to a split up Belgium – was given free hand to counterbalance the separatist aspirations of the Flemish (collaborating) nationalists by raising a Rexist (royalist and Belgicist) *Walloon Legion*; interview Frans Hellebaut, Aarschot, 25 August 1981.
2. The number of Walloon volunteers that enlisted during 1941–45 did not exceed 8,000. Most recent (1999) figures show 7,126 identified men; list P. Canva via J.-P. Roba.
3. Fearing the number of volunteers might be insignificant, pressure was made upon the members of the *Formations de Combat*. The cadres who nevertheless refused to volunteer were reduced to a lower rank.
4. In 1941, the *AGRA* (Les *Amis du Grand Reich Allemand* – The friends of the Greater Reich), a grouping opposed to Degrelle (as only Hitler was recognized as their leader), recruited for the *Waffen-SS*.
5. Dr Miesse, a prominent *AGRA* member, was expelled from the Legion on grounds of anti-Degrelle propaganda.
6. In 1943, to set an example, a legionnaire was tried by court-martial and shot at Wildflecken barracks in the presence of the whole Brigade.
7. The only people Degrelle never got a grip on were those imprisoned in concentration camps.
8. That is ... the very ones who had preferred to step into (better paid) military collaboration in Belgium rather than join the *Légion Wallonie* and ... face the dangers of the Russian front.
9. Only a small number of these willy-nilly *Waffen-SS* was put into action. The remainder was demobilized at Plauen (April 1945) and given false papers of civil workers; E. De Bruyne, *Dans l'Etau de Degrelle – Le Service du Travail obligatoire ou de l'usine à la Waffen-SS*, Foxmaster, Verviers, 1994.
10. This was the case of former *SS-Sturmbannfüher* and *Kdr 69Rgt/28. SS. – Freiw. -Gren. Div. Wallonien* Jules Mathieu; – Interview J. Mathieu, Ciney, 1989; – Personal Papers J. Mathieu.

Notes to appendices

I

1. An incomplete list drawn up in October 1968 shows:
   2 *SS-Ostubaf.*;
   6 *SS-Stubaf.*;
   16 *SS-Hstuf.* (2 killed, 1 missing);
   26 *SS-Ostuf.* (1 killed, 1 missing);
   102 *SS-Ustuf.* (15 killed, 5 missing);
   6 medical doctors, 2 chemists, 1 dentist;
   3 Chatholic chaplains;
   1 veterinarian.
   Among them 11 career officers (2 killed, 2 missing) and 15 officers belonging to the Reserve Corps (2 killed).
   N.b. A small number of White Russian *Sonderführer* must be added to this list.
2. Except for G. Tchekhoff who recovered his actual rank. Mention must be made that he obtained Belgian citizenship before the outbreak of the war.
3. The *11. Kriegslehrgang* at Bad-Tölz took place from 6 September 1943 to 15 March 1944. Mention must be made that although official documents indicate the date of 21 June 1944 as promotion day to the rank of *SS-Ustuf.*, all Walloon graduates of the *11. Kriegslehrgang* were given permission to wear their *SS-Ustuf.* insignias from 1 April 1944 onwards, this as a favour obtained by Degrelle as a direct result of the Cherkassy breakout.
4. Note that Degrelle's *Soldbuch* (see Wim Dannau, *Ainsi parla Degrelle*, Vol. 11, p. 27) mentions 14.09.1944 as the date for the Oakleaves, the Close Combat Clasp in Gold and the German Cross in Gold.

II

1. In a letter dated Aarschot, 17 March 1975, and directed to Jules Mathieu, Frans Hellebaut wrote that he never met any other appellation than *28. SS-Freiw. -Gen. Div. Wallonien* as mentioned in the German document he received at Gronau on 19 October 1944 (*Umgliederung der SS-Frw. Sturmbrigade Wallonien – Tgb. No. 3712. g. Kdos*). According to Hellebaut, even Dr Klietmann from Berlin could not clear up this mystery (letters December 1968); arch. E. De Bruyne. (However, prior to the creation of the *28.SS-Freiw.-Gren.Div.Wallonien*, the *SS-FHA* had plans to create the 26., 27., and *28. SS-Panzer Divisionen*. The 26. was to be created from the *SS-PG Brig. 49*, the 27. from *SS-PG Brig 51*, and the 28. from *SS-Pz Brig.'Gross'*. The first two brigades were instead used to rebuild the *17 SS-PGD GvB* and the *Gross Brigade* was distributed to the divisions of the *6. Panzerarmee*. The *26.* and *27. Divisionen* almost began creation, while the *28.* never did).

III

1. M. Momin & J. P. Denil, *Etudes sur la Poste de campagne de la Waffen-SS*, 1988.
2. CB indicates that the mail was to be delivered to an officer having a safe at his disposal.

IV

1. Von Rabenau was also in charge of the military instruction of the second contingent.
2. *SS-Standartenführer* (posthumously with retrospective effect from 30 January 1944 on).
3. Lehe Wesermünde, 19.08.1897.
   SS-Nr: 98835
   SS-Standartenführer of the *Allgemeine SS* (30.01.1940).

Successively:
E/SS Germania (15.04.1941–10.07.1941) as platoon CO/*4. Kp. Ers. Btl. Germania/ SS-Kampfgruppe Nord/SS-Geb. Jg. Rgt. 6 R. Heydrich* (10.07.1941–15.09.1942) as Co/CO of the *4. (M.G.) Kp/ Kompanie SS-Inf. Rgt (mot) 6 /,*
SS-Geb. Jäg. Er. Btl. Nord (15.09–25.03.1942) as *Btl. Kdr I/SS-Geb. Jg. Rg. 6 R. H.,*
Stab Befehlshaber d. Niederlande (25.03.1942–13.02.1944), *Btl. Kdr der Landwacht Nederland,*
SS-Pz. Gren. A.u.E.Btl. 36,
Kdt Pi. Schu. Hrdischko *(17.07. –21.07.1944).*

4. Lack of specialized Walloon personnel to man the different non-combatant services of the Division, meant that most of them were in the hands of Germans. It was Heilmann's task to make them operational. Walloon affairs, including military instruction at Delligsen, Alfeld and Grünenplan, was in the hands of the Walloons. However, mention must be made that German personnel assisted them; interview F. Hellebaut, Aarschot, 23.08.1982. *Hptm* Pohl was the only exception. As in Belgium he had been in charge of the military instruction of the *G.W.* and *NSKK,* and having evacuated with them, he held his appointment after September 1944.

VIII

1. Sources:
   a. Belgian Handbook-Part II-Post invasion.
   b. *Nachlaß* Baumann, CEGES, Brussels.
   c. Eddy De Bruyne, *Le Recrutement d'éléments étrangers au sein de la Légion Wallonie,* Herstal, 1986.

X

1. Document F. Hellebaut.
2. 1,850 would be more accurate (cfr. *Nachlaâ Baumann,* CEGES, Brussels).
3. Former *SS-Ostuf. Gé. Pé* mentions a number of 450. By the end of the next day 96 were left; cf. letter (36.34.1989) to E. De Bruyne.
4. Estimation by Hellebaut were made more than 25 years ago. In the meantime documents ascertain the presence of 7,500 to 8,000 Walloon legionnaires 1941–45.

XVIII

1. Source Georges De Bongnie.

XIX

1. Source J.-L. Roba.

Bibliography

A. Unpublished Sources

1. Centre de Recherches et d'Etudes Historiques de la Seconde Guerre Mondiale – CREHSGM / CEGES /.

Archives Rex C13 – Archives Walloon Collaborating Groupings.

2. Berlin Document Center – BDC.

Personal records in the matter of Walloon officers of the *Waffen-SS*, including Léon Degrelle's.

3. Military Court / Brussels.

Index of wanted individuals (8 volumes).

Memoir Victor Matthys.

War Crimes. Explanatory statement in the matter von Falkenhausen, Reeder, Bertram and von Claer.

Various criminal records of individuals condemned in pursuance of art. 113, 114, 116, 118bis, 119, 121bis of the Penal Code (Military, Political and Cultural Collaboration).

4. Military Court / Liège.

Sipo Liège and Arlon – War Crimes – Explanatory statements in the matter Strauch, Lippert and jointed interested parties.

Geschichte der Sicherheitspolizei und des SD in Belgien 1940, insonderheit der Dienststelle Lüttich und Arel. (Böttcher Memoir).

5. Archives Roland Devresse.

Papers John Hagemans (*Prévôt* of the *Jeunesse Rexiste*).

Memoir Roger De Goy (J. Hagemans' private secretary).

Memoir Roger Gondry (10 March 1942 contingent).

Memorandum Pierre Pauly (2nd Commander of the *Légion Wallonie*).

Roland Devresse, *Un Mouvement de Jeunesse dans la Tourmente 1940–1945: Histoire de la Jeunesse Rexiste, des volontaires de la Jeunesse à la Légion Wallonie, de la Jeunesse Légionnaire, de la fin et de l'après-guerre.*

Factual account of the Schillersdorf counter-attacks (20–23.04.45).

6. Documents Francis Balace.

Grimm report.

7. Archives Eddy De Bruyne.

Various memoirs of *Légion Wallonie* veterans:

Memoir Georges Tchekhoff, (via Mrs Tchekhoff/Brazil);

Memoir André Régibeau, (via A. Régibeau);

Memoir Jules Mathieu, (via J. Mathieu);

Memoir René Ladrière, (via R. Lemaire);

Memoir Raymond Lemaire, (*idem*);

Memoir Paul Kehren, (via P. Kehren);

Memoir Alphonse Van Horembeke, (via R. Van Leeuw);

Memoir Abel Delannoy, *Confession d'un SS-Assassin;*

Memoir Charles Generet, (via J.-L. Roba);

Memoir Georges Delrue, *Journal de Campagne*, (via E. Muller);

Franz Hellebaut, *Papers and Documents*, (via F. Hellebaut);

Memorandum Heinz Forsteneichner, (via H. Forsteneichner);

Private post-war correspondance Henri Derriks-André Régibeau, (via A. Régibeau);

A l'Est coule l'Oder. – Memoir Gé. Pé., (via *Gé. Pé.*);

Jean Dinant, *La bataille de Poméranie*, (via E. Muller);

Marcel Drion, *Ma Campagne d'Estonie*, (via E. Muller);

Memoir Albert Steiver: *Rescapé du poteau d'exécution, aide de camp du Général Degrelle, commandant de la 28. SS-Division Wallonie raconte!* (via A. Steiver);

Georges Gilsoul, *Documents;*

Louis Fierens, *Ce n'est qu'un journal, rien qu'un journal.* – CEGES;

Jean Frisschen, *Mémoires de l'hiver 1941–1942*, (via Jean Frisschen);

Philibert Canva , *Documents;*

Robert Nivelle (L. Lippert's secretary during Cherkassy campaign), *Documents;*

Robert Hirsoux, La défense de l'Olschanka;

Fernand Kaisergruber, Mémoires Donetz-Caucase-Tcherkassy;

***, Commémoration des événements du 1er septembre 1944 vu cinquante ans après par un ancien de la division SS Wallonie (Oct. 44-Avril 45);

Henri Philippet, factual account of the Estonian Campaign/*Kampfgruppe Ruelle.*

B. Oral and Written Sources

1. Letters by:

Dr Alfred Albert, Albert Busiau, Philibert Canva, Paul Chenut, Georges De Bongnie (France), Léon Degrelle (Spain), Mrs Derriks-Warnimont, Roland Devresse (France), Florent E., Dr Heinz Forsteneichner (Germany), Jean Furnelle, Roger Gondry, Marcel Henry, Thérèse Leroy, Robert Nivelle, Jules Mathieu, *Gé. Pé.* Léo Poppe (Argentina), Jean-Pierre Quoirin, André Régibeau, Paul Relick, Adolphe Renier (France), Mrs Dr Stahl (France), Albert Steiver (Germany), Mrs Georges Tchekhoff (Brazil), Raymond Van Leeuw (Spain), Albert Vidick, Roger Wastiau, Jacques Wautelet (Germany).

2. Interviews:

Philibert Canva, Yves Boulangé, Mathieu De Coster, Léon Degrelle (Spain), Pierre Dengis, Abel Delannoy, Robert de Surlémont, Roland Devresse, Henri Feldbuch, Jean Frisschen, Roger Gondry, Marthe Henry, Frans Hellebaut, René Henrottay, Robert Hirsoux, Fernand Kaisergruber, Paul Kehren, Jacques Leroy, Jules Mathieu, Emile Muller, *Gé. Pé.*, Henri Philippet, André Régibeau, Paul Relick, André Poulet, Adolphe Renier, Paul Schreiber, Alex Stroïtnowski (Spain), Raymond Van Leeuw (Spain), Jean Vermeire, Jacques Wautelet.

C. Memoirs, Diaries, Souveniers

BRONCKART J., *Cinq années d'occupation. Verviers pendant la Guerre 1940–1945*, 3 vols, n.d.

BRONCKART J., *Bombes, Obus et Robots. Ce qui troubla la quiétude des Verviétois du jour de la libération à la fin de la Guerre*. Verviers, October 1945.

BOURGUET Jean, *Histoire de la 31° Cie de l'Armée Belge des Partisans*, PL Editions, Tilf, 1983.

DE BECKER Raymond, *La Collaboration en Belgique (1940–1944) ou une révolution avortée, Courrier Hebdomadaire du CRISP*, no. 497/498, Brussels, 1970.

DEGRELLE Léon, *Folie de la Répression*, Madrid, June 1980.

DEGRELLE Léon, *Le fascinant Hitler!*, Imprimé dans la Communauté européenne, n.d.

DE LANDSHEERE Paul & OOMS Alphonse, *La Belgique sous les nazis.* – 4 volumes Brussels, Editions Nouvelles, 1946, 1947.

DELVO Edgar, *Sociale collaboratie – pleidooi voor een volksnationale sociale politiek*, Ned. Boekhandel, Antwerpen, 1975.

GILSOUL Georges, *Gil raconte – Période 1922 – 1982.* privately published.

GRUBER F. K., *Nous n'irons pas à Touapse – Du Donetz au Caucase. De Tcherkassy à l'Oder*, privately published, 1991.

MOREAU de MELEN Henri, *Au Terme de la Route – Mémoires*, 1988.

PHILIPPET Henri, *Et mets ta robe de bal*, privately published, 1983.

STRUYE Paul, *L'Evolution du sentiment public en Belgique sous l'occupation allemande*, Ed. Lumière, 1945.

TERLIN Paul, *La Neige et le Sang.* Ed. Gergovie, 1998.

D. Collaborating Press and Periodicals

L'Amicale de la D.W.M.

Les Annales – publication of the Division *Wallonie.*

L'Avenir – Berlin Edition.

Berkenkruis, Maandblad van de Oud-Oostfrontstrijders, 1983–1988.

Bulletin des Maisons Wallonnes.

Le Combattant Européen – Organe mensuel de la Brigade SS Wallonie.

L'Effort Wallon.

Etre – Revue de la C.N.E.E. pour l'Education et la Grandeur de Notre Peuple.

Informations politiques et administratives de Rex, published by the HQ of the Rexist Movement.

Jeune Europe.

Le Front Allemand du Travail – Nature – But – Voies, Verlag der Deutschen Arbeitsfront, Brüssel, 1942.

Le Pays Réel.

Le Militant – Bulletin de l'Ordre des Militants de l'UTMI.

Le Rempart – Organe officiel de l'épuration, Ligue anti-maçonnique belge.

Le Téméraire – Organ of the Walloon Eastern Front Veterans, issues 1 to 42.

La Toison d'Or.

Revue de la Presse publiée par le Service de Presse de l'Etat-Major de Rex – Service intérieur du 19.08.44.

Wallonie – Cahiers de la communauté culturelle wallonne.

E. Audio-Visual Sources

DE WILDE Maurice: *De Nieuwe Orde* (Flemish television, 1986).

Na september 1944 – De Droom is uit … (Flemish television, 30 November 1990).

Face et Revers (Walloon television, 1986).

F. Inventories

MASSON H, *Archives Rex et Mouvements wallons de collaboration* – CREHSGM, 1981.

G. Work Tools

Annuaire Officiel de la Presse Belge édité par l'Association générale de la Presse belge.

Basic Handbook, Part II. Post-Invasion, London. Foreign Office, 1944.

BEKAERT Herman, *Le Code du Conseil de Guerre*. Les Editions Lumière.

S. BERNSTEIN & P. MILZA, *Dictionnaire Historique des Fascismes et du Nazisme*, Ed. Complexe, 1992.

Bundeszentrale für politische Forschung: Nationalsozialistische Diktatur, Band 912, – Bonn,1983.

Cahiers de la Seconde Guerre Mondiale, (15 volumes), CREHSGM.

Collection of the *Bulletin usuel des Lois et Arrêtés. Législation promulguée par le Gouvernement Belge en exil – mai 1940 – décembre 1943*, Bruylant, Brussels, 1946.

Collection of the *Bulletin des Tribunaux.*

Collection of the *Revue de Droit et de Criminologie.*

Dictionnaire d'Histoire de Belgique, Les hommes et les faits, Ed. Didier Hatier, Brussels, 1988.

Encyclopedie van de Vlaamse Beweging, Lannoo, Tielt, 1973.

Eddy DE BRUYNE, *Collaboration politique, culturelle, intellectuelle et militaire francophone belge 1940–45. Index explicatif de documentation générale*, Housse, 2002.

JACOBSEN H. A. – *Der zweite Weltkrieg in Chronik und Dokumenten 1939–1940, Wehr und Wissen Verlaggesellschaft*, Darmstadt, 1961.

German Military Symbols, Military Intelligence Division War Department, Washington – Directorate of Military Intelligence War Office, London, 1 April 1944.

La Collaboration, Les noms, les Thèmes, les Lieux. (Henri ROUSSO, MA Editions, Paris, 1988).

Le Petit Dictionnaire des Belges, Ed. Le – Cri, RTB F, 1993.

Lexicon Politieke & Jeugdkollaboratie – BRT – *Instructieve omroep*, 1985.

Moniteur Belge. Issues from 1945 to 1952.

National Socialism – Basic principles , their applications by the Nazi Party's Foreign Organization, and the use of Germans abroad for Nazi aims, Department of State, Washington, 1943.

Nationalsozialistische Diktatur 1933–1945. Eine Bilanz (BRACHER / FUNKE / JACOBSEN), *Schriftenreihe der Bundeszentrale für politische Bildung, Band* 192, 1983.

Philip REES, *Biographical Dictionary of the Extreme Right since 1890*, Simon & Schuster, New York, 1990.

Louis L. SNYDER Dr, *Encyclopedia of the Third Reich*, Paragon House, NY, 1989.

H. Institutions

Centre de Recherches et d'Etudes Historiques de la Seconde Guerre mondiale – CREHSGM, Brussels (*CEGES* since 1 March 1997)

Berlin Document Center, Berlin.

Bundesarchiv, Bonn.

Department of the Army. The Chief of Military History and the Center of Military History, Washington D.C.

Militärarchiv, Freiburg im Breisgau.

Rijksinstituut voor Oorlogsdokumentatie, Amsterdam.

I. Dissertations and Articles

BARTETZKO, Alois Akon, *Military Collaboration in the Germanic countries 1940–45*, University of California, Los Angeles, 1966.

COLLARD Fabian, *Les Formations de Combat de Rex (1940–1944) – De la propagande à la répression*, University of Liège, Thesis, 1998.

COLIGNON Alain, *Les Anciens Combattants en Belgique Francophone 1918 – 1940*, Thesis. ULg, 1984.

COLIN Françoise, *Les Mouvements wallons de collaboration pendant la Seconde Guerre Mondiale* (à *l'exception de Rex*), Thesis, ULB, Brussels, 1980.

CONWAY Martin, *The Rexist Movement in Belgium 1940–1944*, D.Phil. Thesis, Oxford, 1989.

CORNIL P, *Considérations générales sur le régime des condamnés pour incivisme, Etudes et Documents* – Revue de Droit Pénal et de Criminologie.

CREVE Jan, *Het Verdinaso en zijn Milities – Militievorming tussen beide Wereldoorlogen in Vlaanderen en Nederland (1928 – 1941)*, University of Ghent, Thesis, 1985.

CREVE Jan, *Recht en Trouw – De Geschiedenis van het Verdinaso en zijn Milities*. Soethout & Co, Antwerp, 1987.

DAUTRICOURT Joseph, *La Jurisprudence Militaire*, 2 volumes, Larcier, 1946.

DAUTRICOURT Joseph, *La Trahison par Collaboration avec l'Ennemi occupant le Territoire National, Etude préparatoire et pratique de la répression, dans le cadre des lois pénales belges complétées par les arrêtés-lois des 17 décembre 1942 et 6 mai 1944*, Larcier, Brussels, 1945.

DE BENS Els, *De Belgische dagbladpers onder Duitse censuur 1940–44*, De Nederlandse Boekhandel, Antwerpen, 1973.

DE BRUYNE Eddy, *Les Crises internes de la Légion Wallonie*, CREHSGM, TH388, 1990.

DE BRUYNE Eddy, *Le S.V.T.W. rexiste (mai 44-sept. 44) et le S.T.W. (oct. 44 – avril 1945)*, CREHSGM, B3309.

DE BRUYNE Eddy, *La difficile naissance d'une légion perdue – Jours de Guerre*, tome VIII, Crédit Communal, 1993.

DE BRUYNE Eddy, *Un aspect de la collaboration militaire dans la partie francophone du pays*. 1985, CREHSGM – JP 732.

DEGRELLE Léon, *Front de l'Est 1941 – 1945*, La Table Ronde, 1969.

DE JONGHE Albert, *La lutte Himmler – Reeder*, Cahiers CERHSGM.

DE JONGHE Albert, *Hitler en het politieke lot van België*, Uitgeverij de Nederlandse Boekhandel, 1972.

DELAUNOIS Jean-Marie, *Vie et combat de José STREEL* (1911–1946), Thesis, UCL, 1990.

DELMOTTE Guy, *La Légion Nationale 1922 – 1942*, Thesis, Ulg. 1965.

DEVAUX Jean-Philippe, *Degrelle et le Rexisme*, Thesis, University of Neufchâtel, 1986.

DUMON Frédéric, *La Collaboration politique et administrative*, Etudes et Documents – Revue de Droit Pénal et de Criminologie, no. 10, 1946–1947.

ESTES Kenneth William, *A European Anabasis: Western European Volunteers in the German Army and SS, 1940–1945*, Thesis, University of Maryland, 1984.

FLAHAUX Jean-Jacques, *Le Service des Volontaires du Travail pour la Wallonie (1940–1944) – Un mouvement dans la tourmente de la Belgique occupée*, Thesis, UCL, 1979.

German Order of Battle 1944. Arms and Armour Press, London, 1975.

GILISSEN John, *Etudes statistiques de la répression de l'incivisme*, Revue de Droit Pénal et de Criminologie, February 1951.

GANSHOF VAN DER MEERSCH Walter, *Réflexions sur le répression des crimes contre la Sûreté extérieure de l'Etat Belge*, Etablissements Emile Bruylant, 1946.

GROEN Koos, *Landverraad – De berechtiging van collaborateurs in Nederland*, Fibula Nieuwste Geschiedenis, Unieboek b. v., Weesp, 1984.

HANSSENS William, *La Rééducation des inciviques – Journée d'Etude du 14 juillet 1947 de la commission Internationale permanente pour l'Etude de la Répression des Crimes contre le droit des gens et des faits commis dans l'intérêt de l'ennemi*, Brussels, June 1947.

HAUPT Matthias Georg, *Der Arbeitseinsatz der belgischen Bevölkerung während des zweiten Weltkrieges*, Rheinische Friedrich-Wilhelm Universität, Bonn, 1970.

HOMZE Edward, *Foreign Labor in Germany*, Princeton University Press, 1967.

KNÖBEL, *Racial Illusion and Military Necessity in the Germanic Countries – A Study of SS political and manpower objectives in occupied Belgium*, Michigan, 1969.

LAHAYE Ghislain, *Le Parti Rexiste dans l'Arrondissement de Liège 1935–1940*, Thesis, ULg, 1979–80.

LOBET Albert, *Collaboration policière sous l'Occupation – La Brigade B de Charleroi (Police Merlot – 1943 –1944)*, Thesis, UCL, 1995.

LUYCKX A., *Les Porteurs d'armes*, Etudes et Documents – Revue de Droit Pénal et de Criminologie, tome XXVII, 1947, pp. 834–855.

MAES Philippe, *Un aspect de la collaboration dans la région du Centre: les formations policières et représailles en 1944*, Thesis, ULg, 1988–89.

MEYERS Willem C. M., *La Vlaamse Landsleiding – Un gouvernement d'émigrés en Allemagne après septembre 1944*, CREHSGM, Oct. 1972.

MOMIN, M. & J. P. DENIL, *Etude sur la Poste de campagne de la Waffen-SS. Marcophilie et Histoire Postale Militaire 1939 – 1945*, 1988.

PAPELEUX L., *Milieux collaborateurs et presse censurée en régions francophones (1940–1944), La Vie Wallonne*, no. 356, 1976.

PAQUOT Eric, *Sicherheitsdienst Lüttich et organisation policière allemande à Liège (1940–44)*, Thesis, ULg 1984–85.

PETRI Franz, *Die Niederlande (Holland und Belgien) und das Reich, – Volkstum – Geschichte – Gegenwart*, Ludwig Röhrscheid. Verlag Bonn 1940.

PETRI Franz, *Germanisches Volkserbe in Wallonien und Nordfrankreich*, Ludwig Röhrscheid Verlag Bonn, 1937.

PHOLIEN Joseph, *La Répression – Méditations sur la nécessité d'une politique dans la répression pour faits de guerre.*

REYNVOET Vincent, *La vie quotidienne à Auvelais sous l'occupation allemande* (1940- 1944*), Thesis, UCL, 1994.*

ROBA Jean-Louis, *La Section carolorégienne de la Défense du Peuple*, n.d.

ROMIJN Peter, *Snel, streng en rechtvaardig. Politiek beleid inzake de bestraffing en reclassering van "foute" Nederlanders 1945 – 1955*, 1989.

SCHÄRER R. Martin, *Deutsche Annexionspolitik im Westen. Die Wiedereingliederung Eupen-Malmedy im zweiten Weltkrieg*, Peter Lang, Bern, 1978.

SELLESLAGH Frans, *De Tewerkstelling van Belgische Arbeidskrachten tijdens de bezetting. – Dokumenten I & II*, Navorsings- en Studiecentrum voor de Geschiedenis van de Tweede Wereldoorlog, 1970–1972.

SIMON Michel, *Les Organisations de Jeunesse d'Ordre Nouveau en Belgique francophone 1940–1944*, Thesis, ULg, 1987–88.

SIMON Michel, *Jeunesses rexistes & Légionnaire* (1940 – 1945), La Gleize, 1995.

SIMON Michel, *Jeux sans Piste – Les Organisations de jeunesse d'Ordre Nouveau non rexistes en Belgique francophone sous l'Occupation*, Stoumont, June 2000.

TIMMERMANS Bernard, *Légion Wallonie 1941–1945 – Les Motivations des Volontaires pour le Front de l'Est*, Thesis / Criminology, ULg, 1992–93.

TRIFFAUX Jean-Marie, *Une page d'histoire de l'occupation allemande à Arlon : le Deutscher Sprachverein*, Cahiers no. 14, CREHGSGM, 1991.

TRIFFAUX Jean-Marie, *Arlon 1939 – 45*, Arlon, 1994.

VANBRABANT Eric, *Actes de violence dans neuf communes de la région liégeoise et études sur les bourgmestres de ces communes*, Thesis, Ulg, 1994.

VANDERLINDEN Jean-Marc, *Problèmes de reclassement et de cheminement socio-professionnels des anciens de la Légion Wallonie*, Thesis, UCL, 1988.

VAN DER STRAETEN, *Réflexions sur la collaboration intellectuelle*, – Mémoire, – Revue de Droit Pénal et de Criminologie, 1956–1957.

WILLEMS Hubert, *Pangermanisme pragmatique? Critères d'Identification – Godefroid Kurth, le Nationaliste de Henri Bischoff, l'annexionniste 1914–1918 / 1940–1944. A l'Ombre des extrémistes allemands – Bravade ou voltige Saint-Vithoise* (Essai Historique), 1989.

WILLEMS Hubert, *Le Ministre libéral Albert Devèze et Eupen – Malmédy – Saint-Vith – L'Amour sacré de la Patrie*, 1989.

WILLEQUET Jacques, *Les fascismes belges*, Revue d'Histoire de la Deuxième guerre mondiale, April 1967.

WILLEQUET Muriel, *Un mouvement Antijuif en Wallonie: La Ligue de la Défense du Peuple sous l'Occupation allemande (1940–1943*), Thesis, ULg, 1993–1994.

J. Books

ASSOULINE Pierre, *Hergé*, Plon 1996.

BALACE F. & COLIGNON A, *Quelle Belgique dans l'Europe allemande* dans *Jours de Guerre*, tome 10, Crédit Communal, 1994.

BALACE Francis, *L'Aventure des Volontaires du Travail* dans *Jours de Guerre*, tome 10, Crédit Communal, 1994.

BALACE Francis, *Les Hoquets de la liberté* dans *Jours de Guerre*, tome 20, Crédit Communal, 1996.

BARTHELEMY Victor, *Du Communisme au Fascisme – L'Histoire d'un engagement politique*, Albin Michel, 1978.

BAUDHUIN Fernand, *L'Economie Belge sous l'Occupation allemande 1940–1944*, Ed. Bruylant, 1945.

BENJAMIN Mico & DETHY J.-M., *L'Ordre Noir – Les Néo-Nazis et l'extrême droite en Belgique*, P. De Méyère Editeur, Brussels, 1986.

BUSS Ph & A. MOLLO, *Hitler's Germanic Legions*.

BREES Gwenaël, *L'Affront National – Le Nouveau visage de l'extrême droite en Belgique*, EPO, 2ème Ed., 1992.

BRIGNEAU François, *L'Aventure est finie pour eux*, Librairie Gallimard, 1960.

BRISSAUD André, *Pétain à Sigmaringen*, Librairie Académique Perrin, Paris, 1957.

BECQUET Charles-François, *L'impossible Belgique, d'une guerre à l'autre*, U.W.E.A., 1986.

(Collective) *De l'Avant à l'Après-Guerre. L'Extrême Droite en Belgique Francophone*, De Boeck Université, 1994.

BUCHBENDER O. & HAUSCHILD R., *Radio Humanité – Les émetteurs allemands clandestins 1940*, Ed. France-Empire, 1984.

CAILLET Hubert & DEFRERE Robert, *Les Maquisards wallons*, Ed. L'Horizon Nouveau, Liège, 1945.

CABALERRO Carlos, *El Batallón Fantasma – Españoles en la Wehrmacht y Waffen-SS 1944- 45*, Valencia, 1987.

CHARLES, Jean-Léon & Philippe DASNOY, *Les Secrétaires Généraux face à l'Occupant 1940 – 1944*, Collections Inédits, De Meyer, Bruxelles, 1974.

COLIGNON Alain, *Ostkantone*, *Jours de Guerre*, tome 2, Crédit Communal, 1990.

COLIGNON Alain, *Secours d'Hiver, Secours d'Hitler, Jours de Guerre*, vol 6, Crédit Communal, 1992.

COLIGNON Alain, *C.N.A.A., L'agriculture en rangs d'oignons, Jours de Guerre*, vol. 7, Crédit Communal, 1993.

COLIGNON Alain, *Première page, cinquième colonne, Jours de Guerre*, vol. 8, Crédit Communal, 1992.

CROUQUET Roger, *La Bataille des Ardennes au jour le jour*, Ed. Libération 44, Brussels, 1944.

CHANSON Paul, *Les Droits du Travailleur et le Corporatisme*, Desclée-DeBrouwer & Cie, Editeurs, 1934.

DANTOING Alain, *La 'Collaboration' du Cardinal – L'Eglise de Belgique dans la Guerre 40*, De Boeck, 1991.

DEAT Marcel, *Mémoires Politiques*, Denoël, 1989.

DE BRUYNE Eddy, *La Collaboration francophone en exil, septembre 1944 – mai 1945*, Housse, 1997.

DE BRUYNE Eddy, *Les Wallons meurent à l'Est*, Ed. Didier Hatier, Brussels, 1991.

DE BRUYNE Arthur, *De Kwade jaren*, Uitgeverij De Roerdomp Brecht/Antwerpen, 1973.

DEGRELLE Léon, *La Cohue de 40*, Ed. R. Crausar, Lausanne, 1949.

DEGRELLE Léon, *Lettre à mon Cardinal*, Editions de l'Europe Nouvelle, Brussels, 1975.

(DEGRELLE) – *In Memoriam – Léon Degrelle et le Rexisme*, Les Editions de la Toison d'Or, Paris, 1995.

DEGRELLE Léon, *La Guerre en Prison*, Editions Ignis, Brussels, 1941.

DE LENTDECKER Louis, *Tussen twee vuren*, Davidfonds, Leuven, 1985

DE MAN Henri, *Après Coup*, Ed. de la Toison d'Or.

DE MAN Henri, *Cavalier Seul*, Ed. Le Chaval Ailé.

DEVOS Luc, *La Libération de la Normandie aux Ardennes*, GEV, 1994.

DE WEVER Bruno, *Greep naar de Macht – Vlaams nationalisme en Nieuwe Orde – Het VNV 1933 – 1945*, Lannoo Perspectief Uitgaven, 1994.

DE WEVER Bruno, *Oostfronters – Vlamingen in het Vlaams Legioen en de Waffen-SS*, Reeks Retrospectief. Lannoo/Tielt/Weesp, 1984.

DE WILDE Maurice, *België in de Tweede Wereldoorlog – De Kollaboratie 1*, tome 5. Uitgeverij Nederlandse Boekhandel, Antwerpen/Amsterdam, 1985.

DUJARDIN Jean, *Le service "Boucle"*, Cahiers no. 10, CREHSGM.

DUMONT Serge, *Les brigades noires – L'extrême-droite en France et en Belgique francophone de 1944 à nos jours*, EPO, Ed. Vie Ouvrière, Bussels, 1983.

DIRR Dr J, *Belgien als französische Ostmark – Zur Vorgeschichte des Krieges*, Max Kirstein Verlag, Berlin, 1917.

DOUBLET Jean, *Le Front du Travail allemand*. Centre d'Etudes de Politique Etrangère, Section d'Information no. 10, Ed. Hartmann, 1937.

DUMON Frédéric, *La Répression de la Collaboration avec l'ennemi 1944–1952, La Revue Générale*, 1/96, 1996.

ERB H. GROTE, Freiherr, *Konstantin Hierl. Der Mann und sein Werk*, München Zentralverlag der NSDAP, 1942.

FALKENHAUSEN, Alexander *Freiherr* von, *Mémoires d'Outre-Guerre. Comment j'ai gouverné la Belgique de 1940 à 1944*, Ed. De Méyère, Brussels, 1974.

GARCON Maurice, *Les Procès de la Radio: Ferdonnet, Jean Hérold-Paquis, Compte rendu sténographique*, Ed. Albin Michel, Paris, 1947.

GARCON Maurice, *Les Procès de la collaboration: Fernand de Brinon – Joseph Darnand – Jean Luchaire. Compte rendu sténographique*, Albin Michel, Paris, 1948.

GEORIS-REITSHOF Michel, *Extrême Droite et Néo Fascisme en Belgique*, Pierre De Méyère, éditeur, Brussels,1962.

GERARD – LIBOIS J. & J. GOTOVITCH, *L'An 40 – La Belgique occupée*, CRISP, 1971.

GIHOUSSE Marie-Françoise, *Mouvements wallons de résistance. Mai 1940 – septembre 1944*, Institut Jules Destrée, 1984.

GORDON BERTRAM, M., *Collaborationism in France during the Second World War*, Cornell University Press, Ithraca and London, 1980.

GOTOVITCH José, *Du Rouge au Tricolore – Résistance et Parti Communiste*, Archives du Futur /Histoire, 1992.

HEROLD-PAQUIS Jean, *Des illusions ... désillusions*, Bourgoin Editeur, Paris, 1948.

HERREMANS Maurice-Pierre, *Personnes déplacées (Rapatriés, disparus, réfugiés)*, Ed. Marie-Julienne Ruisbroeck, Brussels, 1948.

HIRSCHFELD Gerhard, *Nazi Rule and Dutch Collaboration – The Netherlands under German Occupation 1940–1945*, New-York, 1988.

IN 'T VELD N.K.C.A., *De SS en Nederland*, Slijthof/Amsterdam, 1976.

KOCH Julius, *Kampfzeit im Ausland – Die Entwicklung der Auslands-Organisation der NSDAP in Belgien*, Brussels, Sept., 1942.

HAEGY, *Angoisse! Bombes et Robots – Quand l'offensive von Rundstedt menaçait Verviers*, Ed. Vinche, Verviers, n.d.

HOTON L., *Y eut-il un activisme wallon durant la guerre?* Ed. du Journal de Liège, 1936.

HUYSE Luc & DHONDT Steven, *– 1942 Onverwerkt verleden 1952 -*, Uitgeverij Kritak, Leuven, 1991.

LALMAND Edgar, *Le Parti Communiste de Belgique dans la Lutte pour la Libération – Rapport présenté au Comité Central du Parti Communiste de Belgique, le 21 octobre 1944.*

LAMBERT Pierre Philippe & LE MAREC Gérard, *Paris et Mouvements de la Collaboration –* Paris 1940 – 1944, *Jacques Granger, Paris, 1993.*

LAROCK Victor, *Un aspect de la Question Royale – A quand la vérité?* Ed. du Peuple et du Monde du Travail, (circa 1950).

LEMAIRE Alfred, *Le Crime du 18 août ou les journées sanglantes des 17 et 18 août 1944 dans la région de Charleroi*, Couillet, 1947.

LONCHAY André, *L'Effondrement des Ministères Wallons – Départ des Saltimbanques*, Brussels, Lamertin, 1919.

MAJERES Pierre, *Le Luxembourg Indépendant – Essai d'histoire contemporaine et de droit international public*, Imprimerie de la Cour J. Bedforr, Luxembourg, 1946.

MICIN Melchior, *La Vérité sur la tragédie de Forêt*, Press, Verviers, 1946.

NEULEN Hans-Werner, *Europas Verlorene Söhne – Die Tragödie der Freiwilligen im Zweiten Weltkrieg*, Universitas Verlag, München, 1980.

MOTTARD Gilbert, *Des Administrations et des hommes dans la tourmente – Liège 1940–45*, Crédit Communal, 1987.

NOGUERES Louis, *La dernière étape à Sigmaringen*, Librairie Arthème Fayard, 1956.

NOVICK Peter, *L'Epuration française 1944 – 1949*, Balland, Paris, 1985.

ORY Pascal, *Les Collaborateurs 1940 – 1945*, Seuil, 1976.

POTARGENT, P., *Déportation – La mise au travail de la main-d'oeuvre belge dans le pays et à l'étranger durant l'occupation*, Edimco S. A., Brussels, n.d.

PULINGS Jean, *Visages du Corporatisme*, Les 3 Ecrits, Paris-Brussels, 1941.

REX Hier et Aujourd'hui, Enquêtes et Reportages, no. 2, 1985.

RIKMENSPOEL Marc, *Soldiers of the Waffen-SS: Many Nations, One Motto*, J. J. Fedorowicz, Winnipeg, 1999.

RIKMENSPOEL Marc. *Waffen-SS: The Encyclopedia*, New-York, Bookspan, 2002.

ROBA J.-L. & J. LEOTARD, *La Région de Walcourt-Beaumont pendant la seconde guerre mondiale*, tomes I (1940–1941), II (1942–1943) & III (1944–1945), Cercle d'Histoire de l'Entité de Walcourt, 1984–1996.

RUTH HERMANN Dr Paul, *Luxemburg*, Ferdinant Hirt in Breslau, 1942.

SAINT-PAULIEN, *Histoire de la Collaboration*, Nouveau Esprit, 1961.

SCHILLEMANS G.-T., *Philippe Pétain – Le Prisonnier de Sigmaringen*, Editions mp, 1965.

SCHNEIDER, Jost, *Their Honor was Loyalty. An illustrated and documentary history of the Knight's Cross holders of the Waffen-SS and Police 1940 – 1945*, R. James Bender Publications, 1977.

SCHULZE-KOSSENS Richard, *Militärischer Führernachwuchs der Waffen-SS – Die Junkerschulen*, Munin Verlag, Osnabrück, 1982.

SKORZENY Otto, *Missions secretes*, Flammarion, 1950.

STEIN George, *The Waffen-SS*, Cornell University Press, 1966.

STRASSNER Peter, *Europaïsche Freiwillige. Die 5. SS-Panzerdivision Wiking*, Munin Verlag Osnabrück, 1977.

TAUGOURDEAU Alain, *Les Organisations Nationales-Socialistes 1920 – 1945*, 1991.

VAN COPPENOLLE E, *Wat ik nog te zeggen heb. – Het Belgisch beleid inzake de handhaving van de openbare orde gedurende de duitse bezetting 1940–1944*, Boekengilde Brederode, Antwerpen, 1953.

VAN DEN WIJNGAERT Mark, *L'Economie belge sous l'occupation. La politique d'Alexandre Galopin, gouverneur de la Société Générale*, Document Duculot, 1990.

VAN DER BORGHT Corneille, *Le Scandale des disparus – Guerre 1940 –1945*, n.d.

VAN GEET W. J. D., *De Rijkswacht tijdens de bezetting 1940–1944*, De Nederlandse Boekhandel, 1985.

VAN OVERSTRAETEN Raoul, Gen. *Sous le Joug. Léopold III prisonnier*, Ed. D. Hatier.

VAN ROY Louis, *Het Taboe van de Kollaboratie*, DNB-Uitgeverij Pelckmans Kapellen, 1987.

VERHOEYEN Etienne, *La Belgique occupée – de l'An 40 à la Libération*, De Boeck – Westmael, 1994.

VERSCHAEVE Cyriel, *In 't verre land vreeselijk alleen*, Boekengilde Brederode Antwerpen, tweede druk, n.d.

VINCX Jan, *Vlaanderen in Uniform 1940–1945* (7 vol), Etnika, Antwerpen, 1980.

WEGNER, Bernd, *Hitlers Politische Soldaten – Die Waffen-SS 1933–1945*, Ferdinand Schöningh, Paderborn, 1982.

WILLEQUET Jacques, *La Belgique sous la botte – résistances et collaborations 1940–1945*, Ed. Universitaires, 1986.

WARMBRUNN Werner, *The German Occupation of Belgium 1940–1944*, Peter Lang Publishing, New-York, 1994.

WULLUS-RUDIGER J.-W., *En marge de la Politique Belge 1914–18*, Editions Berger-Levrault, 1957.

WYNANTS Jacques, *Mémoire d'une région. Verviers libéré – septembre 1944 – janvier 1945*, Librairie Derive, 1984.

K. Degrelle

BRASILLACH Robert, *Léon Degrelle et l'avenir de Rex*, Plon, Paris, 1936.

CHARLIER, Jean-Michel, *Léon Degrelle: Persiste et Signe*, Jean Picollec, 1985.

CONWAY, Martin, *Le Rexisme de 1940 à 1944: Degrelle et les autres*, Cahiers, CREHSGM, Brussels, 1986.

d'YDEWALLE, Charles, *Degrelle ou la triple imposture*, Pierre de Méyère,1968.

DANNAU Wim, *Ainsi parla Degrelle* (13 vol.), Byblos, Brussels, 1972.

DANNAU Wim, *Degrelle, face à face avec le Rexisme*, Ed. Le Scorpion, Brussels, 1971.

DAYE Pierre, *Léon Degrelle et le rexisme*, Fayard, Paris, 1938.

DE BRUYNE Eddy, *Degrelle-Post-september 1944*. Interview Philippe Van Meerbeeck for the BRT (Flemish Television), February 1990. *Le dossier Léon Degrelle*, Dossier du mois no. 6/7, Ed. du Ponnant, 1963.

FREROTTE Jean-Marie, *Léon Degrelle, le dernier fasciste*, Legrain, Brussels, 1987. *In Memoriam: Léon Degrelle et le Rexisme*, Les Editions de la Toison d'Or, Paris, 1995.

LEGROS Usmard, *Un homme, un chef, Léon Degrelle*, Ed. Rex, Brussels, 1938.

MAGIN Marc, *Léon Degrelle – Un Tigre de Papier*, Didier Hatier, 1988.

MATHIEU Olivier, *En réponse à la presse lors de la mort de Léon Degrelle*, Ed. Aux Bâtons de Bourgogne.

MIGNOLET Djosef, *Leyon Degrelle? On fré*, Rex, Brussels, 1938.

NARVAEZ Louise, *Degrelle m'a dit*, Ed. Morel, Paris, 1961.

Recueil: Organe semestriel du Fonds Européen Léon Degrelle.

VANDROMME Paul, *Le Loup au cou de chien – Degrelle au service d'Hitler*, Ed. Labor, 1978.

L. Legion Wallonie

BONNIVER Marcel, *La Campagne d'Estonie*, unpublished.

DE BRUYNE Eddy, *Les Campagnes militaires de la Légion Wallonie, de la 5ème Brigade d'assaut et de la 28ème Division Wallonie*, unpublished.

DEGRELLE Léon, *Feldpost*, Ed. Rex, Brussels, 1944.

DEGRELLE Léon, *La Campagne de Russie*, Le Cheval Ailé, 1949.

DEGRELLE Léon, *Le Front de l'Est 1941–1945*, La Table Ronde, 1969.

DERRRIKS Henri, *La Légion Wallonie*, unpublished manuscript.

DEVRESSE Roland, *Les Volontaires de la Jeunesse à la Légion Wallonie*, unpublished.

HAGEMANS John, *Mémorial Prévôt de la Jeunesse 1914–1942*, Ed. de la Jeunesse, 1943.

HEINDERYCKX Ph, Captain, *L'Organisation et l'Equipement de la LEGION WALLONIE 1941–1945*, 1992, unpublished.

HELLEBAUT Frans (and a group of 'Wallonie' officers), *Légion 'Belge' Wallonie – Historique*.

HELLEBAUT Frans, *Historique sommaire de la Légion Wallonie*, unpublished.

HENROTTAY René, *Chemin d'Idéal – Ukraine – Caucase -Tcherkassy*, Aux Bâtons de Bourgogne, 1999.

LANDWEHR Richard & Jean-Louis ROBA, *The Wallonien – The History of the 5th SS-Sturmbrigade and 28th SS volunteer Panzergrenadier Division, Siegrunen Magazine*, 1984.

Le Téméraire (42 issues), organ of the Walloon Eastern Front veterans.

LITTLEJOHN David, *Foreign Legions of the Third Reich*, Vol. 2, R. James Bender Publications, 1981.

MABIRE Jean, *Légion Wallonie – au Front de l'Est 1941–1944*, Presses de la Cité, 1987.

MABIRE Jean, *Division Wallonie sur la Baltique 1944- 1945*, Troupes de Choc, 1989.

MABIRE Jean, *Brigade d'Assaut Wallonie – La percée de Tcherkassy*, Jacques Granger, 1995.

MABIRE Jean & Eric LEFEVRE, *Légion Wallonie*, Art et Histoire d'Europe, 1988.

MATHIEU Jules, *Historique de la 1ère Cie du Wal. Inf. Btl 373, de la 1ère Cie de la 5ème Brigade d'Assaut et du 69ème Régiment de la 28ème Frw. Gren. Div. Wallonien*. Unpublished; – arch. Eddy De Bruyne.

PAULY Pierre, Capt. B.E.M., *Mémorandum sur les combats du 28 février 1942*, unpublished manuscript.

POULET André, *Récit de la patrouille Van Eyser*, unpublished manuscript.

ROBA Jean-Louis, *The First months of the Sturmbrigade Wallonien*, *Siegrunen*, vol. II, no. 2 (May 1978) and Vol. II no. 3 (July 1978).

ROBA Jean-Louis, *L'Honneur et la Fidélité. Essai de biographie de Lucien Lippert*, Uitgeverij De Krijger, 1997.

SAINT-LOUP, *Les Hérétiques. Les SS de la Toison d'Or – Flamands et Wallons au combat*, Presses de la Cité, 1975.

TIMMERMANS Bertrand, *Légion Wallonie 1941–1945 – Les Motivations des Volontaires pour le Front de l'Est*, Thesis, Ulg, 1992–1993.

VAN POUCKE Guido, Major BEM, *De Vlaamse en Waalse Waffen-SS aan het Oosfront*, unpublished, December 1967.

M. Rexism

BODELET Jean-Michel, *Le rexisme dans la province de Luxembourg (1940 –1944)*, Ulg, 1996.

BRUSTEIN William, Prof. Dr., *The Political Geography of Belgian Fascism: The Case of Rexism*, Annual Meetings of the Social Science History Association, New Orleans, Louisiana, 1987.

BUTTGENBACH André, *Le Mouvement Rexiste et la situation politique de la Belgique*, Ets. Emile Bruylandt, 1987.

DANNAU Wim, *Degrelle face à face avec le Rexisme*, Ed. Scorpion, 1971.

DEGRELLE Léon, *Le Message de Rex*, Editions de Rex, 1936.

DENIS Jean, *Bases doctrinales de REX*, Editions Rex, Brussels, 1936.

DENIS Fréderic, *Rex est mort*, Editions Labot, 1937.

ETIENNE J.-M., *Le Mouvement Rexiste jusqu'en 194*, Presse de la fondation nationale des sciences politiques, 1968.

GERARD-LIBOIS Jules, *Rex 1936–1940, – Flux, reflux, tensions et dislocations*, CRISP no. 1226, 1989.

GRUNNE, Count Xavier de, *Pourquoi je suis séparé de Rex*.

LAHAYE Ghislain, *Le Parti rexiste dans l'Arrondissement de Liège 1935–1940*, Thesis, ULg, 1988.

LEVAUX Léopold, *Devant le Rexisme*, Centrale d'Edition et de Propagande.

PFEIFFER Robert et Jean LADRIERE, *L'Aventure rexiste*, Pierre de Méyère, éditeur, 1966.

STREEL José, *Ce qu'il faut penser de Rex*, Les Editons Rex, Brussels.

STREEL José, *Positions rexistes*, Editions Rex, Brussels.

STREEL José, *La Révolution du vingtième Siècle*, Nouvelle Société d'Editions, Brussels, 1942.

VROYLANDE de Robert, *Quand Rex était petit …*, Editions Lovanis, 1936.

List of Authors' Publications

Eddy de Bruyne

Les Wallons meurent à l'Est – Degrelle et les légionnaires wallons au

front russe 41–45. *Didier Hatier, Brussels, 1991.*

La difficile naissance d'une légion perdue – Jours de Guerre No. 8.

Crédit Communal, Bruxelles, 1992.

Dans l'Etau de Degrelle – Le Service du Travail Obligatoire ou de l'usine

à la Waffen-SS. *Foxmaster. Verviers, 1994.*

La Collaboration francophone en exil, mai 44- sept. 45. Housse,1997.

"A propos d'un carnet" in MEMOR, Bulletin d'Information No. 33/2001 - Université Charles-de-Gaulle – Lille 3.

La Sipo-Sd à Liège 1940 – 1944 – Composantes et lignes de Force. CHLAM,

Liège, 2003.

Unpublished research:

Les campagnes de la Légion Wallonie, de la 5. SturmbrigadeWallonien et de

la 28. SS-Frw. Gr. Div. Wallonien. 600p.

Un aspect de la collaboration militaire dans la Belgique francophone – Le recrutement d'éléments étrangers. 53p.

Les Crises internes de la Légion Wallonien. 233p.

Les Polices rexistes de l'Occupant à Liège 1940–44.101p.

Le Recrutement dans les Stalags et Oflags en faveur de la Légion Wallonie. 41p.

Une certaine Wallonie, un certain wallingantisme. vus d'enface.

Wallingants francophiles, germanophiles, hitlérophiles etgermanolâtres. 53p.

Quelques aspects de l'Univers collaborationniste à Liège 1941 – 1945. 348p.

Collaboration politique, culturelle, intellectuelle et militaire

francophone belge 19040–45 – Index explicatif de documentation générale. 320p.

Marc Rikmenspoel

Soldiers of the Waffen-SS : Many Nations, One Motto. JJ Fedorowicz, 1999.

Waffen-SS : The Encyclopedia. Bookspan, 2002.

Also available from Helion & Company Limited

Twilight of the Gods: A Swedish Waffen-SS Volunteer's Experiences with the 11th SS-Panzergrenadier Division 'Nordland', Eastern Front 1944–45

Thorolf Hillblad (editor) – 144pp, b/w photographs, map. Hardback – ISBN 1-874622-16-7

For the Homeland! The History of the 31st Waffen-SS Volunteer Grenadier Division

Rudolf Pencz – 288pp., b/w photographs, maps. Hardback – ISBN 1-874622-01-9

To Battle. The Formation & History of the 14th Waffen-SS Grenadier Division

Michael Melnyk – 400pp, b/w photographs, ills, maps. Hardback – ISBN 1-874622-41-8

A selection of forthcoming titles

Hitler's Last Levy: The Volkssturm 1944–45
Hans Kissel — ISBN 1-874622-51-5

Military Operations of the Dutch Army, 10th–17th May 1940
P.L.G. Doorman, O.B.E. — ISBN 1-874622-72-8

Hitler's Miracle Weapons: The Secret History of the Rockets and Flying Craft of the Third Reich
Volume 2 – From the V-1 to the A-9: Unconventional short- and medium-range weapons
Friedrich Georg — ISBN 1-874622-62-0

Some Additional Services From Helion & Company

BOOKSELLERS

- over 20,000 military books available
- four 100-page catalogues issued every year

BOOKSEARCH

- Free professional booksearch service. No search fees, no obligation to buy

Want to find out more?
Visit our website – www.helion.co.uk

Our website is the best place to learn more about Helion & Co. It features online book catalogues, special offers, complete information about our own books (including features on in-print and forthcoming titles, sample extracts and reviews), a shopping cart system and a secure server for credit card transactions, plus much more besides!

HELION & COMPANY

26 Willow Road, Solihull, West Midlands, B91 1UE, England
Tel: 0121 705 3393 — Fax: 0121 711 4075
Email: publishing@helion.co.uk — Website: http://www.helion.co.uk